CONTEMPORARY
ISSUES IN
CANADIAN POLITICS

CONTEMPORARY ISSUES IN CANADIAN POLITICS

Frederick Vaughan

Patrick Kyba

O.P. Dwivedi

Department of Political Studies, University of Guelph

P

PRENTICE-HALL ❦ OF CANADA, LTD.
Scarborough, h *Ontario*

© 1970 by Prentice-Hall of Canada, Ltd.
Scarborough, Ontario

PRENTICE-HALL, INC., ENGLEWOOD CLIFFS, NEW JERSEY
PRENTICE-HALL INTERNATIONAL, INC., LONDON
PRENTICE-HALL OF AUSTRALIA, PTY., LTD., SYDNEY
PRENTICE-HALL OF INDIA PVT., LTD., NEW DELHI
PRENTICE-HALL OF JAPAN, INC., TOKYO

Library of Congress Catalog Card No. 70-109493
0-13-169813-3 (pa.)
0-13-169821-4 (cl.)
1 2 3 4 5 74 73 72 71 70

PRINTED IN CANADA

Contents

Preface

Students and teachers of Canadian politics have often expressed a desire for a book which bridges the gap between textbook material and the issues of immediate political concern to Canadians. *Contemporary Issues in Canadian Politics* is intended to fill this need, and to this end we have presented a number of scholarly articles about current problems and their possible solutions. Each section of the book treats an important feature of government and politics in Canada – federalism, constitutional issues, parliament and the executive, the public service, and the judiciary. We have attempted to select those articles which will acquaint our readers with the major issues in each area.

This book does not cover all issues of concern to Canadians today. Limited space alone would have prevented this, but a more fundamental reason was the dearth of articles, both behavioural and non-behavioural, on several current issues.* Moreover, we were not always able to obtain issue-oriented articles and, where necessary, we have included articles of a more descriptive nature in order to provide background to the problems.

We wish to express our gratitude to all those who in any way assisted in the preparation of this book, especially to the authors and publishers who generously permitted us to reprint their articles.

FREDERICK VAUGHAN,
PATRICK KYBA,
O. P. DWIVEDI.

*For a good discussion of the lacunae in Canadian political science research, see Donald V. Smiley, "Contributions to Canadian Political Science Since the Second World War", *Canadian Journal of Economics & Political Science*, XXXIII, No. 4, November, 1967, Toronto: University of Toronto Press.

CONTEMPORARY
ISSUES IN
CANADIAN POLITICS

SECTION ONE

FEDERALISM

If one can say that Canadian federalism has evolved over the past one hundred years, one must surely say that that evolution was influenced by the concept of federalism held by the Prime Ministers throughout those years. Certainly no one doubts that the present Prime Minister has a clear idea of what Canadian federalism is and how it should function in the future. The first essay in this section is, therefore, Mr. Trudeau's controversial statement concerning the theory and practice of federalism.

And for those who believe that "Canada's future lies in the direction of co-operative federalism", W. R. Lederman's essay on the limitations of this approach will prove particularly instructive.

No discussion of Canadian federalism would be complete without a statement by a French Canadian on the difficult problem of special status for Quebec, a problem to which both Prime Minister Trudeau and W. R. Lederman allude in their essays. Claude Ryan's balanced statement on the form such special status might take is a significant contribution to the resolution of the problem.

And, perhaps as a reminder that the problems of Canadian federalism are deep and serious, Donald Smiley's previously unpublished essay on the resolution of federal-provincial conflicts brings this section to a close.

1

I

The Practice and
Theory of Federalism*

PIERRE ELLIOTT TRUDEAU

Goals have no more reality than the means that are devised to reach them. As every reformer discovers sooner or later to his chagrin, it is not sufficient to conceive ideals lofty enough, and to desire them strongly enough, for them to be automatically attained through some due process of history. And there exists no 'Operation Boot-straps' whereby dedicated parties can lift themselves by sheer force of will into the realm of justice triumphant.

Therefore inevitably, the electoral failings of democratic socialism in most industrial societies have led the partisans of social democracy in recent years to reappraise their ends and their means in the light of changing social and economic reality. For example, the nationalization of the instruments of production is now being considered less as an end than as a means, and one that might in many cases be replaced by more flexible processes of economic control and redistribution.

In Canada, the Regina Manifesto of 1933 was replaced in 1956 by the Winnipeg statement of principles which purported to fit more adequately the social and economic temper of the times. Socialist strategy likewise has been radically altered, as is shown by the recent resolutions of the C.C.F. and of the Canadian Labour Congress to launch a new party. But unfortunately socialists in Canada have seldom been guided in their doctrine and their strategy by a whole-hearted acceptance of the basic political fact of federalism.

Left-wing thinkers have too often assumed that fundamental reform is impossible without a vast increase, in law or in fact, of the national government's areas of jurisdiction; C.C.F. parliamentarians have repeatedly identified themselves with centralism, albeit within the framework of a federal constitution; party strategists have planned accordingly; and the general public can rarely praise or damn Canadian socialism without referring to its centralizing tendencies.

In this essay, I will state my belief that the foregoing assumptions and inclinations have considerably harmed the cause of reform. Section I will

---

*This article originally appeared in Michael Oliver (ed.) *Social Purpose for Canada*, Toronto, University of Toronto Press, 1961. By permission of the publishers.

show that, other things being equal, radicalism can more easily be introduced in a federal society than in a unitary one. Section II will claim that the dynamics of history are not urging the Canadian nation towards centralization any more than they are towards decentralization. Section III will argue that the theory of democratic socialism can make no unassailable case for centralization.

In consequence, it should follow that Canadian socialists must consider federalism as a positive asset, rather than as an inevitable handicap. However, that is not to say – and I hope the point will remain present in the reader's mind throughout – that this essay pleads *for* provincial autonomy and *against* centralization in absolute terms. My plea is merely for greater realism and greater flexibility in the socialist approach to problems of federalism: I should like to see socialists feeling free to espouse whatever political trends or to use whatever constitutional tools happen to fit each particular problem at each particular time; and if my argument is taken to mean that the present socialist preconception in favour of centralism should permanently be replaced by a preconception in favour of provincial autonomy, I shall have completely failed to make my point.

ON STRATEGY AND TACTICS

If the whole of the Canadian electorate could miraculously be converted to socialist ideals at one fell swoop, there would be no reason to discuss strategy in the present context. Socialism would be achieved with or without federalism, and socialist administrations would be installed at every level of governmental affairs, no matter what the form of the constitution.

But such is not the case. In a non-revolutionary society and in non-revolutionary times, no manner of reform can be implanted with sudden universality. Democratic reformers must proceed step by step, convincing little bands of intellectuals here, rallying sections of the working class there, and appealing to the underprivileged in the next place. The drive towards power must begin with the establishment of bridgeheads, since at the outset it is obviously easier to convert specific groups or localities than to win over an absolute majority of the whole nation.

Under a system of proportional representation the argument might run differently, and indeed that is why so many reformers have stood for P.R. But it is obviously unrealistic to suppose that the governing parties will introduce electoral régimes that would hasten the accession to power of the oppositions. Consequently, radical strategy must be designed to operate under the present electoral system of one-man constituencies.

In the absence of P.R. it seems obvious that the multi-state system of a federal constitution is the next best thing. (Indeed the experience of that superb strategist Mao Tse-tung might lead us to conclude that in a vast and heterogeneous country, the possibility of establishing socialist strongholds in certain regions is the very best thing.) It is strange that on the one hand C.C.F. tacticians often argue that the road to power at the national level might have to pass through the election of socialist administrations at the municipal level, but that on the other hand, by casting themselves as very unenthusiastic supporters of provincial autonomy, they make it difficult for themselves to follow the provincial highroads towards national power. Such subservience of the tacticians to the postulates of the 'theory class' is amazing, in face of the fact that the C.C.F. has become the Government or the official Opposition in several Provinces, whereas it has never come within sight of such successes in the national Parliament.

True, the successes of socialism at the provincial level, especially around the middle 1940s, did stimulate somewhat more interest in the provincial cause. But, for all that, a change of attitude to federalism still seems to be required within the ranks of Canadian socialism. No longer must our federal constitution be regarded as something to be undone, the result of a costly historical error which is only retained at all because of the 'backward areas' of Canada. Federalism must not only be accepted as a datum with which Canada is stuck, as is many another country of semi-continental size. Federalism must be welcomed as a valuable tool which permits dynamic parties to plant socialist governments in certain Provinces, from which the seed of radicalism can slowly spread.

Economists readily accept the fact that different areas have reached different stages of economic growth, and consequently that theories cannot be implemented everywhere in identical fashion.[1] Sociologists accept similar facts with similar consequences. It is urgent that socialist politicians give wider recognition to the fact that different regions or ethnic groups in Canada are at vastly different stages of their political development, and that it is folly to endorse strategies that are devised to swing the whole country at the same time and in the same way into the path of socialism.

I have heard socialist leaders in Canada state with indignation that they would never 'water down' their doctrines to make them more palatable to this or that part of Canada. Such an approach, I must admit, always puzzles me; for socialism, like every other political theory, has been diluted at different times and in different places to a great variety of strengths. And in terms of political tactics, the only real question democratic socialists must answer is: 'Just how much reform can the majority of the people be brought to desire at the present time?'

The main distinction between the conservative and the progressive mind is that, in seeking the solution to the foregoing problem, the progressive will tend to overestimate the people's desire for justice, freedom, and change, whereas the conservative will tend to err on the side of order, authority, and continuity. The true tactical position of the *democratic* socialist is on the left, *but no further.*

Such a line of thought leads to the conclusion — unpleasant only for the doctrinaires — that socialists must stand for different things in different parts of Canada. Of course there is a need for doctrinaires of a sort; or at any rate for theoreticians who will constantly expound what they think to be the nearest thing to 'pure' socialism. For, as it has been often observed, the dreamers of today frequently become the realists of tomorrow; and the educational value of painting utopias has repeatedly been established by the eventual realization of such goals through the democratic process.

Yet, so long as socialism is to seek fulfilment through parliamentary democracy, with its paraphernalia of parties and elections, there will be a constant need for the tactician as well as the theorist. And both will have to be reconciled by the strategist.

Now it should be obvious to all these groups that no national party can keep its integrity while preaching a gospel which varies as it moves *a mari usque ad mare*; neither can it keep its status as a national party if it seeks support only in narrow regionalism. Yet, on the other hand, if the party preaches the same gospel everywhere, its partisans in some areas will desert it as being too reactionary, whereas in other areas the party will fail to find adherents because it appears too revolutionary.

That dilemma can easily be solved by making full use of our federative form of government. Socialists *can* stand for varying degrees of socialism in the various Provinces of Canada by standing in autonomous provincial parties. Indeed, since the strength of a national party is largely determined by the strength of its component parts, sufficient priority must be given to the building of such parts. In other words, in building a national party to the left, consideration must be given to what is provincially possible as well as to what is nationally desirable. The policy of the national party will thus be the result of a compromise between the most and the least advanced socialist thinking in various parts of Canada.

It is perhaps no coincidence that during the twentieth century — that is to say, during the period when Canada has effectively developed into a vast and heterogeneous nation spreading from coast to coast — the one national party that has been strongest and governed longest is the party that has traditionally stood for provincial rights and embraced in its ranks such provincial free-stylers as Taschereau, Hepburn, Angus Macdonald, and Smallwood. For even while the Liberals at Ottawa were riding the wave of centralism, Liberal leaders in provincial capitals were stoutly defending the cause of autonomy.

By contrast, the C.C.F. has reaped little electoral reward for its studied application in speaking with one voice and acting with one purpose in all parts of Canada. In Quebec alone, where the socialist vote has usually hovered around 1 per cent of the total, a book could be filled with the frustrations of former members of the C.C.F. who felt or imagined that provincial affairs must always be subordinate to the *raison d'état* of the national party.

In the postwar era the Quebec organization squandered its efforts and made itself ridiculous by running spurious candidates in two or three dozen ridings at each federal election, partly in order to obtain free time on the air-waves, but mainly in order that the electorate of the rest of Canada might be momentarily fooled into believing that the party was strong in Quebec. Then in 1956 and 1957, when efforts were being made to enlarge

1. See Scott Gordon's chapter in M. Oliver (ed.) , *Social Purpose for Canada*, Toronto: University of Toronto Press, 1961, wherein he accepts the possibility that the wage rate in the Maritimes will be lower than the Canadian average, provided the rate of growth is not. See also W. W. Rostow, *Stages of Economic Growth*, Cambridge: The University Press, 1962, *passim*.

the left in Quebec by grouping all liberal-minded people in the *Rassemble-ment,* members of the C.C.F. – on the grounds that the C.C.F. was here to stay – refused to envisage any orientation that might lead to the setting up of a left-wing political group, newer and stronger than the C.C.F. Finally, in 1958 and 1959, when the C.C.F. had decided it was no longer here to stay but here to merge into a new party, the Quebec branch of the C.C.F. – on the grounds that it had to wait for the new party – rejected the *Union des forces démocratiques,* with the consequence, in June 1960, that the *Union nationale* party was defeated by the Liberals alone rather than by a coalition of the left and of liberal-minded people.

The historical events briefly recited in the foregoing paragraph were the result of discussion and decision by honest men. If I refer to them in the present context it cannot be with the intention of displaying hindsight; for who knows what good or evil would have followed from the contrary decisions? But such references are necessary to illustrate what great pains were taken by the C.C.F. in Quebec in order to avoid 'nationalist devia-tionism'. In view of Quebec's past, such a course was not without some justification, but it obviously went too far when it precluded the Quebec left from exploiting the same type of elementary opportunity as that which permitted the launching by Mr. Ed Finn of *a* new party in Newfoundland, even though *the* new party had not yet fired the starting gun.

In short, the C.C.F. in and out of Quebec always seemed to take the position that once it had become a powerful party at the national level it would easily find support in each Province. Such an approach smacks of paternalism, if each Province is taken singly; and it obviously begs the principle, if the situation is considered as a whole.

A great amount of freedom for the left appears to be necessary at the provincial level. Just as each Province must evolve towards political and economic maturity in its own good time, likewise radicalism in different parts of Canada must be implanted in different fashions. For a time, parties with the same name may find themselves preaching policies differing in scope from one Province to the other. Perhaps even parties with different names may preach the same ideology in different Provinces. And for a time, the situation of the left in Canada will not be cut and dried. It will be confused and challenging; and its diversity from Province to Province will stimulate competition and perhaps even establish a system of checks and balances, while at the national level the left will adopt strategies and tactics based on possibilities rather than on mere desirabilities.

The socialist mind is a planning one, so in all likelihood it will not respond enthusiastically to the pragmatic approach to strategy which is suggested here. Consequently, it may be well to point out that the present argument does not do away with the possibility of, or with the need for, planning at every level of politics; but it does lend emphasis to the im-portance of the plan at the provincial level, and hence it makes planning more effective.

Obviously, a strategy limited to Saskatchewan (or Quebec, or British Columbia) will be less exciting than one covering the whole of Canada. But it will also be less exciting than a plan applicable to the Socialist In-ternational. And much more telling than either!

It is sometimes argued by Canadian socialists that their opposition to the United States is not based on narrow nationalism, but on the fact that complete American domination would tend to prevent Canada as a community from realizing values good for human beings. In other words they believe that socialism can more easily be established in Canada, as a smaller unit, than on the whole North American continent. Surely, then, they should not underestimate the importance of trying to realize socialism in the even smaller units of the Provinces, which have, within the limits of the constitution and particularly of Section 92, many of the prerogatives of sovereign states.

ON HISTORY, PAST AND FUTURE

Of the countries of the world, Canada has the eighth oldest written constitution, the second oldest one of a federal nature, and the oldest which combines federalism with the principles of responsible government.

Yet some of our fellow Canadians have an even more illustrious record as pioneers in constitution-making: the Confederation of Six Iroquois Nations was founded in 1570, or thereabouts, and is still in existence today. Anthropologists and sociologists have marvelled at the keen political sense of Canada's earlier inhabitants. And the question arises whether historians will have the same opinion of the subsequent settlers!

If it be true that the first hundred years are the hardest, I see no cause to despair of the future of Canadian federalism. True, its erratic advance has caused many misgivings. There has been endless discussion as to the nature of the British North America Act, whether it be of the essence of a law or of a contract; and we have heard much argument from the lawyers and the senators, deploring the provincial bias given to the constitution by the Privy Council.

In reference to practical politics, such discussions can become tedious. It should be a sufficiently workable proposition to hold that the Act of 1867 was a law of the Imperial Parliament, but a law based on an agreement between federating parties, and consequently a law which can best be understood and interpreted (and eventually amended) by referring to the spirit of that agreement.

As to the criticism of the Privy Council's interpretation of the B.N.A. Act, it is basically in the same category as the criticism of the Supreme Court interpretations by a late premier of Quebec. In the final analysis, the ultimate decisions of the courts in matters of public concern always affect someone's politics adversely and will always be attacked on that basis.

Such criticism of the Privy Council by socialists is of course a political right. But I wonder how useful it is to the cause of socialism when it can be fairly construed as an opposition to provincial autonomy. For, as I shall argue later on, in section III of this essay, socialists do not stand to gain very much in theoretical terms from vastly increased centralization. And in practical terms, I have tried to show in section I that they stand to lose a great deal. In point of fact, had the C.C.F. been less identified with centralization I doubt whether it would have been weaker as a national party.

On the contrary, its national strength might have benefited from the improved fortunes of the provincial parties. And I do not see how democratic socialism could have been adulterated in the process.

True, in present-day politics, there exist a number of built-in centralizing forces. The combination of external pressure and of improved internal communication may tend to unify large countries to a greater extent than in the past. Legislation may tend to become as broad as the problem with which it is meant to deal, and a federal constitution may not appear to be the best instrument for dealing with a non-federal economic society. The countervailing power to a corporate élite which is nationwide in strength may have to be a government which is nationwide in jurisdiction. And for all these reasons, the socialist will be tempted to enhance the power of the central government at the expense of the Provinces.

But the true socialist will also be a humanist and a democrat, and he will be quick to realize that Canada is very much a federal society from the sociological point of view; people from various parts of Canada *do* hang together on a regional basis which very often supersedes the class basis. And the understanding of Canadian political history would be very incomplete indeed if it ignored the existence, for instance, of the Maritimer, the Quebecker, or the Westerner. In the first part of this chapter I have argued that the existence of such regional fidelities provided a tactical asset to the spread of radicalism. But I add here that they may eventually, in times when cybernetic planning is becoming a possibility, prove to be the main bulwark of democracy against a central government's *New Despotism,* its *Law and Orders* or its 'parliamentary bureaucracy'.

For there are physical limits to the control which may be exercised over the central bureaucracy by the people's representatives and by the judiciary. The executive power may tend to increase its control by increasing the number of ministers; but the Cabinet will quickly reach that size beyond which deliberation becomes useless and decision impossible. (Thus, in the United Kingdom, out of some five dozen ministers, perhaps only half of them will be of Cabinet rank and only twenty-odd will actually sit in the Cabinet proper.) The legislative power can increase its control over the bureaucracy by increasing the length of the parliamentary session, but there again British experience shows that the entire year eventually proves too short; besides, in as large a country as Canada, Members of Parliament would lose all contact with the electorate if they had to sojourn in the federal capital indefinitely.

As regards the judiciary, its terms of reference are limited by the statutes themselves, which are generally prepared by the bureaucracy before being adopted by Parliament; the judiciary is powerless to exercise an over-all control of the bureaucracy as long as our system of administrative law remains in its present embryonic state.

In time, it is hoped that administrative law will be expanded and perfected, that Parliament will learn to use the committee system with greater effectiveness, and that other devices will be developed to protect democracy against bureaucracy. But in the meanwhile, and even after, it would be folly to disregard the device of federalism which we already have in our possession and which may be the most effective of all, since it reduces the magnitude of the task allotted to one central government.

Furthermore, in the age of the mass society, it is no small advantage to foster the creation of quasi-sovereign communities at the provincial level, where power is that much less remote from the people and where political education (and general creativeness) is related to more homogeneous and manageable groups of citizens.

Finally, it might be added that at a time when the uncontrolled production of thermo-nuclear weapons has made total war a gruesome possibility, the case for decentralization in terms of defence extends far beyond the mere scattering of industries.

Caught between centripetal and centrifugal forces, Canada's future, like its past, may continue to oscillate between times of federal and times of provincial predominance, depending upon the immediate needs of the people and the temper of their various politicians. (For it must not be forgotten that these latter have a vested interest in strengthening *that* level of government at which *they* operate.) Or – more likely – the political future of Canada will lie in the direction of greater centralization in some areas and greater decentralization in others. But at all times, co-operation and interchange between the two levels of government will be, as they have been, an absolute necessity. In that sense, I doubt whether federalism in the classical sense has ever existed, that is to say a federation which would have divided the totality of its sovereign powers between regional and central governments with such sharpness and adequacy that those governments would have been able to carry on their affairs in complete independence of one another.

Applied to Canada, the foregoing statement is easily proved. The constitutional provisions of the B.N.A. Act established intergovernmental relationship as indispensable from the outset, among the executive, the legislative, and the judicial organs.

Concerning the executive, the office of Lieutenant-Governor was designed to ensure a permanent bond between the federal and the provincial governments: the Lieutenant-Governor was definitely a federal official, appointed, paid, and in some cases dismissed by the Ottawa government. The powers of reservation and disallowance also provided a link between the two levels of government. Finally the financing of the respective administrations was established as an area of indispensable co-operation: by Confederation the Provinces gave up the bulk of their sources of revenue, retaining only direct taxes and various fees; in exchange the central government pledged itself to make the four different types of payment referred to in sections 111, 118, and 119 of the B.N.A. Act.

As regards the legislative function, relations were inevitable in the areas of subordinate jurisdiction and in those of divided jurisdiction. Under the first heading fall sections 93, 94, and 95 of the B.N.A. Act, relating to education, uniform legislation, agriculture, and immigration; in that area we might also add cases of conditional legislation or of legislation by reference (but not of legislation by delegation, which is deemed unconstitutional). Under the second heading (jurisdiction divided between the federal and the provincial legislative powers) fall four types of laws: first, laws concerning matters which can be regulated either by criminal or by civil law, such as the Sunday Observance Acts; second, laws concerning matters which fall partly under the federal residual clause ('peace, order and good government') and partly under the provincial residual clause ('all matters of merely local or private nature'), such as Temperance Acts; third, laws concerning matters which, according to their extension, are either 'regulation of trade and commerce' or 'property and civil rights', such as company laws, marketing laws, and industrial legislation; fourth, laws concerning matters allocated (without subordination) to both federal and provincial jurisdiction, either by the letter of the B.N.A. Act, such as direct taxation, or by judicial interpretation, such as fisheries.

Finally, in judicial matters, co-operation was of vital importance. By Section 92, paragraph 14, the Provinces were given exclusive jurisdiction over the administration of justice; by 96 the Governor General appoints 'the Judges of the Superior, District and County Courts in each Province'; and by 101 the central government may establish a general court of appeals and any additional courts. If these sections in their application had not been reasonably well integrated, the judiciary would have ceased to function: rival tribunals would have been set up, *res judicata* would have had no meaning, and clash between executive powers would have been inevitable.

From the foregoing analysis of the B.N.A. Act it is obvious that intergovernmental co-operation is not only possible but that it is in many ways consitutionally indispensable. It is not surprising therefore that the federal and provincial governments have developed many instruments for dealing with subjects of joint concern.

First in order of importance are the meetings of governments at ministerial level: the federal-provincial conferences of 1906, 1910, 1915, 1918, 1927, 1931, 1932, 1933, 1934, 1935, 1941, 1945-6, 1950, 1960 (not to be confused with the inter-provincial conferences of 1887, 1902, 1910, 1913, 1926, 1960).

Second come the meetings of departments at ministerial level. This category includes, for example, the agricultural conferences, the Ministers of Mines Committee, the tourist conferences, all of which are generally annual meetings of the appropriate ministers and other personnel. Also included in this group are the Old Age Pension Interprovincial Board, the conferences set up for the exchange of statistical material, and those convened to discuss the Trans-Canada Highway.

Third, at the purely administrative level, there exists a great variety of agreements and continuing organizations to deal co-operatively with specific matters of common concern. Typical examples include the Canadian Association of Administrators of Labour Legislation, the Conference of Commissioners on Uniformity of Legislation, the Committee on Security Frauds Prevention Law, the Committee on Uniform Company Law, the Fisheries Development Committee, the Fur Advisory Committee, the Provincial Boundary Commission, the Canadian Council on Nutrition, the

Canadian Wild Life Conference, the Vocational Training Committee. Other examples might include the recently established 'Resources for To-morrow' Conference; co-operation in the fields of agricultural and forestry research and control; arrangements concerning citizenship training classes; co-ordination of health programs; agreements whereby provincial officers administer the federal Migratory Birds Convention Act or some of the fisheries regulations enacted by the Government of Canada; agreements whereby certain Provinces delegate the policing of certain towns and rural districts to the R.C.M.P.[2]

Finally, and in a category apart, one must consider the various types of financial arrangements between the federal government and the Provinces. As was stated above, the B.N.A. Act made provision for certain types of federal payments. But government finance remained ever a problem: the subsidy basis was thoroughly altered by constitutional amendment in 1907, and in various ways since then. Federal grants-in-aid to help the Provinces with specific tasks were also resorted to, though rather sparingly at first, since it was generally felt that the spending of funds should not be divorced from the perception thereof. This category also includes the tax rental agreements, first begun during the Second World War, and periodically renewed, with varying degrees of provincial acceptance, the history of which is fairly well known.

The purpose of the foregoing paragraphs is to show that the story of Canadian federalism is one of constant intergovernmental exchange and co-operation. It is also in part a story of sometimes subtle, sometimes brazen, and usually tolerated encroachments by one government upon the juris-diction of the other. For instance, the federal government (which has always shirked using the jurisdiction over education it held under Section 93, paragraph 4, of the B.N.A. Act) has used grants-in-aid to enter reso-lutely into the areas of technical and university education. Indeed the federal 'spending power' or so-called 'power of the purse' is at present being construed as a federal right to decide (at the taxpayers' expense!) whether provincial governments are properly exercising any and every right they hold under the constitution.[3]

2. The foregoing enumeration is apt to appear long and tedious to the layman. But in order that he truly grasp the tremendous scope of federal-provincial relation-ships, I will add that in 1950, at the request of the Privy Council Office, I made a summary of existing federal-provincial co-operative arrangements which covered more than fifty pages.

3. In a brilliant chapter published in A. R. M. Lower, F. R. Scott, et al., Evolving Canadian Federalism, Durham, N.C., 1958, Professor Corry finds it 'extraordinary that no one has challenged the constitutionality of the assumed spending power before the Supreme Court' (p. 119). I share his wonderment; but I find it even more extraordinary that political scientists fail to see the eroding effect that the 'power of the purse' will have on Canadian democracy if the present construction continues to prevail, and in particular what chaos will result if provincial govern-ments borrow federal logic and begin using their own 'power of the purse' to meddle in federal affairs.

On the other hand, examples can be given of provincial encroachments upon federal jurisdiction. The invasion, supported by legal fiction, into the field of indirect taxation might be one case. Another example is the appointment of judges of provincial courts whose jurisdiction far exceeds the limits beyond which only that of federal judges was supposed to go, under Section 96 of the constitution[4].

In short, it almost seems as though whenever an important segment of the Canadian population needs something badly enough, it is eventually given to them by one level of government or the other, regardless of the constitution. The main drawback to such an approach is that it tends to develop paternalistic instincts in more enterprising governments, at the expense of democratic maturation in others. In areas where there exists a clear division of responsibilities between the federal and provincial levels, there is no doubt that the only proper censor of a government which incompetently discharges its obligations is the electorate of *that* government, and not some other government responsible to some other (level of) electorate.[5] And if, for example, federal politicians are convinced that by their very nature the totality of the provincial governments *cannot* discharge their duties in some area, surely the proper procedure is for those politicians to seek the overt transfer of such areas into federal jurisdiction, either by way of constitutional amendment (as in the case of unemployment insurance), or by invoking federal powers under Section 92, paragraph 10 (c).[6]

It might be wise to labour this point further, since it will illustrate how certain policies, though conceived in terms of the general welfare and applied in a spirit of co-operation, can in reality be paternalism in disguise.

Thus far in this essay I have studiously avoided making a special case for French Canada. But at this time it is necessary to discuss the special case English-Canadian writers sometimes make on its behalf.

It has been very ably argued that 'the initial survival of French culture in Canada did not depend upon provincial autonomy'; and further that 'the possession of provincial autonomy was a relatively minor factor in the growth of French culture and influence during the first half century after 1867.'[7] Both facts are quite true; but not true is the inference that many people draw from them, to wit, that the survival and growth of French-Canadian culture do not (at the present time) depend upon the existence of provincial autonomy. Such an inference might only be true if culture were defined to exclude the art of self-government. As a matter of fact, if the ability to govern themselves is such a minor facet of the French Canadians' cultural make-up today, it is precisely because in the past French Canadians never learned to make proper use of their elective governments as servants of the whole community.

Typically, Quebec's two most recent champions of provincial autonomy, Premiers Taschereau and Duplessis, were socially and economically conservatives. They barely exercised many of the powers given to them by the autonomy they so loudly affirmed and, as a result, social and cultural legislation was the product of the central government over which the French-Canadian electorate had no absolute control.

Now there is no need to remind me that the central government is not foreign, but is the government of all Canadians. And I do not find good legislation distasteful merely because it originates in Ottawa as opposed to Quebec.[8] The real question lies elsewhere: can a cultural group, which by virtue of the Act of 1867 received the right to govern itself in many areas of jurisdiction, ever mature democratically if it persistently neglects or refuses to exercise its right? And are not such omissions or refusals inevitable if the lacunae they create are constantly and adequately filled up by a central government which is largely representative of another cultural group? To give but one example: from the Quebec point of view, the most serious objection to federal grants to universities was obviously not that the universities had enough money or that federal money had a peculiar odour; it was that once the universities had their bellies filled with federal grants they would see no reason to oppose that provincial government which had persistently failed in its constitutional duties by leaving education in such an impoverished state; and Quebeckers would chalk up another failure in their struggle to master the art of self-government.

At this point, a comment may well be forthcoming: should the universities of the poorer Provinces be faced with starvation simply because Quebec is showing signs of embarking upon the slow process of political maturation? The objection is typical of all those which keep Quebec nationalism alive. For it is basically emotional and misses the point that the university grants were not equalization grants since they were handed to all Provinces, rich and poor, on the same basis. Nor, for that matter, were they anti-cyclical in nature since they were initiated and continued in times of inflation, when the central government should have been trying to reduce its spending. To the average Quebecker, therefore, the

4. I first heard this point raised by Mr. Benno Cohen of the Montreal Bar.

5. I will consider the case of disallowance and of reservation later on. But it might avoid considerable misunderstanding if I state immediately and unequivocally that I hold equalization grants (enabling poorer provinces to keep pace with the richer ones) and counter-cyclical fiscal policies to be within the jurisdiction of the federal government.

6. In this respect it might be remarked that if these latter means are infrequently used, it is partly because central governments, who occasionally like to meddle in provincial affairs, do not necessarily relish the prospect of being saddled with some new responsibility for ever. It is interesting to note that while it took over sole responsibility for unemployment *insurance*, the federal government has always scrupulously avoided the claim that unemployment *in general* was a matter within the jurisdiction of the federal government.

7. F. R. Scott, "French-Canada and Canadian Federalism" in A. R. M. Lower, ed., *Evolving Canadian Federalism* Durham, N.C.: Duke University Press, 1958 pp. 57 and 59.

8. As a matter of fact I might be prepared to argue that some day, if and when *inter alia* the political maturity of all Canadians had reached a very high level, a more centralized state would be acceptable for Canada.

university grants appeared to be an invasion pure and simple of provincial rights.[9]

Most English Canadians fail to realize that it is their attitude (as in the above example) which exactly determines the extent and force of Quebec nationalism. Central government encroachments, which are accepted in other Provinces as matters of expediency, cannot be so viewed in Quebec. For French Canadians are not in any important sense represented in the Canadian power élite, whether governmental or financial,[10] and any attempt at unilateral transference of power from the Quebec élite to the Canadian one will naturally set the corresponding defence mechanisms in motion. On the contrary, a scrupulous respect of the postulates of federalism – by rendering such mechanisms obsolete – will lend greater force to the efforts of those Quebeckers who are trying to turn their Province into an open society. And perhaps more important still, it will create a climate where the debate between autonomy and centralization can be solved through rational rather than emotional discussion.

The upshot of my entire argument in this section is that socialists, rather than water down (to use a previous expression) their socialism, must constantly seek ways of adapting it to a bicultural society governed under a federal constitution. And since the future of Canadian federalism lies clearly in the direction of co-operation, the wise socialist will turn his thoughts in that direction, keeping in mind the importance of establishing buffer zones of joint sovereignty and co-operative zones of joint administration between the two levels of government.

The establishment of such areas of confidence is very important; for when parties stand as equals at negotiations, the results are invariably better and fairer. That perhaps is why there has been a great deal of effective co-operation between federal and provincial departmental officials; each feels that he is answerable only to his own sovereign' government. Might not machinery be established to extend this feeling to meetings at the highest levels with similar beneficial result?

There have been many proposals for setting up machinery to ensure better co-operation between the federal and the provincial governments. The most frequent concern the desirability of having periodic federal-provincial conferences with a permanent secretariat to ensure their successful functioning. A less frequent proposal advocates the establishment of a secretary of state for the Provinces at Ottawa, and a department of federal relations in each Province. It has also been suggested that if governments were constitutionally permitted to delegate legislative powers to one another there would be much greater co-operation between them.

Of course there exist many more devices for promoting co-operative federalism.[11] And others still await discovery. By way of example I might single out a rather neglected piece of co-operative machinery: royal commissions of inquiry could become a very important medium of co-operation between governments in Canada, rather than the causes of friction they sometimes are now. Reliable information upon matters of joint concern is essential to the pursuance of harmonious federal-provincial relations;

it is therefore surprising that in such matters royal commissions tend[12] to be the exclusive creation of the executive branch of *one* government, which in effect exercises inquisitorial activities over acts within the jurisdiction of other governments. Surely, in such cases, some method should be devised for the setting up of joint commissions of inquiry, appointed by the several governments and reporting back to them.

But unfortunately there is here neither time nor place to discuss these matters further. It would be regrettable, however, if Canadian socialists found too little time to discuss them. For if it be true that Canada's future lies in the direction of co-operative federalism, it will be guided there by those parties and politicians who will have proven themselves most realistic and far-seeing in that regard.

ON THEORY

It would seem at first glance that many of the more important economic policies of socialism can only be applied with thoroughness under a unitary form of government. Economic planning and control have little meaning

9. There is here neither time nor place to deal at length with the subject of federal grants to universities. However, I wish to make it quite clear that the Quebec argument is based on the explicit position of the federal authorities that they have no jurisdiction whatsoever over education. (*Cf.* St. Laurent's speech at Sherbrooke in October 1956, and one on November 12 of that year.) Since the grants cannot be justified on grounds of federal jurisdiction over education, nor in terms of macro-economic stabilization, nor for reasons of equalization policy, there only remains the argument of 'the power of the purse'. That prerogative is interpreted to mean that any government can raise money by taxation for purposes outside of its jurisdiction, provided it gives the money without any attempt to legislate. In my view such an interpretation is not only wrong but dangerous: for it would, for instance, authorize the provinces to tax in order to pay a large bonus to any federal civil servants or military personnel who could prove their mastery of the French language; or to any federal judge whose philosophy was 'sound'. And so on.

10. See John Porter's work on economic and bureaucratic élites, *Canadian Journal of Economics and Political Science*, Toronto: University of Toronto Press, August 1957, p. 386, and November 1958, p. 491. For other references, see P. E. Trudeau (ed.), *La Grève de l'amiante*, Montreal: Les Editions Cité Libre, 1956, p. 77.

11. Thus in Australia co-operative action has been greatly faciliated by such institutions as the Premiers' Conferences and the Loan Council. The United States, which, it might be argued, is more centrally controlled than Canada, has also experimented with many devices of inter-state co-operation: the Governors' Conferences, the Regional conferences of Governors, the Council of State Governments, the American Legislators' Association, the different national associations of Secretaries of State, of Supervisors of State Banks, etc.

12. Quasi-exceptions — to rare to create a contrary tread — have existed. For instance, Mr. Mackenzie King in 1909 obtained the approval of all provinces before proceeding with the appointment of a Commission on Industrial Training and Techical Education. In 1948 the Fraser Valley Commission included commissioners nominated by federal and provincial governments, and was asked to report to both.

unless they are part of a unified, well-integrated process. Therefore, the argument goes, a socialist must, in essence, be a centralizer.

Fiscal and monetary policies, for instance, are bound to have little beneficial effect if various central and regional governments are at liberty to cancel out each other's actions by contradictory policies. Thus a deficitary federal budget would have but slight effect upon national deflationary trends if provincial surpluses added up to an amount equal to the federal deficit.

However, it must be pointed out that from that point of view socialists are no worse off than neo-capitalists or Keynesian liberals. The stabilization policies of these latter groups might also be easier to apply in a unitary state; but in its absence, those groups do not throw up their hands in despair, nor do they cast political caution to the winds by becoming crusaders against provincial rights. They merely set out to find ways of adapting their economic theories to the political realities.

In Canada, there exists no constitutional problem as regards monetary policy, since money, banking, and the interest rate all fall under the single jurisdiction of the central government. However, regarding fiscal policy the difficulties are great, since provincial governments have autonomous budgets and consequent taxing, borrowing, and spending powers. And, for instance, Canadian postwar inflation was no doubt aggravated to the extent that certain provincial deficits operated against federal surpluses.

It is to the credit of the Liberals that they devised and implemented tax rental agreements between the central and regional governments which curtailed the degree to which the fiscal practices of the various governments might operate at cross-purposes. But as time went by it became obvious that Liberal logic, as expressed during the 1945 Conference (and in the Green Book), was in reality a vicious circle: the federal government – because it had greater financial resources – argued that it should bear greater social responsibility and therefore that its financial powers should be correspondingly increased.

It is to the credit of the reactionaries (I am referring to Mr. Duplessis and his Union Nationale) that they refused to be deceived by a system whereby the federal government could, in lieu of the provincial government, tax the citizen in all the Provinces in order to spend money (on a scale far in excess of that which might have been required for stabilization or equalization policies) for purposes within provincial jurisdiction. But it is not to the credit of the socialists that they should have been little more than bystanders, goading the Liberals on, during this whole episode.[13]

At the present time, when Canadian public opinion, led by the Liberal Premier of Quebec and the Conservative Premier of Ontario, apparently unopposed by the socialist Premier of Saskatchewan, seems to be running amok in favour of extreme provincialism, as witnessed by the federal-provincial conference held in the summer of 1960, there is a greater need than ever for an enlightened socialist approach to the fiscal problems of a federal form of government. If the swing towards centralism, which began with the Depression, is not now to be countered by a long swing towards excessive regionalism, there will be an urgent need for solutions based on co-operation.

It is quite conceivable that Canadian fiscal policy could be considered from month to month and year to year by a joint continuing committee of federal and provincial officials and experts. Confronted with comprehensive sets of statistical material and forecasting data, such a committee – if it were immunized against all forms of political interference – could make policy recommendations as well as any body of purely central officials; and perhaps even better, since they would take greater cognizance of such problems as regional bottle-necks, local unemployment, and immobility of labour, and since the hitherto purely federal control over money and banking would be examined in the light of provincial budgetary needs.

Of course, it would be up to the several provincial and central governments to decide what they would do with the policy recommendations. And this is where co-operation at the executive levels would appear to be of extreme importance and would have to be recognized as such. But one could count, in the first place, on some degree of moral suasion to which the governments might find themselves subjected. And in the second, the various electorates – when the time came to judge the financial policies of their respective governments – would be less inclined than now to condone incompetence or ignorance.

For there is no escape from politics, nor should there be. There is always one point where the most expert economic advice must be submitted for implementation to the political representatives of the people. 'I know no safe depository of the ultimate powers of society but the people themselves; and if we think them not enlightened enough to exercise this control with a wholesome discretion, the remedy is not to take it from them, but to inform their discretion by education' (Thomas Jefferson). And as I have shown in sections I and II of this essay, the people can 'exercise their control' just as well under a federal state as under a unitary one, and perhaps even better.

Consequently, the economic aspects of socialist theory might be a guide towards a more efficient distribution of powers under the constitution; but they need never be considered as an invitation to turn Canada, any more than all of North America or the whole world itself, into a unitary state. Planning is a possibility at any and every level of government. It may be more costly (in economic terms of outlay, leakage, multiplier effect, and

13. Exception should be made for the group which headed the Quebec Federation of Industrial Unions (C.C.L.). Their *Mémoire à la Commission royale d'enquête sur les problèmes constitutionnels*, Montreal, 1954, was the first document or statement I know of which reconciled the rationale of provincial tax deductibility with that of equalization grants and macro-economic stabilization. And the preface to the second edition showed that the formulae which had just been worked out by the St. Laurent and the Duplessis governments were wrong, in that they were based on unilateral action and in that they betrayed the very principles of anti-cyclical budgeting.

so on) at one level of government than at another.[14] But the incidence of political cost (in terms of freedom, self-government, local pride, and ingenuity) might be completely the reverse.[15] The true planner is the one who tries to minimize cost and maximize satisfaction, in every way and not only in dollars and cents.

The foregoing argumentation can be applied to every aspect of economic theory. Investment planning and resource development, for instance, both become in the last analysis matters for political decision. In economic terms it may be possible to compare the costs of building and operating a zinc mine at Hay River, a railway in Labrador, a steel mill near Verchères, and a university in Prince Rupert, and the marginal productivity of each. But the social value of such enterprises can only be appreciated with reference to political realities. And the final choice will have to be a political one.

Consequently, in such matters, there is no reason to presume that the federal government will be more enlightened than the sum of the provincial governments, or even than one provincial government acting alone. Since ultimately the decisions are political rather than economic, it follows that they can be taken by Provinces as well as by the central government. And a (socialist) Province with a planning board might be more likely to plan wisely than a (reactionary) central government with no such board.

In other words, economic planning must eventually be reduced to political planning. And the economic theory of socialism cannot be divorced from its political theory, which is largely bound to strategy and tactics.

Thus we revert to the first section of this chapter, which recommended pragmatism, condemned paternalism, and paid great heed to the different stages of political maturity. Since regionalisms do exist in Canada, such feelings should be exploited to further the cause of democracy: each community might enter into a state of healthy competition with the others in order to have better 'self-government'; and thus the whole Canadian system of government would be improved by creative tensions between the central, the provincial, and even the municipal administrations.

Regarding such tensions and competition, it is not for the socialist to cast his lot irrevocably with one level of government as opposed to another. (It is not, for instance, because the reactionaries have in the main opposed centralization that socialists should necessarily favour it!) Since the sum total of governments has the sum total of powers, the first task of the socialist is to educate all of the people to demand maximum service from all of their governments. And his second task is to show how any unhealthy tensions can be resolved through co-operation.

Since every Canadian has a right to the good life, whatever the Province or community he lives in, the socialist should define the minimum conditions required for that life, and make them a part of the socialist program. But such goals must first be stated without any preconception as to whether they should be realized at the federal or at the provincial level. It is often said that the concept of provincial autonomy is favourable to corporate wealth, since it weakens the power of the (central) state. But it can just as easily be shown that it favours socialism, as in the case of Saskatchewan.[16] And, as was pointed out earlier, there is certainly no reason to believe that socialism in Canada is nearer to realization at the federal than at the provincial level.

Federalism then must be regarded as a *chose donnée* of Canadian politics; and in the debate which opposes centralization to autonomy, socialists should be as detached and pragmatic as they hope to become in the debate over public versus private ownership; those are all means, and not ends, and they must be chosen according to their usefulness in each specific case.

Of course, it should not be adduced from the foregoing paragraph that the division of sovereign powers under a federal constitution is held to be purely a matter of arbitrariness and indifference. Obviously some laws and some areas of administration should, by their very nature, come under one level of government rather than under the other. And there is surely some good in trying to improve upon, or modernize, the rational but perhaps ageing division of powers adopted by the Fathers of Confederation. I am inclined to believe, however, that Canadian socialists have exaggerated the urgency of rewriting or reinterpreting the B.N.A. Act.

Personally, I cannot share the views of those people who seem to feel that, had the trend of Privy Council decisions favouring provincial autonomy been different, the fate of the Canadian people would have been immeasurably improved in the past. Neither can I agree with those who, having read long-run centralizing trends into our political future, predict the virtual withering away of Canadian federalism and oblige the political party to which they belong to stand or fall on the fulfilment of such prophecies.

As I have shown above, most of the reforms that could come about

14. Even in strictly economic terms, however, it is too readily assumed that planning should necessarily be a centralized function. Recent studies of planning in the Soviet Union underline 'les nécessités de la décentralisation' and the importance of 'des centres de décisions autonomes' (Cahiers de l'I.S.E.A., No. 86 (Paris, 1959)). And in this connection I am grateful to my friend Mr. Fernand Cadieux for having pointed out to me certain recent trends in the study of social institutions: in their book *Organizations*, New York, 1958, March and Simon invoke 'the principle of bounded rationality as an important force making for decentralization' as opposed to central planning; in other words, 'given realistic limits on human planning capacity, the decentralized system will work better than the centralized' (pp. 203–9).

15. The first effect of centralization is to make every sort of indigenous characteristic disappear in the different parts of a country; while it may be thought that this is the way to exalt political life in the country as a whole, it is really destroying it in its constituent parts and even in its elements.' Proudhon.

16. The riots that occurred in Belgium during the first days of 1961 underline the importance of a decentralized state to the cause of socialism. According to Jean Lambion, an outstanding socialist trade-union official, "federation [instead of a unitary state] would give us Walloons a socialist government to carry out long overdue social and economic reforms we desperately require. There is no other way we can get those things." Montreal *Star*, January 7, 1961.

through greater centralization could also follow from patient and pains-taking co-operation between federal and provincial governments. And the remaining balance of economic advantage that might arise from forcefully transferring more power to the central government is easily offset by the political disadvantages of living under a paternalistic or bullying government.

Granted the foregoing statement, it is difficult to see why socialists devote such energy to constitutional might-have-been's or ought-to-be's, instead of generally accepting the constitution as a datum. From the point of view of 'making available to all what we desire for ourselves', it is not of such momentous consequence that the subject matter of some particular law falls within the jurisdiction of the federal as opposed to the provincial governments, since in either case the governments are responsible to one electorate or another. In other words, laws – whether they issue from one central government or from ten provincial governments – benefit the same sets of citizens. The only important thing, then, is that these latter clearly know which level of government is responsible for what area of legislation, so that they may be aroused to demand good laws from *all* their governments.

A sound rule for Canadian socialists would be to insist that, if need be, they are prepared to carry out their ideals under the present constitution. Thus, they would be encouraged to educate and organize at *all* levels of the electorate. And the various federal or provincial socialist parties and programs would tend to concentrate on that part of the socialist ideals that can be implemented at *their* level of government.

This would not prevent socialist parties from stating in certain limited cases that reforms might be carried out more efficiently if the constitution were amended. But in such cases, amendments would be clearly mentioned, and not sly encroachments which inevitably result in confusing the electorate as to which level of government is responsible for what. Nor would the proposed amendments all, and as a matter of course, tend to be in the direction of centralization.

For instance, provincial socialist parties should stand for provincial labour codes, and for co-operation between the various governments under the constitution to establish minimum labour standards from coast to coast. But that would not necessarily prevent the same men, as members of the socialist party at the national level, from standing for a constitutional amendment permitting Parliament to legislate upon a national labour code if and when the Provinces should fail to arrive at one through co-operative action. There are even some cases where socialists at all levels could unite in advocating *joint* federal-provincial legislation.[17]

For example again, when socialists advocate a constitutional amendment enacting a bill of rights for all Canadians and all governments in Canada, they might simultaneously advocate the abolition of the federal right to disallow and to reserve provincial laws, since such safeguards would then be obsolete.[18] For example also, socialists might well prove their lack of bias between central and regional governments by proposing that the Supreme Court be really established as an impartial arbitrator in constitutional cases. This could be done by making the Court independent of the federal and the provincial governments, just as the Privy Council used to be. Thus the Supreme Court Act would cease to be a federal statute, and could be entrenched in the constitution. And the judges might be chosen alternately from panels submitted by the federal and the provincial governments.

To sum up and conclude this essay, it might well be said that the basis of a socialist ideology is to work out a certain set of human values, for the fostering of which society is held collectively responsible.

The basis of a socialist program is to state what minimum standards of the good life must ensue from that set of values, and to demand that those standards be made available to all, given the federal data that some like to live by the sea, some in the plains, and that some prefer to speak French.

The basis of a socialist critique is to state clearly what the provincial governments can do and fail to do, and what the federal government can do and does not do, each within its respective jurisdiction.

Finally, the basis of socialist action is to define the various ways of striving towards socialist goals under a federal constitution, and to lead each community towards such goals as it can hope to attain.

To many an idealist, it may appear that socialism within a federal structure of government is not as pure, as exciting, and as efficient as socialism in a unitary state. That may be so, just as democratic socialism may be less efficient and far-reaching than the totalitarian brand. But just as democracy is a value in itself, which cannot be sacrificed to considerations of expediency, likewise at certain times and in certain places federalism may be held to be a fundamental value, and the penalty for disregarding it may be the complete collapse of socialism itself.

17. This is spelt out in some detail on pp. 23–4 of the *Mémoire* cited in n. 19.

18. Personally I would be prepared to argue that they are obsolete in any case.

2

The Limitations of
Co-operative Federalism*

W. R. LEDERMAN

FEDERALISM AS CO-OPERATIVE

In the world of today, any federal system needs in considerable measure to be a co-operative federalism. In Canada, for example, we have seen increasing necessity for agreements or understandings between the federal government and provincial governments concerning specified uses of their respective powers and resources on many matters. These agreements or understandings take many forms, operate in many ways and occur at every official level – specifically at the legislative, ministerial or civil service levels, or some combination of them. Such co-operation has been and is going on to a surprising degree.

But the success of these co-operative measures is not just a matter of a sufficient upsurge of good will in Ottawa and the provincial capitals. At times the life or death of particular ministries may be at stake, and in any event hard bargaining is frequently to be expected. Such bargaining necessarily takes place against the background of basic definition provided by the federal constitution. There must be initial definition of the powers and resources of each government in the federation before there can be bargains or agreements among them about what each government is to do or refrain from doing with its respective powers and resources. Co-operation and mutual good will we certainly need, but no amount of them will do away with the absolute necessity for a primary authoritative distribution of powers and resources in our federal constitutional document. At present this is the British North America Act, and, unless and until it is amended or replaced, its present scheme sets the basic framework within which co-operative measures between governments in Canada must be undertaken. So the text of the federal constitution is of continuing importance, but of course this point should not be pressed to extremes. Changing the wording of the constitution in this or that respect, for example, or even rewriting it wholesale, would not be a cure-all for everything that may be wrong in Canada. On the other hand, the opposite

---

*Reprinted, with permission from *The Canadian Bar Review*, Vol. XLV, 1967.

extreme should also be avoided — this is the idea that the text of the federal constitution, whatever it may be, really means little or nothing in the ongoing life and government of the country. Here the concept seems to be that the constitutional text is just a façade which can be made to give a legitimate front to any arrangements whatever arrived at among those in power for the moment in the political life of Canada and the Provinces.

As usual, the truth does not lie at either of these extremes. Much change and adjustment can be brought about by official agreement and practice, and it is essential to flexibility and efficiency of federal processes of government in the modern state that this should be so. Nevertheless, the text of the federal constitution as authoritatively interpreted in the courts remains very important.[1] It tells us who can act in any event. In other words, constitutionally it must always be possible in a federal country to ask and answer the question – What happens if the federal and provincial governments do not agree about a particular measure of co-operative action? Then which government and legislative body has power to do what? And even though federal-provincial agreement on some matter may come at the end of difficult negotiations, the question and answer just referred to will have influenced the result because the answer is a primary element in defining the bargaining power of the federal government on the one hand and the provincial governments on the other. . . .

One example of the relation of basic constitutional definition to bargaining power can be seen in the history of federal-provincial taxation agreements. There have been several federal-provincial conferences, to settle these agreements from time to time, but on each occasion the federal government seems to have made the essential decisions and proposals, thus setting what the terms of the agreement were to be if there was to be agreement at all. The Provinces, particularly the economically weaker ones, have in the main found themselves in a 'take-it-or-leave it' position respecting the federal proposals. . . . The question arises then – Why has the federal government been able to make its views prevail in these situations? No doubt many factors are at work, but the most important one is simply that, under the federal constitution, the federal taxing power is a much more potent instrument than is the taxing power of a Province. The latter must be direct and is confined territorially to a subject in the Province. The federal taxing power is not limited as to type and takes for its territorial base the whole of Canada, thus matching in jurisdiction the national or inter-provincial operations of many tax payers, particularly corporate ones. Thus, at least in the fields of personal and corporate income, the federal government is able to operate a taxation system that is both more effective and more fair than are the taxation systems of the respective Provinces operating independently. The federal and provincial taxpayers are the same persons or corporations, and they are very sensitive to considerations

1. Concerning the importance of judicial interpretation, see W. R. Lederman, "The Balanced Interpretation of the Federal Distribution of Legislative Powers in Canada (The Integrity of the Process of Interpretation)" in Crépeau and Mac-Pherson (ed.), *The Future of Canadian Federalism*, 1965, pp. 91-112.

of effectiveness and fairness and also to the inconvenience and expense of multiple income tax returns.

A contrasting example with the same lesson is provided by the story of the Canada and Quebec pension plans. In 1951, for the first time and so far the only time in Canadian constitutional jurisprudence, a principle of provincial paramountcy in a concurrent field was expressed when the British North America Act was amended to allow the federal Parliament to make laws relating to old age pensions. Section 94A . . . reads as follows:[2]

The Parliament of Canada may make laws in relation to old age pensions and supplementary benefits, including survivors' and disability benefits irrespective of age, but no such laws shall affect the operation of any law present or future of a provincial legislature in relation to any such matter.

The original Canada Pension Plan as proposed by the federal government differed in basic ways from the Quebec Pension Plan as proposed by the Quebec government. It will be recalled for instance that the latter was a fully-funded plan providing large sums for investment while the former was not. The Lesage government was able to insist on the scheme of the Quebec Pension Plan for Quebec to the exclusion of the Canada Pension Plan primarily because of the principle of provincial paramountcy in this respect, in section 94A of the British North America Act. Constitutionally this gave them the last word in any event for Quebec. Accordingly, to achieve the necessary degree of uniformity across the country, the federal government and the governments of the other Provinces accepted a revised Canada Pension Plan that was in harmony with the Quebec Pension Plan. . . .

The text of our constitution, then, does set the basic terms that provide definition and context for the various forms of intergovernmental co-operation that have developed in the field of Canadian federal-provincial relations. . . .

We must now ask – What is the characteristic first principle of any federal constitution? It is an original distribution by subjects of primary legislative powers between provincial or state governments on the one hand and a central government on the other. It means the territorial sub-division of the country to give a number of states or provinces, and also an original distribution by subjects of legislative powers between the central government in respect of the whole national territory on the one hand and the several sub-regional governments for their respective fractions of the national territory on the other hand. This division of law-making powers by territorial sub-divisions and subjects means that the respective state governments and the central government develop in certain respects a peculiar involvement with and dependence on one another. In Canadian terms this leads to certain measures of intergovernmental co-operation in the field of federal-provincial relations. It is vital to realize that the conditions underlying these measures are in the main peculiar to a full-fledged federal system, so that we do not have here just another species of international relations.

To speak in more detail, the point is this: independent countries like

France and Britain can meet their needs for co-operation by international treaties or less formal agreements between their governments. But France and Britain are mutually exclusive as to territory and bodies of citizens, and each government for its own population and territory has the full range of legislative powers. This is not so between the federal government and the provincial governments of Canada. In the Canadian federation, Province by Province, the federal government and the respective provincial governments are responsible for the same territories and the same populations. The only separation is in the realm of ideas, the division of law-making powers by subjects between the federal government . . . and the provincial governments. . . . *Note that these conditions all differ from those obtaining between governments of independent countries in international relations.* The federal and provincial governments have joint responsibility for the same territories and populations, but each is limited to its own list of subjects of power for the purpose. Ideally the federal and provincial lists of powers should be crystal clear and mutually exclusive. But, as we shall see later, such perfection is not attainable in power-distribution systems and the exigencies of imperfection are the roots of many of the problems of federal-provincial relations. In any event, it should be quite clear that federal governmental institutions in Canada are *not* just a sort of Canadian United Nations Organization (or United Provinces Organization) created by the Provinces and dependent for continued existence on the collective sufferance of the Provinces. Where federal subjects of power are concerned, provincial sub-division boundaries simply disappear and the federal government operates as a matter of original constitutional right in the whole of Canadian territory. Likewise the provincial governments operate concerning provincial subjects of power as a matter of original constitutional right in their respective sub-divisions of the national territory. In total operation this provides a system of government for the whole of the Canadian people and territory on all legislative subjects, a system that is vastly superior to anything possible by agreement between independent countries under the present régime of international law. Specifically, under the Canadian federal constitution, where intergovernmental co-operative measures are desirable in federal-provincial relations, both federal and provincial ministers and legislators are under the salutary political pressures of the need to respond to the wishes of the *same electoral bodies of citizens in the same territory.* Moreover, if an agreed solution for some problem situation in federal-provincial relations is not forthcoming, our federal constitution makes provision in several ways for a national solution by federal legislation in any event, if the need is sufficiently urgent.[3] Accordingly, a federal constitution like ours compared to the régime of international law provides much more effective pressure for governments to reach agreement in the

2. British North America Act, 1951, 14-15 Geo. VI, c. 32 (U.K.) as added to by British North America Act, 1964, 12-13 Eliz. II, c. 73 (U.K.).

3. For example, the federal general power in the opening words of section 91 of the British North America Act, and the doctrine of Dominion paramountcy in the event of conflict between federal and provincial statutes in a concurrent field.

first place, and in addition often provides an alternative of over-all (national) legislative action in the absence of agreement, an alternative the like of which is altogether missing among governments of independent countries under the régime of international law. The proposal that the Province of Quebec should become an "Associate State" of the rest of Canada is nothing more nor less than a proposal to destroy the Canadian federal constitution in favour of the greatly inferior sort of thing that is possible in the way of inter-governmental arrangements among independent States under international law. There is no essential constitutional difference between the proposal for an Associate State and complete separation. . . .

CANADIAN FEDERALISM UNDER JUDICIAL REVIEW

Earlier I said that the main separation between the federal government on the one hand and the provincial government on the other was in the realm of ideas – the division or distribution of law-making powers by subjects. If the federal and provincial lists of powers could be effectively clear, complete and mutually exclusive in all circumstances, each would tend to his own business and the need for federal-provincial co-operative measures would be at a minimum. But this is just not the situation in real life. Inevitably the lists of categories have conflicting and overlapping features. . . . Nearly all laws or legislative schemes have a multiplicity of features, characteristics or aspects by which they may be classified in a number of different ways, and hence potentialities of cross-classification between the various categories of the federal and provincial lists are ever present. The more complex the statute, the greater the number of logical possibilities in this regard. So, in the case of a particular law challenged for validity, one aspect of it will point to a federal category of power with logical plausibility, but, with equal logical plausibility another aspect points to a provincial category of power. Or, one can say the same thing another way. The respective federal and provincial classes of laws often overlap one another as general concepts in many important respects, and thus compete, so to speak, through this partial coincidence of categories to control the statutes to be classified. The courts have had to face these problems because of their final responsibility to interpret the federal distribution of powers, and have developed the all-pervasive aspect theory of interpretation to meet the situation. "Subjects which in one aspect and for one purpose fall within Section 92, may in another aspect and for another purpose fall within Section 91."[4]

In the course of judicial decisions on the British North America Act, the judges have basically done one of two things. First they have attempted to define mutually exclusive spheres for federal and provincial powers, and they have had considerable though partial success in doing this. But, where mutual exclusion did not seem feasible or proper, the courts have implied concurrency of federal and provincial power in the overlapping area, with the result that either or both authorities have been permitted to legislate, provided in the latter event that their statutes did not in some way conflict one with the other in the common area. In the event of conflict, the judicial doctrine of dominion paramountcy is to the effect that federal legislation prevails and provincial legislation is suspended or inoperative.[5] The interpretative course followed then might be summed up as follows — mutual exclusion if feasible but concurrency where necessary.

An example of the mutually exclusive result is offered by the *Inter-Provincial Bus Lines* case of 1954.[6] Here the Judicial Committee of the Privy Council held that the power to regulate interprovincial or international motor vehicle enterprises carrying goods or persons across boundaries was exclusively federal, whereas the power to regulate such enterprises when they operated only within the boundaries of a single Province was exclusively provincial. The former were connecting undertakings (a federal responsibility), the latter were local undertakings (a provincial responsibility).

By contrast, the Unconscionable Transactions Relief Act of the Province of Ontario was upheld as valid by a judicial finding of concurrency in the field of interest charges.[7] This statute provides that, if in all the circumstances the cost of a loan is excessive and the transaction harsh and unconscionable, the court may order the contract reformed so as to make its terms fair and reasonable. Clearly this statute concerns the whole range of undue influence in contract . . . and so logically falls within the provincial category of "Property and Civil Rights" under the British North America Act.[8] Also, it is equally obvious that insofar as it deals with interest charges it falls within the federal category of "Interest" under the British North America Act.[9] Thus the statute in question has both its federal and its provincial aspects, and its validity depends, under the present system of interpretation, on determining whether one of these aspects is primary, or whether the two aspects are equivalent in their relative importance in accordance with the social and economic responsibilities of both levels of government. If the federal aspect of interest is primary, then only the federal Parliament can enact a law dealing with interest in this way, and the provincial statute falls because it deals with interest as well as other things. On the other hand, if the provincial aspect of interest, as part of the whole picture of undue influence in contract, is of equivalent importance to the federal concern with interest, then the provincial statute stands in its entirety, unless there is actually inconsistent federal legislation on interest — and the Supreme Court of Canada found this not to be so in the Ontario

---

4. *Hodge* v. *The Queen* (1883-84), 9 A.C. 117, at p. 130.

5. For a detailed analysis of what is involved in concurrency, conflict and paramountcy, see W. R. Lederman, *The Concurrent Operation of Federal and Provincial Laws in Canada* (1962-63), 9 McGill L.J. 185.

6. *A.G. for Ontario* v. *Winner*, (1954) A.C. 541.

7. R.S.O., 1960, c. 410, and *A.G. for Ontario* v. *Barfried Enterprises Ltd.*, (1963) S.C.R. 570.

8. 1867, 30-31 Vict., c. 3 (U.K.).

9. *Ibid.*

case. In other words, the Province is responsible for general undue influence laws in contract, and no such law is complete unless it includes remedies concerning undue interest rates as well as other facets of undue influence. Hence the judicial finding that, *in this context*, there is a provincial power to deal with interest concurrent with the federal power. Incidentally the decision on the Ontario Unconscionable Transactions Relief Act has very important implications – it has opened the way for the Provinces to enact comprehensive schemes for the protection of consumers generally, which some of them are now doing.

In any event, the point for present purposes is that the conditions governing federal-provincial co-operation differ to some extent, depending on whether one is talking of co-operation concerning mutually exclusive fields of power or concurrent fields of power. In either case, of course, there may simply be federal-provincial agreement that each will exercise its own powers for itself, but in a particular way that complements and does not frustrate the operation of legislation of the other. So far as form is concerned, this is no doubt the simplest type of federal-provincial co-operation. Indeed this is all that is formally necessary to effect co-operation in a concurrent field, but more of this later. In relation to exclusive fields of power, there is a further consideration, that of the delegation of legislative powers between the federal government on the one hand and provincial governments on the other.

LEGISLATIVE AND ADMINISTRATIVE DELEGATION

The intergovernmental delegation that concerns the Canadian federal system has taken two forms which, for lack of better terms, might be designated as legislative and administrative. The legislative type involves the federal Parliament attempting to delegate directly to a provincial legislature power to make laws respecting some portion of an exclusive federal category of power, or vice versa. The administrative type of intergovernmental delegation involves the federal Parliament attempting to invest provincial officials with power and responsibility to apply federal laws, and this may at times include wide regulation-making powers for the provincial officials in part of an exclusive federal legislative field. As in the case of direct legislative delegation, administrative delegation may also be attempted between a provincial legislature and federal officials. The Supreme Court of Canada has ruled that legislative delegation is invalid and that administrative delegation is valid. This difference in result has its difficulties because, when wide regulation-making power is given, for example, by the federal Parliament to a provincial board or commission, it is difficult to see much distinction between legislative and administrative delegation. Nevertheless, it will be argued here that the distinction is a valuable one though it does have its gray areas.

First, as to legislative delegation, the leading authority is the *Nova Scotia Inter-delegation* case[10] in the Supreme Court of Canada in 1950. In this case the proposed Delegation of Legislative Jurisdiction Act of the

Province of Nova Scotia had been referred as Bill 136 to the Supreme Court of Nova Scotia, which held it to be *ultra vires* of the Province. Appeal was taken to the Supreme Court of Canada which unanimously affirmed the decision of the Supreme Court of Nova Scotia *en banc*. Chief Justice Rinfret described the terms of Bill 136 as follows:[11]

By virtue of this Bill, if it should come into force, by proclamation, as therein provided, the Lieutenant-Governor in Council, may from time to time delegate to and withdraw from the Parliament of Canada authority to make laws in relation to any matter relating to employment in any industry, work or undertaking in respect of which such matter is, by s. 92 of the B.N.A. Act, exclusively within the jurisdiction of the Legislature of Nova Scotia. It provided that any laws so made by the Parliament of Canada shall, while such delegation is in force, have the same effect as if enacted by the Legislature.

The Bill also provides that if and when the Parliament of Canada shall have delegated to the Legislature of the Province of Nova Scotia authority to make laws in relation to any matter relating to employment in any industry, work or undertaking in respect of which such matter is, under the provisions of the B.N.A. Act, exclusively within the legislative jurisdiction of such Parliament, the Lieutenant-Governor in Council, while such delegation is in force, may, by proclamation, from time to time apply any or all of the provisions of any Act in relation to a matter relating to employment in force in the Province of Nova Scotia to any such industry, work, or undertaking.

Finally, the Bill enacts that if and when the Parliament of Canada shall have delegated to the Legislature of the Province of Nova Scotia authority to make laws in relation to the raising of a revenue for provincial purposes by the imposing of a retail sales tax of the nature of indirect taxation, the Lieutenant-Governor in Council, while such delegation is in force, may impose such a tax of such amount not exceeding 3% of the retail price as he deems necessary, in respect of any commodity to which such delegation extends and may make Regulations providing for the method of collecting any such tax.

This certainly raised the essential issues squarely, and the reasons of the judges for their negative decision are best given in their own words. Chief Justice Rinfret:[12]

The constitution of Canada does not belong either to Parliament, or to the Legislatures; it belongs to the country and it is there that the citizens of the country will find the protection of the rights to which they are entitled. It is part of that protection that Parliament can legislate only on the subject-matters referred to it by s. 91 and that each Province can legislate exclusively on the subject-matters referred to it by s. 92. The country is

10. *A.G. of Nova Scotia* v. *A.G. of Canada*, (1950) 4 D.L.R. 369.

11. *Ibid.*, at pp. 370-371.

12. *Ibid.*, at pp. 371-372.

entitled to insist that legislation adopted under s. 91 should be passed ex-
clusively by the Parliament of Canada in the same way as the people of
each Province are entitled to insist that legislation concerning the matters
enumerated in s. 92 should come exclusively from their respective Legis-
latures. In each case the Members elected to Parliament or to the Legisla-
tures are the only ones entrusted with the power and the duty to legislate
concerning the subjects exclusively distributed by the constitutional Act
to each of them.

Mr. Justice Taschereau:[13]

If the proposed legislation were held to be valid, the whole scheme of the
Canadian Constitution would be entirely defeated. The framers of the
B.N.A. Act thought wisely that Canada should not be a unitary state, but
it would be converted into one, as Mr. Justice Hall says, if all the Prov-
inces empowered Parliament to make laws with respect to all matters ex-
clusively assigned to them. Moreover, it is clear that the delegation of legis-
lative powers by Parliament to the ten provinces on matters enumerated
in s. 91 of the B.N.A. Act could bring about different criminal laws, differ-
ent banking and bankruptcy laws, different military laws, different postal
laws, different currency laws, all subjects in relation to which it has been
thought imperative that uniformity should prevail throughout Canada.

Mr. Justice Rand made the same point in a somewhat different way.
The relationship of delegation involves subordination of the delegate to
the delegating body, and so is simply not an appropriate relationship between the federal Parliament on the one hand and the provincial legislatures on the other. They are primary and co-ordinate legislative bodies
under the constitution.[14]

Subordination implies duty: delegation is not made to be accepted or acted
upon at the will of the delegate; it is ancillary to legislation which the
appropriate Legislature thinks desirable; and a duty to act either by enact-
ing or by exercising a conferred discretion not, at the particular time, to
act, rests upon the delegate. No such duty could be imposed upon or
accepted by a co-ordinate Legislature and the proposed Bill does no more
than to proffer authority to be exercised by the delegate solely of its own
volition and, for its own purposes, as a discretionary privilege. Even in the
case of virtually unlimited delegation as under the Poor Act of England,
assuming that degree to be open to Canadian Legislatures, the delegate is
directly amenable to his principal for his execution of the authority.

In other words, handing over a plenary and primary legislative discretion
in this manner, even on a bilateral basis subject to revocation, is not really
delegation at all, it is amendment of the federal constitution, however
partial or temporary such amendment may be. . . .
So much for legislative delegation – it is a necessary implication of our
federal constitution that primary legislative powers cannot be traded or
transferred, even with consent on both sides, between the federal Parliament and a provincial legislature.[15]

In spite of this strong stand against intergovernmental delegation at the primary legislative level, the Supreme Court of Canada soon made it clear, in the *Prince Edward Island Potato Board* case of 1952,[16] that delegation to officials of the other government at the subordinate levels of the administration of laws and regulation-making was a different matter and was valid. The Legislature of Prince Edward Island had by statute provided for a Potato Marketing Board of provincially appointed persons empowered to make rules for the marketing within Prince Edward Island of potatoes produced there, the board itself to be the sole marketing authority. This was valid legislation, being concerned with the intraprovincial marketing of local produce. Meanwhile, the Federal Agricultural Products Marketing Act of 1949,[17] dealing with the federal subject of interprovincial and export marketing of agricultural products, provided as follows:

2(1)The Governor in Council may by order grant authority to any board or agency authorized under the law of any province to exercise powers of regulation in relation to the marketing of any agricultural product locally within the province, to regulate the marketing of such agricultural product outside the province in interprovincial and export trade and for such purposes to exercise all or any powers like the powers exercisable by such board or agency in relation to the marketing of such agricultural product locally within the province.

(2)The Governor in Council may by order revoke any authority granted under subsection one.

The Governor in Council made an order delegating this power respecting Prince Edward Island Potatoes to the Provincial Board and the Supreme Court of Canada held the delegation to be valid and operative. As Mr. Justice Taschereau put it:

The Supreme Court of Prince Edward Island relied upon A.-G. N.S. v. A.G. Can., [1950] 4 D.L.R. 369, [1951] S.C.R. 31, to answer in the negative, but I do not think that that case supports the view that has been adopted. The judgment merely decided that neither Parliament nor the Legislatures can delegate powers to each other so as to change the distribution of

13. *Ibid.*, at p. 382.

14. *Ibid.*, at p. 386.

15. This is subject to the exception to be found in section 94 of the British North America Act in favour of the federal Parliament at the expense of the legislatures of the common law provinces. Section 94 allows no revocation once the step has been taken of passing provincial powers to the federal Parliament—perhaps this is one reason why it has never been used. In any event, its presence in the British North America Act implies that there is to be *no other way* of transferring primary legislative powers by bilateral consent under the British North America Act. The Supreme Court of Canada in the *Nova Scotia* case noted and approved this implication.

16. *P.E.I. Potato Marketing Board* v. *H. B. Willis Inc. and A.G. of Canada*, (1952) 4 D.L.R. 146.

17. S.C., 1949, c. 16.

powers provided for in ss. 91 and 92 of the B.N.A. Act. *Here the issue is entirely different. The federal legislation does not confer any additional powers to the Legislature but vests in a group of persons certain powers to be exercised in the inter-provincial and export field. It is immaterial that the same persons be empowered by the Legislature to control and regulate the marketing of natural products within the Province. It is true that the Board is a creature of the Lieutenant-Governor in Council, but this does not prevent it from exercising duties imposed by the Parliament of Canada:* Valin v. Langlois, 5 App. Cas. 115.[18]

Thus, a means was found to combine in the hands of one regulatory body control over the whole marketing process of an agricultural product within and beyond the Province of production – a desirable result much sought after for years in constitutional practice. . . .

The administrative type of intergovernmental delegation has been widely used in our constitutional practice and has brought valuable and indispensable elements of flexibility to our federal system. Indeed, some of it is called for by the very terms of the British North America Act itself. For example the federal Parliament is charged by section 91 (27) with the making of criminal law, both substantive and procedural, whereas each provincial legislature is charged by section 92 (14) with arranging for "The Administration of Justice in the Province". Accordingly, ever since 1867, provincial Attorneys-General and the permanent officials of their departments, including the Crown Attorneys, have administered the federal Criminal Code in their respective Provinces. Moreover, most of the criminal trials under the Criminal Code of Canada are conducted by provincially-appointed magistrates who are given their authority in this respect by the procedural section of the Criminal Code of Canada. Furthermore, while Ontario and Quebec provide their own police forces so that in these two provinces provincial police officers enforce the federal Criminal Code, the situation differs in the other eight Provinces. In them the provincial governments, by contract with the federal government, employ the Royal Canadian Mounted Police for enforcing provincial as well as federal offences in their respective territories. There are of course other examples of useful administrative delegations, but space does not permit their exposition here.

THE FUTURE OF DELEGATION

Before attempting an opinion on the merits of legislative or administrative delegation in our federal system, there is one further development to note. Part II of the Fulton-Favreau Bill for amendment of the Canadian constitution purported to establish a new procedure for direct intergovernmental delegation at the primary legislative level that would, if put into effect, reverse to an important extent the decision in the *Nova Scotia Inter-delegation* case. For one or two of the Provinces at least, this was apparently very important in inducing the agreement of 1964 on the formula as a whole. Briefly, the Fulton-Favreau Bill's draft delegation sections were to this effect.[19] The federal Parliament could enact a statute concerning the provincial subjects of prisons, local works and undertakings, property and civil rights and matters of a merely local or private nature in the Province, provided that:

(a) *prior to the enactment thereof the legislatures of at least four of the provinces have consented to the operation of such a statute . . . or,*

(b) *it is declared by the Parliament of Canada that the Government of Canada has consulted with the governments of all the provinces, and that the enactment of the statute is of concern to fewer than four of the provinces and the provinces so declared to be concerned have under the authority of their legislatures consented to the enactment of such a statute.*

Likewise, a provincial legislature could enact a statute relating to any subject of Federal power provided that:

(a) *prior to the enactment thereof the Parliament of Canada has consented to the enactment of such a statute by the legislature of that province, and*

(b) *a similar statute has . . . been enacted by the legislatures of at least three other provinces.*

Revocation of these delegations at any time by the delegating legislative body was provided for. Thus the agreement of the federal Parliament and four provincial legislatures would be necessary for a delegation either way under this scheme. The only exception was that there might be fewer than four provincial consents required concerning a provincial delegation to the federal Parliament if seven, eight or nine Provinces said they had no interest in the matter. But, so far as a delegation of federal power to the Provincees was concerned, it was to be mandatory that at least four Provinces should agree and enact "similar" statutes before any of those statutes could have effect.

It is now necessary to attempt some assessment of these various alternatives of intergovernmental delegation. My view is that the decision in the *Nova Scotia* case is correct and that direct bilateral trading or transfer of primary legislative powers between the federal Parliament and a provincial legislature should not be permitted. The substantial reasons for this were given by the judges in that case and typical extracts have already been quoted. It would be all too easy to engage frequently in such delegation under strong but temporary political pressures of the moment, thus creating a patch-work pattern of variations Province by Province in the relative

18. *Supra,* footnote 16.

19. See The Amendment of the Constitution of Canada (Ottawa, 1965), a White Paper issued under the authority of the Honourable Guy Favreau, Minister of Justice. Appendix 3 contains the text of the so-called Fulton-Favreau Bill or Formula.

   I am in favour of Part I of the Fulton-Favreau Bill as a means of bringing the constitution home. As indicated, though, I am opposed to the delegation proposals in Part II and think they should be dropped.

powers and responsibilities of the federal Parliament and the provincial legislatures. This could seriously confuse the basic political responsibility and accountability of members of the federal Parliament and the federal Cabinet, and too much of this could destroy these federal institutions.[20] Not much more can be said for the delegation proposals of Part II of the Fulton-Favreau Bill. They seem to be either dangerous or useless. If the proposed delegation procedures could be worked readily, then the dangers to federal institutions just spoken of are present. If the procedure were to prove unworkable, and it *is* very complex, then it is a waste of time. Certainly it can have no attraction to those who desire to develop a particular status for Quebec, because the consent of four Provinces would be required for a delegation of federal powers, and where are Quebec's three companions in the circumstances?

The previous remarks refer to the passing of primary and plenary legislative discretions by intergovernmental delegation, but administrative delegation, as the term has been used here, forms quite a contrast. Here we are often concerned only with the application of laws the substance of which has already been determined in the proper legislative forum under the existing distribution of powers – Canadian Parliament or provincial legislature as the case may be. The administration of laws already formulated, that is, their interpretation and application to the persons and circumstances contemplated by their terms, still involves at times important discretions, but they are much lesser discretions than the primary legislative discretions exercised when laws are first formulated. Delegation at this administrative level is a proper and useful division of labour in government and does not threaten the situs of, or the political accountability for, primary legislative discretions in our federal system. Even when regulation-making power is involved for the subordinate delegate body, if that regulation-making power is properly limited, still there is no threat to responsibility for primary legislative discretions under our federal system. The courts have shown more disposition to control regulations of subordinate boards or commissions than to control statutes of Parliament or a provincial legislature.

While it is true . . . that a subordinate provincial board might be given a dangerous extent of regulation-making power by the federal Parliament, the courts could insist that this stop short of the sort of thing attempted in the proposed Delegation of Legislative Jurisdiction Act of Nova Scotia, described earlier. To take an extreme hypothetical example, if the federal Parliament proposed to delegate power to make criminal law generally to provincial Criminal Law Boards composed of provincially appointed officials, surely the courts would find this invalid as a colourable attempt to bring about the objectionable type of direct primary legislative delegation under the guise of administrative delegation. At least where intergovernmental administrative delegations are concerned, the courts should be strict about this and confine permissible regulation-making powers for the delegate body to developing the detail of the legislative scheme in the master statute concerned, which should in these circumstances contain the main standards or guide-lines to be followed. Indeed, two master statutes are involved in these cases, one federal and one provincial. Neither should be a mere skeleton statute.

Mention of the two master statutes suggests another possibility that should be noticed as a final point in this consideration of intergovernmental delegation. The subordinate delegate body in such cases could be made up of federal and provincial officials. This seems to be quite within the scope of the precedent set by the *Potato Board* case. For example, in the field of the sale of company securities, given that part of the field is within exclusive provincial jurisdiction and part within exclusive federal jurisdiction, it would be constitutionally possible to compose a joint board of federal and provincial appointees with delegations of powers to the board that gave it a complete range of control over the sale of securities. Probably this would only work, as a matter of political accountability, if the federal and provincial governments were fully agreed in some detail on the nature of the controls to be exercised. If this were so and were sufficiently expressed in the master statutes, then the board members could no doubt get on harmoniously with the execution of their common tasks regardless of whether they were federal or provincial appointees. In any event, though it is highly speculative whether a joint board would work, it is clear that intergovernmental delegations of many kinds at the levels of administration of laws and subordinate regulation-making bring a very valuable element of flexibility to the Canadian federal system.

While delegation, as in the fields of agricultural marketing and motor vehicle enterprises, has given provincial governments some entry to exclusive federal fields of legislative jurisdiction, the federal government has in the main relied on other techniques to exert an influence in certain exclusive fields of provincial legislative jurisdiction. Conditional grants and federal crown corporations have been used to this end, and may properly be considered as distinct co-operative forms in the area of federal-provincial relations. What is here involved is the use of federal resources for undertakings that usually fall within provincial powers so far as legislative regulation of that type of undertaking is concerned. In the case of federal conditional grants, the offer of funds and the conditions attached, when accepted by the Province, amount to a federal presence and influence of some sort in a field legislatively provincial. For example, the federal government offered the provincial governments grants of federal money for the construction of the trans-Canada highway in the respective Provinces. Highways have always been considered local works under section 92 (10) of the British North America Act. Nevertheless it was federal policy that there should be a trans-Canada highway and that it should measure up to certain standards and dimensions in construction. Accepting Provinces were required to meet these standards and to pay a relatively small proportion of the cost by matching grants from provincial funds. There

20. Dr. Eugene Forsey has warned of this danger with great force and clarity. See his paper on The Legislatures and Executives of the Federation in Volume 1 of Background Papers and Reports of the Ontario Advisory Committee on Confederation (Toronto, 1967).

have been many federal conditional grant programs, and some are very complex. A detailed examination of them is beyond the scope of this essay, but certain general considerations concerning them require examination.

CONDITIONAL GRANT PROGRAMS

Professor G. V. LaForest in his recent treatise on *The Allocation of Taxing Power under the Canadian Constitution* gives the opinion that these grants-in-aid are constitutionally valid and permissible.[21]

Federal statutes authorizing the grant of money to the provinces on condition that the provinces adopt legislation described in federal statutes, regulations or Dominion-provincial agreements constitute a well-worn route for implementing federal policies. Examples are blind and disabled persons' allowances, hospital insurance and the trans-Canada highway arrangements. One of the usual conditions is that the provinces should bear a definite proportion of the costs of the schemes. Since offers of money, especially for social service schemes, are difficult to refuse, the Dominion is thereby able not only to implement its policies by use of its own resources but also to divert the resources of the provinces to these ends as well.

The validity of these schemes has never been tested; thus far neither the provinces nor the Dominion have demonstrated any inclination to refer the matter to the courts, and a private individual would seldom have the standing to question it. However they appear to be valid. Certainly payments to the provinces are constitutionally unobjectionable. Dominion subsidies to the provinces are provided by several constitutional provisions and (though these rest on no firmer foundation than an opinion of the Law Officers of the Crown) by several Dominion statutes. These, it is true, are given free of conditions, but in complying with the conditions attached to grants the provinces are merely exercising their own legislative powers. Whatever political implications these may have, therefore, it seems very doubtful if their constitutional validity could be successfully challenged.

It should be noted that the federal legislation concerned in these cases makes conditional offers of money, it does not contain compulsory regulations. For example, the hospital insurance scheme mentioned is in the permissible category Professor LaForest describes because the compulsory features of it, so far as members of the public are concerned, are found in the provincial legislation of the accepting Provinces. . . .

The question should now be asked whether conditional grants do not lead to different states of federal-provincial relations with different Provinces, if some accept certain grants while others do not? Does this not confuse political accountability and responsibility for members of the federal Parliament and cabinet? In this connection Professor Donald V. Smiley has made an important point in his treatise on *Conditional Grants and Canadian Federalism.* Federal conditional grants have not been primarily concerned with legislative regulation, they have been primarily concerned with providing resources for desirable social services, public works and the like. The emphasis is on the use and management of funds belonging to the federal government, and federal policies are thus pursued as a matter of managerial decisions and conditions set by the owner of the necessary funds, because he is the owner. For example, the federal government's Crown Corporation, Central Mortgage and Housing Corporation, cannot directly impose building codes on the construction industry in the Provinces; such legislative regulation is within provincial jurisdiction. But the corporation can say that it will not lend the federal government's money to home builders unless its specified construction standards are met. After all, private lenders go this far. In any event, federal standards thus make themselves felt through the medium of contracts with builders. No builder can be told that he *must* meet the federal standards, but if he is not prepared to do so he does have to borrow his money elsewhere. Accordingly, dislocation of primary legislative power and confusion of the relevant political accountability is not much of an issue so far as conditional grants are concerned. But other matters of great importance to the Provinces are involved. To a considerable extent provincial priorities in the use of provincial revenues and resources are put under federal influence through the need for matching provincial payments in some proportion to qualify for federal grants. Also, the matter of who gets credit for welfare schemes the public wants may well be vital to the political survival of particular provincial or federal governments. Nevertheless, I consider that the advantages of conditional grants greatly outweigh any disadvantages for the federal government and provincial governments. . . . Federal initiative through conditional grants has brought great benefits to Canadians in every Province. Necessary welfare schemes have usually come more quickly, at better standards and in more places than would otherwise have been the case.

Accordingly, federal conditional grants have brought beneficial elements of flexibility to our federal system, elements that do not pose a threat to the essential basis of federal institutions or the autonomy of the Provinces. Each party has real bargaining power under the constitution, and so should be able to take care of itself in the intergovernmental negotiations about the terms of conditional grant programs. The federal government has superior revenue-raising and financial power for the reasons given at the beginning of this essay. The provincial governments and legislatures have the essential powers of compulsory legislative regulation that many of these programs require at some point, as well as some of the revenues.

Furthermore, it seems that the federal government is always going to be in the position of having more revenue than it needs to carry out its direct responsibilities under the constitution. Federal taxing power is more effective and more fair than provincial power, in the types of taxes available and in the territorial extent of the power. Also, to a very significant degree, the federal Parliament needs to keep such taxes as those on corporation and personal income in its own hands as levers for managing the national economy in aid of full employment and prosperity. Finally, only the federal government can effect the net transfers of public funds to

21. Toronto, 1967, pp. 40-1.

the Provinces located in the poorer regions of Canada to help them to improved conditions. And such improvement is one of the basic aims of Confederation. In the face of these considerations, it is no use to say that the revenue-raising capacities of the provincial legislatures and the federal Parliament should be precisely matched to the direct legislative responsibilities of each, by changes in the allocation of taxing powers under the constitution. This simplistic solution is impossible. My view is then that there will always be a surplus of funds in federal hands that should be dispensed to the Provinces in a mixture of conditional and unconditional grants. Conditional grants then, as a form of co-operative federalism, are with us indefinitely. It may be that we have reached a period when there should be more room for provincial influence on the nature of these schemes, and more sympathy at Ottawa for this. The inherent flexibility of this form of co-operative federalism means that new and different arrangements could be developed as the need or desire for them became clear. Better federal-provincial agreements concerning both conditional and unconditional federal grants-in-aid is one of the ways to real constitutional improvement.

CONCLUSION

We have reviewed some of the more important forms of official federal-provincial co-operation in Canada, and have assessed some of their implications for our federal system. Inevitably and increasingly, federal and provincial governments are involved with one another and dependent on one another. Federal-provincial conferences and major consultations of various kinds go on constantly at all official levels. In 1966 there were almost as many formally scheduled federal-provincial conferences of some kind or other as there were days in the year.[22] On some days of any year there are no doubt more provincial cabinet ministers in Ottawa than federal ministers. Such wide-ranging official co-operative activity is a sign of health and vitality in our federal system. Moreover such co-operative federalism contains important elements of flexibility for meeting some of the needs of change. It provides opportunities for innovation that may help greatly to establish more satisfactory relations between the federal government on the one hand and the provincial governments on the other. In particular, the legitimate forms of co-operative federalism have a continuing role of importance to play in developing a satisfactory relationship between the Parliament and Government of Canada on the one hand, and the Legislature and Government of the Province of Quebec on the other. Nevertheless, these co-operative measures take place and can only take place against the background of basic definition provided by the first principles of our federal constitution. There are essentials here at this fundamental level that must be honoured and preserved if Canada is to continue and to progress as a federal country in her second century.

22. The Financial Post for May 21st, 1966, carried a listing of federal-provincial conferences of all types held or to be held in 1966. It covers almost two newsprint pages.

3

The Possible Contents of
Special Status for Quebec*

CLAUDE RYAN

For several years, a lively constitutional debate has been carried on in
Canada. Although some people consider this debate a waste of time and
energy, the fact remains that changes in the Constitution are being widely
discussed. It is in Quebec that the debate is most animated and radical.
Where formerly constitutional debates were reserved for the experts, in
Quebec they are now the object of public attention. Is it possible that the
whole controversy is merely the result of a cleverly orchestrated piece of
agitation on the part of a few visionaries? To ask the question is to answer
it. What is happening is more serious than is generally supposed. Some of
the highest authorities in the political sector and in other spheres of
activity are questioning whether they should continue to accept a Constitution that is a hundred years old. Previously, this self-interrogation took
the form of electoral protest and discussion. Since the 1960 renaissance,
the discussion has completely changed direction. It now represents the
desire of a people for freedom and a flourishing culture.

In the face of such a movement, one can cling to the status quo, as most
of English Canada has done, in the hope that the storm will pass. Or, as
Le Devoir has tried to do, one can adopt a positive attitude by admitting
the existence of the movement, understanding the feelings behind it, and
seeking the changes which could or should be made. Having tried constantly to keep abreast of new ideas here and elsewhere, we now wish to
present these ideas to our readers before passing judgment on them. We
have tried to determine whether ideas somewhat opposed to our own do,
in fact, express that ever-elusive will of the majority in Quebec.

Constitutions are not immutable and sacrosanct. They exist to serve
people. They are instruments rather than ends in themselves. In order to
be relevant and vital, constitutions ought to be documents with which
the people may identify, which express their aspirations and, as a result,
which engender their spontaneous loyalty and respect. Some time ago we
concluded that the present document, the British North America Act, does

---

*Reprinted, with permission of the author, from "Quebec in the Canada of Tomorrow".
Translated from *Le Devoir* Special Supplement, (Montreal, 1967).

not fulfil these requirements. This supplement is intended to elucidate our arguments and, more important, is an attempt to clarify proposals for eventual revision.

It is impossible for us, of course, to present all the opinions we have published in the past or to prepare a new draft constitution. Our objectives are more modest:

1. To verify that our views on the necessity for constitutional revision stem from a genuine need;
2. To examine the possibility of revision which would revolve around the search for special status for Quebec within a renewed federal system.

THE PRESENT CONSTITUTION HAS HAD ITS DAY

The mere survival of the B.N.A. Act over the last century is a tribute to the practical wisdom of its authors and subsequent interpreters. However, grave injustices were committed in its name against the French-Canadian population, especially outside Quebec. Often, the B.N.A. Act also served the ends of centralist forces in threatening the basic institutions of French Canada. Nevertheless, it has permitted Canada to enjoy a century of relative peace and considerable progress. These are facts which it would be a mistake to overlook.

In spite of this, the fact remains that the Constitution is so tainted with weaknesses that render it obsolete, is so ambiguous and so ineffecual, that it could not be corrected by minor alterations. It is the document as a whole and the general inspiration of the text which must form the basis of a new constitution.

Here, we will simply give a brief outline of the most important changes:

1. Where it refers to the division of powers, the present text is ambiguous. It says nothing of activities which did not exist in 1867. In addition, it contains very general clauses which usually favour the central government and which may be interpreted to the detriment of the legitimate interests of the member Provinces.
2. By its tone, the present text reflects the colonial period in which it was written. It is full of references to the British Empire and other entities which have no meaning today.
3. The present text lacks certain elements which are essential to a truly autonomous and complete constitution. It contains no provision for constitutional amendment and no satisfactory mechanism for arbitrating constitutional disputes.
4. The present text does not lend itself to bringing English-Canadian nationalism, which tends to polarize around a desire for a strong central government, together with French-Canadian nationalism which, without wishing to be cut off from the rest of Canada, will, at least in the near future, be more Quebec-oriented. Within the present system, English Canadians think French Canadians are unco-operative, while French Canadians think of English Canadians as inveterate centralists. The result is tension between the two "isms" mixed with confronta-

tions and never-ending quarrels over procedure and laws. All of this impedes action. Many projects are set aside, are postponed indefinitely, or are undertaken despite opposition from one of the two groups.

5. The fundamental intention of the text has remained ambiguous. Did the Fathers of Confederation wish to create a true association between two peoples who were considered equal at the outset? Or did they think of creating a "new nation" which would permit no more than the continuance, within a territory called Quebec, of certain religious, cultural and linguistic particularities? Neither the B.N.A. Act nor history holds the answer. The historian Creighton has flatly contradicted anyone who thinks that the problem has been resolved. The Anglo-Canadian history specialist on Confederation has rivals in Quebec who have reached conclusions similar to his but by very different routes.

The opinions presented in this collection are proof of the feeling among French Canadians that the present constitutional text is unsatisfactory. An increasing number of English Canadians are becoming aware of the need for change though the majority would most probably be satisfied with the status quo. To them we can only repeat – for the thousandth time: listen to the other point of view in the hope that the chance of a new dialogue will not be lost by your refusals and indifference. You have asked for several years: What is it that Quebec wants? What is it that French Canada is asking for? The first thing that we ask is that you recognize with us the existence of problems which arise from the present constitutional confusion. We do not ask that you accept from the start all that we suggest. We are prepared for vigorous and detailed negotiations. All we wish is that you recognize the *facts* from the beginning.

QUEBEC IN A NEW CANADIAN SYSTEM

The failure of the Fulton-Favreau formula proved once again that Quebec is the Gordian knot in the Canadian question. Had it not been for Quebec, the formula would have become law. The rest of Canada would have welcomed this as a definite sign of progress. Similarly, in the major constitutional conflicts of recent years, the protagonists have been Quebec and the central government. Evidence would show that other Provinces were frequently involved in constitutional conflicts with the central government; however, the conflicts involving Quebec were the ones which gave rise to the most serious political problems.

Since 1867, Quebec has occupied a special place in the Canadian federation. Rather than diminishing, this status has become increasingly confirmed. Before 1960, Quebec took a defensive attitude to discussions of constitutional matters. The attitude of the "Quiet Revolution", on the other hand, is decidedly one of dynamic affirmation.

Some people have concluded that Quebec is moving inexorably towards separatism or a vague confederalism which, for all practical purposes, would give it complete sovereignty. We are not of this opinion, but think it desirable and possible, for at least one or two generations, to maintain a federal system in Canada on condition that such a system ensures by law and in practice a distinct position to Quebec by granting it "special status".)

Thousands of English Canadians shudder at the thought of "special status". This concept has nothing heretical about it, nor does it entail anything that is really new. The germ of the idea exists in the B.N.A. Act not only insofar as Quebec is concerned but also insofar as other Provinces are concerned. The concept of special status has been tried repeatedly in both unitary and federal systems. It does not necessarily imply privileges or special favours as one is too easily led to believe, but rather it entails realistic recognition of diversities which are so pronounced that they are incompatible within a system that aims at uniformity.

CONCRETE FORMS OF SPECIAL STATUS

A discussion of the principles of special status would not be of much use. It is better to show illustrations of such status for Quebec. Here are several suggestions which could form the basis of further research:

1. In the preamble of a new constitution one would have to state clearly that Canadian political society is founded on the principle of cultural duality. If this duality is to become meaningful, special responsibility for the "distinct society" will fall on the government of Quebec. Means must also be found to write into the constitutional text the major observation of the Dunton-Laurendeau Commission – that is, that there exist in Canada two "distinct societies" one of which is centred mainly in Quebec. Cultural duality in Canada is a noble ideal worthy of the most generous efforts. However, if Quebec is not made the focal point of our second culture, there is no chance of achieving this ideal. History has proven this amply.

2. We would be inclined to leave the central government nearly all the precise powers that it exercises now by virtue of Section 91 of the B.N.A. Act. However, to this general provision, we would add precise clauses concerning the recognition of the wider latitude that Quebec must enjoy. Here are concrete examples:

   a. In Quebec's case, one would have to foresee the possibility of delegation of powers which could be effectuated without modifying the constitutional text each time. Articles in this supplement deal with the sharing of costs and responsibilities in sectors such as the placement of labour, agricultural credit, detention, rehabilitation work for delinquents and police services. Without making this a question of absolute principle, we are of the opinion that nothing should stand in the way of such services being guaranteed to Quebeckers by the Quebec government for obvious social and cultural reasons. In an eventual constitutional amendment formula, given Quebec's special status, provision would have to be made for the possibility of such transfers. This was the most serious omission of the Fulton-Favreau formula.

b. For matters of a social or cultural nature which were not assigned exclusively to one or the other levels of government in 1867, there must be the possibility of either national solutions or the right of Quebec to declare its prerogatives and, as a result, withdraw from federal programs in exchange for fiscal compensation. In this category we would include the following matters:

(a) family allowances;
(b) old age pensions and the Canada pension plan;
(c) social welfare and assistance;
(d) housing;
(e) scholarships and bursaries to students;
(f) financial institutions, insurance and trust companies, commercial societies, with the exception of the banks and the other institutions which would be especially entrusted to Ottawa's care;
(g) regional and urban development;
(h) scientific research in the universities.

c. In sectors which have traditionally fallen within the jurisdiction of the federal government, certain legal interpretations that until now have been too rigid would have to be revised, and the need must be recognized for a new division of responsibilities that would take into account legitimate aspirations – notably those of Quebec. Can one, in 1967, continue to argue that Ottawa ought to have exclusive and complete power in international relations, broadcasting and immigration? Already, the courts have undertaken to define limits on its jurisdiction in these areas. Reasonable and thorough consideration of each of these areas of jurisdiction should give rise to fresh distinctions more in line with life in 1967. Since Quebec has jurisdiction over education and social security, and the development of French culture in Quebec, why should it not have the right to create the international ties necessary to the full and intelligent exercise of these powers? How can it be argued that Quebec should entrust Ottawa with exclusive control over radio and television in the Province? If Quebec is largely responsible for French cultural development within the Province, is it even conceivable that the federal government be allowed to exercise full authority over immigration?

The three areas of federal power which are questioned have, because of the ambiguous terms under which they were laid down, been used to the advantage of the central government. All of them merit more careful scrutiny.

3. In certain areas the British North America Act must frankly be altered. Substitutions must be made for sections which have become obsolete or ambiguous so that the new terms take Quebec's particular position into account. In this respect, here are some examples:

a. Jurisdiction should be given to Quebec over matters such as marriage and divorce which are intimately connected with property and civil rights.

b. The organization of the courts should be revised to encourage more uniform development of the Civil Law and to give Quebec more clearly defined guarantees in matters of arbitration, particularly those concerning constitutional questions.

c. Quebec's right to have its own language policy should be more clearly established in the same way as exists in the other Provinces. By this we do not mean to advocate unilingualism, a concept to which we do not personally subscribe. We will, however, use all our energy to protest against a constitution which entrusts French-language rights to the other Provinces, but shackles Quebec with English-language guarantees.

d. In the present constitution, the central government possesses several very general powers, notably: taxation; the right to make laws for peace, order and good government in Canada; the power to act in the national interest; and the residual power. Ottawa's interpretation of these powers has created discontent in Quebec on many occasions. The central government often used its interpretation as an excuse for interfering in areas of provincial jurisdiction – at least in Quebec's case. A new constitution should define more rigidly the contents and the exact limits of these general powers. It should also be specified that Quebec has the power to disassociate itself without being penalized by Ottawa financially or otherwise. Quebec would be free to take this step except in grave situations such as a state of war or rebellion within the country. In case of a constitutional dispute, only a constitutional tribunal that had been accepted by all parties should have the authority to decide the case.

e. Finally, a constitutional discussion would provide a chance to examine completely the role and the composition of the Canadian Senate which, in its present form, hardly corresponds to the requirements of wholesome federalism.

4. As to the implications that the concept of special status would have for economic policy, particularly monetary and fiscal policy, Quebec should be allowed to exercise its jurisdiction without undergoing loss of revenue – in other words, receive appropriate fiscal compensations by right. It should also be a rule in a normal federal system that each level of government should have direct access to the sources of revenue that it needs to fulfil its responsibilities properly.

Having established this, one must recognize that until further inquiry has been made, a minimum number of essential powers must be left with the federal power. Without these, it could not influence, as it must, general economic trends.

A prudent and realistic approach in this respect has been suggested. For the moment, we will simply present some considerations in line with this thinking:

1. We must undertake studies which consider in detail the relation of the Quebec economy with that of the rest of Canada, the United States, and other countries. We lack specific facts on this subject, and our discussions end in ambiguity shortly after they begin.

2. We must accept the fact that a limit should be set on the proportion

of direct taxes that Ottawa can give up to the provinces. According to certain experts, this limit could vary from 50 to 80 per cent. In practice, it could not reasonably fall below 35 or 40 per cent. The role of direct taxes is too closely interconnected with general economic progress and growth to eliminate justifiably from this field of taxation the government which has the general responsibility of ensuring a balanced economy. In any case, there is no reason why the proportion should be identical for all provinces. It could remain about 40 per cent for the other provinces and be lower for Quebec so that the latter could fulfil the special responsibilities we have mentioned above. In any case, the deciding factor must be the provision of a federal intervention mechanism so that the central government retains its influence over the economy. Mr. Sharp's experience in 1965 with the 10 per cent tax reduction provides a very useful illustration of this point.

3. Apart from direct taxation, an important transfer of resources could also be achieved through indirect taxation, particularly through the federal sales tax and certain other taxes, e.g., on tobacco and alcohol. The idea has already been put forward repeatedly by Robert Bourassa, a contributor to this collection. It has also been taken up by the Advisory Committee on Confederation established by the Ontario government. On this subject, one would find it well worthwhile to refer to a study contained in the second volume of *Background Papers and Reports* prepared on behalf of the Robarts' government.

4. On matters which concern monetary policy and foreign commerce, Ottawa should retain prime responsibility and have the powers to fulfil it as befits a sovereign government. Increasingly, frequent consultations will have to take place with the Provinces. Besides, one cannot rely too completely on the effectiveness of provincial representation on federal decision-making bodies.

5. Centralists must realize, after all, that four-fifths of public investment expenditure in Canada will be, from now on, the responsibility of the provincial and municipal authorities; also, more than half of the public revenue will be raised in the future by these same authorities. These facts are proof that economic policy cannot be thought of as the exclusive responsibility of the central government.

Today, economic policy is the essence of government action at all levels. Surely we must define the aspects of this policy that ought to stem primarily from one authority or the other. An attempt to confer the exclusive responsibility of all economic policy on any one level of government would be to deny the premise on which federalism and the division of powers are based.

Two Important Questions

In discussions about special status, two objections are often raised:

1. How could Quebec provide completely different services within its boundaries while participating in national equalization programs?

2. How could Quebec participate fully in the decisions of the federal Parliament if such decisions apply only to the other Provinces after Quebec withdraws?

For the first question, we have often suggested a double answer. First, particularly in the field of social security, Quebec ought to offer its citizens a whole scheme of services which could differ appreciably from national schemes in the method of implementation, but would be of a standard equivalent to those available throughout the rest of Canada. More specifically, it should devote a fair portion of its total revenue to social security expenditures to match the standard in the rest of Canada – taking into account, of course, differences in the level of employment, education and economic development.

If Quebec's politicians, under the pretext of false progressivism, offer social security programs at a level much superior to those of the rest of the country, the Province will have difficulty claiming its share of equalization benefits. The protection of the citizen, in this case, takes precedence over the affirmation of national values. The essential condition on which Quebec's distinctive position rests is that the Province provide the same protection to its citizens at a rate equivalent to that available in other parts of Canada.

Second, in anticipation of the day when Quebec will be among the most developed Provinces, it ought to assume the responsibility of its share of equalization payments now made to the less favoured provinces.

These provisions are basic and should be written into a new constitution, probably under fundamental rights.

It is not very difficult to answer the second question satisfactorily. The fact is that Quebec would not, at any time, receive special favour. It would have the right to receive compensation for the plans which it undertakes itself and which the other Provinces prefer to entrust to Ottawa. It would have a right to its share of equalization payments. It would have to tax itself more heavily for projects that it alone feels are essential. We do not see how Quebec's representatives to the Commons could be embarrassed by the kind of special status that we envisage. In view of these considerations, if, for example, Ottawa decided to modify the Canada pension plan, any modification would inevitably have repercussions on Quebec's social security system. Similarly, any change in the equilibrium of federal expenditures would have definite effect on the equilibrium of the Quebec economy.

Because of these effects, and even more because of politics, we do not see the need for concern over the role of Quebec's representatives to Ottawa when one is considering a more clearly defined special status for the Province. As we see it, it is logical that Ottawa should retain the bulk of its present powers, and that it should continue to play a very important role in international affairs, defence, economic policy, etc. Frankly, the arguments used in all sincerity by men like Donald Smiley and Alvin Hamilton do not stand up to analysis.

WHERE ARE THE VEHICLES OF REFORM TO BE FOUND?

We speak of constitutional revision as if it were to take place in the very near future. In fact, one should not be too optimistic. In English Canada, a general preference for the status quo will work against the idea of change. In French Canada, certain divisions which have always harmed us will continue to do so and will facilitate the maintenance of the status quo.

In English Canada, only those groups which are not now in power will militantly support change. The leaders of the Liberal Party, and the upper echelons of the federal civil service favour pragmatic evolution rather than fundamental revision. The Conservative Party will not have a policy on this subject as long as it cannot resolve its leadership problem. The English-speaking press, the business world, the bourgeois elite, and the labour movement in the Provinces other than Quebec are almost all in favour of the status quo. There are, however, two main elements in English Canada which may serve to promote research into a new system: the New Democratic Party and a growing number of intellectuals in the universities. It would, perhaps, be well to add to these the political leaders of several English-speaking Provinces; but, in the light of recent statements, one is led to question whether a man like Mr. Robarts will not be as conservative in these matters as are the present Ottawa leaders.

On the French-Canadian side, one cannot anticipate our Liberal representatives in Ottawa taking a stand which is at all specific. Left to their own devices, a high proportion of representatives in the Quebec Liberal caucus would gladly study the means of achieving a new status for Quebec. But they are not free to say publicly what they think. Their English-speaking leaders have placed them under the authority of Mr. Trudeau, a man whom it is unlikely they would have chosen themselves. Whatever may be their personal opinions, it is quite understandably in their best interests to act as if they shared the views of the new orthodoxy which rules Ottawa. They were looking for leadership on this subject from a man like Mr. Marchand. The latter, however, instead of setting out a clear line of reasoning seems to go out of his way to establish, in public, the fact that he has not worked out a policy, by attacking a couple of times each week, strawmen that even an editorial writer starved for material would not dare resort to more than once a month.

Within the next few months, there will surely be interesting initiatives shown in the private sector as, for example, the meeting of the Estates-General at which hundreds of French Canadians will participate without soliciting Mr. Trudeau's good wishes. However, the main impetus ought to come from Quebec, in other words from the Quebec Legislature. After the promising beginnings of three or four years ago, the Legislative Assembly has procrastinated on constitutional matters. It is time, for its own sake, that it stop putting off till tomorrow matters which are obviously of great urgency. It is time that it appraise Quebec's expectations, that it define them as concrete proposals in order to provide the basis for serious negotiations with the rest of the country. One can only hope that the two major parties of Quebec will reach some understanding as soon as possible, so as to get the problem out of the political thicket. If all that Mr. Johnson and Mr. Lesage have been saying over the last few years were sincere, there could be no other outcome.

4

Canadian Federalism
and the Resolution of
Federal-Provincial Conflict

DONALD V. SMILEY

My argument is straightforward. More than at any time in the history of Confederation, contradictory claims are now being made by the federal and provincial governments about their respective responsibilities in many important spheres of public policy. These disputes would not in themselves challenge either the effectiveness of these governments in discharging their duties or the continuing existence of the federal system. What is more crucial is the absence of authoritative procedures for resolving these claims. Despite the apparent immobility of the Canadian government regarding this aspect of constitutional reform, a redefinition of the respective roles of the federal and provincial governments and their relationships is of urgent importance.

Broadly defined, a constitution is a group of authoritative procedures for regulating (a) the relations between citizens and government, (b) the relations among the constituent organs of the government. In 1965 Pierre Elliott Trudeau wrote: ". . . in a democratic country the constitution is the shield protecting the weak from the arbitrary intervention of power."[1] As Minister of Justice, and now as Prime Minister, Mr. Trudeau has directed the policies of the federal government toward the more effective protection of individual rights as a matter of urgency. But this is a partial view of a constitution. A constitution is at the same time a shield *and* a sword; it *protects* individuals against government, and it *confers* power on the component organs of government and determines their respective privileges and responsibilities. It is these latter aspects of the Canadian constitution, i.e. the respective roles of the federal and provincial governments and the relations between them, which most directly threaten the continuing viability of the Canadian constitutional system.[2]

A workable constitution must offer authoritative procedures for the resolution of conflicting claims and these procedures must be acceptable to the parties concerned. In respect to the federal aspects of a constitution, these parties are of course the central and the regional governments. Authoritativeness is of far greater importance to the continuing survival of a political system than any other characteristic of the constitution – more important than whether the constitution is new or old, whether it is highly codified and explicit or whether it leaves a great deal to convention and tradition, or whether it is a focus for popular loyalties to the polity. No constitution will ever meet the criteria of authoritativeness fully. There is a simplistic view of democracy which presumes agreement on the "rules of the game," i.e. the constitution, with the possibility of any amount of disagreement on the actual conflicts resolved through these procedures.[3] Stable democracies are not like that. Within every democratic polity there are continuing debates about what the constitution is or should be, and since parties to important substantive disputes often believe that the existing procedures for resolution are not neutral, then try to alter these ground-rules. Presumably, there are also some limits in any political system on the kinds of substantive conflicts that can be resolved by constitutional means. Some clashes of aspirations and interests are so profound that men will not agree to resolutions reached through constitutional procedures.

Although the stability of a democratic system does not require consensus on the constitution the capacity of a polity to survive depends greatly on its ability to give authoritative resolution to some disputes so that political decision-makers can give their attention to others. A quick demonstration of this capacity can be given by an examination of the issues that were agitating the politicians and the politically influential public five or ten years ago. Most of these disputes are no longer in the forefront of political conflict. Usually a law was enacted, and a new administrative agency was created to implement it. Those most directly affected adjusted, willingly or grudgingly, to the new situation, and the matter was removed from direct political attention. This process of the successive resolution of conflicting claims is, of course, impeded or completely obstructed when the disputants disagree on the procedures by which these conflicts can be authoritatively resolved. We have reached this point in Canadian federalism.

THE RISE AND DECLINE OF CO-OPERATIVE FEDERALISM

Canadian federalism in mid-1970 can be understood only against the background of developments in the recent past. In broad terms, we are in

1. Pierre Elliott Trudeau, "Quebec and the Constitutional Problem", *Federalism and The French Canadians*, Toronto: The Macmillan Company of Canada, Ltd.
2. I am not asserting that the survival of the Canadian federation is my ultimate political value. I believe it is a valid criticism of functional analysis that its preoccupation with systems—maintenance gives a fundamentally conservative perspective. However, it is not my purpose in this essay to discuss the final ends that I believe the continuing existence of Confederation will serve. For some analyses of my position on this see *The Canadian Political Nationality*, Toronto: Methuen and Company Ltd., 1967, particularly pp. 128-135.
3. For an interesting account along these lines see the pamphlet by Abe Fortas, *Concerning Dissent and Civil Disobedience*, New York: Signet Books, 1968.

the process of ending a constitutional experiment which developed subsequent to the election of the Pearson government in the spring of 1963. It reached its zenith about the end of the next year and began to disintegrate from the summer of 1965 onward. This short-lived regime was called co-operative federalism. Its operating assumption was that even the most fundamental federal-provincial differences could be resolved through the continuing procedures of intergovernmental consultation and negotiation.

The establishment of co-operative federalism was a response of the federal and provincial governments to circumstances under which they were increasingly inter-dependent. Their respective jurisdictions often overlapped, and the federal authorities had in large measure lost the capacity to dominate the Provinces which they had acquired during the Second World War and perpetuated in the subsequent years. From the summer of 1963 onward there was a rapid though piecemeal development of institutions and procedures for high-level intergovernmental collaboration; more frequent meetings of Prime Ministers dealing with a broader range of matters than before; annual meetings of Ministers of Finance; specialized agencies for intergovernmental relations in the federal administration and several Provinces; regular meetings of Ministers and Deputies in many policy fields where most interaction had been at the technical level; more regularized procedures of interprovincial corporation.[4] During this period the federal authorities showed an unprecedented willingness to consult with the Provinces where the latter's interests were involved, even regarding such matters as trade policies which were, according to the constitution, within the exclusive jurisdiction of the central government.

By the end of 1964 there were three major achievements of co-operative federalism. First, the Tax Structure Committee was established in the summer of 1964. Its members were federal and provincial Ministers of Finance (who were given a specialized staff and wide-ranging powers to inquire into the most fundamental aspects of federal-provincial financial relations. They were directed to report to a Federal-Provincial Conference early in 1966.[5] Never before had there been arrangements for federal-provincial consultation about fiscal matters at the ministerial level been institutionalized in this way.

Second, on October 14, 1964 a Conference of Prime Ministers and Premiers unanimously accepted a procedure for amending all aspects of the Canadian constitution without resort to the Parliament of the United Kingdom.[6] This was a major break-through in federal-provincial relations, since the governments had been discussing this matter since 1927, intensively since the fall of 1960.

Third, during 1964 there was federal-provincial agreement on several contracting-out arrangements[7] which the federal authorities hoped would satisfy Quebec's demands for greater financial and administrative autonomy than that desired by the other Provinces, and would simultaneously provide for the maintenance of Canada-wide service standards. Following the Federal-Provincial Conference of March 1964, there were detailed discussions of a procedure by which Provinces might, without financial penalties, choose not to participate in certain established conditional grant programs. Provisions to this effect were subsequently enacted by Parliament, but only Quebec accepted these alternatives. Also in 1964, the federal and Quebec governments agreed to arrangements whereby that Province would undertake programs of youth allowances, guaranteed loans to university students and public contributory retirement pensions – programs which, elsewhere in Canada, were financed and administered by the federal authorities.

It would thus have been possible by early 1965 for a reasonable observer to believe that even such seemingly intractable problems of federal-provincial dispute as constitutional reform and the allocation of tax sources and revenues between the two levels might be resolved by the procedures of cooperative federalism. But, after the middle of that year, the new constitutional regime began to disintegrate. The elements of this continuing process can be outlined briefly.

The Federal Medicare Plan

At the Federal-Provincial Conference of July 1965, Prime Minister Pearson announced the desire of the federal government to give financial support to provincial medical insurance plans which met certain conditions.[8] Specifically, the provincial schemes were to provide universal coverage and were to be publicly administered; all services normally provided by physicians were to be included, and benefits were to be portable among participating provinces. Legislation providing for the federal proposal was enacted by Parliament late in 1966. To take advantage of the federal offer would have put the Provinces to great expense when none could afford it.[9] and when most did not assign public medical insurance the highest priority in their expenditure plans. The federal authorities showed some willingness to modify the original proposal in response to provincial opposition, and in particular to agree that 90 per cent rather than universal coverage

4. For analyses òf these developments see E. Gallant "The Machinery of Federal-Provincial Relations", VIII, No. 4 *Canadian Public Administration*, Dec. 1964, pp. 515-26, and D. V. Smiley "Public Administration and Canadian Federalism", VII, No. 3 *Canadian Public Administration*, Sept. 1964, pp. 371-88.

5. For these terms of reference, see *Federal-Provincial Tax Structure Committee Report*, Ottawa, Sept. 14-15, 1966, pp. 5-6.

6. *The Amendment of the Constitution of Canada*, issued under the authority of the Honourable Guy Favreau, Minister of Justice, Ottawa: Queen's Printer, 1965.

7. See J. S. Dupré, "Contracting-Out: A Funny Thing Happened on the Way to the Centennial," *Report of the 1964 Conference of the Canadian Tax Foundation*, Toronto, 1965, pp. 209-18.

8. For the original federal proposal, see *Opening Statement by the Prime Minister of Canada* to *The Federal-Provincial Conference* beginning on July 18, 1965, mimeo., pp. 21-28.

9. The Canadian Tax Foundation estimated that the total shortfall of provincial revenues in terms of expenditures in 1967-'68 would be $427 million. Six of the ten Provinces were expected to have over-all deficit in the 1968-'69 fiscal year. There were tax increases in 1968-'69 budgets of seven of the ten Provinces. *Tax Memo.*, No. 45, June 1968, The Canadian Tax Foundation, Toronto.

would render a plan eligible for support and that the inauguration of the scheme could be delayed one year until July 1, 1968. However, Ottawa refused to be moved from the basic features of the 1965 proposal, and when the scheme came into operation only Saskatchewan and British Columbia had programs which qualified for federal assistance. It seems likely, though, that now all the other Provinces will find the political and financial costs of non-participation too high to remain outside the national plan. The federal medicare scheme, which was evolved and announced without consultation with the Provinces, and which was enacted over the opposition of most of them, was a direct challenge to the emergent understandings of co-operative federalism which posited a mutual respect by all governments regarding matters within the jurisdiction of the other level.

The Apparently Insatiable Demands of Quebec for autonomy[10]

Prior to, say, the fall of 1965 it was reasonable to hope that the evolving procedures of co-operative federalism would lead to an equilibrium in the distribution of powers and responsibilities between Ottawa and the Provinces. The federal government and the Provinces other than Quebec delineated their respective roles to as large an extent as they could agree. In its role, Quebec would, without financial penalties, choose not to participate with the federal authorities in joint programs whose subject-matter was within provincial legislative jurisdiction. From the federal viewpoint and that of the other Provinces, it was understood in the contracting-out arrangements that Quebec would undertake specific commitments to provide these services at standards similar to those prevailing elsewhere in the country; and in the health and welfare schemes Quebec was to ensure Canada-wide portability. By late 1965, however, it was apparent that Quebec would, as a matter of policy, demand "fiscal equivalents" for future joint programs in which the Province chose not to participate without assuming commitments to proceed according to national standards. There were new directions in Quebec welfare policies aimed directly at replacing federal family allowance and old age security schemes by provincial ones. In the fields of manpower policy, agriculture, and regional development, it became clear that Quebec was intent on extending its sphere of autonomy, in some instances by ousting the federal government from some of its activities and in others by bringing federal policies into harmony with provincial objectives. The Lesage government clearly wished to extend the Province's involvement in international affairs, and through Mr. Paul Gérin-Lajoie, the Minister of Education, it adopted the position that these activities should not be subjected to federal supervision or control as long as they dealt with matters within provincial legislative jurisdiction. In these and other matters, Quebec's demands for autonomy appeared to be insatiable.

The Rejection of the Fulton-Favreau Formula by Quebec

On January 20, 1966 Premier Lesage wrote to Prime Minister Pearson informing him that the government of the Province had decided to postpone indefinitely the submission to the Quebec Legislature of the Fulton-Favreau formula for constitutional amendment.[11] The reasons given by the Premier for this action were extremely unconvincing. The real motivation seems to have been that the Union Nationale and other politically influential groups in Quebec had created a climate of opinion hostile to the proposed procedure and had made an important partisan issue of the government's acceptance of it. Thus what had seemed a major breakthrough in Canadian constitutional development ended abruptly in failure. What is more, the reversal of Quebec policy challenged directly what might reasonably have been understood about co-operative federalism: that a government was committed to bring before its Legislature an agreement which it had accepted at a Federal-Provincial Conference.

The Election of the Union Nationale Government

The unexpected victory of the Union Nationale in the Quebec general election of June 1966 was a decisive event in the disintegration of co-operative federalism. Although the demands for autonomy of Premier Lesage and his colleagues were extensive, the administration had chosen for the most part to pursue its objectives within the framework of intergovernmental negotiation. Prime Minister Pearson and Premier Lesage had been colleagues in the federal cabinet prior to the 1957 election, and between these leaders as well as between senior officials of their two governments there had developed a pattern of relations characterized by continuous consultation and a mutual appreciation of the constraints operating on each administration.[12] All this was now changed. The new Union Nationale government, unlike its predecessor, was committed to an early and radical rewriting of the constitution, and it showed much less confidence that Quebec's objectives could successfully be pursued through the piecemeal processes of federal-provincial negotiation. Further, Mr. Johnson and his colleagues were relatively unknown in Ottawa and the other Provinces, and what was known of the new leadership gave cause for apprehension. The close pattern of relations between the federal and Quebec governments that had developed prior to June 1966 has not been re-established.

The New Allocation of Revenues and Responsibilities proposed by the Federal Government in the Fall of 1966

At a meeting of the Tax Structure Committee in September 1966 and at a Federal-Provincial Conference convened the next month to deal with the financing of post-secondary education, the federal government proposed a comprehensive re-allocation between the two levels, of revenues,

10. See Donald V. Smiley, *The Canadian Political Nationality*, Toronto: Methuen & Company Ltd., 1967, pp. 66-78.

11. *House of Commons Debates*, January 28, 1966. The Pearson-Lesage correspondence is printed in Paul Fox, (ed.), *Politics: Canada*, Second Edition, Toronto: McGraw-Hill Co. of Canada Ltd., 1966, pp. 146-49.

12. See Smiley, *op. cit.*, pp. 66-78.

revenue sources and responsibilities.[13] It was the first such attempt that Ottawa had made since the Dominion-Provincial Conference on Reconstruction in 1945-46. The essential elements of the new plan were:

(a) *A radically new equalization formula which took into account provincial tax yields from all sources;*

(b) *The gradual termination of a large number of shared-cost programs with unconditional fiscal compensation to the Provinces;*

(c) *Federal ' withdrawal from direct capital and operating grants to institutions providing post-secondary education with unconditional compensation to the Provinces based on 50 per cent of the operating costs of these institutions;*

(d) *Complete federal financial responsibility for the occupational retraining of adults.*

The motivations behind the federal initiative were complex. Ottawa undoubtedly wished to change the system whereby pressures on the Provinces for increased expenditures were almost immediately translated by their governments into pressures on the federal authorities for financial concession. The extent of federal responsibilities for interprovincial financial equalization made more crucial than ever a more precise measurement of provincial fiscal need. Rapidly increasing university expenditures required a clearer definition of the respective roles of the two levels in financing post-secondary education. Perhaps most crucially, the various contracting-out arrangements had resulted in a situation where Quebec had attained a *de facto* special status among the Provinces and, as we have seen, the appetites of successive Quebec governments for autonomy appeared insatiable. The federal initiatives in the fall of 1966 coincided in time with the increasing influence of Pierre Elliott Trudeau in the constitutional policies of the federal government. Before and after entering federal politics in 1965, Trudeau consistently opposed any form of special status for Quebec and favoured a clearer definition of federal and provincial responsibilities. The federal proposals of 1966 were in basic harmony with his position. Most importantly, in terms of co-operative federalism, these proposals as they related to the financing of education were adopted and announced as government policy as a unilateral federal initiative without extensive prior consultations with the provinces.

The Convening of the Confederation of Tomorrow and Constitutional Conferences

Co-operative federalism proceeded by *ad hoc* and piecemeal devices to seek agreement on particular matters without much concern for more fundamental ones. The initiative taken in November 1967 by the government of Ontario[14] in convening the Confederation of Tomorrow Conference, and the response to this invitation by the other Provinces, indicated that among the provincial administrations there was a prevailing sentiment that piecemeal evolution should be accompanied by more general discussions of the directions in which the Canadian federal system was developing. Apparently in response to this, the federal government announced in the fall of 1967 that the Federal-Provincial Conference, originally called for February 1969 to deal only with the proposal for a Canadian Charter of Human Rights, would be opened up to broader considerations of constitutional reform. These two conferences have in part turned the attention of the governments away from the resolution of specific problems to discussion of more general matters.

Federal-Quebec Relations and the General Election of 1968

The effective operation of co-operative federalism requires that for the most part political leaders refrain from seeking popular mandates for the positions they have taken in federal-provincial conflicts. It is probably unrealistic to expect that this requirement will ever be fulfilled completely, and it is a standard partisan technique of provincial leaders to attempt to demonstrate that their government has been dealt with unfairly by Ottawa. However, early in the election campaign of 1968, the publication by the federal government of the White Paper entitled *Federalism and International Conferences on Education*[15] propelled federal-Quebec relations into partisan politics in an unusually dramatic way. The White Paper was, for the most part, an elaboration of Ottawa's position on federal and provincial roles in international affairs which had been announced at the Constitutional Conference the previous February.[16] However, the discussion included the federal version of Ottawa's continuing dispute with Quebec concerning the Province's participation in international conferences dealing with educational matters. The circumstances under which the White Paper was released, and the emphasis that Prime Minister Trudeau and his Liberal colleagues gave to their constitutional policies in the 1968 election campaign, make it reasonable to suppose that the government was deliberately seeking a popular ratification of these policies in future relations with the Provinces, and in particular with Quebec.

In summary, co-operative federalism has failed. There are still a great many unresolved disagreements about the respective roles of the federal and provincial governments – disagreements about Quebec's role in international matters; the scope of federal powers over credit-granting institutions; federal and provincial responsibilities in educational broadcasting; medicare; jurisdiction over off-shore mineral development; Indian affairs; the nature and extent of federal responsibilities in interprovincial fiscal equalization; the federal responsibility (if any) for making equal opportunities available to individual Canadians; responsibilities in regional economic development, in housing, etc. It is significant to note that in the past decade the sources of tension moved more and more from the alleged

---

13. *Federal-Provincial Tax Structure Committee*, Toronto: Queen's Printer pp. 11-30, and *House of Commons Debates*, October 31, 1966, pp. 9289-92.

14. See the statement of Premier Robarts, *Debates, Legislature of Ontario*, May 23, 1967, Toronto: Queen's Printer, pp. 3566-68.

15. Ottawa, Queen's Printer, 1968.

16. The Honourable Paul Martin, *Federalism and International Relations*, Ottawa, Queen's Printer, 1968.

encroachment of Ottawa on matters within provincial jurisdiction, to such areas of dispute as banking, broadcasting, Indian affairs and international relations, which were formerly recognized to be almost exclusively federal concerns. More than in the immediate past, governments are now inclined to discuss particular matters within some framework of general principle, and so long as constitutional discussions go on this will almost inevitably continue to be so. However, these substantive conflicts would not in themselves threaten the viability of Canadian federalism. In fact, the maintenance of a federal system requires a continuing tension between centripetal and centrifugal influences, and in conditions of their interdependence, the absence of conflict between central and regional governments could only signify that one level had attained a temporary or permanent dominance over the other. The circumstance of contemporary Canadian federalism is, however, that conflicting claims are being made about some of the most important areas of jurisdiction at the same time as the governments concerned have failed to reach agreement on the appropriate procedures for resolving these claims and regulating the relations between federal and provincial governments.

PROCEDURAL AMBIGUITIES AND DISAGREEMENTS

There are five major areas of unresolved procedural disagreements in federal-provincial relations.

The Authority and Nature of the Federal-Provincial Conference

In the broadest of terms, has the Federal-Provincial Conference of Prime Ministers and Premiers become the sovereign authority in Canada? – sovereign even over the written constitution because such a Conference could decide how the constitution was to be amended? Has the Conference any collective authority apart from its members, or is it analagous to an international gathering in which each participating government retains its full freedom of action? Is the Conference, or any subordinate agency it creates, the appropriate body for resolving conflicts between Ottawa and only one Province? – as Mr. Stanfield asserted in the 1968 election campaign when he suggested that the Ottawa-Quebec international affairs dispute be referred to the Continuing Committee on the Constitution established by the Conference the preceding February. What are the operating procedures for Federal-Provincial Conferences? Can they be convened only by the federal government? Must decisions be unanimous? How, if at all, can effective co-operation of governments at this level be reconciled with the constitutional tradition that governments are accountable to their respective elected legislatures and through these legislatures to national and provincial electorates? Are there inherent incompatibilities between the Federal-Provincial Conference and the constructive activity of legislatures and their committees in those areas with which Conferences now deal?[17] What relationship can be established between the Conference and various interprovincial groups, particularly between the Federal-Provincial Continuing Committee on the Constitution and the five-Premier committee set up to carry on the discussions begun at the Confederation of Tomorrow Conference? There is no agreement among the participating governments on these and other fundamental questions about what has become a central operating institution of Canadian federalism.

The Nature of the Consultative process

With the increasing interdependence between federal and provincial governments, more effective procedures of consultation are necessary if each level is not to frustrate the objectives of the other. But there is no agreement on the nature of the consultative process or on the subjects to which it should apply. In this decade, successive Quebec governments have asserted the obligation of the federal government to consult with the Provinces on certain matters which usually come under federal jurisdiction. Premier Lesage at the Federal-Provincial Conference of November 1963 elaborated a view of co-operative federalism which combined provincial autonomy and extensive federal-provincial consultations, through specialized institutions concerning trade, transportation, and monetary policies where provincial objectives were directly engaged.[18] In this protest about the Canada-Belgium cultural agreement signed in May 1967, Premier Johnson asserted that the federal authorities had an obligation to consult with Quebec on cultural and educational relations with the French-speaking world.[19] The Premier has also insisted that Ottawa should have consulted with the Provinces prior to the enactment by Parliament of legislation dealing with educational broadcasting.[20] There are also conflicts about appropriate procedures of consultation. In the debates of this decade it has sometimes seemed that the obligation to consult was exclusively Ottawa's. However, Prime Minister Pearson asserted at the 1965 Federal-Provincial Conference that the Provinces had a corresponding obligation where federal interests and objectives were involved.[21] Successive Quebec governments have been committed to the establishment of specialized institutions for federal-provincial consultation;[22] Ottawa and the other Provinces have preferred to proceed otherwise. There are unresolved difficulties about timing. When one government is taking the initiative and is disposed to

17. There have been repeated suggestions, mainly from members of the Official Opposition, that the House of Commons be more directly involved in federal-provincial matters by the establishment of a standing committee on these matters, and that the Opposition should somehow be associated with federal-provincial meetings on constitutional reform. Nothing has come of these proposals.

18. *Proceedings*, Ottawa, Queen's Printer, 1964, pp. 44-6.

19. *Le Devoir*, 9 Mai, 1967.

20. *Le Devoir*, 20 Novembre, 1967.

21. Opening Statement to the Federal-Provincial Conference, July 19, 1965, *mimeo*. p. 3.

22. *Proceedings of the 1963 Federal-Provincial Conference*, and *The Government of Québec and the Constitution*, L'Office d'Information et de Publicité du Québec, 1968, pp. 42-4.

consult with others, should such consultations take place before a bill has been introduced into the legislature, debated on principle, and passed on second reading? Or is it more appropriate that the legislature be asked to ratify a detailed proposal arrived at after consultations? At what point should consultations with the Provinces take place concerning treaties and other international agreements in which provincial action is necessary to the full implementation of these accords? These and other questions about the scope and nature of consultation remain unresolved.

Judicial Interpretation of the Constitution

During this decade of profound conflicts about jurisdiction, there has been little desire on either level to seek judicial clarification. The Federal-Provincial Conference of March 1964 saw a severe breakdown in the relations between Quebec and the other governments, and at the end an angry Premier Lesage asserted that he would submit several areas of disputed jurisdiction to the courts for determination. He did not subsequently do so, but it is a significant indication of how judicial review of the constitution is viewed, that the Premier's statement was everywhere regarded as a threat and as a dramatic escalation of federal-provincial conflict. In December 1964, the federal cabinet submitted a reference to the Supreme Court concerning jurisdiction over mineral resources off the coast of British Columbia.[23] This matter had been the subject of unresolved disagreement between the central and British Columbia governments for some years. Those Provinces with coastlines all vigorously protested that the action of the federal authorities was an inappropriate way of resolving this dispute. In its 1967 decision the Supreme Court upheld the federal claim.[24] The government of British Columbia has defied this ruling, and some petroleum companies are apparently paying lease fees to both the federal and B.C. governments.[25] A more generalized attack on the legitimacy of the Supreme Court as an arbiter of the constitution has come from certain quarters in Quebec. It has been argued that because the unilateral action of the federal Parliament established the Court as the final court of appeal in all Canadian cases the Supreme Court cannot legitimately interpret a constitution which is essentially a pact between the federal government and the Provinces.[26] The incumbent Quebec administration has not stated this point of view explicitly, but at the 1968 Constitutional Conference Premier Johnson asserted: ". . . because of the way in which the Supreme Court is constituted, it is difficult to accept this court as a constitutional tribunal of the last resort."[27] There are thus profound disputes among the federal and provincial governments about the legitimacy of the Supreme Court as a constitutional arbiter and the appropriate role, if any, for judicial review in questions of disputed jurisdiction.

Partisan Politics and the Resolution of Federal-Provincial Conflict.

The federal election of 1968 brought into sharp relief contradictory opinions about the appropriate relation between partisan politics and federal-provincial conflict. As we have seen, the publication by the government of the White Paper on *International Conferences on Education* brought the important Quebec-Ottawa dispute into the campaign. The

Prime Minister and his colleagues maintained that the issue raised contradictory conceptions of Canada and that, because it was so fundamental, the electors were entitled to know where the parties stood. Mr. Stanfield, on the other hand, insisted that the issue was too complex to be adequately debated during an election campaign, that it had been grossly over-simplified by the government,[28] and that it should have been referred to the Constitutional Committee on Constitutional Matters established at the Federal-Provincial Conference of February 1968. Furthermore, claimed the Conservative leader, the conflict could not be resolved by whatever verdict the national electorate gave. Its introduction into the federal political arena could only serve to harden Quebec attitudes and might well precipitate a provincial election. Even if the Union Nationale were somehow defeated in the process begun by the Prime Minister, the other major parties in Quebec had more rigid views on constitutional matters.

Conflicts about the nature and urgency of Constitutional reform

The Constitutional Conference of February 1968 revealed fundamental differences among the eleven governments about the urgency and nature of possible reforms in the constitution. There are three fairly well-defined positions:

– The federal government says that constitutional reform should proceed in three successive steps: (1) the constitutional entrenchment of various classes of individual rights; (2) the possible reform of certain "central institutions of Canadian federalism" – more particularly the Senate, the Supreme Court, the federal public service, and the national capital; (3) the division of powers between the federal and provincial governments.[29] This order appears to be a matter of firm federal policy, and the government has strongly resisted Quebec's demands for an earlier discussion of proposals for a radical redistribution of federal-provincial powers.

– The Quebec position is: that a radical and early rewriting of the constitution is necessary.[30] The first and overriding priority in such a procedure is the effective constitutional recognition of the bi-national nature

23. For a lucid account of the issues involved see Edwin R. Black, "Oil Offshore Troubles the Waters", LXXII *Queen's Quarterly*, Winter 1966, pp. 589-603.

24. (1968) 62 W.W.W. 21.

25. For the B.C. position see *The Province*, Vancouver, March 26, 1968.

26. For an analysis to this effect see the speech of Mr. Maurice Allard (Sherbrooke) in the House of Commons, *Debates*, February 21, 1966, pp. 1545-49. Mr. Allard is a former professor of constitutional law. In several articles in *Le Devoir* Paul Sauriol has taken the same position, see *Bloc Notes*, 16 Février, 1965, 24 Août, 1965, and 19 Novembre, 1966.

27. *The Government of Québec and the Constitution*, p. 86.

28. For the position of Mr. Stanfield see the interview with George Bain, *The Globe and Mail*, Toronto, June 5, 1968 and also the press statement of the Conservative leader on May 11, 1968 and his Halifax Speech of May 16, 1968.

29. The Right Honourable L. B. Pearson, *Federalism for the Future*, Ottawa, Queen's Printer, 1968, pp. 18-36.

30. Statement of Premier Daniel Johnson at the February Constitutional Conference, reprinted in *The Government of Québec and the Constitution*, pp. 61-2.

of Canada and the assignment of new and more extended powers for Quebec.

– The position of the other Provinces is: that constitutional reform, either as conceived by Ottawa or Quebec, is not urgent. At the Confederation of Tomorrow Conference Ross Thatcher of Saskatchewan asserted a view which is probably shared by many of the other Premiers: "I suppose in Saskatchewan if we had a hundred problems, the Constitution would be the hundred and first, but we also realize that from a national point of view this may not be the case." This immobility is not evenly distributed among the Provinces. It is most profound in the three westernmost Provinces, and somewhat less so in Newfoundland, Prince Edward Island and Nova Scotia. Ontario and New Brunswick are significantly more tolerant of discussions on constitutional revision. Except in Quebec, however, there is no widespread dissatisfaction with the constitution, and it was undoubtedly to meet this sentiment that the agenda of the 1968 Conference included "Questions of Regional Disparity," an item which in the narrow sense does not relate directly to the constitution.

Under conditions of great secrecy, the federal and provincial governments began in the summer of 1968 to discuss proposals for constitutional reform. It is impossible of course for an outsider to know what progress is being achieved, but it seems likely that many of the governments involved remain unconvinced of the urgency of fundamental constitutional reform.

Possible Procedures for Resolving Federal-Provincial Conflicts

How can the profound conflicts in Canadian federalism be resolved? It is unrealistic to contemplate a solution where there are no important matters under dispute between federal and provincial governments. But what the continuing viability of the system appears to require is a group of authoritative procedures for the successful resolution of particular conflicts. In this section, the possibilities of several alternatives such as procedures in the immediate future are examined.

The Employment of the Quasi-Unitary Features of the Constitution

A determined federal government which wished to press to the limit its claims against the Provinces would have a formidable arsenal of legal weapons. It might exercise widely its powers to disallow provincial legislation. It might bring a large number of important provincial "Works and Undertakings" under the jurisdiction of Parliament through the provisions of Section 92 10(c) of the British North America Act. It might exercise extensively the federal power to spend and lend in matters within provincial legislative jurisdiction and enforce its own conditions on those accepting these funds – whether Provinces, local authorities, private groups or individuals. It could press to the limits its jurisdiction over defence, navigation and shipping, trade and commerce, banking, agriculture and other areas of power as advised by legal experts. It could use aggressively its financial powers to bring the provinces into harmony with national objectives. It could cause to have changed the jurisdiction and procedures of the Supreme Court and "pack" that body to ensure decisions favourable to the federal government. As a last resort, the federal authorities might change the distribution of legislative powers between Parliament and the provinces – it is almost certain that the United Kingdom Parliament would assent to any such request.

The situation which I have described is of course constitutional science-fiction, a deliberate destruction of Canadian federalism by legal means. There has in fact been a movement away from the employment of what might be called the quasi-unitary features of the Canadian constitution. Disallowance is in abeyance, probably permanently. Parliament has shown no disposition in recent years toward enhancing its jurisdiction over important spheres of activity through Section 92 10(c). Federal spending power has been exercised in a more discriminating way in the past ten years. Federal fiscal powers have become a less effective means of control, with the long-term trend toward a smaller proportion of total public expenditures being made by the central government. Judicial review of the constitution is being used with moderation. It appears to have become a constitutional convention that no amendment altering the distribution of legislative powers will be sought without the unanimous consent of the provinces. In brief, there are few immediate possibilities for resolving outstanding disputes over jurisdiction though the federal government is resorting to a group of powers which makes the Canadian constitution, in its purely legal aspects, a quasi-unitary one.

Judicial delineation of spheres of disputed jurisdiction

Several proposals have recently been made about reforming the court of final appeal in Canadian constitutional cases. The minimum kind of reform would go no farther than establishing common law and civilian panels in the Supreme Court so that Civil Code appeals coming from Quebec would be decided by specially trained judges. More far-reaching proposals would create a tribunal whose jurisdiction was limited to constitutional cases with part of its membership chosen by the Provinces.

It is prudent not to make sweeping predictions about the future role of judicial review in delineating spheres of disputed jurisdiction, whether there are major reforms in the structure and functioning of the Supreme Court and other parts of the judicial system or not. I tend to believe that the courts will continue to play a relatively minor role in determining the shape that Canadian federalism will take, although in defining certain federal and provincial legislative powers and in validating certain forms of federal-provincial delegation, the judiciary has acted constructively.[31] J. A. Corry pointed out a decade ago that private businesses had become less willing than in the past to enter into litigation challenging federal powers,[32] and it is unlikely that, in the near future, many private persons or groups will be motivated to undertake the lengthy and expensive legal

31. See W. R. Lederman, "Some Forms and Limitations of Co-operative Federalism", XLV *Canadian Bar Review* (September 1967), pp. 409-36.

32. A. R. M. Lower, F. R. Scott et al., "Constitutional Trends and Federalism," *Evolving Canadian Federalism*, Durham, N.C.: Duke University Press.

action involved in such a challenge. As far as governments themselves are concerned, it is difficult to foresee the changes that could make them seek more extensive judicial review or even – as the results of the reference involving off-shore mineral rights seem to indicate – to accept judicial decisions which they believe to be to their disadvantage.

Constitutional Reform

Will the period of federal-provincial constitutional discussions which is now beginning produce in the foreseeable future an authoritative resolution of some of the areas of jurisdiction now in dispute? Again, one must make cautious predictions. It so happens that as discussions go on, and as the governments involved are increasingly frustrated by jurisdictional conflicts, new patterns of intergovernmental relations and a restatement of the respective roles of each level will emerge. On the other hand, there appear to be several influences inhibiting this outcome:

– As we have seen, the federal and provincial governments are in deep disagreement both about the necessity of comprehensive constitutional reforms and whether, if they are necessary, they should include a radical redefinition of powers between the two levels. The Constitutional Conference of February 1968 saw stated two contradictory directions for constitutional reform – that of Quebec and that of the federal government – with varying degrees of immobility among the nine other Provinces. Any comprehensive restatement of federal-provincial powers will require a very great will to do so among the governments involved. This will has not yet been created.

– Comprehensive revision of the constitution seems to require agreement on symbolic matters, and such agreement is difficult. Those most intent on reform insist that a new Canadian constitution should be a focus for popular loyalties. The flag debate has demonstrated the deep disagreements among Canadians about their common political symbols, and this issue, unlike that of the constitution, was capable of resolution by Parliament alone. Marcel Faribault has been one of the most persistent proponents of a new constitution, partly on the grounds that the symbolism of the existing one is inappropriate. Most Canadian politicians, however, are not very adept at political metaphysics, and one of the least enlightening exercises in which a future Federal-Provincial Constitutional Conference might engage would be to try to make something of a formulation like the opening of the preamble to the Faribault-Fower constitution "We the people of Canada, recognizing that all authority is from God, Supreme Lawgiver, Judge and Ruler of Heaven and Earth . . ."[33]

– Any serious discussions of comprehensive reform will inevitably involve a renewal of debate about a procedure for constitutional amendment, and the prospects for agreement seem remote. The Fulton-Favreau formula was an extraordinarily intricate series of compromises. The position of the Union Nationale has consistently been: that any amendment procedure whose result would be to prevent Quebec from attaining a wider scope of autonomy than the other provinces wish is unacceptable. Prime Minister Trudeau has maintained that a differential distribution of legislative powers among the provinces is ultimately destructive of Confederation, and on this basis he opposed the delegation provisions of the Fulton-Favreau formula.[34] Among the other Provinces than Quebec, there is no doubt an understandable resentment about the failure of the solution to which all eleven governments agreed in 1964 and a hesitation about reopening the issue.

Federal-Provincial Agreement on Particular and Limited Matters

Can co-operative federalism be re-established? It is an essential characteristic of viable federal systems that central-regional relations are organized so that profound disagreement on some matters does not preclude agreement on others.[35] To take a recent and dramatic example of this organization, Prime Minister Trudeau and the Honourable Maurice Sauvé took a few hours out on May 26, 1968 from their election campaign in Quebec, which was widely interpreted as the pursuit of a mandate for federal constitutional policies, to participate with Premier Johnson in a ceremony at Rimouski where an Ottawa-Quebec agreement was signed for the expenditure of $258 millions on a depressed areas development program in Eastern Quebec.[36] Studies of Canadian and American federalism have shown a high degree of functionalism in central-regional relations[37] where major decisions concerning important public activities are made by groups of specialized personnel from both levels of government.

In the present context, the insulation of those areas of federal-provincial relations where agreement is possible, from those where it is not, is more difficult than in the past. The successful working of co-operative federalism requires among those involved a high degree of pragmatism, even opportunism — a profound disposition to consider specific issues without raising broader questions of principle. However, the discussions begun in the Confederation of Tomorrow Conference and the Constitutional Conference almost inevitably mean that federal and provincial politicians will discuss particular problems within a more general framework than in the

---

33. Marcel Faribault and Robert M. Fowler, *Ten to One: The Confederation Wager*, Toronto/Montreal, McClelland and Stewart Limited, 1965, p. 119. For a collection of Mr. Faribault's writings on the constitution see *Vers Une Nouvelle Constitution*, Ottawa, Editions Fides, 1967.

34. Trudeau, *op. cit.*, pp. 40-2. This critique of the Fulton-Favreau formula was made shortly before Mr. Trudeau entered politics. So far as I know, he has not spoken directly of the problem of amendment procedure since that time but it is central to Trudeau's constitutional thought that any differential distribution of legislature powers between the provinces is unacceptable.

35. Smiley, *op. cit.* pp. 371-388.

36. *The Globe and Mail*, Toronto, May 27, 1968.

37. Donald V. Smiley, *Conditional Grants and Canadian Federalism*, Canadian Tax Paper No. 32, Canadian Tax Foundation, Toronto, 1963, pp. 37-42 and Edward W. Weidner, "Decision-Making in a Federal System," in Aaron Wildavsky (ed.) *American Federalism in Perspective*, Little, Brown and Company, Boston, 1967, pp. 229-56.

past. During this decade, Quebec's quest for autonomy has been single-minded, and it seems that even the most specific kind of federal-provincial matter has been dealt with in these terms. Functionalism, almost by definition, is featured by decisive influence being wielded with relatively homogeneous perspectives by groups of officials from both levels. Also during the 1960's there has been a movement among most of the governments to subordinate specialized individuals and agencies involved in federal-provincial relations to those with broader concerns. The conditions for co-operative federalism are not auspicious.

The Resolution of Federal-Provincial Disputes Through Partisan-Political Processes?

In the light of the decisive results of the federal general election of June 1968 is it reasonable to suppose that the new federal administration will be more effective than its recent predecessors in imposing its will on the Provinces and thus resolving several of the more crucial areas of disputed jurisdiction? Or, to put it another way, will a range of conflicts which have not been susceptible to resolution through executive and judicial procedures be resolved through the processes of the partisan-political system? An affirmative answer to these questions is indicated on the following grounds:

– Both the relative decisiveness of the electoral result, and the prominence that Mr. Trudeau and his colleagues gave to the constitutional issue in the campaign, make it reasonable to suppose that the government has a mandate for its constitutional position. The content of this mandate is imprecise, but it seems to include opposition to the demands of Quebec for special status in the Canadian federal system.

–Within Quebec, the Liberal victory may cause both federal and provincial politicians to question the assumption on which most of them have proceeded in this decade: that only some variation of Quebec nationalism is electorally popular. The provincial Liberal party appears to be undergoing a radical assessment of its position on constitutional matters and may come to support a federalist alternative. Among the federal parties, it seems unlikely that in the forseeable future there will be the kinds of compromises with Quebec nationalism which were so electorally unsuccessful in the campaign.

– None of the provincial governments was able to influence the election decisively in the way it desired. It is significant that, in the Provinces with provincial Liberal administrations, the federal Liberals won only 8 of the 34 seats at stake. In Newfoundland and New Brunswick the Liberal percentage of the popular vote decreased from the 1965 election, in Saskatchewan there was no significant change and in P.E.I. there was a slight gain. The unfavourable Liberal results in Newfoundland and Saskatchewan have been attributed to the current unpopularity of their incumbent provincial governments. On this basis, one could almost conclude that there are net disadvantages for a federal party to have provincial governments of the same complexion in power. In the other Provinces, governments were similarly impotent. The support of the Ontario Conservatives and Quebec Union Nationale for the federal Conservative party resulted in only 16 of 162 Conservatives being elected from these two Provinces. In Alberta and British Columbia, the Manning and Bennett governments were totally incapable of affecting federal election results in any significant way. So far as the immediate future is concerned, federal-provincial conflict will proceed within a framework where provincial governments are unable to harm the federal administration politically, except under those circumstances where the latter is thwarted by the unpopular actions of a provincial government of the same partisan complexion.

It is by no means certain, however, that Mr. Trudeau's personal popularity and the decisive results of the 1968 federal general election will predispose the provinces toward accepting the leadership of Ottawa. At the Annual Conference of the Canadian Bar Association held in Vancouver in September 1968, the Prime Minister criticized what he regarded as the immobility of the provinces in constitutional matters.[38] In particular, he expressed disappointment at the failure of the Premiers at their August meeting to take a stand on the Quebec position of extending provincial powers into international affairs. Of the general discussions of constitutional reform, Mr. Trudeau said: "Several Provinces have shown enthusiasm for the review. Others have appeared more hesitant, reluctant perhaps to embark wholeheartedly on a journey whose destination is uncertain. But this is not a journey on which one can afford to leave several parties behind."

There is scattered evidence of the increasing federalization of the Canadian party system in the sense that federal and provincial parties in several dimensions are increasingly independent of each other:

– Electoral successes of a party at one level are by no means always or even characteristically followed by its success at the other level. The following table, for example, gives the results in succeeding provincial elections after the wake of the Diefenbaker victory in the federal general election of 1958.

		Conservative % of popular vote compared with previous prov. election	Liberal % of popular vote compared with previous prov. election
Newfoundland	Aug. 20, 1959	– 6.7	– 8.3
P.E.I.	Sept. 1, 1959	+ 5.9	– 5.9
Nova Scotia	June 7, 1960	– .3	– 5.6
New Brunswick	June 27, 1960	– 6.0	+ 7.3
Quebec	June 22, 1960	did not contest	+ 6.8
Ontario	June 11, 1959	– 2.4	+ 3.4
Manitoba	June 16, 1958	–19.5	– 6.0
Saskatchewan	June 8, 1960	+12.0	+ 2.4
Alberta	June 18, 1959	+14.7	–17.2
British Columbia	Sept. 12, 1960	+ 3.6	– .9

38. Press Release (mimeo.), September 3, 1968.

As we have seen, incumbent provincial governments do not seem to have been able to affect decisively the results of the 1968 federal general election. Although careful analysis of these "coat-tail" effects is necessary[39] it is reasonable to suppose that a successful federal or provincial party must secure a base of electoral support somewhat different from that of its counterpart at the other level.

– There are and have been in the recent past, several successful political parties which are exclusively or almost exclusively oriented toward one level or the other. The incumbent governments of Alberta, British Columbia and Quebec are exclusively provincial. In terms of electoral success, the Conservative parties of the three westernmost Provinces are almost exclusively federal in orientation. The federal and provincial Liberals in Quebec consummated an almost complete organizational separation in 1964, and in that Province where, in formal terms at least, the autonomy of federal and provincial parties is most complete, the Creditistes, who do not participate provincially, are the most effective opposition to the federal Liberals.

– Apparently these are developments toward increasingly autonomous federal and provincial parties in terms of party finance.[40] Until recently, party finance in Canada was highly centralized, and the major contributors were corporations in Toronto and Montreal who wished one kind of concession or another from the federal government. This situation has changed. Part of this change is, of course, the result of the breakdown of the two-party system and of the incumbency of parties which are exclusively or almost exclusively provincial. In 1963 the Legislature of Quebec enacted a program for direct public subsidies to recognized parties. The result was to disentangle the federal and provincial from their mutual financial dependence. Perhaps more crucially, the increasing importance in the economy of natural resource development has led corporate contributors to be more willing than before to support provincial parties.

In general terms, then, federal and provincial political systems appear to be evolving toward separation, and within particular provinces successful parties must command resources of electoral support, organization, and finance, independent of the party at the other level. Thus the party system is, less than in the past, an integrative force along nation-wide lines. The general election of June 1968 appeared to indicate the relative impotence of the provincial Premiers in affecting the federal results, but it is possible that Mr. Trudeau and his colleagues would have equally little influence over the political fortunes of provincial political parties.

39. See Howard Scarrow, "Federal Provincial Voting Patterns in Canada", *Voting in Canada*, John C. Courtney (ed.), Scarborough, 1967, pp. 82-9, and D. H. Wrong "Patterns of Party Voting in Canada", *Public Opinion Quarterly*, XXI, (1957).

40. See the provocative analyses of Khayyam Z. Paltiel in *Studies in Canadian Party Finance*, Committee on Election Expenses, Ottawa, Queen's Printer, 1966, pp. 1-21.

SECTION TWO

CONSTITUTIONAL ISSUES

So much of Canadian politics of late has involved specific constitutional issues that it was deemed appropriate to devote an entire section in this book to a few of the major constitutional problems.

Few issues have initiated more debate among politicians, political scientists and lawyers than the proposal for a constitutional bill of rights. Kenneth Kernaghan's essay surveys the problem of the protection of basic civil liberties and shows that support for a constitutional bill of rights is growing. Peter H. Russell responds to this and similar suggestions with a case for a "more democratic approach" to the protection of civil liberties.

This section would be incomplete without Prime Minister Trudeau's "Charter of Human Rights" since he is the main advocate of an entrenched bill of rights. It is not unreasonable to expect that forthcoming proposals for a constitutional bill of rights will probably include many of the items enumerated in the "Charter of Human Rights."

The final issue covered in this section involves the thorny problem of treaty-making and treaty-implementation. Mr. Justice Bora Laskin places the issue in perspective with a cogently argued paper originally prepared for the Ontario Advisory Committee on Confederation. Jacques-Yvan Morin replies, by implication, with a case for the special claim of Quebec to enter into treaties with foreign governments in certain matters.

5

Civil Liberties and
a Constitutional
Bill of Rights

KENNETH KERNAGHAN

In the Canadian House of Commons on July 1, 1960, John George Diefenbaker, then Prime Minister, uttered these words in support of the enactment of a bill of rights for Canada:

I am a Canadian, a free Canadian, free to speak without fear, free to worship God in my own way, free to stand for what I think right, free to oppose what I believe wrong, free to choose those who shall govern my country. This heritage of freedom I pledge to uphold for myself and for all mankind.[1]

The purpose of this essay is to examine the validity of Mr. Diefenbaker's eloquent statement as a description of either the historical or existing status of Canadian freedoms. Integral to this inquiry is an account of the events and personalities associated with the movement toward the enactment in 1960 of the Canadian Bill of Rights[2] and toward the current proposal for a Canadian charter of human rights.

I

THE BILL OF RIGHTS AND THE CONSTITUTION

Unlike the United States Constitution, the British North America Act makes little provision for the defence of civil liberties.[3] The few scattered references to the subject in the Confederation Debates indicate that the Fathers of Confederation saw little need for the provision of explicit constitutional protection of Canadian freedoms.[4] John A. Macdonald, in speaking of the benefits the Provinces received from their association with England, claimed that "so long as that alliance is maintained, we enjoy, under her protection, the privileges of constitutional liberty according to the British system".[5] This view is reflected in the preamble to the British North America Act which expresses the desire of the federating

Provinces to establish "a Constitution similar in Principle to that of the United Kingdom".

If Canada's written constitution is modelled "in principle" on the British Constitution, which has not in modern times incorporated a statutory bill of rights, why does Canada require greater legislative safeguards to civil liberties than Great Britain? Professor F. R. Scott has answered that the elements of "parliamentary restraint in legislation, bureaucratic restraint in administration, and a strong and live tradition of personal freedom among the citizens generally",[6] which are conducive to the preservation of civil liberties in Great Britain, are present in the Canadian milieu only in part. Moreover, Canada, in distinct contrast to Great Britain, is a vast country inhabited by a heterogeneous people. The British tradition of respect for civil liberties is, therefore, only one among many Canadian traditions, some of which are less concerned with the preservation of basic freedoms. There is, in Canada, less toleration of dissenting views and, consequently, a more willing disposition to restrict the freedoms of expression and activity. In addition, the federal nature of the Canadian governmental system demands the scrutiny of the enactments of not one, but eleven separate governing bodies. In Great Britain, legislative authority over civil liberties lies with Parliament alone, but in Canada this authority is divided between the Federal Parliament and the provincial legislatures.

The oft-repeated statement that Canada has inherited adequate guarantees to civil liberties from British traditions of common law is an invalid, even a dangerous, assumption. Certainly, the British people have, during

1. *Debates (Commons)*, 3rd Sess. 24th Parl. (1960), 5649-50.

2. *An Act for the Recognition and Protection of Human Rights and Fundamental Freedoms*. Canada, *Statutes*, c. 44 (1960).

3. One of the most widely approved classifications of civil liberties in Canada is that set down by Bora Laskin in *Canadian Constitutional Law* 3rd ed., Toronto, The Carswell Co., 1966, p. 974. This classification includes:
   a) "the traditional political liberties, i.e. freedom of association, of assembly, of utterance and communication and of conscience and religion",
   b) "legal liberty, such as freedom from arbitrary arrest, or arbitrary search and seizure; protection from self-crimination and protection of fair and impartial adjudication",
   c) "economic civil liberty, involving a transfer to the economic sphere of the notion of individual rights developed in the political sphere",
   d) egalitarian civil liberties, "involving not state abstention but affirmative intervention to secure such things as equality of employment opportunity or of access to services or amenities without discrimination on account of religion or colour or origin".

4. See for example *Parliamentary Debates on the Confederation of the British North American Provinces*, Quebec, Hunter Rose and Co., Parliamentary Printers, 1865, pp. 1, 29, 31, 833 and 1027.

5. *Ibid.*, p. 44.

6. F. R. Scott *Civil Liberties and Canadian Federalism* Toronto, University of Toronto Press, 1959, p. 13.

their history, produced such declarations of rights and liberties as the Magna Carta of 1215, the Petition of Rights of 1629, and the Bill of Rights of 1689. This British heritage has admittedly been valuable in promoting a spirit of liberty in Canada, but it has not been, and cannot be, sufficient to deter recurrent violations of civil liberties.

Although the British North America Act merely assumes the existence of human rights and fundamental freedoms, it does contain a few clauses which can be interpreted in a broad manner as basic guarantees to civil liberties. Section 20 of the Act declares that there must be an annual session of Parliament; separate school provisions in section 93 restrict absolute provincial power over education; section 99 secures the autonomy of the justices of the Provincial Superior Courts through a stipulation for tenure during good behaviour; and section 133 ensures the use of the English and French languages in the federal and Quebec legislatures, in Quebec courts, and in courts established by the Federal Parliament.

The absence of precise constitutional allocation of legislative jurisdiction over civil liberties to either the federal or provincial governments has given rise to much legal controversy in Canada. The debate has centred on the question of whether the constitutional authority of the Provinces over "Property and Civil Rights in the Province"[7] gives the Provinces any jurisdiction in the civil liberties field. In the United States, the term "civil rights" is popularly understood to be an acceptable alternative to the expression "civil liberties". This American usage is inappropriate in Canada, however, since the courts have not yet clearly delineated the extent to which provincial jurisdiction over "property and civil rights" extends to the whole area of human rights and fundamental freedoms. The justices of the Canadian Supreme Court in their decisions on civil liberties questions, and leading constitutional authorities in their writings, have disagreed on this difficult constitutional issue.[8] Clearly, all federal or provincial legislation affecting civil liberties must be drafted with painstaking regard to this jurisdictional dispute.

II

MOVEMENT TOWARD A BILL OF RIGHTS

The first formal resolution proposing the enactment of a Canadian bill of rights was presented to the House of Commons on October 10, 1945 by Mr. Alistair Stewart, a member of the Co-operative Commonwealth Federation (C.C.F.).[9] Nevertheless, concern for the preservation of civil liberties had been expressed much earlier. During the period between Confederation and the First World War, religious and racial conflicts within the federation gave the crucial questions of minority and cultural rights priority over the political, legal, economic and egalitarian liberties. After 1914, however, the Conservative Government was subjected to harsh criticism for its encroachments on individual liberties under the War Measures Act[10] and for the restrictive legislation enacted in the wake of the

Winnipeg Strike in 1919. This legislation ruled that non-Canadians could be deported,[11] and any members of associations could be imprisoned,[12] if convicted of advocating forcible overthrow of the government.

James Shaver Woodsworth, one of those arrested during the Winnipeg Strike, won election to Parliament in 1921 and served as the leading Parliamentary champion of civil liberties until his death in 1942. As leader of the C.C.F., Mr. Woodsworth presented his party's program, popularly known as the Regina Manifesto, to the House of Commons on February 5, 1934. Section 12 of this program read as follows:

Freedom of speech and assembly for all; repeal of Section 98 of the criminal code; amendment of the Immigration Act to prevent the present inhuman policy of deportation; equal treatment before the law of all residents of Canada irrespective of race, nationality or religious beliefs.

This statement reflected the demands that Mr. Woodsworth had been pressing for more than a decade before the founding of the C.C.F. The members of this party (now the New Democratic Party) have been continually more zealous than those of other Canadian political parties in keeping the civil liberties issue before Parliament and the people.

Mr. Woodsworth was especially critical of the Liberal Government's refusal to disallow Quebec's Padlock Act. This statute, formally entitled An Act Respecting Communistic Propaganda,[13] received the unanimous vote of the Quebec Legislative Assembly on March 24, 1937. The Act declared illegal the preaching of communism or bolshevism in buildings or houses of Quebec and outlawed the distribution of literature which propagated these views in any area of the Province. The Attorney-General had the authority to close and "padlock" for one year any building suspected of being employed for such a purpose. All this government activity could take place without the trial and conviction of the accused in the regular courts. In a commentary on the Padlock Act, a committee of the Canadian Bar Association stated:

It gives the Attorney-General great powers which he can exercise in the first instance without the slightest judicial restraint, and takes away all of the safeguards which even an ordinary criminal enjoys before conviction. . . . possibly it is under laws such as this that in other lands the homes of respectable and law abiding citizens are ransacked simply because their owners do not wear a brown or a black shirt.[14]

---

7. Sec. 92(13).
8. See Walter S. Tarnapolsky, *The Canadian Bill of Rights* Toronto, The Carswell Co., 1966, pp. 9-12 and D. A. Schmeiser, *Civil Liberties in Canada* London, Oxford University Press, 1964, pp. 13-16.
9. *Debates (Commons),* 1st Sess. 20th Parl. (1945), 900.
10. Canada, *Revised Statutes,* c. 288 (1952).
11. *An Act to Amend the Immigration Act.* Canada. *Statutes* c. 25 (1919).
12. *An Act to Amend the Criminal Code.* Canada, *Statutes,* c. 46 (1919).
13. Quebec, *Revised Statutes,* c. 52 (1941).
14. *Annual Proceedings of the Canadian Bar Association,* XX (1937), p. 258.

The Act was employed extensively against persons and associations suspected of participation in communistic activity. The grave danger to civil liberties lay in the omission of a definition of "communism" or "bolshevism" and in the Quebec government's loose application of these terms, and of the Act itself, to political enemies.

The federal government's reluctance to disallow the Padlock Act was not understandable to Mr. Woodworth and his associates in view of the disallowance several months later of three Alberta statutes enacted by the Social Credit Government. Three other proposed statutes were reserved by Alberta's Lieutenant-Governor for consideration by the federal government. One of these bills, An Act to Ensure the Publication of Accurate News and Information, proposed to force newspapers to print corrections of news stories critical of the government and to reveal the sources of their information. Upon reference to the Supreme Court, all three bills were declared *ultra vires* the provincial government as an integral part of a whole range of Social Credit legislation encroaching upon federal powers.[15]

Notwithstanding Mr. Woodworth's contribution in bringing such civil liberties transgressions to the attention of Parliament, John Diefenbaker has been the man most closely associated with achieving the Canadian Bill of Rights. In fact, the subject of Mr. Diefenbaker's maiden address to the House of Commons was the preservation of civil liberties. On this occasion, Mr. Diefenbaker admitted the necessity for the abrogation of certain freedoms in time of war, but he denounced the Liberal Government for the excessive arbitrary prosecutions which occurred under the War Measures Act.[16]

Under this Act, authority was delegated to the Governor-in-Council to issue "such orders and regulations as he may by reason of the existence of real or apprehended war, invasion or insurrection deem necessary or advisable for the security, defence, peace, order and welfare of Canada". This delegation of emergency powers from Parliament to the Executive enabled the Canadian Cabinet to exercise almost unrestrained power over all aspects of the economy and of society associated in any significant way with the defence of the realm. During the war, the Canadian Criminal Code was supplemented by the Defence of Canada Regulations made by order-in-council under the authority of the Act.[17] Canadian citizens as well as enemy aliens were subjected to the strict execution of these Regulations. Such associations and societies as the Jehovah's Witnesses and the Communist Party were declared illegal; newspapers and other publications were censored or suppressed; formidable barriers to free speech were erected in the form of heavy penalties for any unfavourable statement, report or opinion likely to prejudice the defence of Canada or the efficient prosecution of the war; the right to trial by jury was curtailed; trials were held in secret; and the writ of *habeas corpus* was suspended. Professor A.R.M. Lower has written that "a Liberal Government, which had always stood for the utmost freedom to the individual and for the maintenance of all his traditional civil rights, was the government that cut into freedom and abrogated civil rights to a degree not equalled in any other English-speaking nation".[18] It is noteworthy that, despite Mr. Diefenbaker's criticism of the Defence of Canada Regulations, the great majority of the Conservative members called for more stringent enforcement of the Regulations.[19]

Under the National Emergency Transitional Powers Act,[20] the use of certain emergency powers and the delegation of these powers to the Governor-in-Council continued into the postwar period to meet "emergency conditions in the period of reconstruction".[21] Most of the Defence of Canada Regulations restrictive of individual liberties were revoked in August and September, 1945, but more than forty regulations concerning such subjects as enemy aliens and the custody of Japanese persons were retained.

Canadians who had witnessed government's wartime invasions of civil liberties found further cause for alarm in its postwar policy toward the Japanese. In 1942, under intense pressure from most of British Columbia's federal and provincial politicians and from such interest groups as labour unions and veterans' organizations, the federal government evacuated more than twenty-one thousand Japanese from that Province to other parts of Canada. Confused as to what choices were actually available to them,[22] 10,295 Japanese subsequently signed requests for repatriation to Japan. Then, on December 17, 1945, the federal government presented to the House of Commons three orders-in-council[23] affecting the Japanese. One of these orders authorized the deportation to Japan of over ten thousand Japanese, more than half of whom were Canadian-born or naturalized citizens. The rest were Japanese nationals.[24] Many of those who had requested repatriation now wished to remain in Canada but were to be deported unless they had revoked their signed request before September 1, 1945 – "the day before the unconditional surrender of the armed forces of Japan".[25] Thus, Canadian citizens of Japanese descent were to be

15. *Reference Re Alberta Statutes*, S.C.R. 100 (1938).

16. *Debates (Commons)*, 1st Sess. 19th Parl. (1940), p. 748.

17. See Ewell E. Murphy Jr., "The War Power of the Dominion", *Canadian Bar Review*, XXX October, 1952, pp. 791-806 and H. McD. Clokie, "Emergency Powers and Civil Liberties", *Canadian Journal of Economics and Political Science*, XIII August, 1947, pp. 384-94.

18. A. R. M. Lower, *Colony to Nation*, Toronto, Longmans, Green and Co., 1957, c. 1959, pp. 532-33.

19. Mr. Diefenbaker was assisted in his criticism of the Regulations by the Conservative member A. H. Bence; four of the C.C.F. members – M. J. Coldwell, T. C. Douglas, Angus MacInnes, and J. W. Noseworthy; and the Unity member Dorise Nielsen.

20. Canada, *Statutes*, c. 25 (1945).

21. *Debates (Commons)*, 1st Sess. 20th Parl. (1945), p. 2448.

22. See F. E. La Violette, *The Canadian Japanese and World War II* Toronto, University of Toronto Press, 1948, pp. 238-245.

23. P. C. 7355, 7356, and 7357.

24. La Violette, *op. cit.*, p. 272.

25. Order-in-council P.C. 7355.

deported despite the fact that Prime Minister Mackenzie King himself admitted that:

. . . no person of the Japanese race born in Canada has ever been charged with any act of sabotage or disloyalty during the years of the war.[26]

In the face of outraged public and Parliamentary opposition to the deportation, the Liberal Government asked the Supreme Court for an advisory opinion as to whether the three orders-in-council were within the constitutional jurisdiction of the federal government.[27] The Supreme Court ruled that the federal government had authority under the *War Measures Act* to pass such orders-in-council. On appeal, this decision was sustained by the Judicial Committee of the Privy Council.[28] Eugene Forsey commented later that:

. . . in effect, the Judicial Committee held that so long as the orders-in-council purported to be based upon the existence of an emergency, of "real" or "apprehended" war, that (sic) they could provide for the exile of any Canadian citizen at any time to any place, without trial and with or without proof of the commission or alleged commission of any offence.[29]

The Liberal Government, legally vindicated by the judicial decision, but politically wounded by its deportation policy, reversed its previous decision so that only those Japanese who still wished to return to Japan actually left Canada.[30] With a few notable exceptions among Canada's federal politicians, the record of the Liberal and Conservative parties on the Japanese question was deplorable. Again, the C.C.F. members demonstrated their customary concern for civil liberties by defending the rights of the Japanese.

While the debate raged over the government's treatment of the Japanese, the Canadian public learned, on February 15, 1946, of another governmental encroachment on civil liberties. On September 6, 1945, Igor Gouzenko, a cipher clerk at the Soviet Embassy, turned over to the Royal Canadian Mounted Police a number of documents taken from the Embassy, which revealed a widespread espionage network in Canada. Consequently, by order-in-council,[31] the Acting Prime Minister or Minister of Justice received powers of interrogation and detention to prevent any person "from communicating secret and confidential information to an agent of a Foreign Power or otherwise acting in any manner prejudicial to the public safety or of the safety of the State". Then, by a second order-in-council,[32] Supreme Court Justices Taschereau and Kellock were appointed members of a Royal Commission to hear evidence and to prepare a report on the state of Soviet espionage in Canada. Twenty-six persons, whose identities were revealed through the Embassy documents, were arrested. They were held incommunicado but without being formally charged with any offense, and without access to families or legal counsel. Following interrogation by the Royal Commissioners, charges were laid against thirteen of the persons detained. In the Interim Reports and the Final Report[33] released by the Commission, evidence of the guilt of certain persons charged with espionage was published before they were brought to trial. When the untoward methods of the inquiry were revealed to the public, the Liberal Government was severely castigated by Canadian civil libertarians. The Civil Liberties Committee of the Canadian Bar Association questioned whether the "safety of the State" was sufficient justification for the "radical departures from the normal and long established procedure" in the espionage cases.[34]

The religious sect, the Witnesses of Jehovah, also had good cause to be concerned with the preservation of civil liberties. Under the Defense of Canada Regulations, the federal government has banned the Jehovah's Witnesses for three years during the war. Then, in the postwar years, the Witnesses experienced mob violence and arbitrary arrests in the Province of Quebec. The Witnesses' efforts to win religious converts in the Province had included door-to-door visits and the distribution of literature in which the Roman Catholic Church in particular was strongly denounced. The provincial government took strict measures to curb the proselytism of the Witnesses. Many of these restrictions seriously compromised the religious liberty to which the Witnesses were entitled.

It is evident that in this immediate postwar period there was in Canada an urgent need for improved legislative safeguards to civil liberties. A central event in the progress toward this end was the adoption by the General Assembly of the United Nations on December 10, 1948 of the Universal Declaration of Human Rights. Signators to the United Nations Charter in 1945 had pledged to support the Charter's reaffirmation of "faith in fundamental human rights, in the dignity and worth of the human person, in the equal rights of men and women and of nations large and small".[35] One of the foremost purposes of the United Nations was to achieve international co-operation "in promoting and encouraging respect for human rights and fundamental freedoms for all without distinction as to race, sex, language or religion".[36]

During the next decade Mr. Diefenbaker and a number of C.C.F. members kept the theme of civil liberties alive. The Liberal Government

26. *Debates (Commons)*, 5th Sess. 19th Parl. (1944), 5915.
27. *In the Matter of a Reference as to the Validity of Orders in Council . . . in Relation to Persons of the Japanese Race*, S.C.R. 248 (1946).
28. *Co-operative Committee on Japanese-Canadians v. Attorney-General for Canada*, A.C. 87 (1947).
29. *Proceedings of the Special Senate Committee on Human Rights and Fundamental Freedoms*, (1950), p. 85.
30. 3,964 Japanese returned to Japan. La Violette, *op. cit.*, p. 273.
31. P.C. 6444 of October 6, 1945.
32. P.C. 411 of February 5, 1946.
33. *Report of the Royal Commission to investigate . . . the communication, by public officials and other persons in positions of trust of secret and confidential information to agents of a foreign power*. Ottawa. June 27, 1946.
34. *Annual Proceedings of the Canadian Bar Association*, XXIX (1946), p. 143.
35. Preamble to the *Charter of the United Nations*.
36. Chap. 1, art. 1(3) of the *Charter*.

maintained its now characteristic inactivity in the face of Opposition demands for a Canadian bill of rights. Government spokesmen insisted that few of the vociferous advocates of such legislation comprehended the constitutional complexity of the issue. In a prolonged debate in February 1955 on Mr. Diefenbaker's periodic resolution for a bill of rights, Minister of Justice Stuart Garson contended that there was not a single right or freedom contained in the articles of the resolution that was "not amply protected by the existing laws of Canada at the present time, if those laws are properly invoked and administered".[37]

III

THE SUPREME COURT AND CIVIL LIBERTIES

The Justice Minister's statement was partly substantiated by the performance of the Supreme Court in the 1950's. In a series of celebrated civil liberties decisions, the Court interpreted the British North America Act and existing Canadian statutes in a manner designed to provide firm judicial protection of Canadian civil liberties. At the beginning of the decade, Canada's renowned libertarian justice, Ivan C. Rand, anticipated in the following statement the momentous civil liberties decisions to come:

. . . in the present upheaval, what must be increasingly affirmed is that the courts, in the ascertainment of truth and the applicability of laws, are the special guardians of the freedom of unpopular causes, of minority groups and interests, of the individual against the mass, of the weak against the powerful, of the unique, of the non-conformist . . . our liberties are largely the accomplishments of such men.[38]

Most of the civil liberties cases which came before the Supreme Court during the 1950's grew out of those alleged violations of political and legal liberties which occurred in the Province of Quebec. Five decisions between 1951 and 1959 involved relations between the Jehovah's Witnesses and the Province of Quebec. The Supreme Court cleared a Witness from a sedition charge for distributing an issue of the sect's official magazine *Awake!*, which denounced in abusive language the persecution of Jehovah's Witnesses by Quebec authorities.[39] The right of a Witness to distribute religious tracts in the streets of Quebec City was upheld by the Court.[40] Damages were awarded against police officers who broke up a peaceful meeting of Witnesses in a private home[41] and against a single police officer who arrested a female Witness for the distribution of religious literature, imprisoned her for two days without making a formal charge, denied her counsel, and then offered her freedom in exchange for a release from all liability for her detention.[42] Finally, the Court ordered the Premier and Attorney-General of Quebec, Maurice Duplessis, to pay damages for the arbitrary cancellation of the liquor licence of a restaurant owned by a

Witness who had acted on close to 400 occasions as bailsman for his religious cohorts.[43]

In the case of *Birks v. City of Montreal*,[44] the Supreme Court found *ultra vires* a Quebec statute which empowered municipalities to require storekeepers to close their shops on Roman Catholic holy days. Then, in the case of *Switzman v. Elbling*,[45] Quebec's Padlock Act was declared to be beyond the jurisdiction of the provincial government because its subject matter came under the federal control of criminal law.

The Supreme Court obviously served as the chief guarantor of civil liberties during the decade preceding the enactment of the Bill of Rights. The judicial philosophy of the Court was evolving toward vigorous protection of Canadian freedoms. Professor Edward McWhinney has referred to the Court's contribution as "a Bill of Rights to be implied by the Supreme Court from the general terms of the Canadian Constitution and the basic premises . . . of political life in Canada".[46]

IV

THE FINAL STEPS

Many of the proponents of a Canadian bill of rights were delighted in June, 1957 by the elevation of Mr. Diefenbaker, chief Parliamentary spokesman and leader of the Conservative Party, to the position of Prime Minister.

Several choices as to the form of a bill of rights were open to the new government: (1) a constitutional amendment guaranteeing protection of civil liberties in those areas within federal jurisdiction; (2) a bill of rights enacted by the federal government which would override any provincial legislation which threatened to violate its terms; (3) a constitutional amendment restricting the powers of both the federal and provincial governments to legislate in violation of civil liberties; (4) complementary federal and provincial legislation covering the whole field of rights and freedoms; and (5) an ordinary statute of Parliament applicable only to

37. *Debates (Commons)*, 2nd Sess. 22nd Parl. (1955), 909.

38. "The Role of an Independent Judiciary in Preserving Freedom", *University of Toronto Law Journal*, IX (1951), p. 13.

39. *Boucher v. The King*, S.C.R. 255 (1951).

40. *Saumur v. City of Quebec*, 2 S.C.R. 299 (1953).

41. *Chaput v. Romain*, S.C.R. 834 (1955).

42. *Lamb* v. *Benoit*, S.C.R. 321 (1959).

43. *Roncarelli v. Duplessis*, S.C.R. 121 (1959).

44. S.C.R. 799 (1955).

45. S.C.R. 285 (1957).

46. "Mr. Justice Rand's 'Rights of the Canadian Citizen' – the 'Padlock' Case". *Wayne Law Review*, IV, 1957-1958, p. 120.

federal legislation. The Opposition parties concentrated their criticism of Mr. Diefenbaker's draft bill of rights – Bill C-79 – on the fact that the Government chose the fifth and, to them, the least attractive, alternative.

Mr. Diefenbaker's persistent campaign for adequate legislative protection of Canadian civil liberties was finally rewarded in August, 1960. By this time, Mr. Diefenbaker was enjoying widespread public support for his efforts. Nevertheless, the Parliamentary Opposition, interest groups, and legal scholars continued to advocate that the bill of rights take the form of a constitutional amendment ensuring protection to civil liberties within both federal and provincial legislative jurisdictions. Despite these indications that renewed efforts by the government might well have resulted in a more efficacious bill of rights than that encompassed by Bill C-79, the Prime Minister would permit no further delay. The Bill of Rights received the unanimous vote of the House of Commons on August 4 and passed the Senate the very next day without a recorded vote. No Member of Parliament wanted to go on record as an opponent of the Canadian Bill of Rights. This bill, under the formal title of An Act for the Recognition and Protection of Human Rights and Fundamental Freedoms, became law with the granting of loyal assent by the Governor-General on August 10, 1960.

The first section of part I of the Act declares that a number of human rights and fundamental freedoms "have existed and shall continue to exist" in Canada "without discrimination by reason of race, national origin, colour, religion or sex".[47] Section 2 states that Canadian laws, unless otherwise specified, "shall be construed and applied" in such a way that the rights and freedoms set down in section 1 are not violated and that seven specific legal liberties listed in section 2 are preserved.[48] Section 3 instructs the Minister of Justice to ensure that all subsequent bills and regulations are consistent with the Bill of Rights. Section 4 provides that part I is to be known officially as the Canadian Bill of Rights.

Part II, section 5 of the Act provides that any freedom existing in Canada but not recorded in the Bill of Rights is not abrogated thereby and that the Act is applicable only to federal legislation. Section 6 proclaims that when the Cabinet declares, under the War Measures Act, that "war, invasion, or insurrection, real or apprehended, exists" the declaration be submitted to Parliament. Nevertheless, any government action, order, or regulation authorized by the War Measures Act is not to be considered an encroachment upon the rights and freedoms embraced by the Bill Rights.

A consequence of the government's adoption of the Bill of Rights as an ordinary statute of the Federal Parliament is that Canadian citizens can invoke the provisions of the Bill only when the application of a federal law or regulation is involved. The Bill cannot be applied to provincial statutes or municipal by-laws.[49] Yet the evidence suggests that violations of Canadian civil liberties are more likely, particularly in peace-time, to issue from provincial or municipal governments than from the federal government. Indeed, the Bill of Rights does not furnish protection of civil liberties where it is most urgently required.

V

APPLICATION AND EVALUATION OF THE BILL OF RIGHTS

The courts' utilization of the Canadian Bill of Rights in the brief period since its enactment has been generally disappointing to the Bill's proponents. Moreover, if the limited effectiveness of the Bill has not been gratifying to its critics, it has at least fulfilled their pessimistic predictions. For most of the decade since 1960 the performance of Canadian courts suggested that effective protection to civil liberties was unlikely to emerge from judicial interpretation of the Bill of Rights in its existing form.

47. Part I, Section 1 reads:
    1. It is hereby recognized and declared that in Canada there have existed and shall continue to exist without discrimination by reason of race, national origin, colour, religion or sex, the following human rights and fundamental freedoms, namely,
       (a) the right of the individual to life, liberty, security of the person and enjoyment of property, and the right not to be deprived thereof except by due process of law;
       (b) the right of the individual to equality before the law and the protection of the law;
       (c) freedom of religion;
       (d) freedom of speech;
       (e) freedom of assembly and association; and
       (f) freedom of the press.

48. No law of Canada shall be construed or applied so as to
    (a) authorize or effect the arbitrary detention, imprisonment or exile of any person;
    (b) impose or authorize the imposition of cruel and unusual treatment or punishment;
    (c) deprive a person who has been arrested or detained
        (i) of the right to be informed promptly of the reason for his arrest or detention,
        (ii) of the right to retain and instruct counsel without delay, or
        (iii) of the remedy by way of *habeas corpus* for the determination of the validity of his detention and for his release if the detention is not lawful;
    (d) authorize a court, tribunal, commission, board or other authority to compel a person to give evidence if he is denied counsel, protection against self crimination or other constitutional safeguards;
    (e) deprive a person of the right to a fair hearing in accordance with the principles of fundamental justice for the determination of his rights and obligations;
    (f) deprive a person charged with a criminal offence of the right to be presumed innocent until proved guilty according to law in a fair and public hearing by an independent and impartial tribunal, or of the right to reasonable bail without just cause; or
    (g) deprive a person of the right to the assistance of an interpreter in any proceedings in which he is involved or in which he is a party or a witness, before a court, commission, board or other tribunal, if he does not understand or speak the language in which such proceedings are conducted.

49. A Toronto lawyer commented facetiously that "the Diefenbaker Bill of Rights provided protection to all Canadians just so long as they don't live in any of the Provinces." Reported in Peter C. Newman, *Renegade in Power: The Diefenbaker Years*, Toronto, McClelland and Stewart Limited, 1963, p. 230.

Civil Liberties and a Constitutional Bill of Rights 79

Indeed, in a 1968 government white paper, Justice Minister Pierre Elliott Trudeau, now Prime Minister, expressed the prevailing view of Canadian legal scholars that the Bill

... has in practice had a limited application because the Courts have held that it does not expressly over-ride any provisions inconsistent with it which may be contained in earlier federal statutes. While conceivably the 1960 Bill could have been interpreted so as to alter previously enacted statutes, the courts have not done this. There have been some conflicting opinions in various lower courts, but there has on the whole been a strong judicial tendency to assume that Parliament did not intend by the Bill of Rights to alter specific, pre-existing, inconsistent statutory provisions. The Courts have said instead that Parliament would have made an express amendment had it intended to alter its own previously enacted laws.[50]

During the ten years before the passing of the Bill of Rights the Supreme Court had, through case law, begun to develop a "judicial" bill of rights for Canadian citizens. Since the retirement of Justice Ivan C. Rand in 1959 and the enactment of the Bill of Rights in 1960, however, the Court's decisions concerning civil liberties, and particularly those relating to the Bill of Rights, have tended to be more restrictive of individual and collective freedoms.[51]

Then, in November 1969, a Supreme Court decision[52] pointed the way to a possible revolutionary change in the interpretation and application of the Bill of Rights. By a 6 to 3 vote, the Court ruled that section 94(b) of the Indian Act, providing penalties for an Indian unlawfully intoxicated off a reserve, is inoperative because it denies "equality before the law" guaranteed by section 1(b) of the Bill of Rights. The Court also held that section 2 of the Bill means

... that if a law of Canada cannot be "sensibly construed and applied" so that it does not abrogate, abridge or infringe one of the rights and freedoms recognized and declared by the Bill, then such law if inoperative "unless it is expressly declared by an Act of the Parliament of Canada that it shall operate notwithstanding the Canadian Bill of Rights."[53]

If Canadian courts now rule that Parliament did intend "by the Bill of Rights to alter specific, pre-existing, inconsistent statutory provisions", there may be a significant shift of authority in the civil liberties sphere from Parliament to the judiciary. Moreover, one of the primary arguments for constitutional entrenchment of the Bill of Rights will be lost. Since the Bill applies only to federal legislation, however, statutory or constitutional restrictions on the provincial legislatures may still be desirable.

Despite the failure of the Bill to realize the lofty expectations and confident assurances of the Diefenbaker Government that it would provide solid legal protection to Canadian freedoms, the Bill has been immensely valuable to Canadian society. The widespread publicity surrounding the debate over the desirability and the feasibility of a bill of rights has made Canadians sensitive to possible infringements of civil liberties. The Bill has substantive merit as an educational instrument – a means of informing

Canadians of rights and freedoms that should exist and of making each individual more careful not to be deprived of them. Unfortunately, the performance of Canadian courts since 1960 suggests that effective protection of these rights and freedoms is unlikely to emerge from judicial interpretation of the Bill of Rights in its existing form.

To remedy this problem, the Liberal Government proposed in February 1968 that the federal and provincial governments co-operate in the entrenchment of political, legal, egalitarian, linguistic, and, eventually, economic rights in the British North America Act.[54] The addition of linguistic rights to the Laskin classification outlined above is in accord with the *Report of the Royal Commission in Bilingualism and Biculturalism* recommending constitutional recognition of English and French as the two official languages of Canada.[55] The Government suggested that the issue of protecting economic rights be postponed because "it might take considerable time to reach agreement on the rights to be guaranteed and the feasibility of implementation".[56] At a federal-provincial conference on the Constitution held later in February, five provincial premiers endorsed the proposed charter of human rights and five premiers took the matter into consideration. The conference marked the beginning of continuing discussions on constitutional questions – including the possible incorporation of a charter of human rights in the British North America Act.

While public interest in recent years has centred primarily on civil liberties activity at the federal level, the provincial legislatures have furnished statutory protection in those areas in which they enjoy constitutional competence. Virtually all the Canadian provinces have enacted legislation against discriminatory practices in employment and accommodation. The Saskatchewan Bill of Rights Act, passed as early as 1947, is still in effect. Since 1960 the Provinces of Alberta, Nova Scotia and Ontario have consolidated their various anti-discrimination statutes into human rights acts. And in March 1968, the Ontario Government released the first three volumes of a comprehensive report of the *Royal Commission of Inquiry into Civil Rights.*

50. *A Canadian Charter of Human Rights*, Ottawa, Queen's Printer, 1968, pp. 13-14. See also Schmeiser, p. 52 and Mark R. MacGuigan, "The Development of Civil Liberties in Canada", *Queen's Quarterly*, LXXII, Summer, 1965, p. 273.

51. See *Oil, Chemical and Atomic Worker's International Union v. Imperial Oil Ltd.*, S.C.R. 584 (1963); *Robertson and Rosetanni v. The Queen*, S.C.R. 651 (1963); and *Saumur v. A.-G. of Quebec*, S.C.R. 252 (1964). Two other more libertarian decisions, carried by a five to four majority of the Court, are *Brodie v. The Queen*, S.C.R. 681 (1962) and *McKay v. The Queen*, S.C.R. 798 (1965). For an excellent summary of judicial interpretation of the Bill of Rights, including an analysis of the decisions of the Supreme Court, see "The Effect of the Canadian Bill of Rights on Canadian Law" in Tarnopolsky, *op. cit.*, pp. 90-111.

52. The Queen v. Joseph Drybones. (Unrecorded at time of pub.)

53. Ibid.

54. *A Canadian Charter of Human Rights*, Ottawa, Queen's Printer, 1968.

55. Book I — *The Official Languages*, Ottawa, Queen's Printer, 1967.

56. *A Canadian Charter of Human Rights*, p. 27.

This nation-wide concern for the preservation of human rights and fundamental freedoms indicates that federal-provincial accord on a bill of rights enshrined in the British North America Act may soon be achieved. Nevertheless, it is crucial that the optimism founded upon recent accomplishments in the legislative defense of civil liberties does not become complacency, for there are many areas of Canadian society where freedoms are still in jeopardy. There are still such critical problems as the rights of Canadian Indians, the arbitrary and secret decision-making processes of administrative boards, the frequent charges of police brutality, the peremptory censorship of films by provincial authorities, and the invasion of privacy by wiretapping and eavesdropping.

It is clear that legislative or even constitutional guarantees alone are not adequate to ensure the defense of civil liberties. The ultimate efficacy of all civil liberties legislation, including a charter of human rights, lies in the extent to which such statutory directives conform to strong national sentiments. Canadians can be proud of the existing status of civil liberties in their country. But the sporadic infractions of Canadian freedoms that have occurred, and the many areas where positive legal protection is still needed, point to the necessity for continued vigilance.

6

A Democratic Approach
to Civil Liberties*

PETER H. RUSSELL

In our society the phrase "civil liberties" is apt to conjure up the image of
the great popular majority, the demos, crushing the sacred rights of the
individual or the small minority. For, traditionally "The Tyranny of the
Majority" has been the great peril which has inspired our active civil libertarians to seek safeguards for the fundamental rights and freedoms of the
individual. For this tradition of civil liberty the most attractive panacea
has been the instrument of a bill of rights – a fundamental code of basic
rights enforced by a group of wise and independent judges against the
illiberal demands of legislative majorities and their executives. In Canada
it has been the common mission of a whole generation of civil libertarians
to press for a bill of rights which would effectively guarantee that neither
national nor provincial majorities could ride roughshod over minority
rights.[1] Now with Pierre Elliott Trudeau, a staunch champion of a constitutional bill of rights, in power in Ottawa, this movement is closer than
ever before to realizing its prime objective.

Those of us who are concerned about the quality of liberty in our civil
society should step back for a moment and take a good long look at the
approach to civil liberty which the bill of rights proposal represents. How
realistic is it as a diagnosis of the main threat to our liberty? How plausible
is its prescription for our emancipation? Do you feel menaced by the prospect of the great Canadian majority, acting through its elected representatives in Ottawa, steam-rolling over your basic rights and liberties in pursuit
of its own interests? Are you comforted by the possibility that soon the
Canadian Bill of Rights may be "entrenched" in the Constitution enabling

---

*Reprinted with permission of *The University of Toronto Law Journal*

1. See, for example, F. R. Scott, *Civil Liberties and Canadian Federalism*, Toronto,
University of Toronto Press, 1959; D. A. Schmeiser, *Civil Liberties in Canada*,
London, Oxford University Press, 1964; Bora Laskin, 'The Supreme Court and Civil
Liberties' 1955, 41 *Queen's Quarterly*, at 455; F. W. Bowker, 'Basic Rights and
Freedoms: What are They?' 1959, 37 *Can. Bar Rev.*, at 43; Mark R. MacGuigan,
'Civil Liberties in Canada' 1965, 72 *Queen's Quarterly*, at 270.

our judiciary to veto these strident majoritarian demands and secure your liberty? If you ask yourself these questions and can honestly answer them in the affirmative, what you surely need is a psychiatrist, not a bill of rights.

When we confront the realities of democratic life in the modern state, we recognize at once the fantasy quality of the paradigm of majority tyranny and minority rights. In no significant way does the majority conduct the government of a large modern democracy. Certainly governments in democracies govern in the name of the people, or of the majority; also in a vague sort of way the exigencies of periodic elections, legislative debates, public discussion, and pressure-group activity make it incumbent on our democratic governments to be sensitive to a larger range of claims and interests than they might otherwise consider. But the majority of citizens themselves do not, and indeed cannot, deliberately rise up and seize the power formally granted to them by democratic constitutions to realize their ends at the expense of severe deprivations of the minority's freedom. It has been a central preoccupation of western political science for more than half a century to explain that this is so. One suspects that even civil libertarians of the classical mould have heard that message, in at least one of their ears, and yet they continue to fulminate about the need to check the will of the majority by a judicially enforced code of basic rights.

Of course, there may very well be reasons other than the dangers of majority tyranny for supporting the bill of rights idea, and we shall look at some of these later in this essay. But at this point what we are principally concerned with is the tendency in the classical civil libertarian tradition to deflect our attention from the issue which has the most fundamental bearing on our civil liberty – that is, the quality of our democracy. In Canada, as in the United States, nearly all of the books and articles formally devoted to discussions of "civil liberties" are written by lawyers, whose data about "civil liberty" are derived almost exclusively from court cases in which judges have been concerned with balancing the claims of the state (national or local) against the claims of private persons. The common thrust of this literature is the advocacy of laws and judicial decisions which treat the latter claims more generously than the former. What we miss in the literature is any real consideration for the quality of public life beyond the fragmentary episodes which turn up in the law reports. What this means in terms of conceptualizing the problem of civil liberty is that no consideration is given to the extent to which the claims of the state represent the interests of the people; no real concern is given to the possibilities which our society permits outside the court room for its members to influence the powers by which they are governed.

But this surely should be the central issue. In the history of political ideas it was the guiding instinct of democratic theory to seek a design for power which by virtue of popular participation would make government less coercive. From the Renaissance until the emergence of "mature liberal democracies" in relatively modern times, this was the path along which the main core of western political thought sought to provide for a maximum of liberty in an ordered society. But in our century and in our society it has very nearly become an abandoned path. This is because we have lost the thread of democratic theory as our guide to the enlargement of our civil liberty. For the most part we have become either disillusioned or complacent about the democratic character of our system of government. We no longer are armed with a theory of democracy which we can use as a critical device for liberalizing the exercise of public authority.

THE DECLINE OF DEMOCRATIC THEORY

It is useful to reflect briefly on the major stages through which democratic ideas have evolved in western culture. The point of this exercise is to understand the intellectual grounds for the current mood of acquiescence or despair with democracy. We will then examine those grounds critically, in the hope that this will yield a revitalized approach to democracy which can serve as a theoretical basis for expanding our civil liberty.

In our own western history the original impulse of democratic thought was a protest against an aristocratic society which denied large sections of the public any formal right to participate in politics. The essential demand was for a transfer of political power vertically downwards, from the landed aristocracy at least to the middle ranks of society if not to the masses. The classical democratic theorists of the seventeenth, eighteenth, and early nineteenth centuries provided various justifications for this transfer of power. It might be justified in terms of the individual's "natural right" to consent to the force by which he is governed (John Locke), or in the hope that by submitting to the General Will of all, the individual would enjoy a new and more perfect kind of freedom (Jean-Jacques Rousseau), or as the most direct way of ensuring that government pursues the greatest happiness of the greatest number (Jeremy Bentham). But all of these democratic philosophies were cast in the classic mould of social criticism and political prophecy: the political order they described was the aristocratic undemocratic system which they condemned. The democratic order they proclaimed was known only by its ideal possibilities, not by its operational reality.

By the mid-nineteenth century the context of democratic theory was being radically altered. The democratic theorist was now being confronted with the existence of "democracy" in America and, to an increasing degree, in Britain and continental Europe. Exposed to the reality of democracy, the immediate response of democratic theory was to acknowledge that the mere shift of political power to larger numbers of the population, from the higher to the lower orders, did not remove all the ethical dilemmas of power. The Madisonian concern for checks and balances in the American polity, Alexis de Tocqueville's poignant warning of the egalitarian excesses of democracy in America, and John Stuart Mill's analysis of majority tyranny in *On Liberty* all shared the conviction that the crucial problem of the new age was not how to make democracy possible but how to prevent it from going too far. The contemporary civil libertarian concern for the protection of the individual's rights against majority tyranny is the legacy of this particular strand of liberal-democratic thought.

But while liberal thinkers were uttering their warnings against mobocracy, a growing number of social scientists were responding in a quite different way to the experience of democracy. What struck many of those who

looked closely at the distribution of power in the new democratic structures was that despite the formal rules of democratic constitutions a small
number of people continued to hold the bulk of political power. Democratic procedures might alter the composition of the governing elite but
they could not overcome the force of what Robert Michels, one of the foremost writers of this tradition, called the Iron Law of Oligarchy: "The
majority is thus permanently incapable of self-government . . . The
majority of human beings, in a condition of eternal tutelage, are predes-
tined by tragic necessity to submit to the dominion of a small minority,
and must be content to constitute the pedestal of an oligarchy."[2] Contrary
to the liberals' fear of democratic excesses, the central message of this
body of thought was that the classical democratic ideal of popular rule
and political equality could never be realized in any large scale political
organization.

In the twentieth century democracy has become for most of the world
the legitimate form of government. Even regimes which seem to be authoritarian and non-democratic try to increase their appearance of legitimacy
by cloaking themselves with the rhetoric of democracy. But the ironical although natural side of this development is that while democracy has
become the principal form of orthodox government, the theory of democracy, especially in the West, has become a conservative force. As a theory
of government it functions mainly as a rationalization for the existing
social and political mechanisms; as an ideal it serves not as a guide to
reform but as a conscience, warning of the iniquities of radical political
action and social change.

Orthodox democratic thought in the Anglo-American world has fallen
heir to the elitist tradition. It accepts the "realistic" conclusion of Michels
that the masses cannot rule. The complexity and range of decisions made
by any large modern state, the apathy and ignorance of great numbers of
the electorate, the control of major communications media by a few interests, and the unavoidable hierarchies of power concomitant with large
bureaucratic structures – all of these factors conspire to render impossible
the fulfillment of the democratic ideal of giving every citizen an equal
amount of power to influence governmental decisions. Despite constitutions which give one man one vote and formally bestow controlling authority on the people's representatives, some will inevitably have much more
power than others.

But the modern breed of democratic theorist, while accepting the Iron
Law of Oligarchy, has insisted on the distinctiveness of the elitist system
produced by democratic rules and institutions. The essence of that distinctiveness is that the democratic elite is a pluralist elite; the chief purpose of
democratic institutions is to ensure that a number of would-be rulers participate in popularity contests to determine who in fact will rule. Joseph
Schumpeter has provided the governing definition of this conception of the
democratic process: "The democratic method is that institutional arrangement for arriving at political decisions in which individuals acquire the
power to decide by means of a competitive struggle for the people's vote."[3]
According to this image, democracy's unique value is not the realization of

the classical ideals of self-government, political freedom, or political equality, but the avoidance of a system which guarantees a monopoly of power to a single group. In the words of Robert Dahl, one of the most influential contemporary exponents of this view of democracy:

Elections and political competition do not make for government by majorities in any significant way, but they vastly increase the size, number, and variety of minorities whose preferences must be taken into account by leaders in making policy choices. I am inclined to think that it is in this characteristic of elections – not minority rule but minorities rule – that we must look for some of the essential differences between dictatorships and democracies.[4]

The "minorities rule" approach to democracy finds a positive philosophic base in the more sophisticated, twentieth-century version of the liberal "majority tyranny" phobia – the "mass society" anxiety. The cassandras of mass society and totalitarian democracy have made a virtue out of the necessity revealed by the elitist tradition. According to their prophecy the great forces of industrialization, urbanization, and materialism, by destroying the roots of meaningful community and group life, threaten, to an ever-increasing extent, to melt individuals into an unarticulated social mass. It is in the context of this "mass society" that the modern totalitarian dictatorship has arisen and staged its "popular" revolutions in the name of the people. The warning is clear: radical social change engineered by "popular" governments on behalf of an undifferentiated "people" is not democratic at all, but on the contrary involves the authoritarian imposition of an all-embracing pattern of life on society and the eradication of the individual's freedom.

Thus we have arrived at the present state of democratic thought in our culture. "Democracy," we are now told, is here and it is good. It isn't all that the classical philosophers dreamed it might be, but then they were naive: they knew far more about the system they rejected than the one they called into being. But we are wiser. We know that in terms of their ideals we can never have more than a "little bit of democracy." Political power in our system is a little less unequally distributed, governmental decisions are a little more responsive to public opinion, the composition of the governing elite changes a little more rapidly – what more can reasonable men expect? And above all, the whole complicated institutional net of elections, legislatures, bureaucracies, courts, and communication media in which the decision-making process is enmeshed prevents any one party, group, or mass from going off half-cocked without negotiating its demands

2. Robert Michels, *Political Parties* (Translated by Eden and Cedar Paul), New York, Dover Publications, 1959, p. 390.

3. Joseph A. Schumpeter, *Capitalism, Socialism and Democracy*, 3rd ed., New York, Harper & Row, 1950, p. 269.

4. Robert A. Dahl, *A Preface to Democratic Theory*, Chicago, The University of Chicago Press, 1956, p. 132.

with the claims of other interests. To quote the apostles of this realistic democratic creed:

In point of fact the development of democratic constitutionalism has largely consisted in extending or inventing institutions before which conflicting interests could be made to confront one another under conditions leading to successful negotiation and orderly regulation.[5]

or,

A central guiding thread of American constitutional development has been the evolution of a political system in which all the active and legitimate groups in the population can make themselves heard at some crucial stage in the process of decision.[6]

The trouble with this conception of democracy is that it provides a barren model, a sterile ideal. Its exponents take this model of democracy seriously only because they can entertain the possibility of a completely monolithic society with a decision-making system devoid of any bargaining or negotiating process among different interests. Presumably, existing communist systems qualify in their view as the prototypes of "minority" rule states and "unplural" societies. But the arrogance involved in assuming this contrast is blatant. An uneven distribution of economic wealth and educational opportunity can reduce the bargaining opportunities of social groups in the political process just as surely as can a prohibition against opposition political parties. Whether the one produces more severe inequalities of political influence than the other is a nice unanswered question. And it is a question for which neither the pluralist ideal itself nor the notion of "minorities rule" can provide an answer. Even a society as small and monolithic as a family is in some sense "pluralist", and even masters must "bargain" with their slaves.

TOWARDS A PROGRAM OF DEMOCRATIZATION

If we apply the conventional notions of democracy shared by most western political scientists to our institutions of government, we end up simply rationalizing the status quo by means of an ideal which in hard empirical terms is virtually devoid of prescriptive or descriptive force. Instead, we should return to the original inspiration of democratic philosophy to find effective ways of enlarging the citizen's liberty or preventing its diminution. Such a course means seriously examining the possibility of overcoming or at least reducing the barriers to fulfilling the underlying aspiration of democracy – the ideal of diminishing coercion and expanding freedom by making government responsive to the interests of the governed.

To explore thoroughly the various avenues towards a more thorough democratization of our public life would be an enormous task, far exceeding the scope of this paper. Much of the idealism of the "New Left" is already directed along this path. The principal point which I wish to urge here is that this orientation rather than the conventional advocacy of judicial checks on popular power is the correct approach to civil liberty. The fundamental libertarian problem is not too much democracy but too little democracy.

Still it is worth while suggesting some of the more promising means for increasing the democratic character of our system of public authority. Within the context of our large modern governments, there are two factors of crucial importance to our democratic possibilities – the scale and the scope of governmental activity.

The scale of government is likely to have a decisive influence on the degree to which government policy coincides with the preferences of the governed. Where individuals have different preferences concerning policy issues, the larger the group to be governed the more likely it is that some dissenting portion of the group will be subject to a governmental decision contrary to its members' interests.[7] Or, to put the same point another way, smaller units of government have a better chance of coinciding with groups of people that are more nearly homogeneous in their policy preferences. This, of course, is the essential justification for federal systems of government, and for the decentralization of authoritative decision-making generally.

But there are obvious limitations on the extent to which decentralization can be used as a vehicle of democratization. In a society which is increasingly subject to technological and economic integration it becomes ever more unrealistic to isolate the governmental decisions of one unit from those of its neighbours. Larger units of government are clearly required to deal with what the political economists call the externalities – the interrelated interests – of the smaller units. Nor would it be feasible to design units of government which could exactly match the distribution of opinion on each and every public issue. There is a very low limit to the number of levels of government by which a community can be governed. Inevitably, any level of government will have to carry out a cluster of activities not all of which are conducted on the optimum scale.

Still, while acknowledging these limitations, it is essential that the libertarian have a bias for small-scale government and a suspicion of centralization. For a federal country such as Canada this bias would demand a careful explanation of the reasons for subjecting any social problem to a uniform solution by the central government. In this country the articulation of the provincial rights position is already effective enough. It needs little encouragement. Currently, a more vital concern is the political impotence of our cities. For most of our citizens, the public policies that have the most direct bearing on the quality of their lives are carried out at the municipal level. But the citizen often finds that he has less opportunity to

5. George A. Sabine, "The Two Democratic Traditions", 1952, 61 *Philosophical Rev.* p. 470.

6. Robert A. Dahl, *supra* note 4, p. 137.

7. For an exposition of the logic of this proposition see Roland Pennock, "Federal and Unitary Government – Disharmony and Frustration", 1959, 4 *Behavioural Sciences*, pp. 147-57.

participate effectively in influencing policy here than at the higher levels of political organization. This is partly because city governments have little autonomy. In Ontario, for instance, final determination of questions concerning city planning – questions which will have a crucial effect on the kind of neighbourhood in which people live – is not in the hands of the citizens at all, but is controlled by the Ontario Municipal Board, an appointed provincial authority. And, where decision-making authority does exist at the municipal level there is a lack of political organizations capable of aggregating interests and focussing the citizen's attention on the major policy alternatives. That is why the recent movement of political parties into the arena of municipal politics could have far greater benefits for civil liberty than would a bill of rights.

Turning to the question of the scope of government activities – the range of social activities subjected to government control and regulation – we confront the central preoccupation of the traditional dialogue between "left" and "right" in western politics. We cannot presume to offer here a categorical answer to the question of whether more or less governmental activity is required to enhance our liberty. As anyone who has even a nodding acquaintance with this issue will appreciate, an individual's or group's freedom may be increased or diminished by government intervention in social life. It all depends on the persons and activity involved, whether enforcement of values by public authorities positively or negatively affects the capacity for self-development.[8] As to taking a broad general stand on the issue, it is difficult, given the paucity of hard empirical knowledge about the distribution of power and opportunity in our society, to be other than agnostic.

However, if as liberals we are genuinely committed to maximizing the individual's capacity for self-development, we should recognize that in our day and age it is as essential to be critical of unnecessary exercises of governmental coercion, as it is to attack avoidable sources of private coercion. Indeed one of the liberal's key areas of concern should be precisely those forms of government intervention in the broad fields of social welfare and education, where the objective is to provide individuals with vital economic or cultural opportunities which they would not otherwise enjoy. All too often the regulatory side of governmental activity in these fields has been extended far beyond the point required to redress the mal-distribution of opportunity in society. Old-age assistance programs, designed to assist the few who cannot save for their old age themselves, unnecessarily dictate how all shall invest a significant portion of their wealth for their retirement years. Public departments of education, in the process of enabling the economically underprivileged to obtain a good education, effectively block other groups from developing educational experiments outside the public sector.

No doubt there are those who will brand this expression of concern for dismantling unnecessary extensions of public authority, coupled with a strong bias for reducing the scale of government, as simply a manifestation of old-fashioned laissez-faire liberalism. But surely the true conservatives these days are those who continue to believe in the simple equation of radicalism with state intervention. Today in both the communist world and the western democracies, the most distinctive currents of radical thought share a common interest in decentralization, and a greater reliance on voluntary social activity. One finds, for example, a very close affinity between those communist theorists who are seeking ways of creating market relationships in various sectors of their economies and economic liberals in the West such as Milton Friedman who summon their contemporaries to re-examine the reasons for supplanting voluntary contractual relationships with mandatory governmental regulation in a wide range of social and economic activities.[9]

As important as the scope and scale of government activity are to the citizen's liberty they can never be ideally adapted to maximize the freedom of all members of the community. There will always be a good deal of public authority which is directed towards ends upon which not all can agree. Thus the question of improving and expanding the democratic qualities of the decision-making processes of government must remain of vital concern to the civil libertarian.

Here the central interest must be the unequal distribution of power and influence in the liberal-democracies of the West, including our own. It was the genius of the elitist tradition to teach us that the constitutional rule of "one man, one vote" does not guarantee that each person will be equally capable of influencing his government's decisions. Now it should become the goal of the committed democrat to overcome the grossest sources of social and economic inequality in order to give some real content to the constitutional guarantee of political equality. Even in terms of merely voting in elections, the evidence suggests that the distinction between voter and non-voter corresponds with basic social differences. As E. E. Schattschneider pointed out in his classic analysis of the limits of organized politics in the United States, "Every study of the subject supports the conclusion that non-voting is a characteristic of the poorest, least well-established, least educated stratum of the community."[10] Or again, as Rober Dahl wrote in acknowledging the prime social barriers to the effective realization of political equality, "By their propensity for political passivity the poor and uneducated disfranchise themselves."[11]

8. Perhaps the most thorough and thoughtful contemporary analysis of the factors affecting the individual's capacity for freedom is presented by Christian Bay in *The Structure of Freedom*, New York, Atheneum, 1965. It should be noted that Bay concludes "It is still largely a matter of conjecture and sweeping interpretation just how different types of stable social institutions affect the individual's capacity for self-development", p. 232.

9. Compare for instance the reform program put forward by Friedman, in *Capitalism and Freedom*, Chicago, University of Chicago Press, 1962, with recent Yugoslav efforts towards economic decentralization. For information on the latter, see George W. Hoffman and Fred W. Neal, *Yugoslavia and the New Communism*, New York, Twentieth Century Fund, 1962, especially ch. 14.

10. E. E. Schattschneider, *The Semisovereign People*, New York, Holt, Rinehart and Winston, 1960, p. 105.

11. Robert A. Dahl, *supra* note 4, p. 81.

The focal point of any program aimed at raising the political efficacy of the socially disenfranchised must be the educational system. This is so not simply in the obvious sense that the extension of educational opportunities is an essential step in removing the most severe social and economic disabilities of the disenfranchised; in a more fundamental way, the content of education must direct people towards the effective exercise of their political rights. Universally accessible public education up to any level will do little to improve the democratic quality of our system if that education is conducted in an authoritarian way.

What is required as a bare minimum in this area is the removal of any barriers to voluntary political activity by students themselves. Canadian civil liberties buffs, who have fretted so much about the absence of a constitutional bill of rights forbidding our legislators to circumscribe our political freedom, would have been much more constructively occupied resisting the local school authorities who have out-lawed the organization of political parties and clubs in the secondary schools of many Canadian communities. I doubt whether the freedom of many Canadians has been seriously jeopardized by lack of an effective bill of rights, but the latter practice has done much to condition generations of Canadian school children to view organized politics as a semi-illicit activity, rather like sex or liquor, best left to a coterie of irredeemable adults. Rather than pinning gilt-edged copies of Mr. Diefenbaker's Bill of Rights to the classroom wall assuring the student that all his rights and freedoms are secure, we should endeavour to teach the student, or at least give him some respect for, the rudimentary arts of political organization and agitation without which the practical exercise of his rights is likely to be illusory.

For if the individual is to have some opportunity to have his preferences and interests taken into account by the decision-making system, it is essential that he acquire some of the primary skills and interests of political activity. To quote Schattschneider again: "The struggle is no longer about the *right to vote* but about the organization of politics. Nowadays the fight for democracy takes the form of a struggle over theories of organization, over the right to organize and the rights of political organizations, i.e., about the kinds of things that make the vote valuable."[12] Our educational system, in both its formal and informal channels, instead of fostering taboos about political activity, should encourage the cultivation of political skills, including an understanding of the major media of communication. It is the nurturing of a positive capacity for self-expression and critical judgment which is likely to serve as the best defence against restrictions on communicative freedoms – whether those restrictions stem from public or private control.

We should recognize that the object of this broad educational endeavour to promote active political participation extends beyond the utilitarian ideal of ensuring that government policy coincides as closely as possible with the preferences of the majority. That is certainly part of the democratic ideal. But if it were all, then we might achieve utilitarian democracy through the magic of some giant computer capable of accurately aggregating our preferences and identifying policies designed to maximize our individual satisfactions. But the fuller democratic vision has also regarded a positive improvement in the quality of life as part of the justification for the equalization of political power and responsibility. We can hardly improve on John Stuart Mill's formulation of this conviction when he wrote:

A person who is excluded from all participation in political business is not a citizen. He has not the feelings of a citizen. To take an active interest in politics is, in modern times, the first thing which elevates the mind to large interests and contemplations; the first step out of the narrow bounds of individual and family selfishness, the first opening in the contracted round of daily occupations.[13]

To be concerned about the citizen's liberty is first and foremost to be concerned about his capacity for active citizenship. It is this which should be the primary occupation of those Canadians who wish to enhance our civil liberties.

On a completely different front there is another proposal which I think should be considered as a way of increasing the responsiveness of government to the interests of the governed. This proposal, I am sure, would not have gained the support of John Stuart Mill or, I suspect, that of most Canadian liberals. But the very hostility such a proposal engenders is evidence, I think, of the deep elitist instincts of so much of the liberal intelligentsia. For what I wish to advocate is a much larger and more systematic use of public opinion polls.

The need for information about public attitudes to policy issues is greatest in the inter-election period. In large modern "democracies" an ever-increasing range of important policy decisions is decided between elections in situations which are somewhat insulated from the pressures of electoral politics. There are those who welcome this development, but they are not democrats and should reject the entire thesis of this article. But for the democrat the insulation of government decision-making from the broad range of public opinion is a serious problem.

The classical solution to the inter-election problem was the practice of representative government: it was the function of the elected representatives to sensitize government to public opinion. More recent political science has included the activity of organized pressure groups and lobbies as an essential component in the process of exposing government to the demands and interests of the governed. But neither the elected legislature nor the network of organized interests is able to provide a fair indication of the range of opinion on many policy issues. Parliamentary parties and members of parliament are often notoriously out of touch with large segments of the community; all too often they are overly sensitive to the interest of some special group in the community. Pressure groups tend to be highly elitist within their own structures; anyone who has belonged to

12. E. E. Schattschneider, *supra* note 10, p. 102.

13. John Stuart Mill, "Thoughts on Parliamentary Reform," in *Dissertations and Discussions*, London, J. W. Parker & Son, 1867, p. 17.

a trade union or a professional organization should realize how frequently there is little correspondence between the views of the organization's officials and those of its rank and file members. And then there are a host of interests and preferences which, for a variety of reasons, never become well enough organized to enter into the so-called "bargaining" process of modern pluralistic government at all.

In advocating frequent and systematic consultation of public opinion polls by government, I am not calling for a system of government by plebiscite. I am not suggesting that government automatically adjust its policy to follow the results of the latest gallup poll. The use of opinion polls which I favour is as a counter-weight to the unbalanced character of the influences to which government is subject through parliamentary and pressure-group activity. Well-conducted polling is the only way to give public representation to that body of opinion which, because of the maldistribution of political efficacy in our society, does not gain access to the established channels of political communication.

It is true that the government, with future elections in mind, will, on occasion, look past the organized interests and attempt to gauge the general state of public opinion on an issue. But in the absence of reasonably reliable information about public attitudes, these exercises in "testing the public's pulse", especially when conducted by civil servants, are likely to be highly misinformed and may result in decisions that are not at all in keeping with the public's general view of its interests.

The difficulties involved in establishing polling techniques which can provide meaningful and accurate accounts of the distribution and intensity of preferences are unquestionably enormous. Also, the most careful consideration must be given to finding means whereby private interests or government itself can be prevented from controlling the polls and their outcomes. But these problems are surely not insurmountable. Indeed, in terms of political technology, the evolution of such institutions is a fitting challenge for our age. Several centuries ago the question of establishing judicial tribunals for the impartial adjudication of private disputes was a central challenge to the political technology of England. That challenge was successfully met and today we enjoy the advantages of a system which enables us to submit our quarrels with our neighbour to the generally careful and disinterested arbitration of our courts. In terms of political technology the development of an independent judiciary is a magnificent achievement. But for most of us today this achievement is rarely relevant to our most important rights and interests. These, today, are much more likely to be directly dependent on positive decisions of government than on the outcome of litigation in the courts. Thus it is now as appropriate to concern ourselves with the integrity and accuracy of institutions designed to measure public preferences for alternative government policies, as it once was to be concerned with securing fair and independent courts of law.

I have only touched here on two of the directions in which we should strive to increase the real quotient of democracy in our system of government. There may be many other more practical and fruitful proposals which can be made. But, in the context of our general discussion of civil liberties, the essential point to emphasize is that our future libertarian prospects depend fundamentally on realizing a much higher degree of democracy in our system of government, rather that establishing procedures for preventing government from abrogating the norms of a democracy which is presumed to exist already.

THE LIMITED VALUE OF A BILL OF RIGHTS

But it would be utopian to expect the most militant commitment to democracy to achieve anything approaching the complete democratization of government. There will always be a significant range of governmental outputs felt by some to be highly coercive. It is to the mitigation or overcoming of these coercive acts of government that the classical notion of a bill of rights has been applicable.

Even in this area of concern it is questionable whether the bill of rights is a useful technique. Indeed, it might turn out to have extremely illiberal consequences. Certainly it deflects attention from the areas of governmental activity and the remedial devices which are most vitally related to civil liberty.

The underlying philosophy of the bill of rights advocate is the notion that there are certain fundamental norms – especially the various freedoms of expression, freedom from ethnic, racial, or religious discrimination, and certain procedural practices in law enforcement and the administration of justice – which should never be abrogated by positive acts of government. While these fundamental social values are regarded as inherent in the mainstream of our political culture, it is feared that the elected legislature will in a moment of haste or absence of mind enact laws or authorize governmental procedures which are inconsistent with these norms. Many of those who agitated for a bill of rights in Canada argued that the comparatively heterogeneous ethnic composition of the Canadian population meant that there was a much greater danger of popular governments violating these rights and freedom in Canada than there was, for instance, in Great Britain.[14] Thus a bill of rights was required to codify these fundamental values and empower the courts to overrule any act of government which transgressed them.

Any assessment of the bill of rights idea must begin by recognizing that a really effective bill of rights would entail a transfer of power from the legislative branch of government to the judiciary. This implication raises the fundamental question of whether such a transfer of power is politically possible. There is no question that such a transfer can be formally made. If, instead of being cast in the form of an ordinary act of parliament as the

14. This, for instance, was one of the major arguments advanced by Dr. Eugene Forsey in advocating the incorporation of a bill of rights in the Canadian constitution. See his testimony to the Canadian Senate's Special Committee on Human Rights and Fundamental Freedoms, 1950, pp. 79-80 of its *Proceedings*.

present Canadian Bill of Rights is, it were to be incorporated in the written constitution, then theoretically the courts could veto legislation which was deemed to contravene the provisions of the bill of rights, and such a veto could only be overridden by the difficult process of constitutional amendment. However, it seems to me highly unlikely that in terms of real political power a legislative majority strongly committed to a policy would succumb before a judicial veto. Certainly American experience, which Canadian supporters of a constitutional bill of rights are so eager to emulate, indicates that judicial enforcement of a bill of rights is, in the long run, ineffectual against a national legislative majority bent on gaining its ends. As Robert Dahl has shown in reviewing Congressional responses to Supreme Court vetoes in the United States, "There is . . . no case on record where a persistent law-making majority has not, sooner or later, achieved its purposes."[15]

But it is unlikely that the grand strategy of the bill of rights device is politically feasible, a more modest version of it may be practicable. Indeed, it is the more modest version which the most thoughtful Canadian advocates of a constitutional bill of rights have usually had in mind. For instance, in 1955 M. J. Coldwell, then the national leader of the C.C.F., explained the purpose of writing a bill of rights into the B.N.A. Act in these terms: "Written into our constitution the rights and freedoms would ensure the people of Canada that temporary legislative majorities . . . would be prohibited from, or at least, if not prohibited would find more difficult the setting aside of . . . our fundamental rights."[16] It might well be possible for the courts, temporarily, to make it difficult for the legislature to enact laws which infringe the judiciary's version of the rights and freedoms enshrined in a bill of rights. But this raises the more important half of my doubts about an effective bill of rights – is it desirable to grant the judiciary even this modest accretion of power?

To answer this question intelligently it is essential to recognize the kind of decision-making which is involved here. The process of applying the general ideals inscribed in a bill of rights involves a delicate balancing of social priorities. As anyone who has given this question a little thought must acknowledge, "fundamental rights and freedoms" cannot be treated as ethical absolutes. Those who subscribe in a general way to these values will invariably insist that in practice they must be circumscribed: exponents of freedom of speech will make an exception of laws against slander and libel or obscenity; advocates of religious freedom will endorse the prohibition of the "religious experience" associated with LSD; opponents of racial discrimination will support laws restricting the distribution of liquor to Indians; adherents of fair trial procedures do not usually insist that all administrative agencies affecting the rights of the citizen follow all the "fair hearing" requirements of normal courtroom procedure; and so on. Reasonable, liberal persons will certainly disagree on which exceptions to allow, but the question raised here is who should resolve these issues – the courts or the legislature?

A simple majority-rule democrat might conclude that the answer is obvious – the legislature which represents the majority must settle these issues as it should settle all others, for otherwise we would have a system of minority rule. As it stands, this is not a very convincing answer, even for the democrat. For it assumes that the majority's views are expressed through the decisions of the elected legislature – a most dubious assumption in the light of hard-headed political science which has shown us how unlikely it is that the host of decisions made by elected officials in the modern democratic state will always reflect the views of a majority of its citizens. Besides, some of the rights and freedoms asserted in bills of rights, especially the communicative freedoms, refer to social practices which are essential if a genuine majority will is to be articulated in the political process.

But the majority-rule democrat is on the right track. For a society that aspires to be democratic should formally resolve the most important questions of public policy through its elected legislature. And the delicate balancing of social priorities involved in adopting the fundamental concepts of political freedom and civil rights to the other goals of public policy is certainly among the most important issues of government. Granted that the representative legislature may not always be truly representative, it is still the branch of government whose deliberations are most thoroughly exposed to public purview and whose decisions enter most immediately into political debate and discussion. The concrete determination of the degree to which the state should permit its citizens to enjoy the kinds of rights and freedoms listed in a bill of rights is among the most significant of a community's policy-making tasks. It is far too important an exercise in social ethics to be left to appointed judges in the cloistered sanctuaries of judicial tribunals.

Some, caught up in the mass-society phobia which has preyed on the minds of so many western intellectuals, may fear that the legislative majority in hot pursuit of its policy objectives will lack the requisite degree of sensitivity to the bill of rights values. I think this fear is unjustified. In our political culture today there is no more potent charge for an opposition party to make against the government than to accuse it of violating a fundamental right or freedom. Mr. Diefenbaker's political success in sponsoring the Canadian Bill of Rights, however inconsequential in practice that Bill may be, demonstrates how much popular political mileage can be made by appearing before the public as a staunch defender of fundamental rights and freedoms.

The complete and instant legislative defeat of the notorious Ontario "Police Act" in 1964 provides graphic evidence of the popular appeal of civil liberties. Here was a provincial government riding high with an overwhelming majority, when suddenly the press and the opposition parties jumped on a section of a bill introduced by the government to strengthen the powers of the Police Commission in investigating organized crime

15. Robert Dahl, *supra* note 4, pp. 110. For a more detailed presentation of the evidence supporting this contention see also his, "Decision-Making in a Democracy: The Supreme Court as a National Policy-Maker," 1958, 6 *J. Public L.*

16. *Canada, House of Commons Debates*, 1955, p. 916.

(normally a popular objective) as authorizing procedures which entailed severe deprivations of fundamental civil liberties. Within twenty-four hours of the bill's introduction in the legislature, the premier was assuring the house that he would "not tolerate any legislation which infringes upon or jeopardizes the basic, fundamental, personal rights and freedoms of the individuals of this province,"[17] the minister who introduced the bill had resigned, and the government had accepted an opposition amendment deleting the impugned section of the bill. Indeed this episode suggests that the public might sometimes be overly susceptible to allegations that government policy infringes their basic rights. Often, from a political point of view, it is extremely difficult to make the case for circumscribing the enjoyment of certain rights in order to pursue more important policy goals.

But, on the whole, not only is the popular branch of government as sensitive to the importance of basic rights and freedoms as are the courts, but it is also more likely to give careful attention to balancing the competing values involved in civil liberty issues. Here we must refer to the quality of the judiciary. All too often the bill of rights advocate's scepticism of the integrity of elected representatives blinds him to the short-comings of the judiciary. This is a particularly important point for Canadians to consider.

In Canada neither the history of judicial appointments nor the traditional style of jurisprudence practised by judges should give anyone grounds for feeling confident about the superior capacity of the judiciary for sensitively and intelligently settling vital questions of civil liberties. Canadian judges right down to the county court level are all selected by a small clique of federal politicians in one or other of the two major national parties.[18] These appointments have seldom gone to lawyers or jurists who in their earlier careers have manifested a lively interest in or association with the social issues surrounding civil liberties questions. The judicial selection system is itself an exercise in ethnic and political discrimination: at the Supreme Court level only Christians of Anglo-Saxon or French-Canadian backgrounds have been appointed, while most of the Supreme Court judges have had connections with either the Liberal or Conservative parties, none has ever been associated with the C.C.F.–N.D.P., the Social Credit, or any other minor political party.

With a few notable exceptions, such as Duff C.J. and Rand and Kellock JJ., the Supreme Court of Canada has followed an extremely conservative, legalistic brand of jurisprudence which leaves little scope for the exploration of the social dimensions of legal issues, including civil liberties issues.[19] Judicial interpretations of the substantive provisions of Mr. Diefenbaker's Bill of Rights do not demonstrate a deep interest on the part of Canadian judges in civil liberties matters. As Professor Bora Laskin (as he then was) concluded, after exposing the narrow unreflective framework within which the majority of the Supreme Court of Canada cast its first attempt to elucidate the substantive meaning of one of the freedoms listed in the Bill of Rights, "this self-imposed horizon of reference is not calculated to inspire much confidence in the depth analysis of the issues confronting the court."[20] If Bora Laskin were typical of the men appointed to Canada's highest judicial tribunals, then we might have some reason to assign our courts the major responsibility for balancing the competing claims of freedom and order. But he clearly is not, and, so long as that is so, those who care deeply about the manner in which questions of civil liberty are resolved would be most unwise to transfer a major share of policy-making in this area to our courts.

While, then, for a variety of reasons, I cannot support the basic purpose of a constitutional bill of rights, there may be other functions which such a bill might serve. One of these would be to confront the legislature in a systematic way with the implications of legislative and executive policies for fundamental rights and freedoms. Partial provision for this is already contained in section 3 of the existing Bill of Rights. This section requests the minister of justice to submit all draft bills and regulations to the clerk of the Privy Council to ascertain whether they contain any provisions inconsistent with the Bill of Rights and to report any inconsistencies to the House of Commons. While this section points in the right direction, as it stands it is virtually a dead letter for it entrusts the government itself with the responsibility of testing its own proposals against the Bill of Rights. So far, to the best of my knowledge, and surely to no one's surprise, the minister of justice has not reported that a government proposal is in violation of the Bill of Rights.[21] To put real teeth into such a provision, a standing committee of the House of Commons would have to be established to review the possible effects of legislative and executive initiatives on fundamental rights and freedoms.[22] The establishment of such a committee would provide Canadian citizens with a more reliable and accessible device for examining the libertarian aspects of public policy than would the opportunity to appeal to a judicial system, which not only might fail to take the libertarian's concerns seriously, but will charge him thousands of dollars and make him wait several years to find this out. And we should remember that in Canada, unlike the United States, there are as yet no large well-financed civil liberties associations able to finance the

17. Quoted in John Saywell (ed.), *Canadian Annual Review 1964*, Toronto, University of Toronto Press, 1965, p. 111.
18. For an analysis of the political and cultural background of Supreme Court judges, see Peter H. Russell, *Bilingualism and Biculturalism in the Supreme Court of Canada*, Ottawa, The Queen's Printer, 1969, ch. 3.
19. This aspect of our judicial system has been widely discussed in recent literature. See for example, Dean Horace E. Read, "The Judicial Process in Common Law Canada", 1959, 37 *Can. Bar Rev.*, p. 265, and Edward McWhinney, "Legal Theory and Philosophy of Law in Canada", in *Canadian Jurisprudence*, McWhinney, (ed.), Toronto, Carswell, 1958.
20. Bora Laskin, "Freedom of Religion and the Lord's Day Act – The Canadian Bill of Rights and the Sunday Bowling Case", 1963, 41 *Can. Bar Rev.*, p. 152. (Ed. note: Mr. Justice Bora Laskin was appointed to the Supreme Court, March, 1970.)
21. An examination of the Canadian Bill of Rights and its results does not record any instances: see G. Tarnopolsky, *The Canadian Bill of Rights*, Toronto Carswell, 1966.
22. An amendment to the Bill of Rights along these lines was put forward by Hubert Badanai, but was defeated by the government majority. *Canada, House of Commons Debates*, 3 August, 1960, at 7492-3.

litigation of the individual or group who wishes to challenge allegedly illiberal acts of government.

In the Canadian context, or in the context of any society within which local majorities possess attitudes to civil liberties deviating sharply from the prevailing attitudes of the national majority, an effective bill of rights might serve yet another purpose; it might enable the interests dominant in national decision-making to impose, through the judicial branch of government, their particular conception of civil liberties on deviant local legislative majorities. To some extent this appears to be one of the principal results both of recent Supreme Court decisions in the United States relating to racial discrimination, and also of a series of prominent Canadian Supreme Court rulings in the 1950s against the Quebec government's persecution of Jehovah's Witnesses. Certainly, throughout the long series of parliamentary debates and committee hearings which preceded the enactment of the Canadian Bill of Rights in 1960, the actual infringements of basic rights and liberties most frequently cited as evidence for the necessity of a Bill of Rights concerned the intolerant policies of provincial governments towards such minority groups as the Hutterites in Alberta, the Doukhobors in British Columbia, or the Jehovah's Witnesses in Quebec.[23]

Even if we were to assume that it is desirable to have the Provinces subjected to national supervision in those matters covered by a bill of rights, the judiciary might not be the best branch of federal government for formulating all the policies which such supervision entails. Canadians, for example, are apt to forget that (in contrast to the United States where the national Supreme Court's application of the Bill of Rights in part compensates for the states' paramount position in the field of criminal legislation) our constitution gives the federal legislature control over criminal law, and that we have national legislation in the form of a Criminal Code through which many of the procedural rights so highly valued by civil libertarians may be most effectively defined and enforced. But even so, on balance I am not attracted to a greater centralization of decision-making in this area. Where there are no significant external effects, and the local majority's view point is articulated through a reasonably democratic political process, I favour local determination of these issues. In both the American Supreme Court decisions on desegregation and the Canadian Supreme Court decisions pertaining to the Jehovah's Witnesses in Quebec, the second condition which I attach to my preference for local resolution of civil liberties issues was not fulfilled.

It might be argued that judicial enforcement of a national bill of rights, emphasizing those political rights most essential to the practice of democracy, is necessary for the democratization of politics in the constituent units of a federation. But this is doubtful. So far as Canada is concerned, the very large extent to which the "obstacles to democracy in Quebec"[24] have been overcome, has had very little, if anything, to do with the Supreme Court's rulings against the Duplessis government. And we should note that whatever effect they did have was not through the implementation of a formal bill of rights but through the application of provisions already contained in our constitutional system. Today the provincial political process, including Quebec's, is as democratic as are national politics. Consequently I am inclined to leave the resolution of civil liberties questions in provincial fields of authority to the provinces.

Finally, there are some who might contend that decisions concerning civil liberties within the Provinces have a vital impact on the general climate of opinion throughout the whole country, and in this sense have important "external effects". Those who subsibe to this position usually emphasize the broad "educational" impact of a bill of rights. Mr. Diefenbaker and his supporters put great stress on this aspect of the present Bill of Rights. They acknowledged that it could be overruled by a simple act of Parliament and that it would not apply to the Provinces at all, but still they urged that its mere existence and distribution would, to use Mr. Diefenbaker's unelegant phrase, "make Canadians more freedom-conscious". Those who have agitated for a stronger constitutional bill have contended that incorporation in the written constitution would increase its educational potentialities.

But I am not very impressed by the "educational" qualities attributed to formal codifications of fundamental rights and freedoms. Political communities which have them, such as the USSR or the USA, do not appear to me to have derived great educational benefits from them in terms of instructing their citizens in the real significance of civic liberty. If we wish to make our citizens "more freedom-conscious," I much prefer the more direct method advocated earlier in this article, than what is usually little more than a slick piece of governmental "public relations" which, if it works, may produce a population with a blind faith in the social reality of a few pious phrases.

INADEQUACY OF THE LAWYER'S APPROACH AND THE NEED FOR A NEW TECHNOLOGY

Whether the Canadian Bill of Rights continues in its present form or whether it is incorporated in our written constitution, will not make much difference at all to the rights and liberties of many Canadians. And that is precisely the most serious charge to be levelled against the Bill and its devotees: our preoccupation, or at least the preoccupation of our leading politicians with the Bill, has deflected attention from those forms of governmental activity which pose the most serious threat to the citizen's liberty as well as from the most efficient mechanisms for the defence of that liberty.

23. Four special committees of the Canadian parliament have been devoted to the consideration of 'Human Rights and Fundamental Freedom's: special joint committees of the two houses in 1947 and 1948, a special committee of the Senate in 1950, and a special committee of the House of Commons in 1960. All of them concentrated exclusively on the pro's and con's of a bill of rights.

24. This is the phrase used by Pierre Elliott Trudeau as the title of his article in 1958, 24 *CJEPS*, p. 297.

The bill of rights approach assumes that the legislative majority is the most serious threat to civil liberty and that traditional courts of law provide the most effective vehicle for overcoming the illiberal acts of the aggressive majority. This approach is wrong on both counts. It is the executive side of government, the ever-expanding bureaucratic labyrinth, public or semi-public, whose members make those day-to-day decisions which have a vital and immediate effect on what the citizen can or cannot do – it is this side of government, not the legislature, which is most likely to deprive the individual citizen of some fundamental right or encroach unfairly on his liberty. It is true that, according to the legal theory of parliamentary supremacy which our country is supposed to follow, everything this bureaucracy does must ultimately find some authorization in a formal legislative act. It might therefore seem sufficient protection for the citizen to be able to ask a court to determine whether the government official who allegedly mistreated him exceeded the powers given him by the legislature. Unquestionably the citizen has such a legal right which occasionally is effectively asserted in our system. But he might have to spend many years and risk thousands of dollars in legal costs in the process of exercising this right. Besides, our legislatures bestow on the executive vast areas of discretionary power which are beyond review by even the most aggressive of courts.

The legal profession's limited social vision has, I suspect, been the prime factor in blinding many of its members, including so many of those who would describe themselves as civil libertarians, to the inadequacy of traditional judicial techniques for correcting abuses of executive power. The lawyer's professional training in common law in Canada as in Great Britain, conditions him to view social relations through the little slivers of life that are revealed in law reports. He cheers the great liberal judicial decisions in which, after several years of expensive litigation, some distinguished judge in grandiloquent language recognizes the legitimacy of the little man's grievance. And he is likely to conclude that those "landmark" decisions effectively protect all citizens from arbitrary administrative acts. On this score it is difficult to decide who are most mistaken, the lawyers who "would like to see both federal and provincial parliaments permanently prevented from derogating from civil liberties" by "a genuine constitutional Bill of Rights"[25] or those who like Paul Martin (and many of his fellow Liberals) opposed the Diefenbaker Bill of Rights on the grounds that "every human right and fundamental freedom with which this particular measure is concerned is now protected by law in this country. There are now in existence legal remedies to protect these human rights in Canada."[26]

Such legalistic complacency is completely blind to how seldom in fact the traditional legal remedies are relevant or available to the individual who finds himself confronted by what he regards as an unfair or incompetent act by a government official or bureau. In such situations what the individual usually requires, most urgently, is a quick, impartial, and inexpensive investigation of his complaint. A less legalistic, more realistic perspective would surely acknowledge that is is of little avail to inform the individual caught in such a situation that for several hundred dollars he can consult a lawyer to find out whether it is worth going to court and that, in any case, his particular grievance is likely not a "legal" issue but deals with some question of administrative neglect or oversight beyond the court's ken.

It is the great merit of the ombudsmen movement to recognize the short-comings of existing legal devices for reviewing citizens' complaints of abusive administrative acts. Donald Rowat and Henry Llambias, two political scientists who have been in the forefront of the agitation to establish ombudsman-like institutions in Canada, surveyed those instances "of mal-administration, arbitrariness and out-right injustice which had been publicly reported within the past few years and which were not adequately handled by existing machinery," and reported that:

They reveal a bewildering variety of examples of bureaucratic bungling at all three levels of government – federal, provincial and local; they range from simple (but nonetheless serious) cases of red tape such as failure to answer an inquiry or make a decision, to heart-rending stories of some persons incarcerated for years in the cockroach-ridden mental wing of Montreal's Bordeaux jail.[27]

They found about sixty such cases which had occurred over a three-year period, and it should be emphasized that these were only reported cases. As they pointed out "there are countless others that are never brought to light and in which the aggrieved persons may suffer years of heart-breaking frustration."

The ombudsman-like institutions advocated for Canada are, unlike courts, not decision-making institutions – they are primarily investigatory agencies. Their principal function is to investigate the citizen's complaint of of maladministration and to initiate legal action or recommend administrative or legislative reform where remedial action seems to be required. In practice, Scandinavian experience suggests that only a small percentage of grievances, probably under ten per cent, would warrant any corrective action, after initial investigation. But this does not detract from the merits of the scheme, for fundamentally the ombudsman should be regarded as a technique for improving our system of public communication. Above all, he should help to plug that yawning gap in our communications system between the individual citizen affected by a particular governmental act and the elected representatives finally responsible for the acts of all public authorities. It would also do something to counteract the worst consequences of a system which enables the members of a privately run guild,

25. Mark R. MacGuigan, "Civil Liberties in Canada", 1965, 72 *Queen's Quarterly*, p. 277.

26. *Canada, House of Commons Debates*, 5 July, 1960, at 5728.

27. D. G. Rowat and Henry J. Lambias, "Canada-Proposed Schemes", in D. C. Rowat (ed.), *The Ombudsman*, London, George Allen & Unwin Ltd., 1965, p. 187.

the legal profession, to enjoy a monopoly in the distribution of legal knowledge.

Prime Minister Trudeau's bill of rights commitment, for the time being, will likely preclude serious consideration of the ombudsman at the federal level. Still, it is heartening to see that proposals for ombudsman-like institutions have been officially placed before most of the provincial governments and have been adopted by three.[28]

But the Ombudsman is only one example of the more direct ways of achieving many of the values which a bill of rights is designed to secure. To take another example, racial equality, if we learn anything from the American experience it is that a bill of rights like that of the USA does very little to alleviate racial discrimination in the private sector where, in a "free-enterprise" society, it is most serious. For this task an agency such as Ontario's Human Rights Commission which can take the initiative in enforcing egalitarian norms directly on private employers and landlords will be a much more useful instrument than a bill of rights.[29]

What we must recognize is that just as on the input side of collective decision-making our political technology must evolve novel methods for organizing and gauging public demand and interest, so also on the output side we require new institutional techniques for identifying and correcting abuses of public authority. In the future, government, no matter how sensitively and democratically we adjust its range and scale, will penetrate the lives of ordinary citizens so deeply that it would be folly to continue to rely on the thin and sticky trickle of formal court-room litigation as the prime defence of our rights. Today we should be no more inclined to accept the established judicial procedures as adequate for the purpose of mediating between the citizen and the state, than the leading English lawyers of several centuries ago were willing to acquiesce in a system which left the monarch's personal discretion as the final repository of justice between citizens.

In the past the articulate civil libertarians in our culture have too often been traditionalists. This is the price we have paid for leaving our civil liberties almost exclusively to the care of lawyers. And we have certainly paid a price. For the lawyer's perspective has distracted us from the concerns which are most immediately related to the rights and liberty we might enjoy in the modern state. From the lawyer's perspective, the struggle for civil liberty has been portrayed in terms of a sagacious judiciary, periodically prodded by some liberal counsel, restraining the overreaching program of the demos. In fact those who would attend to the citizen's liberty should first and foremost address themselves to the democratic qualities of the state's political process. The most direct means of establishing uncoercive government is to evolve a social and political system in which government decisions correspond as closely as possible to the wishes of the governed. This is the democratic approach to civil liberty. To follow it one must recognize that we do not possess as much democracy as we are capable of enjoying. Where government activity cannot be made thoroughly responsive to public demand, and there are many areas where of necessity this must be the case, the effective civil libertarian must look beyond the traditional legal remedies to new institutional forms that make it equally convenient for all to challenge arbitrary treatment by government. These are the directions in which we might most fruitfully focus our libertarian interests in the future.

28. For a survey of recent developments, see D. C. Rowat, 'Recent Developments in Ombudsmanship', 1967, *Can. Public Admin.*, p. 35.

29. Mr. Trudeau, in stating the case for including egalitarian rights in his proposed charter of human rights, acknowledges the importance of provincial and federal legislation aimed at enforcing such rights in the private sector. See his *A Canadian Charter of Human Rights*, Ottawa, The Queen's Printer, 1968, p. 25.

7

Canadian Charter of
Human Rights*

PIERRE ELLIOTT TRUDEAU

There are many different systems of classification used by writers to group
and describe the various human rights. There is perhaps no classification
system which is completely free of difficulties. The system employed here
is but one of many and is used for the sake of convenience only.

Existing human rights measures in Canada are limited in scope. The
Canadian Bill of Rights emphasizes political freedoms (speech, assembly,
religion) and legal rights (freedom from arbitrary deprivation of life,
liberty or property, and equality before the law). Other federal legislation
and most provincial legislation is confined to prohibitions against discrimination in employment, admission to trade union membership, or the provision of accommodation. Some do go further. The Saskatchewan Bill of
Rights, for example, embraces political and legal rights as well as a wider
range of egalitarian rights, and the old Freedom of Worship Act (enacted
during the pre-Confederation Union and still in effect in Ontario and
Quebec) gives some guarantee of freedom of religion.

It is now suggested that there be included in a constitutional bill those
rights which have been legislatively protected in Canada, and to add to
them those linguistic rights which are recommended by the Royal Commission on Bilingualism and Biculturalism in the first volume of the
Commission's report.

Rights which may be included in a bill of the sort under consideration
here fall into five broad categories: political, legal, egalitarian, linguistic,
and economic. They are discussed in that order below.

1. POLITICAL RIGHTS

This term is used in a broad sense to cover matters of belief, their expression and advocacy. The several political rights (here called "freedoms") are
enumerated; following each there is a short discussion of the major legal
considerations which attach thereto.

---

*Reprinted, with permission, from *A Canadian Charter of Human Rights*, Ottawa,
Queen's Printer, 1968.

(a) Freedom of Expression

These freedoms are presently protected legislatively in Section 1 of the Canadian Bill of Rights and in section 4 of the Saskatchewan Bill of Rights. The cases which have been decided to date indicate that these freedoms are largely subject to control by Parliament in the exercise of its criminal law power. There are, however, aspects of freedom of expression which may be subject to provincial limitation, as for example through the law of defamation, or through laws regulating advertising in provincial and municipal elections. For this reason adequate protection can only be offered in the form of a constitutional bill.

The means of definition of this freedom are of equal importance to its declaration. The question arises whether freedom of expression is best guaranteed in simple terms without qualification, or whether the limitations of this freedom ought to be specified. Opponents of an unconditional declaration fear that such wording might restrict the application of Criminal Code prohibitions against obscene or seditious publications, or provincial laws pertaining to defamation or film censorship. This is unlikely, however, for free speech as it developed in England was never equated with complete license. It has long been recognized, even before the Americans expressly guaranteed this right in their constitution, that free speech was subject to limitations for the protection of public order and morals. The United States courts have given the guarantees of the First Amendment very wide scope, but have upheld laws which prohibit speech inciting to unlawful acts, and laws which punish the publication of matter which is purely obscene with no significant redeeming social value. Defamation laws have also been allowed to operate.

In Canada, existing federal laws against sedition and obscenity have been construed so narrowly that it is unlikely they would be held to conflict with a guarantee of free speech. The obscenity provisions of the Criminal Code have been applied since the enactment of the Canadian Bill of Rights without any conflict being recognized.

It is also unlikely that existing provincial laws against defamation would be upset by a free speech guarantee. As long as such legislation is confined to protecting long-recognized private rights of reputation there would be no conflict with the concept of "free speech". Nor is it anticipated that infringements of provincial laws relating to the regulation of advertising, so long as these are clearly related to some legitimate business regulation, would result. (A provincial protection of a right to privacy, now contemplated in some provinces, should also be possible.)

The alternative to a broad, unqualified description of "freedom of speech" is an enumeration of specific exceptions. An example of this more detailed type of language is found in Article 10 of the European Convention on Human Rights:

Article 10

(1) Everyone has the right to freedom of expression. This right shall include fredom to hold opinions and to receive and impart information

*and ideas without interference by public authority and regardless of
frontiers. This Article shall not prevent States from requiring the
licensing of broadcasting, television or cinema enterprises.*

*(2) The exercise of these freedoms, since it carries with it duties and respon-
sibilities, may be subject to such formalities, conditions, restrictions or
penalties as are prescribed by law and are necessary in a democratic
society in the interests of national security, territorial integrity or public
safety, for the prevention of disorder or crime, for the protection of
health or morals, for the protection of the reputation of rights of others,
for preventing the disclosure of information received in confidence, or
for maintaining the authority and impartiality of the judiciary.*

A similar, detailed, approach has been taken in several constitutions patterned after the European Convention. By specifying the grounds for
permissible limitations upon the right, possible uncertainties have been
removed. The disadvantage of this technique, however, is its lack of flexibility and the difficulty of adapting the language to changed circumstances.
For this reason the simple form of description is recommended.

(b) Freedom of Conscience and Religion

There is some legislative protection now. The Canadian Bill of Rights,
section 1, recites, "freedom of religion". The Saskatchewan Bill of Rights,
section 3, declares the right to "freedom of conscience, opinion, and belief,
and freedom of religious association, teaching, practice and worship". The
Freedom of Worship Act (applicable in Ontario and Quebec) declares
the right to "the free exercise and enjoyment of religious profession and
worship". It is arguable, however, that a guarantee of "freedom of religion"
does not protect the freedom of the person who chooses to have no religion.
To protect such persons, consideration could be given to widening the
guarantee to protect, for example, "freedom of conscience".

Freedom with respect to the individual's internal belief or conscience
might well be considered absolute and not qualified in any way. It is the
external manifestation of the exercise or furtherance of beliefs which may
give rise to problems and the need for limitations in the interest of public
safety and order.

In these areas, for example, no one would dispute that federal laws
should be able to prevent acts in the exercise of religious beliefs which
would constitute obscenity, sedition, bigamy, or homicide. It is more debat-
able, however, what further powers Parliament should possess to permit it
to restrict other religiously-motivated acts. An example is the imposition
of Sunday closing of businesses on Christians and non-Christians alike.
The Supreme Court of Canada has said that The Lord's Day Act is not a
denial of freedom of religion but this is not to say that such limitations are
consistent with freedom of "conscience".

The extent of provincial jurisdiction over matters of religion is far
from clear, but it is evident from Sec. 93 of the B.N.A. Act that the
provincial legislatures have some competence and responsibility in respect
of the religious aspects of education.

Thus, constitutional action is required in order to protect all Canadians from legislative interference with their religious beliefs.

(c) Freedom of Assembly and Association

These freedoms are now legislatively protected by section 1 of the Canadian Bill of Rights and by section 5 of the Saskatchewan Bill of Rights. They are closely related to freedom of expression and many of the comments made with respect to legislative jurisdiction over freedom of expression are equally applicable here. As with freedom of expression, they are not usually considered to be absolute but rather are subject to limitations in the interest of public order. Present federal limitations of this nature are mainly found in the Criminal Code relating to unlawful assembly, riot, conspiracy, watching and besetting, and disturbing the peace. Provincial limitations exist in laws dealing with the incorporation or regulation of commercial, educational, charitable and other organizations otherwise within provincial control, in the use of roads and parks for public assemblies, and the like. All these limitations appear to be consistent with freedom of assembly and association so long as they are clearly related to the preservation of public safety and order.

2. LEGAL RIGHTS

These rights go to the very root of the concept of the liberty of the individual, so highly prized in Canada. They are dealt with now, to a certain extent, in sections 1 and 2 of the Canadian Bill of Rights and in section 6 of The Saskatchewan Bill of Rights. They are recognized as well by other statutory provisions and by rules of statutory interpretation developed by the courts. There is not, however, any constitutional protection of the rights.

These rights and their protection fall within both federal and provincial jurisdiction, depending on the context. Both federal and provincial legislation can deal with deprivations of liberty and property, and with judicial and administrative procedures affecting the citizen's interests. Any constitutional guarantee of security of life, liberty and property, or of fair legal procedures, will affect equally the federal and provincial governments.

The Canadian Bill of Rights lists most of the legal rights which need protection; with modification its provisions could form the basis for similar guarantees in a constitutional bill. Using it as a frame of reference, it is suggested that the rights enumerated below should be guaranteed:

(a) General Security of Life, Liberty and Property

The Canadian Bill of Rights declares

The right of the individual of life, liberty, security of the person and enjoyment of property, and the right not to be deprived thereof except by due process of law.

The phrases "due process of law" and "according to law" or "according to the law of the land" have their origin in Magna Carta. They have been employed in one form or another in England, the United States and many other countries. The words "due process of law" have been given a double interpretation in the United States. The first of these is a guarantee of procedural fairness. In this respect, similar words used in the Canadian Bill of Rights are intended to guarantee the specific requirements of fair procedure. The words "due process" have, in addition, been given a substantive interpretation in the United States' courts with the result that the words have been employed as a standard by which the propriety of all legislation is judged. At one time the words used in this latter sense resulted in the judicial invalidation of minimum wage legislation, laws against child labour, and hours-of-work statutes. They were also used as a basis for courts to review public utility rates set by legislatures or regulatory agencies in order to ensure that the rates were, in the view of the courts, adequately compensatory. While more recently the substantive effect given to "due process" has diminished considerably in the United States, the demonstrated potential of this phrase could create some uncertainty in Canada unless its meaning were clearly recited.

In examining American experience with "due process", it appears that the guarantee as applied to protection of "life" and personal "liberty" has been generally satisfactory, whereas substantive due process as applied to "liberty" of contract and to "property" has created the most controversy. It might therefore be possible to apply the due process guarantee only to "life", personal "liberty" and "security of the person". The specific guarantees of procedural fairness set out elsewhere in the bill would continue to apply to any interference with contracts or property. In this fashion the possibility of any substantive "due process" problems would be avoided.

In the alternative, if "due process" is to remain applicable to "liberty" of contract and to "property", there should be spelled out in some detail what is involved. The European Convention and some modern constitutions use this technique with respect to each of the guarantees of life, liberty and prosperity.

(b) Equal Protection of the Law

The Canadian Bill of Rights, section 1(b) declares "the right of the individual to equality before the law and the protection of the law".

It might be argued that this wording serves to overlap other provisions: "protection of the law" is already assured, for example, by the "due process" clause; "equality" would likely also be protected by a general prohibition against discrimination (such as appears in the Canadian Bill of Rights, and as is proposed for the constitutional bill of rights). There may, however, be rights implied in a general guarantee of equality before the law which are not otherwise specified. Because the basic concept is sound, it is desirable to retain some such guarantee.

The phrase "equality before the law" has at least once been construed narrowly in Canada. It was there taken to mean that if one person is treated the same as all others of his race, this is "equality" even if his race is treated differently from other races. The comparable provision in the Fourteenth Amendment to the U.S. Constitution guarantees "the equal protection of the laws". This has generally been construed in the American courts to prohibit legislative distinctions as between various classes of persons except those rationally related to some legitimate legislative object. If this is the result which is desired, there would likely be some advantage in using the American wording.

(c) Cruel Punishment, etc.

Section 2(b) of the Canadian Bill of Rights now provides that no law of Canada is to be deemed to "impose or authorize the imposition of cruel and unusual treatment or punishment". This provision is similar to one in the English Bill of Rights of 1689. A guarantee against such treatment or punishment is also found in the Eighth Amendment to the U.S. Constitution, where it has caused few difficulties. While a court would likely be extremely reluctant to substitute its opinion of a proper punishment for that of the legislature, the power to do so could prove useful in extreme cases.

(d) Rights of an Arrested Person

Section 2(c) of the Canadian Bill of Rights states that no law of Canada shall be deemed to

. . . deprive a person who has been arrested or detained
  (i) of the right to be informed promptly of the reason for his arrest or detention,
 (ii) of the right to retain and instruct counsel without delay, or
(iii) of the remedy by way of *habeas corpus* for the determination of the validity of his detention and for his release if the detention is not lawful. . .

It is recommended that the same rights be protected in a constitutional bill.
    The scope of Clause (ii) has not yet been determined by the courts, but this jurisprudence will develop in due course. One aspect might better be dealt with more specifically, however, than was done in the 1960 Canadian Bill of Rights. This involves the effect of the denial to an accused of the opportunity to retain counsel. Judicial decisions to date under the Canadian Bill of Rights have held that, in instances where counsel is denied, such denial does not affect the admissibility of evidence obtained from an accused interrogated or examined without benefit of counsel. It might be preferable, and more in keeping with the spirit of the bill, to provide that evidence so obtained is inadmissible and that the resulting convictions are invalid if they cannot stand in the absence of the inadmissible evidence.

(e) Right of a Witness to counsel

Section 2(d) of the Canadian Bill of Rights provides that no law of Canada is to be deemed to

. . . *authorize a court, tribunal, commission, board or other authority to compel a person to give evidence if he is denied counsel, protection against selfcrimination or other constitutional safeguards. . .*

and this right should appear in a constitutional bill.

(f) Fair Hearing

Section 2(e) of the Canadian Bill of Rights provides that no law of Canada shall be deemed to

. . . deprive a person of the right to a fair hearing in accordance with the principles of fundamental justice for the determination of his rights and obligations. . .

This is a fundamental requirement which is already generally recognized in the public law of Canada. In a new constitutional bill of rights it might well be placed in association with the fundamental rights to life, liberty and property.

This kind of guarantee to the impartial administration of justice. The general requirements of a "fair hearing" are well known. There are some uncertainties, however, as to where a "fair hearing" is required. The language of the Canadian Bill of Rights indicates that it is required when a person's "rights and obligations" are being determined. These words appear also in the European Convention on Human Rights and some other constitutions drawing upon it. If construed narrowly, such words would apply only to situations involving a dispute between two parties over pre-existing rights. Wider language may be needed if it is the intention that "fair hearing" requirements be extended to such activities as the granting or withdrawal of licences by government agencies, the certification or decertification of unions, or the conduct of a hearing in an investigation under the Income Tax Act or under a provincial Securities Act.

(g) Presumption of innocence

Section 2(f) of the Canadian Bill of Rights states that no law of Canada is to be deemed to

. . . deprive a person charged with a criminal offence of the right to be presumed innocent until proved guilty according to law in a fair and public hearing by an independent and impartial tribunal, or of the right to reasonable bail without just cause. . .

The reference to "according to law", "fair hearing", and "independent and impartial tribunal" reiterate rights guaranteed elsewhere. The requirement of a "public" hearing need not create difficulties. The courts have not construed the Canadian Bill of Rights as preventing the closed court sittings now authorized by the Criminal Code in cases involving, for example, the protection of young accused persons or the security of the state. If desired, however, specific exceptions could be made along the lines of those contained in the European Convention, and in the constitutions patterned on it.

The presumption of innocence is a fundamental ingredient of Canadian criminal justice, and must be guaranteed. This is not to say that the various federal and provincial penal statutes which contain "reverse onus" clauses (clauses which take the existence of certain facts to be proof of other facts unless the accused can produce evidence to the contrary) will be declared unconstitutional. So far the courts have distinguished this kind of factual presumption from a presumption of guilt, and have allowed such federal statutory provisions to apply in spite of the Canadian Bill of Rights.

A constitutional bill of rights will assure that these provisions regarding presumption of innocence, and fair and public hearings will apply equally to prosecutions under provincial legislation as to prosecutions under federal law. Such protection is not afforded by the 1960 Canadian Bill of Rights.

(h) The Right to an Interpreter

Section 2(g) of the Canadian Bill of Rights states that no law of Canada is to be deemed to

. . . deprive a person of the right to the assistance of an interpreter in any proceedings in which he is involved or in which he is a party or a witness, before a court, commission, board or other tribunal, if he does not understand or speak the language in which such proceedings are conducted.

This is an important right, and should be retained.

(i) Other Legal Rights for Possible Inclusion

There are other legal rights which might be included in a constitutional bill of rights which were not included in the 1960 Canadian Bill. Following are some examples.

(i) Guarantee against *ex post facto* laws creating crimes retroactively. Article I, section 9 of the U.S. Constitution gives such a guarantee, as does Article 7 of the European Convention.

(ii) Guarantee against unreasonable searches and seizures. The Fourth Amendment to the U.S. Constitution provides such a guarantee. Article 8 of the European Convention and some constitutions based on it appear to emphasize protection of the private home against interference. At the present time in Canada, evidence obtained not only by means of an unreasonable search but by actual illegal means (as, for example, by theft) is generally completely admissible in the Courts. It is suggested that this double standard of conduct should no longer be tolerated on the part of law enforcement agencies. Illegally obtained evidence should be as inadmissible as an illegally obtained confession.

(iii) Guarantee of the right of a citizen not to be exiled. This may be provided for in section 2(a) of the Canadian Bill of Rights where it refers to "exile", but that clause only prohibits "arbitrary" exile. It is suggested that any exile, whether arbitrary or not, should be prohibited. Apart from the inhumanity of exile there is serious doubt that, in international law, any country is entitled to banish its own citizens. ("Exile", as used here, is to be distinguished from "deportation", which applies only to aliens. If desired, the definition of exile could be extended to include deprivation of citizenship. If this is done, however, the qualification of "arbitrary" should be retained.)

3. EGALITARIAN RIGHTS

This term as used here refers to guarantees against governmental action which would tend to distinguish certain persons or groups of persons for different treatment on the basis of their race, national origin, or other factors unrelated to the purpose for which the distinction is made.

Existing legislation shows a widespread concern about racial and similar discrimination. The Canadian Bill of Rights declares that the rights listed in Section 1 (due process; equality before the law; freedom of religion, speech, assembly, and the press) exist without discrimination by "race, national origin, colour, religion or sex". Federal legislation and legislation in eight Provinces and both territories prohibit discrimination in employment. Seven Provinces and the two territories also prohibit discrimination in public accommodation. The greater number of these statutory provisions, however, are designed to affect only private conduct. A constitutional bill of rights would serve to limit discriminatory activities on the part of governments as well.

The prohibited criteria of discrimination, as well as the areas of activity where discrimination is forbidden, should be considered in any anti-discrimination clauses:

(a) Prohibited Criteria of Discrimination

It is suggested that the bill should provide that the criteria listed in section 1 of the Canadian Bill of Rights – race, national origin, colour, religion, sex – should be retained as prohibited criteria for discrimination. Additional prohibited criteria might be considered, as for example, ethnic origin.

(b) Areas of Activity Where Discrimination Might be Forbidden

  (i)   voting or the holding of public office;
 (ii)   employment – here it is suggested that there be added a qualification to the effect that distinctions based on a *bona fide* occupational qualification are not prohibited. In this way, possible difficulties concerning, for example, provincial legislation authorizing the hiring of teachers for denominational schools on the basis of their religious belief will be avoided;
(iii)   admission to professions where admission is controlled by professional bodies acting under legislative authority;
 (iv)   education – special provisions will be required here to avoid inconsistencies with the guarantees of separate or denominational schools contained in section 93 of the B.N.A. Act and corresponding sections in other constitutional statutes relating to other provinces, for in some cases these school guarantees authorize religious distinctions in student admission policies. An exception to cover situations where a system of separate or denominational schools exists will suffice if there is added to it a provision for educational institutions run exclusively by religious bodies;
  (v)   use of public accommodation, facilities and services;

(vi)   contracting with public agencies;

(vii) acquiring of property and interests in property.

Admittedly, these anti-discrimination provisions might be considered to be embodied in the "equality before the law" clause. But just as it has been found desirable to detail certain aspects of "due process", it may also be useful to detail certain aspects of equality".

4. LINGUISTIC RIGHTS

Section 133 of the British North America Act, 1867, provides as follows:

Either the English or the French Language may be used by any Person in the Debates of the Houses of the Parliament of Canada and of the Houses of the Legislature of Quebec; and both those Languages shall be used in the respective Records and Journals of those Houses; and either of those Languages may be used by any Person or in any Pleading or Process in or issuing from any Court of Canada established under this Act, and in or from all or any of the Courts of Quebec.

The Acts of the Parliament of Canada and of the Legislature of Quebec shall be printed and published in both those Languages.

Thus there already exists a constitutional guarantee of the use of both languages in governmental processes, but this extends only to the legislature and courts of Quebec and to the Parliament and courts of Canada. In matters of education, it has been held that the guarantees of separate or denominational schools do not include any guarantee of the right to use either language as a medium of instruction.

It is submitted that these language guarantees be extended to other institutions of government and to education as has been recommended by the Royal Commission on Bilingualism and Biculturalism. These guarantees would prove effective, it is suggested, if incorporated into a constitutional bill of rights.

If expressed widely, the proposed rights would obviously give rise at the present time to serious practical problems of implementation. The problems are to a large degree overcome, however, through the employment of a formula based upon population proportions on a unit basis as recommended by the Royal Commission, and here endorsed.

The rights fall into two categories:

(a) Communication with Governmental Institutions—

guaranteeing the right of the individual to deal with agencies of government in either official language. It would be necessary to decide whether this should apply to all agencies – legislative, executive, and judicial – and to all governments – federal, provincial and municipal.

(b) Education—

guaranteeing the right of the individual to education in institutions using as a medium of instruction the official language of his choice.

5. ECONOMIC RIGHTS

The kind of rights referred to here are those which seek to ensure some advantage to the individual and which require positive action by the state. The Universal Declaration of Human Rights, for example, included such rights as the right to work, the right to protection against unemployment, the right to form and join trade unions, the right to social security, the right to rest and leisure, the right to an adequate standard of living, the right to education, and the right to participate in the cultural life of the community. The United Nations Covenant on Economic, Social and Cultural Rights adopted by the General Assembly in 1966 included and elaborated upon these rights.

The guarantee of such economic rights is desirable and should be an ultimate objective for Canada. There are, however, good reasons for putting aside this issue at this stage and proceeding with the protection of political, legal, egalitarian and linguistic rights. It might take considerable time to reach agreement on the rights to be guaranteed and on the feasibility of implementation. The United Nations recognized these problems when it prepared two separate Covenants on Human Rights – one on Civil and Political Rights and one on Economic, Social and Cultural Rights, thus giving nations an opportunity to accede to them one at a time.

It is therefore suggested that it is advisable not to attempt to include economic rights in the constitutional bill of rights at this time.

THE FORM OF THE CHARTER

The rights to be protected in the proposed constitutional bill fall broadly into one of two types:
 (i) rights which are expressed in terms of restrictions on the power of Parliament and the legislatures, and which require no enabling or implementing legislation in order to become effective (the rights described as "political" and "legal" fit into this category), and
 (ii) rights which in order to be fully effective must rely on the support of enabling or implementing legislation because they either anticipate sanctions for their enforcement or require positive government assistance, (the rights described as "egalitarian" and "linguistic" fit into this category).

In order not to be inconsistent with the present constitutional division of powers, an entrenched bill of rights must recognize that any required legislation falls within the competence of Parliament in some respects and within the competence of the provincial legislatures in others. And in order to be effective, the proposed bill must anticipate the varying rates of speed at which the various legislatures may feel able to introduce this legislation.

For these reasons it is suggested that the proposed constitutional bill of rights should assume a form which recognizes these variations, and accommodates them. The first portion of the bill could list the several political and legal rights. Two further parts could follow. One would be concerned with egalitarian rights, the protection of which will require in most respects implementing legislation which does not now exist in all Provinces. The further part would deal with linguistic rights as recommended by the Royal Commission on Bilingualism and Biculturalism.

A discussion about implementation of rights calls of necessity for a discussion as well of their limitation in time of emergency. On the occasion of war or other national crisis, western democracies have found it necessary to interfere drastically with normal private rights. No matter what the constitutional context, the courts have generally permited this interference because they recognized the necessities of state involved. Some consideration should therefore be given at the outset to the extent to which the legislative authority of Parliament should be restored in times of emergency, and the means by which this may be accomplished.

One of three approaches might be employed: (i) some general exemption in the nature of the amendment to the War Measures Act enacted as part of the 1960 Canadian Bill of Rights; (ii) a precise specification of the several rights which may be infringed and, perhaps to what extent (in this way the political and legal rights requiring abridgement could be dealt with while egalitarian and linguistic rights could continue unimpaired); (iii) no mention of any exemption, thus permitting the courts to determine what limitations are made necessary in times of crisis (many of the guarantees in the United States Bill of Rights are stated without qualification yet the American courts have recognized that some of them may be limited in time of war).

8

The Provinces and
International Agreements*

MR. JUSTICE BORA LASKIN

I

The distribution of governmental powers in a federal state cannot be complete without reference in its Constitution to foreign affairs. Normally, the exercise of authority in relation to foreign affairs has two aspects: first, there is the *executive power* of direct dealing with foreign states, involving an internal determination of where that executive power resides and an external determination of international status or personality; and, second, there is the *legislative power* of implementing domestically, if need be, the international accord, a matter which in itself has no international significance save as it is expressly dealt with in the international contract. The legislative power of implementation raises, however, an internal domestic issue which, shortly stated, is whether a federal state must be governed in its international relationships by the distributive character of its constitutional organization. Ordinarily, it would be expected that this issue (as, indeed, the question of executive power to engage in international relations) would be settled by the basic Constitution or, if not clearly settled thereby, would be resolved by the decisions of the highest court competent to bind the central and unit governments of the federation by its judgments.

In considering how these matters stand in Canada, two long-established constitutional doctrines provide a relevant background. First, the distribution of legislative power between Parliament and the provincial legislatures involves a correlative distribution of the accompanying executive or prerogative power. (The formal exercise of these executive or prerogative powers at the federal level by the Queen or by the Governor-General, and at the provincial level by the Lieutenant-Governor in the name of the Queen, must, of course, be seen practically in the context of the conventions of responsible government.) Second, the British North America Act exhausts the whole range of legislative power (or, the totality of effective

*Reprinted from *Background Papers and Reports,* Ontario Advisory Committee on Confederation, (Toronto, Queen's Printer, 1967)

legislative power, to use a more recent judicial exposition of the principle) and, subject to express or implied limitations in the Act, whatever is not given to the provincial legislatures rests with Parliament. (On the question of limitations, see Laskin, *Canadian Constitutional Law*, 3rd ed., pp. 70 ff.). The application of these doctrines to foreign affairs in general, or to international agreements in particular, means that the executive power in relation thereto is a concomitant of the legislative power; and that unless it is unqualifiedly found in the catalogue of provincial legislative powers, the matter is within exclusive federal competence. Is this in fact the case under the Constitution and the judicial decisions which have dealt with foreign affairs and international agreements?

II

British colonial history and law show clearly that a grant of legislative power to implement domestically the obligations undertaken in international negotiations is not necessarily a concession of international status. Thus, from the standpoint of Great Britain's exclusive representation of her colonies abroad, there was nothing incongruous in granting power to a colonial legislature to carry into effect by local legislation the international commitments made by Great Britain on behalf of the local colonial government. Recognition of international personality or status would, however, be involved if a colony were given the power of negotiating international agreements without reference to Great Britain (that is, to the British Government).

The Canadian Constitution, unlike the later Australian one, makes no reference to foreign or external affairs. They are touched upon only in the now obsolete Section 132 which reads as follows: "The Parliament and Government of Canada shall have all powers necessary or proper for performing the obligations of Canada or of any Province thereof, as part of the British Empire, towards foreign countries, arising under treaties between the Empire and such foreign countries." The Section is obsolete because Great Britain (or to use the formal name, the Crown in right of the United Kingdom) no longer makes treaties or any other kind of international agreement for Canada or any Province thereof, and it is unreal to expect the Courts to apply Section 132 in the present circumstance of Canada's undoubted independent international status; the language of the Section is beyond any such redemption. It is important, however, to notice the reference in the Section to the provinces. It underlined that at a time when the central government of Canada had no executive power to conduct foreign relations for itself or any of the units, the British Government might do so, but whether it was Canada as a whole or any province that was affected, the necessary legislative and executive powers to discharge the obligation rested with the central authorities in Canada. For this purpose, it was immaterial that the obligations involved matters that would otherwise have been within exclusive provincial legislative (and executive) competence. So-called "treaty" legislation under Section 132 could be enacted only by the Parliament of Canada.

If the Provinces by 1867 and later had no executive power in relation to foreign affairs, and no legislative power either, did they acquire either the one or the other when, in the course of political evolution, Canada as such attained independent international status? As of 1867 and later, Canadian subservience abroad involved under the Constitution federal or Dominion dominance at home. Would then independence abroad mean subservience at home, that is in the sense of loss of complete legislative power to implement domestically international obligations? International agreements involving matters that were in any event within Parliament's competence did not raise any issue. The only questions, at least in a legal sense, were whether the central government could exercise the executive power of dealing internationally with matters which were domestically within exclusive provincial competence, and whether the central Parliament could legislate on those matters so far as necessary to carry out international obligations.

III

The British North America Act limits provincial legislative power territorially; a provincial legislature must confine its valid enactments to operation within the boundaries of the Province. Prior to 1931 there were judicial pronouncements that the Parliament of Canada as well had no power to legislate extraterritorially but, whether or not these were correct, Section 3 of the Statute of Wesminster, 1931 was express in authorizing Parliament to enact extraterritorial legislation. There is no parallel provision with respect to the provincial legislatures.

This does not mean, however, that the Province in its character as a juridical person (whether acting in a formal way as the Crown in right of the province, or through the Lieutenant-Governor or through an authorized Minister) is unable to make agreements with persons or private agencies in another Province or in another country. (Whether or not such agreements involve implementing legislation commanding action or limiting action of the inhabitants of the Province may be put to one side for the moment.) Nor does the want of provincial extraterritorial legislative power mean that independent (although government-launched) agencies are unable to negotiate across provincial or international boundaries. They are in no different position from ordinary residents of the Province in this respect. In other words, private persons or non-governmental agencies may treat with governments, here or abroad, without thereby raising any immediate external affairs problem. It is unnecessary for the purposes of this paper, to go into such allied questions as whether the private person or agency may, under the law of his or its country, engage in transactions abroad, or whether in case of any wrong-doing or injury in the course of an international transaction there may be intergovernmental consequences or repercussions.

A totally different situation exists, however, where the Province as such, or the Crown in right of the Province, negotiates across provincial or international boundaries with another Province or state or the government thereof, because here the question at once arises whether this is an assertion of power in relation to external affairs.

It is necessary to distinguish here dealings between provincial governments and dealings between a provincial government and a foreign state or a governmental unit thereof. Relations between provincial governments do not involve any issue of international law or international relations. Although there is nothing in the Canadian Constitution that expressly permits interprovincial agreements there is, equally, no prohibition and, indeed, nothing that suggests any prohibition. By Contrast, Article 1, Section 10, Clause 3, of the Constitution of the United States is express that "no State shall, without the consent of Congress . . . enter into any agreement or compact with another State or with a foreign Power . . .". Without enlarging on the situation in the United States, it is enough to say that consent of Congress is not required in such minor matters as adjustment of boundaries, but on important matters such as flood control, allocation of water resources and control of crime (on which there are interstate compacts) such consent is admittedly necessary.

The reference to the position in the United States is important to point to a deficiency in the Canadian Constitution in its failure to prescribe any judicial forum for the determination of litigable issues between the Provinces. Provisions of this kind exist not only in the United States under Article III, Section 2 of its Constitution (reposing jurisdiction in the Supreme Court) but also in Australia under Section 75(iv) of its Constitution (reposing jurisdiction in its High Court). In Canada, there is statutory provision in the Exchequer Court Act for that Court to hear disputes between Provinces with their consent. Presumably, in a contract action at least, one Province might sue another in the latter's courts but legislation of the latter Province would have a telling effect on such suits. This enforcement problem as between Provinces is, however, peripheral to the main concern of this paper. On the substantive side, it is sufficient to say that the Provinces are quite free, independent of the federal executive or Parliament, to enter into agreements with each other and to implement those agreements, if necessary, within their respective boundaries, so far as the agreements deal with matters within provincial legislative jurisdiction or deal with property of the particular Provinces.

Where a Province seeks to deal with a foreign state or with a unit thereof (if the foreign state is a federation), a different situation exists. As a matter of internal constitutional law, there is the question whether the Province may, so to speak, reach out to deal with a foreign government. The Canadian Constitution is silent on the matter, but it is an obvious inquiry whether the admitted prohibition against provincial extraterritorial legislative power means a correlative prohibition against provincial extraterritorial executive power. To refer again, comparatively, to the United States, Article I, Section 10, Clause 1, of the Constitution says flatly that "no State shall enter into any treaty, alliance or confederation". This provision, taken in conjunction with the affirmative grant of treaty-making power in Article II, Section 2, Clause 2, to the national government, and in conjunction with the already quoted Article I, Section 10, Clause 3, respecting compacts with foreign states, and also in conjunction with the supremacy

Clause 2 of Article VI ("treaties . . . shall be the supreme law of the land") makes the ascendancy and exclusive foreign relations authority of the national government of the United States clear.

The issue of provincial extraterritorial executive power is compounded in difficulty by the situation which presently exists, under the governing judicial decisions, with respect to federal or Dominion executive and legislative power in respect of foreign affairs and international obligations. The matter must also be viewed from the standpoint of international law and the enforceability of obligations of an international character. In sorting out the problems that arise here it is well to begin by pointing out that for the purposes of international law there is no difference between a treaty, an international convention or international agreement. The formalities attending the assumption of an international obligation do not as such affect its international validity or enforceability. In my submission the situation is the same in Canadian constitutional law so far as concerns both internal executive power and internal legislative power; neither of these aspects of involvement in foreign affairs undergoes any change by reason of the fact that a treaty in its formal connotation is in contemplation, as opposed to a convention or any other type of intergovernmental agreement. I shall expand on this matter below.

IV

As part of Canada's British inheritance, the conduct of foreign affairs and the acceptance of international obligations have been regarded as matters for the executive (for the Cabinet, to refer to the political authority). True enough, the Cabinet is answerable to Parliament, but the latter has not generally imposed controls in advance to govern the manner and extent to which the Cabinet may embroil the country in international affairs. Undoubtedly, it may do so if it chooses. Another aspect of the British inheritance (exhibiting in this respect a difference from the United States) is that Canadian law does not recognize the self-executing treaty, an international obligation which by its own force and terms becomes operative as domestic law. Thus, although the executive may bind the country internationally, the international commitment cannot as such become a rule of conduct for citizens without implementing legislation. (International involvements may have side effects on domestic transactions, but a review of these effects is not germane to the points under discussion).

It is, of course, possible to have intergovernmental arrangements which do not either envisage or require domestic implementation by legislation binding the citizen, because no change in the existing domestic law is involved. Thus, Canada and the United States might agree on the use or occupation by United States forces of military installations in Canada, or there might be an agreement on the exchange of scientific data. Such agreements can, as a rule, be carried out by executive or administrative direction alone. The blunt question that now arises is whether the federal executive is limited in any way by internal legal considerations in the range of matters on which it may engage in international negotiations. The question may be looked at in two ways: first, from the standpoint of an international obligation which requires no implementing legislation, and, second, from the standpoint of an international obligation that does. In this latter connection, it is relevant to note that by international law, a state is under a duty to make or effect such legislative changes as are necessary to carry out its international obligations.

The answer to the question requires another look at the proposition stated at the beginning of this paper; namely, that the distribution of legislative power carries with it a correlative distribution of executive power. It is clear that first, in the colonial period, and later, in the period of Dominion status, and now, in the period of Commonwealth relations, official contact between the British Government and Canada or any part thereof has been and is through the federal government. It alone has presence or status for intra-Commonwealth dealings, as it alone had such status for dealings with Great Britain in earlier periods. This status was an attribute of external recognition, and not really dependent on anything expressed in the British North America Act. As such, it was not limited by the scheme of internal distribution of legislative power but reflected, in the sense in which it was concerned with "family foreign affairs", that there was only one channel of communication between Canada and the outside world and that was through the central government. Although not dependent on anything expressed in the Canadian Constitution, it had support in such provisions as those giving to the Governor-General-in-Council the power to appoint the provincial Lieutenant-Governor (Section 58), giving all residuary legislative power to the federal Parliament (Section 91), and limiting independent provincial authority to action within the province (Section 92).

The release by the British Government of legal and political control over Canadian affairs (formalized through Imperial Conferences in 1926 and 1930, and by the Statute of Westminister 1931) invited external recognition of a wider kind and led to acceptance of the national government of Canada as the spokesman for Canada in international affairs, and the only channel of communication between Canada or any part thereof and a foreign state. (Remaining legal fetters, such as the problem of constitutional amendment, do not detract from the validity of what is said insofar as it concerns the Dominion and the provinces *inter se*.) Indeed, the general rule of international law is that only "states" may be subjects thereof, and a corollary of this has been that only one juridical personality can be recognized in a federal state. The exceptional departures from this rule in the cases of Byelorussia and the Ukraine, which became original members of the United Nations although being constituent republics of the Soviet Union, arose out of a constitutional change in 1944 by which each of the sixteen Union Republics was authorized to enter into direct relations with foreign states. The fact that only two republics became United Nations members was the result of a diplomatic compromise. Moreover, the two republics in question have limited their participation in international affairs to membership and activity in international organizations; they do not have ordinary diplomatic relations with foreign states. Although there is nothing in the Byelorussian and Ukraine example that, in present circumstances, is any precedent for the Canadian Provinces, it is clear that the break-through to what has been called "marginal international personality" depended on both internal constitutional change and external recognition by acknowledged independent states.

It is a fact that there are no provisions in the Canadian Constitution (such as are found in the Constitutions of United States, Switzerland and the West German Republic) permitting the Provinces to make agreements with foreign states with the consent of the national government. I do not say that the national government may not, in any event, permit them to do so, but the want of power of this kind supports the conclusion that the national executive of Canada is in law free to make any kind of international commitment. Canada as such and it alone is responsible internationally if the commitment is not carried out. If it authorizes a Province to engage in international negotiations, as I believe it can, it will still be Canada as such that will be responsible internationally. A foreign state that purported to deal directly with a Province without going through the national external affairs department would be, in effect, recognizing it as having international personality; certainly, the foreign state could not claim to hold Canada accountable if there was a default in the concluded agreement. Conversely, if a Province were to seek to deal directly with a foreign state, the latter's proper answer would be to refer to the Canadian national authority to ascertain if it agreed and if it would stand behind any agreement that was reached.

If the federal executive is free to act, and act exclusively, in any or all matters, as the Canadian organ of treaty-making or of the making of less formal international agreements, is the federal Parliament equally able to act as fully in implementing domestically the results of its international negotiations? It was empowered to do so under Section 132 of the Constitution when the British Government was the organ for the conduct of Canadian foreign relations, but with the federal executive of Canada now acting as such organ, and Section 132 no longer applicable, the governing rule is presently that laid down by the *Labour Conventions* case in 1937. The principle of that case is (to use the words of the Privy Council which decided it, as Canada's highest court at the time) that "for the purposes of . . . the distribution of legislative powers between the Dominion and the Provinces, there is no such thing as treaty legislation as such. The distribution is based on classes of subjects; and as a treaty deals with a particular class of subjects so will the legislative power of performing it be ascertained." The bifurcation of Canada's implementing power, according to whether the matters covered by a treaty or convention or other agreement are otherwise within federal or provincial legislative power, was seen by the Privy Council as necessary to protect provincial constitutional autonomy, and particularly (the judgment suggests) the exclusive competence of Quebec. In this light it stated that "there is no existing constitutional ground for stretching the competence of the Dominion Parliament, so that it becomes enlarged to keep pace with the enlarged functions of the Dominion executive . . . the Dominion cannot, merely by making promises to foreign countries, clothe itself with legislative authority inconsistent with the constitution that gave it birth. . . ."

What the Privy Council's judgment means is that once Section 132 is left behind, neither the federal residuary authority nor the principle of the exhaustiveness of legislative power is adequate (alone or in combination) to spell out an unlimited power to implement international obligations. Indeed, in the *Labour Conventions* case, what were involved were conventions rather than treaties, and it is clear that regardless of the form of the international obligation, or indeed lack of form (it might arise by an exchange of notes, the power of implementation is governed by the ordinary rules of distribution of legislative power between Canada and the provinces. Earlier case law had likewise recognized that no distinction should be drawn, so far as implementation was concerned, according to the form of the international obligation; an intergovernmental convention (it was said in the *Radio* case) came to the same thing as a "treaty" for purposes of Section 132, and the *Labour Conventions* case shows that they involved the same considerations outside of Section 132. Power to implement international promises was not a constitutional value that could be assigned exclusively to the federal Parliament merely because the federal executive was now managing foreign affairs.

In this respect, the situation is different in the United States (where, however, the Constitution is much clearer), and different too in Australia whose Constitution confers power on the Commonwealth Parliament over "external affairs". In both of these federations, by decisions of their highest courts, full implementing power resides in the central legislature, whether or not the matter of the international obligation is one otherwise within the exclusive competence of the states. Notwithstanding this omnicompetent legal power, both the United States and Australia have been restrained by the centrifugal forces which are present in all federations from pushing their constitutional authority too far. They have also from time to time insisted on inclusion of so-called "federal state" clauses in international agreements to which they are parties, clauses whose purposes generally speaking is to entitle the federation to discharge its international obligation by remitting the agreement for implementation to its constituent states where it deals with matters ordinarily within state competence. It is clear, of course, that Canada, but not the United States or Australia, has ground to put a "legal" face on a request for a federal state clause or on a refusal to participate in multilateral negotiations that envisage agreement on matters that otherwise fall within provincial power.

This is not the place to argue for or against the legal limitation presently operable on Parliament in respect of international agreements. It is supported by so close a student of federalism as Professor K. C. Wheare, but opposed by the late Justice Rand who asserted that he "cannot agree that it is possible to eliminate treaty character from legislation accomplishing its terms", and that "the totality of treaty-making action . . . (is) a discrete and entire subject matter" whose only place of reception is in the residual power of the Dominion. Eighteen years after the *Labour Conventions* case,

Lord Wright, who sat on the case as a member of the Privy Council (which at that time gave only a single and ostensibly unanimous opinion), expressed his dissent from the principle there laid down, and in 1956, a year later, the late Chief Justice Kerwin said in the course of his judgment in *Francis* v. *The Queen* that "it may be necessary . . . to consider in the future the judgment of the Judicial Committee in the *Labour Conventions* case'. No clear opportunity has since arisen for any such reconsideration.

V

In the present state of Canadian constitutional law and applicable international law, a Province can engage in dealings with a foreign government only through the authority of the national government, and it would in that respect be really a delegate of the national government. The latter is entitled to determine how and by whom it will be represented abroad. For example, in the Columbia River negotiations with the United States, the Canadian Government took the exceptional step of including a representative of the Government of British Columbia in the Canadian delegation. It is thus possible for it to give authority to a completely provincially-chosen delegation. But the international responsibility would be that of Canada, not that of the Province.

It is my opinion that if a Province presently purported on its own initiative to make an enforceable agreement with a foreign state on a matter otherwise within provincial competence, it would either have no international validity, or, if the foreign state chose to recognize it, would amount to a declaration of independence on the one hand, and, on the other, to a denial of the exclusive juridical competence of Canada as such in the field of foreign affairs. It would then be for Canada to assert that competence against both the Province and the foreign state. Nor could the Province, in my opinion, give such an agreement domestic validity by implementing legislation because (as a matter of internal constitutional law) such legislation would be vulnerable as being action taken under a non-existing power to enter into international commitments. It cannot be the case that because the plenary federal executive power in foreign affairs is not complemented by a plenary implementing power, the result is that the Provinces are able to implement when they have no antecedent executive power to act independently in foreign affairs.

The presence abroad of provincial agents-general, in the main in Great Britain, does not undermine this assertion. They are not accredited to any foreign government although they do receive what may be called diplomatic courtesies. Essentialy, they are governmental representatives promoting the commercial interests of their respective provinces. Any strictly diplomatic issue, involving intergovernmental dealings, is normally referred to the High Commissioner's office. If the office of agent-general were to develop as a diplomatic one, involving accreditation to another government, this would necessitate a re-writing of both Canadian constitutional law and international law if the Canadian federation was to survive in any way closely resembling its present position.

Again, the assertion in question is not belied by the instances in which provinces have engaged in discussions and entered into various arrangements, reciprocal or otherwise, with foreign governments or units or agencies thereof. The Supreme Court of Canada in *Attorney-General for Ontario v. Scott*, decided in 1955, has recognized a distinction between treaties or international agreements and arrangements which do not involve obligation but which envisage reciprocal or concurrent legislative action. One instance is an arrangement between Ontario and Great Britain (as well as with other Provinces of Canada) for co-operative enforcement by each within its jurisdiction of maintenance orders issued by the other against deserting husbands. The line is thin between such arrangements and international agreements but the Supreme Court left no doubt that the Provinces were competent as to the former but not as to the latter. Even such permissible arrangements require, however, that the federal external affairs department be used as the channel of communication. Other dealings have taken place between provinces and border states of the United States, the latter being authorized by the Congress under the "compact" Clause 3 of Article I, Section 10, of the Constitution. The extent and range of such arrangements (limited, of course, to matters within provincial legislative jurisdiction) may well form the subject of a companion study, and it is enough to say here that, in present circumstances, there can be no international agreement without the participation of and assumption by Canada of international responsibility.

There are legal as well as formal differences in the role that the provinces may play in the kind of arrangements sanctioned by the *Scott* case and the implementation (under the rule of the *Labour Conventions* case) of international agreements made by Canada. The international agreement provides a basis for domestic action but, subject to a "federal state" clause in the agreement or other alleviation, such action is commanded by international law. If provincial implementing legislation is enacted, any repeal or change could involve Canada in a breach of international obligation. No such consequence would, of course, flow from the like action taken in respect of the kind of reciprocal or concurrent (and non-obligatory) arrangements dealt with in the *Scott* case. The situation forces speculation whether the difference in the two kinds of dealings is merely a rationalization of the willingness of the foreign state to forego the legal sanction that ordinarily accompanies an agreement; or, to put the matter in other terms, whether this is a case of trying to find a means of effective co-operation with a unit of a federal state in a matter of local concern to it without disturbing the formal rules of international law. If so, it must be evident that not only the foreign state but Canada as well is willing to make the compromise.

9

*The Treaty-making Power of Quebec**

JACQUES-YVAN MORIN

Since the appearance of the first multilateral treaties in the second half of the twentieth century, and particularly since international organizations have given birth to great conventions that are sometimes referred to already as "international legislation", the question of treaty-making power has assumed a new importance and often gives rise to unexpected difficulties within many federations. The treaty has in fact become a very flexible instrument. There is nothing which cannot be made the subject of international law, once States have chosen the treaty as a means of regulating their mutual relationship, of codifying their norms of behaviour or of achieving uniformity in the standards of social, economic or cultural activity. Whether the subject be working hours in industry; social security; responsibility of the aerial carrier; health, education or culture; driving licenses; or human rights, treaties today touch all fields.

In federal-type States, however, several of these subjects fall, wholly or in part, under the legislative jurisdiction of the member States. One can easily see that the exclusive jurisdiction of the cantons, regions or provinces would steadily lose any real meaning if the central agencies of the federation could, at their will, bring these matters into their own field of competence through the expedient of an agreement with a foreign country or a multilateral convention. Can one accept this situation and still talk of autonomy? On the other hand, can one accept the fact that a great number of subjects, of the utmost importance for the future of the international society, cannot become the object of any multilateral regulation for the simple reason that they are the responsibility of provincial or cantonal governments that are jealous of their prerogatives? Is it admissible to "disarm" the federal State in view of the trend towards regional and international integration by denying it one of the most effective means of reducing local particularity?

These questions have, more than once, plunged the constituent bodies and tribunals of federations into a state of perplexity. There is nothing surprising in this, since a fundamental option of an essentially political nature is involved here, which determines to a large extent the kind of federalism practised within the State.

*Reprinted with permission from the Canadian Bar Review, Vol. XLV, 1967.

In Canada today, the question is raised in all its scope. We have, for several years, experienced the doctrinal perplexities and the jurisprudential confusion which already characterized several other federations. Recently, the Quebec Government officially took position in favour of the right of the Canadian Provinces to exercise a *jus tractatuum* which would extend to all matters falling within their field of legislative competence.[1]

I

In order to grasp the present situation in Canada with respect to international agreements, one must go back to the period when the Provinces-to-be were separate colonies within the British Empire. At that time, the Crown controlled all the foreign relations of its dependent territories and the government in London enjoyed almost unlimited power, particularly in the matter of treaties. On the advice of his Britannic ministers, the King concluded agreements that were applicable either to the entire Empire or to a particular colony. Each governor then had the mission of implementing the treaties in the colony under his jurisdiction, unless such a treaty entailed amending the legislation applicable to the colonies, in which case the Imperial Parliament or the colonial legislature was required to intervene in order to implement the agreement internally.[2]

It was quite normal that a similar rule should be inserted in the imperial law which set up the Canadian Union in 1867. Article 132 of the British North America Act conferred upon the central Parliament of the new federation "all powers necessary or proper" to fulfill obligations towards foreign countries incurred by the Empire in the name of Canada or one of her Provinces.[3]

In other words, whenever there was a treaty to be implemented, the federal Parliament, acting alone, could legislate on all matters, even on those which the constitution placed exclusively under provincial jurisdiction. This was the only rule concerning treaties which appeared in the written constitution of Canada. Obviously, no treaty-making power as such was transferred thereby to the central administration of the federation, but the very wide legislative power thus conferred upon Parliament was soon to serve as an argument on behalf of the federal executive in its efforts to obtain the exclusive right to conclude treaties. The article 132-system in

1. See the speech pronounced before the Consular Corps of Montreal by Mr. Gérin-Lajoie, Vice-president of the Council of Ministers and Minister of Education of Quebec, on April 12th, 1965, and published in *Le Devoir*, on April 14th and 15th, 1965, p. 5.

2. A. B. Keith, *Constitutional History of the First British Empire*, 1930, pp. 220, 247, 253.

3. "The Parliament and Government of Canada shall have all powers necessary or proper for performing the Obligations of Canada or of any Province thereof, as part of the British Empire towards Foreign Countries arising under Treaties between the Empire and such Foreign Countries". British North America Act, 1867, 30 & 31 Vict., c. 3.

effect tended towards centralization, since the division of powers within the federation faded out somewhat in the face of imperial treaties.[4] At the time, however, provincial autonomy was not particularly endangered, since most international treaties dealt with matters falling under the jurisdiction of the federal or imperial authorities.

The situation became quite different when Canada obtained the right to conclude treaties without passing through London. His Majesty did indeed continue, during several years, to conclude agreements on behalf of Canada, since this power, under British law, is a royal prerogative.[5] However, the federal government had in effect gradually substituted itself for the British cabinet in advising the King on whether or not to conclude a particular international agreement. Actually, the royal prerogative in this field had long been of a purely nominal nature, so that the central executive body of Canada found itself sole master of the treaty-making power.

II

With the disappearance of the imperial ties and Canada's accession to full international personality, the question was raised whether article 132, which mentioned only "Empire treaties" was applicable to agreements concluded by the Canadian government. Could the central government, through its new right to make treaties, assume the right to legislate in fields reserved to the Provinces under the British North America Act?

Even though the control exercised by the British Cabinet had been removed, the appeal jurisdiction of the Judicial Committee of the Privy Council was maintained until 1949. It was to this tribunal, the highest in the Empire, that were submitted, on several occasions, the matters we have just outlined. Up to 1937, the policy of the Committee was rather hesitant, but no federal law implementing a treaty was invalidated.

In 1937, however, the Judicial Committee, in the famous *Labour Conventions* case, decided to protect the provinces against federal encroachment. The Ottawa Parliament had just adopted laws implementing three International Labour Organization conventions on the eight-hour day, minimum wages and weekly rest, which had been ratified by the Canadian executive in 1935.[6] The Province of Ontario had attacked the validity of this legislation. The Judicial Committee decided that the central power, although competent in the matter of concluding treaties, could not adopt legislation implementing those treaties whose subject fell under provincial legislative jurisdiction. Lord Atkin established the inapplicability of article 132 to the conventions and gave his opinion on the distinction between the conclusion and the implementation of treaties ("formation" and "performance").

There is no existing constitutional ground for stretching the competence of the Dominion Parliament so that it becomes enlarged to keep pace with enlarged functions of the Dominion executive. . . .

. . . the legislative powers remain distributed, and if in the exercise of her new functions derived from her new international status Canada incurs

obligation, they must, so far as legislation be concerned, when they deal with Provincial classes of subjects, be dealt with by the totality of powers, in other words by co-operation between the Dominion and the Provinces. While the ship of State now sails on larger ventures and into foreign waters she still retains the watertight compartments which are an essential part of her original structure.[7]

The conclusion of a treaty adds nothing to the legislative powers of the federal Parliament; the sharing of powers remains the same, whatever the extent of Canada's international activity. On the point of letting go the last reins, the Privy Council no doubt realised that provincial autonomy faced a precarious existence if the article 132 rule were extended; Lord Atkin clearly suggested this in the lines just quoted.[8] Behind a judicial façade, the judgment contains a political decision of the greatest importance, considered in Quebec to be one of the cornerstones of Canadian constitutional law.

This being said, the Privy Council decision is not without serious drawbacks. There exists in Canada a vast field which cannot in practice be made the object of an international treaty, as the provinces greatly hesitate to place themselves in the hands of the central government. Thus, confronted with the efforts of the International Labour Organization and of the General Assembly of the United Nations to have their members ratify conventions which would commit them to apply international norms in their internal legislation, Canada, together with other federal States, has found herself in a deadlock. On the one hand, the central government has the power to conclude treaties, but cannot enact or implement them whenever the subject of the agreement falls within provincial jurisdiction. On the other hand, the Provinces, although competent to legislate in matters of labour, health, education, natural resources, and so on, have let themselves be out-distanced by the central executive with respect to concluding treaties to the point where it is difficult for them today to negotiate with foreign countries.

We will attempt to outline a possible course of action in the light of solutions found in other federations and of the tendencies which have arisen in Canada in the past few years.

4. *In re Nakane and Okasake* 1908, 13 B.C.R. 370 (C.A.).

5. J.-Y. Grenon, "De la conclusion des traités et de leur mise en oeuvre au Canada," 1962, 40 Can. Bar Rev. 151, p. 153.

6. Convention on Working Hours (Industry), 1919; Convention on Minimum Wages, 1928; Convention on Weekly Rest (Industry), 1921.

7. *Attorney General for Canada* v. *Attorney General for Ontario*, [1937] A.C. 326, at pp. 352-354 *passim*.

8. See also the following passage, *ibid.*, at p. 351: "If the position of Lower Canada, now Quebec, alone were considered, the existence of her separate jurisprudence as to both property and civil rights might be said to depend upon loyal adherence to her constitutional right to the exclusive competence of her own Legislature in these matters". Along the same lines, see A. B. Keith, The Privy Council Decisions, A Comment from Great Britain (1937), 15 Can. Bar Rev. 428, at p. 432.

III

If we turn to the positive law of various federations (of which there are twenty or so at the present time), we will see that the diversity in the constitutional systems is such that an initial review can only leave us perplexed. It would appear possible however to systematise this vast material by taking as a basis the distinction found in most States, whether unitary or composite, between, on the one hand, the conclusion and ratification of treaties, which generally are the responsibility of the executive, and, on the other hand, the approval of these agreements and the power to take the necessary measures to enforce or implement the treaties and integrate them in the internal legislative system.

This distinction, which, as mentioned above, was invoked by Lord Atkin in the decision concerning the international labour conventions, makes it possible to reduce to three general categories the various solutions offered by federal constitutions: (a) Federal States in which the conclusion of treaties and the power to approve or implement them is the sole responsibility of the central authorities; (b) States in which the central government has the power to conclude treaties, whereas the member States retain the power to approve or implement treaties whose subject falls within their legislative field; finally (c) Federations whose members possess, to some extent, the power to conclude treaties.

The majority of federal States fall within the first category, particularly the more recent ones. India, Malaysia, Burma, Austria, Mexico, Brazil, and Lybia may be so classified, as well as three of the federations which will be dealt with in the third category, that is, the Soviet Union, the United States and Argentina.

In these federal States, the central authorities have been granted a veritable monopoly with respect to foreign relations and agreements deriving therefrom. Although it is rarely mentioned in the constitutional texts, the rule that federal treaties take precedence over the powers of the member States constitutes an essential corollary to this monopoly. Only the Upper Houses (Senate, Federal Council) are in a position to put forward the point of view of the member States within the central administration. The efficiency of this method as a protection for local autonomy is in most cases very problematical. The federations mentioned in this first category, therefore, present to the outside world a very definite unitary image.

Very few federations can be classified in the second category. They are Nigeria and Canada, to which we may add Australia. These federations are characterized by the fact that the member States have a right to refuse to act whenever the central executive requests that they implement a treaty or multilateral convention, whose subject matter falls within their jurisdiction. In the case of Australia, although the High Court has granted very wide powers of implementation to the federal government, the States have in fact kept their freedom, especially in connection with international labour standards. This is a makeshift solution which satisfies neither the central government, whose international activities are impeded, nor the member States, whose desire to defend their own autonomy reduces them to the role of perpetual hinderers. This is why some federal States have adopted a more flexible system, which we will now examine.

IV

In the last category, one can group, for purposes of analysis, all those composite States whose constitutions authorize the members to conclude some treaties or compacts, even if they do not in practice exercise this right. These are the Soviet Union, the United States, Argentina, Switzerland and the German Federal Republic.

The federated republics of the Soviet Union were granted in February 1944, the right "to enter into direct relations with foreign States, to conclude agreements with them and to engage in the exchange of diplomatic and consular representatives".[9] Whatever may have been the real purpose of this constitutional amendment, it must be admitted, however, that its effect remains largely theoretical. With the exception of the special international status granted to two federated republics, the Soviet Union should rather be classified in the category of federations in which the *jus tractatuum* is the sole responsibility of the central administration.

In the United States, quite recently, Congress took the initiative of encouraging the States to conclude agreements with neighbouring countries, in particular in the fields of forest protection and civil defence. A doctrinal movement has taken form with a view to encouraging the States to make use of the compact clause of the Constitution, which authorizes them to enter into "compacts" with foreign powers, with the consent of Congress.

Thus, in 1949, Congress approved an agreement dealing with the protection against forest fires in the Northeast, which allows certain States to conclude agreements with neighbouring Canadian Provinces. In 1951, a new initiative of Congress in the field of civil defence invited the participation of Canada and Mexico "or of their States or Provinces" in the signature of agreements with the American States.[10] This initiative was not followed through, however, because Ottawa felt that all co-operation in matters of passive defence should take place within the framework of the policies and agreements established by the central authorities. The evolution taking place in the United States appears to hold promise for the future, although it remains very limited for the present.

In Switzerland, the cantons retain certain powers with respect to treaty-making as defined in article 9 of the Constitution:

Exceptionally, the cantons retain the right to conclude treaties with foreign States in respect of matters of public economy, frontier relations, and police; nevertheless, such treaties must not contain anything prejudicial to the Confederation or the rights of other cantons.

9. Constitution of the U.S.S.R., art. 18a. The text of the decrees of the Supreme Soviet amending the Constitution are published in English in *International Conciliation*, Documents for the Year 1944 (Carnegie Endowment), p. 246.
10. Interstate Civil Defense Compact (1951), 64 Stat. 1251, art. X.

This text has been the cause of a lengthy controversy concerning the nature and extent of the *jus tractatuum* of the cantons. Constitutional practice has evolved continually towards centralization throughout the last century and the Confederation has concluded agreements in several spheres formerly reserved for the cantons, in particular, in the field of double taxation.

On the other hand, the practice of the cantons shows that they have concluded a great number of treaties, several of which exceed the relatively tight limits which article 9 imposes upon the cantonal *jus tractatuum*. While all the cantons have not availed themselves of these powers (Valais, Bern, Freiburg, and Glaris, for instance, have not signed any agreements since 1918), one finds in other cantons agreements concerning double taxation, the protection of literary and artistic property, the construction of railways, the distribution of electric power and the administration of justice, in particular with respect to reciprocity in the enforcing of judgments. However, since the Confederation claims the power to negotiate treaties in all fields, it would appear that a sort of concurrent jurisdiction, with federal priority, has evolved with respect to the relations of the cantons with foreign States. Actually, the Federal Council is trying to monopolize the relations of the cantons with the outside world, except in certain matters of secondary importance. This does not prevent cantonal autonomy from being very real, but it rests, in final analysis, on political and economic factors.

In Germany, the member States possess the *jus tractatuum* to the extent of their power to legislate. The *Länder* of Baden-Württemberg, Rhineland-Palatinate and Bavaria have concluded agreements directly with foreign countries on various subjects. The Rhineland-Palatinate government for instance concluded two agreements with Luxembourg, concerning the construction of hydro-electric dams on boundary waters,[11] whereas Baden-Würtemberg has entered into several agreements with Switzerland or Austria concerning fishing in the reserve basins of the Rhine or the protection of boundary waters against pollution.[12] The Free State of Bavaria, for its part, has signed numerous agreements with Austria, most of them in the form of administrative agreements, and also participated in the 1960 agreement with Switzerland, Austria and the *Land* Baden-Württemberg concerning the protection of the waters of Lake Constance.[13]

If we attempt now to draw an overall picture of the allocation of treaty-making power within federations, our analysis of positive law shows that there is no uniform rule in this matter. In the first group are to be found federations which have settled the question in favour of the central government, certainly the easiest solution, but which tend to reduce the powers of the member States proportionately to the increase in the international activities of the central authority. Then come the federations in which the members have a "right of veto" that allows them to refuse to approve or implement agreements concerning matters under their jurisdiction; this situation contains all the disadvantages, since it tends, in practice, to oppose the federal State and the member States and to hinder the development of international legislation. Finally, we have classified in a third category those federal States whose members have the power, under the constitution, to conclude international agreements themselves. This solution, which is rather complex and varies considerably from one federation to another, appears to be, however, the only one which is really appropriate to a federation composed of resolutely autonomous States.

V

At the beginning of 1965, the Quebec Government decided to raise the question of the allocation of treaty-making power in the Canadian federation. The accelerated evolution which Quebec has experienced since World War II, the developments that have taken place in cultural, social and economic fields, and finally the greater emphasis on the tendency towards increased self-government at the very moment when international law is progressively embracing the fields heretofore reserved to provincial jurisdiction, all these factors have pushed the former colony to turn towards the outside world and to establish ties with foreign States, in particular with French-speaking countries.

On February 27th, 1965, was signed in Paris an "Agreement between Quebec and France on the Program of Exchanges and Co-operation in the Field of Education", the negotiations for which had lasted several months.[14] This document is the first *official* agreement concluded between a provincial government and a foreign State, and, for this reason, gave rise to lively debates both in the House of Commons and in the press. The federal government took this opportunity to recall that, in its view, Canada possessed a single international personality within the community of States and that only the central executive had the power to conclude treaties with foreign countries. To further stress this point, the Ministry of External Affairs exchanged letters with the French Embassy on the same day that the

11. State Treaty concerning the construction of a hydro-electric dam on the Sauer near Rasport-Ralingen, of April 25th, 1950, Gesetz- und Verordnungsblatt der Landesregierung Rheinland-Pfalz (1950), no. 35, p. 239; State Treaty concerning the construction of hydro-electric dams on the Our, of July 10th, 1958, Gesetz- und Verordnungsblatt für das Land Rheinland-Pfalz (1959), no. 4, p. 13.

12. Agreement concerning fishing in the reserve basin of the Rhine near the Rheinau dam, of November 1st, 1957, Gesetzblatt für Baden-Württemberg (1959), p. 39; Übereinkommen uber den Schutz des Bodensees gegen Verunreinigung (1960), Gesetzblatt für Baden-Württemberg (1962), No. 1. See also the Regulation on bird-shooting on the territory of the Untersee and the Rhine; agreement with Switzerland and the Canton of Thurgau of May 23rd – June 5th, 1954, Gesetzblatt für Baden-Württemberg (1954), p. 99.

13. *Supra*, footnote 12.

14. The agreement was signed on behalf of the French government by Messrs. C. Fouchet, Minister of National Education, and J. Basdevant, Director General of Cultural and Technical Affairs of the Ministry of Foreign Affairs. On the Quebec side, full powers had been granted by ministerial decree to Messrs. P. Gérin-Lajoie, Vice-president of the Council and Minister of Education, and Claude Morin, Under-Secretary for Federal-Provincial Affairs.

Paris-Quebec agreement was signed, in which it is said that the Canadian Government gives its consent to the agreement. If Quebec's act had constituted a precedent in favour of a certain international capacity for the Province, Ottawa was immediately opposing it from the point of view of principle.

The Quebec Government therefore raised the issue again, several weeks later, in the person of Mr. P. Gérin-Lajoie, Vice-president of the Council and Minister of Education. Before the Consular Corps of Montreal, the Minister developed the theme of Quebec's international personality, in the following terms:

At the time when the Quebec Government is becoming fully aware of its responsibility in the accomplishment of the particular destiny of the Quebec society, it has no desire to abandon to the federal government the powers to enforce conventions whose subjects fall under provincial competence. It fully realises, furthermore, that there is something absurd in the present constitutional situation.

Why should a State which enforces an agreement be incapable of negotiating it and signing it itself? Is not an agreement entered into with the main purpose of being enforced, and should it not be up to those who have the responsibility of implementing it to draw up its terms? . . .

There was a time when the fact that Ottawa exercised international powers exclusively was in no way detrimental to the interests of the federated States, since the field of international relations was quite clearly delimited.

But nowadays it is no longer so. International relations concern all aspects of the life of society. That is why, in a federation like Canada, it is necessary that the member States who so desire participate actively and personally in the drawing up of international conventions which are of direct interest to them.[15]

The reply of the federal government was given to the press on April 23rd and commented upon in Parliament at Ottawa several days later. The Secretary of State for External Affairs was willing to extend a helping hand to Quebec or any other province in the matter of treaties, providing that these were compatible with the general policy of the central government and that, furthermore, the federal treaty-making power be invoked when the agreements were formally concluded.[16]

Several months later, on November 17th, 1965, Ottawa concluded with Paris a treaty or cultural agreement, the purpose of which was to promote exchanges and contacts between France and all of Canada.[17] To the extent that it concerns higher education, its application could give rise to numerous constitutional difficulties; the parties, therefore, specified that they committed themselves to the extent of their respective competence. The agreement contains no reference to Quebec's claims with respect to treaties. There was annexed to the document, however, an exchange of letters in which it was stated that cultural exchanges could be the object of agreements entered into with the Province of Canada. In effect, this letter contains the principal feature of the agreement, since France probably preferred that no mention be made of a constitutional problem in the main body of the treaty. However, the Government of Quebec was in no way inclined to avail itself of this provision, since federal competence in cultural matters is strongly questioned in the Province.

The exchange of letters with Paris stipulated that the Provinces might sign agreements, either by referring to the Ottawa-Paris agreement, or by obtaining the agreement of the federal government. Thus the agreement on cultural co-operation, signed at Quebec several days later, on November 24th, 1965, by the French Ambassador and the Quebec Minister for Cultural Affairs, makes no mention of the Ottawa-Paris agreement.[18] Ottawa's assent appears to have been obtained, however.

VI

These empirical arrangements, designed to save appearances *a posteriori*, raised a number of problems. They must no doubt be considered as another episode in the constitutional crisis which has been going on for some time in this country. Just what sort of agreement must be obtained from the central government? Will Ottawa be able to exercise control over the very content of the agreement, although it may be within exclusive provincial competence? To this, the Quebec Government has replied, through M. Gérin-Lajoie "that it is no longer admissible . . . that the federal government should exercise a sort of supervision and policy control over the international relations of Quebec".[19]

This attitude does not exclude the control of the constitutionality of the agreements entered into by Quebec. It goes without saying that a similar control should also take place with respect to treaties signed by Ottawa. As long as Quebec remains a member of a federal or confederal State, the question of constitutionality may be raised whenever agreements are concluded by either level of government. Important as it is to remove any policy control over Quebec treaties, it is just as important to accept a control of their legality. Of course, this review should not be carried out by the federal government, but rather by the courts.

The new Quebec requires greater decentralisation as a condition of membership in the Canadian federation. Since it is possible, however, that the English-speaking Provinces will tend towards greater centralisation, the most reasonable solution would be to specify in the special status for Quebec a strictly judicial control over treaties. The other Provinces would

15. See *supra*, footnote 2 (Author's translation). The Minister expressed the same views in an address to a delegation of university professors from Belgium, France and Switzerland, at the Quebec Parliament, on April 22nd, 1965.

16. Press Release No. 25, April 23rd, 1965, *Le Devoir*, Montreal, April 24th, 1965, p. 1.; (1965), 110 *House of Commons Debates* 395 (April 26th, 1965).

17. See (1965), 17 External Affairs 513.

18. See *ibid.*, at p. 520.

19. See *supra*, footnote 2 (Author's translation).

then be free to adopt the method which suits them best and, if need be, reinstate the system inspired by article 132 of the British North America Act, or to borrow a solution from the first category of federations we have described (India, Brazil, Austria).

The preceding considerations lead us to believe that the problem of the *jus tractatuum* cannot be separated from the overall constitutional question. Up to now, agreements concluded by Quebec have concerned only double taxation, technical co-operation and exchanges of researchers, professors and students. It is sufficient, however, to envisage the multiplication of such agreements in all fields that fall under provincial jurisdiction, natural resources for instance, to have an idea of the friction which could arise, under the present Constitution, between Ottawa and Quebec. This dimension of the problem indeed shows that Quebec will eventually come to question the overall Canadian federal system and that, sooner or later, it will be necessary to face the heavy task of redefining the constitutional equilibrium of the country.

SECTION THREE

PARLIAMENT AND THE EXECUTIVE

The institutions governing this country in the latter half of the twentieth century are, for the most part, those established for Canada by the British North America Act. Changes have been proposed, and changes effected, in the past hundred years, but today Canadian political institutions are exhibiting an increasing inability to withstand the pressures exerted by the still-expanding scope of government and the alterations in attitudes toward Canadian federalism. This section introduces the reader to several current problems confronting Parliament and the Executive, and to some suggested solutions of their difficulties. These solutions are of two different types: reform measures, to meet changing circumstances; and replacement or abolition in the light of new conditions.

The value of the Monarchy as an instrument of Canadian government has been debated in Canada for many years. Although "the Monarchy" is not an urgent question today, it is of fundamental importance to our system of government whether Canada remains a monarchy or becomes a republic. This section of the book begins, therefore, with a statement of the arguments for and against retention of the Monarchy as presented by the Government of Quebec and Eugene Forsey.

The problems of governing Canada today are more numerous and no less serious than at any time in our history, and the solutions of these problems will depend, to a large extent, on the ability of the Cabinet to adopt new methods of operation appropriate to the conduct of government in the 1970s. R. G. Robertson and Senator Maurice

---

*Reprinted from, *Background Papers and Reports*, Ontario Advisory Committee on Confederation, Toronto, Queen's Printer, 1967.

Lamontagne describe several of the difficulties faced individually and collectively by Cabinet Ministers in the execution of their functions, and suggest ways by which they may be overcome, some of which have been implemented by the Trudeau Government.

The power and prestige of the House of Commons has been decreasing in recent years, and it is clear that reforms in the role, structure, and functioning of the House are essential if it is to remain an effective instrument of Canadian government. The type of change necessary is indicated in Norman Ward's treatment of the reform of the Electoral Boundaries Readjustment Act. A further area where reform is required, the Speakership, is discussed by Denis Smith.

No institution of Canadian government has been subjected to more unwarranted criticism than the Senate. The Senate, however,. from the moment of its creation, in composition or in power, did not possess the capacity to perform the most important of its functions—the representation of provincial interests at the federal capital. The change during the past decade in attitudes toward Canadian federalism indicates that the Senate must be reformed so that it will be able to perform this function. The opinions of the Governments of Ontario, Quebec, and Canada as to how this reform can be accomplished conclude this section.

IO

A Republican Form
of Government*

THE GOVERNMENT OF THE
PROVINCE OF QUEBEC

It would be preferable for the Canadian Union to become a republic, while remaining in the Commonwealth.

At this point, a Canadian president heading the Union would be more conducive to Canadian unity than is the British Crown.

Because it is more easily identified with sovereignty of the people, the republican form of government is more closely allied with most Canadians' conception of the nature of their political institutions.

Adoption of a republican form of government would provide the ideal opportunity to reform several of our political institutions so as to make them more effective.

A republican form of government would render Canada's sovereignty and independence more evident to the rest of the world.

However, this reform, at the Union level, is not of such importance that an overall priority should be attached to it.

As to Quebec, she would like to have the power immediately to become a republic within the Canadian Union.

---

*Included in the *Working Documents* submitted by the Province of Quebec to the Continuing Committee of Officials on the Constitution, July, 1968.

II

The Monarchy in Canada*

EUGENE FORSEY

The first thing to get clear is that the Provinces are not themselves "monarchies". They are parts of a constitutional monarchy, Canada. The Queen is Queen of Canada, not Queen of Ontario, Queen of Quebec, Queen of British Columbia, etc. She is, of course, Queen *in* all these Provinces. But her title is "Queen of Canada", and it is as such that she is Queen *in* each of the Provinces.

This fact is important, because it has been suggested that Quebec, for example, might be allowed to become a republic, with a president, but still remain part of something called "Canada". The analogy, presumably, would be with India, Pakistan and the other republics which remain part of the Commonwealth. But the analogy is false. India, Pakistan and the other republics within the Commonwealth are distinct political nations; each of the Provinces of Canada is *part* of *one* political nation. No Canadian Province could become a republic without ceasing to be part of the one political nation, Canada.

To propose, therefore, that any one Province should be allowed to become a republic is to propose secession, separatism and total independence for that Province.

If the people of any Province favour republicanism, but want to remain part of Canada, then the only thing they can do is try to make *Canada* a republic.

The second thing to get clear is that Canada is a constitutional monarchy by *deliberate choice*. It is not by accident, nor from absentmindedness, or coercion, or the fear of coercion, that the British North America Act, 1867, Section 9, says "The Executive Government and authority of and over Canada is hereby declared to continue and be vested in the Queen". On the contrary . . . not one of the opponents of Confederation, in any province, advocated republicanism. . . .

It would, indeed, have been very surprising if any British North American of consequence had advocated republicanism in the 1860's. Not one square inch of any of the colonies or Provinces had ever been under a republican form of government. In fact, New Brunswick and Canada West (now Ontario) had been founded by people who fled (or were driven)

---

*Originally entitled, "Constitutional Monarchy and the Provinces", included in the *Background Papers and Reports* of the Ontario Advisory Committee on Confederation, The Queen's Printer of Ontario, 1967.

from the Thirteen Colonies precisely because they refused to live under such a government; and the motto of the Province of Ontario to this day commemorates both the monarchism of its founders and their resolve to maintain it: "Ut incepit, sic permanet, fidelis" – "As she began, so she remains, faithful".... The *Confederation Debates* are sprinkled thick with expressions of horror at American republicanism and "mob rule", and of pious gratitude that British North Americans had been spared such a fate.

Why, then, do we now hear so much talk of republicanism, both in French and in English Canada?

First, because republics are once more the fashion, especially since the Second World War, and a lot of people want to be in the swim. All the countries behind the Iron Curtain are republics. Also India, Pakistan, Ghana, Nigeria, Kenya, Tanzania, Uganda, Zambia, Cyprus, South Africa, Ireland, Singapore, South Korea, South Vietnam, Algeria, Tunisia, Egypt, Syria, Lebanon, Israel, the two Congos, the Sudan, Mauretania, Mali, Senegal, Dahomey, Guinea, the Ivory Coast and Italy, have all, within the last few decades, joined the ranks which had already included the United States, France, and the whole of Latin America. . . .

Second, some Canadians seem to have got it into their heads that people who live in a republic are somehow "freer" than those who live in a constitutional monarchy. It would be interesting to know precisely how and why. It is not obvious that South Africans (especially coloured South Africans), or Ghanaians, or Russians, or Chinese, or Hungarians, or Egyptians, for example, or even Americans, Frenchmen, Italians or Indians, have more freedom than we have.

The same comments apply to the notions that as a republic we should be more "independent", or should have more "dignity". How and why?

Then there is the contention that a republic would be more truly "Canadian". This also is not obvious. No part of this country has ever been a republic or part of a republic and to become one would be an abrupt break with our history. Our monarchy, our British monarchy, our Anglo-French monarchy, our historic monarchy, is part of the Canadian tradition. It is not something alien. It is bone of our bone and flesh of our flesh.

At this point, someone may say: "All very well if you are of British ancestry. British settlers brought the British monarchy with them in their baggage. But what about the French Canadians? What about the people of other origins who have come since: the Germans, the Scandinavians, the Ukrainians, the Hungarians, the Dutch, the Japanese and Chinese, and the rest? Surely the monarchy is no part of their Canada?"

Yes, it is. It is plain enough that British Canadians got their ideas of constitutional government from Britain. But where did the French Canadians get their ideas? From France? From Rome? From the United States? From Latin America? From the Laurentian Shield or the Aurora Borealis or the waters of the St. Lawrence or the Saguenay, or their own inner consciousness, or subconsciousness, or unconsciousness? No. Just as plainly, as definitely and unmistakably as the British Canadians, they got their ideas of constitutional government from Britain; just as plainly, as definitely and as unmistakably they got their Civil Law from France.

As for the others, the Germans, the Scandinavians, the Chinese and

Japanese and the rest: they came here, nearly all of them, of their own free will, knowing that they were coming to a country with a British constitutional monarchy, knowing that they would have to adapt themselves to this fact, just as, if they settled in Quebec, they would have to adapt themselves to a French Civil Law. They deliberately chose to become Canadians, deliberately chose to come to a country whose institutions had already been shaped by the two founding peoples who were here in 1867; deliberately chose to come to a country whose constitution was explicitly declared to be "similar in principle to that of the United Kingdom".[1] That constitution they accepted as part of the Canada of which they chose to become citizens. That constitution they have lived under and worked under and prospered under.[2]

In the working of that explicitly British, monarchical constitution, French Canadians and other, non-British, non-French, Canadians have taken a distinguished part.

This is not to say that the constitution cannot be changed, that we are not free to become a republic if we want to. We were free to do so in 1867; we have been free to do so at any time since; we are free to do so now. But if we are to do it, let it be for good and sufficient reasons, not on the false ground that our existing monarchical constitution is "foreign" or "un-Canadian". . . . Our monarchy is part of our constitution; our constitution is part of our history, which has shaped our character as a people. To get rid of it is to change that character; and such a change is "not by any to be taken in hand unadvisedly, lightly or wantonly, but reverently, discreetly, advisedly, soberly", from deep conviction, grounded on rational examination of the facts.

There is no point in change for its own sake, or just for the sake of having the very latest thing in constitutions. What matters in a constitution is not how new it is but how good it is, how well it works. The bigger the change, the heavier the onus upon those who propose it to prove that it is necessary, or even useful. Changing Canada to a republic would be a very big change, the more so as there is an infinite variety of republics to choose from. The change would be fiercely resisted, at least in the Atlantic Provinces, Ontario and British Columbia. A first-class row for sufficient reason is tolerable, may even be necessary; a first-class row without sufficient reason is criminal folly. What good would this particular first-class row do?

The republicans should be asked not only how their nostrum would make us freer or more independent, but also how it would give us better government, or more welfare.

Would a republic, in and of itself, give us a better distribution of legislative power between the Dominion and the Provinces, stronger provinces, or a stronger Dominion, or a better balance of the two? Would it give us a better Executive (President or Cabinet), wiser, stronger, more responsive to public opinion? Would it rescue us from the tribulations, real or supposed, of minority government? Would it give us a better balance between Government and Parliament, or between either and the Civil Service? Would it give us better municipal government? Would it reduce the dangers of corruption? Would it make government cheaper?

Would a republic, in and of itself, give us more welfare, a higher standard of living? Joining the American republic might; but that is a very different thing.

These are the eminently practical questions the republicans must be made to answer, and answer in detail, with reasons. They have no right to ask us to buy a magic potion.

One alleged reason for changing to a republic is that it would help solve the problems arising out of French Canada's position in Confederation. If it were true, this would be a weighty reason indeed. But is it true? This is precisely the place where it is most necessary to ask how the magic potion would work, what special ills it would assuage or cure.

Would a republic automatically mean more bilingualism in the national administration and public service, or in the provincial or municipal administrations and services, or in private business? Would it automaticaly mean more bilingualism in the courts? Would it automatically mean more top jobs for French Canadians in public administration or private business? Would it automatically mean more French Canadians in the Cabinet, or more of them at the head of important departments? Would it automatically produce any change in the Senate or the Supreme Court of Canada? Would it automatically mean more French education for French-Canadian children outside Quebec? Would it automatically mean wider taxing powers, or more revenue, or wider legislative jurisdiction, or a "special status" for Quebec? Would it automatically add one copper to any French Canadian's pay, or shorten his working day by a fraction of a second? Would the country choose a French-Canadian President oftener than it chooses a French-Canadian Governor-General? Would a republic automatically smooth the path to an "Associate State of Quebec", or an independent Quebec?

An amiable, if rather fuzzy, desire to help the French Canadians is undoubtedly one source of the present talk of republicanism. There are at least two others: the carbon copy theory of Canada, and the rubber stamp theory of the Crown. Both are deep-rooted, but both are false.

The carbon copy theory of Canada assumes that this country really is, and certainly ought to be, a second United States....

There could not be a wilder misconception of the origin and nature of Canada. The Fathers of Confederation were not "a lot of mixed-up kids", who tried to copy the United States and failed. They tried to make a very different kind of country, and they succeeded.

The Americans deliberately broke with their past. We have repeatedly and deliberately refused to break with ours. The most important thing for us about the American Revolution is that we, both French Canadians and British Loyalists, refused to have anything to do with it, and indeed strenuously resisted American efforts to "liberate" us. The most important thing about the rebellions of 1837 is that they failed, and for the same

1. British North America Act, 1867, preamble.
2. This is important in relation to complaints that the phrase "the two founding peoples" relegates the "others" to second-class citizenship.

reason: that most of the people, French Canadians and British Canadians alike, refused to have anything to do with them.

The Americans deliberately set out to make theirs a country of one language and one culture. We deliberately chose to preserve two languags and two cultures.

The Americans chose a decentralized federalism. We set out to create a highly centralized federalism. "They commenced at the wrong end", said Sir John A. Macdonald. "Here, we have adopted a different system."[3]

The Americans left most of their criminal law in the hands of the states. We entrusted the whole of our criminal law to the central Parliament.

The Americans made most of their judges elective, and left most of their courts to the states. We made all the judges of our superior, district and county courts appointive, and placed the appointments in the hands of the central Government.

The Americans provided for no central control of the states, except what might be necessary to preserve a republican form of government. We placed at the head of every provincial Government an official appointed by the central Government, instructed by the central Government, and removable by the central Government; endowed him with the power to reserve assent to provincial bills and send them to the central Government for assent or veto; and, to make assurance triply sure, gave the central Government power to wipe any provincial Act off the statute book within one year.

The Americans in effect forbade denominational schools supported by public funds. We guaranteed their existence, and all Provinces but one gave the central Government and Parliament special powers to enforce the guarantees.

The Americans wrote into their Constitution a very explicit and detailed Bill of Rights. We relied on the "well understood" unwritten "principles of the British Constitution".

The Americans provided for fixed election dates, for their President, Senators and Representatives. We provided only for a *maximum* duration of Parliament, with no "term" at all for the Government. An American President who wins an election has to take a fresh oath of office; Franklin Roosevelt, who held office for a total of twelve consecutive years, was President four times. A Canadian Prime Minister who wins an election does not have to take a fresh oath of office; Sir Wilfrid Laurier, who held office for fifteen consecutive years, was Prime Minister only once.

The American Congress and state legislatures are hedged around by constitutional prohibitions. They cannot, for example, confiscate property, or take one man's property and give it to another, or pass retroactive laws. Our Parliament, within the limits of subject and area laid down by the British North America Act, can do anything; for example, confiscate property, take one man's property and give it to another, or pass retroactive laws. So can our provincial legislatures, subject to the Dominion power of disallowance.

No wonder our constitution does not work like the American! No wonder the "carbon copy" looks smudged! But it does not follow that we should get to work with erasers. The French Canadians, for example, might not be altogether pleased by the erasure of section 133 of the British North America Act, guaranteeing a limited official bilingualism in Quebec and at the centre. The Roman Catholics might not be altogether pleased by the erasure of section 93 and the corresponding sections of the Manitoba, Saskatchewan and Alberta Acts. Very few of us would be pleased to see ten systems of criminal law instead of one, or to have most judges elected by popular vote.

A good many people, weary of a rapid succession of Dominion general elections . . . may think they would like the American system of fixed election dates. They might find the reality disillusioning. In the United States, no matter how unworkable a legislature may prove to be, it must go on till the preordained date; no matter what great new issues may arise, no matter how great the wave of hostile opinion, there is no means of hastening by so much as one hour a fresh consultation of the people. In Canada, a fresh dissolution of the legislature can break a deadlock, as in Quebec in 1936; here, parliamentary obstruction can force a parliamentary majority to go before the people on a great new issue where there is reason to believe public opinion is against that majority, as happened with Reciprocity in 1911. And it is noteworthy that the power to break a deadlock, or to bring the legislature into harmony with a changed public opinion, by dissolution of that legislature, is a power of the Crown.

That brings us to the other great current fallacy, the rubber stamp theory of the Crown. This can be very simply stated: the Crown, or its representative, must always follow the advice of the Cabinet in office at the moment, even if that Cabinet has just been resoundingly defeated in an election; or even if that Cabinet refuses to meet Parliament for more than the single sitting, once a year, that the law requires; or even if that Cabinet cannot muster a majority in Parliament and an alternative Cabinet which could do so is possible.

Parliamentary responsible government is a wonderfully sensitive, flexible and effective instrument, far more so than the American system. But also it can be a far more dangerous system than the American. In the American system, everybody is hedged around with legal prohibitions, which will be enforced by the Courts. In our system, that is not so. If a provincial legislature takes it into its head to prolong its own life by a year, two years, ten years, it can do so. No law prohibits. No Court can say no. If a Prime Minister tries to bludgeon Parliament or a legislature into submission by a series of elections, again no law prohibits, no Court can say so. As far as the law goes, he can dissolve a new Parliament or legislature even before it can meet. If he lets it meet, he can dissolve it any time he thinks it won't vote for him. And he can go on doing it as often as he likes. He can totally prevent Parliament or the legislature from transacting any business at all, or any business except what happens to suit him. He can call elections every few months, till the people,

3. *Confederation Debates*, p. 33.

in desperation, either give him a majority or revolt. Not one shred of illegality, and all the quintessence of democracy: what can be more democratic than appeal to the people? But the result would be that governments would be irremovable except by their own consent, or by force of arms. Fantastic? Impossible? One Canadian Prime Minister, after being defeated at the polls, tried to fill up the Senate and the Bench. Another Prime Minister tried to dissolve Parliament before it could vote against him on a motion of censure. As recently as 1952, there were persistent rumours that a provincial government contemplated dissolving the newly-elected legislature before it could meet.

What does stop this kind of thing happening in Canada? Generally, the sense of decency and fair play and responsibility which we took over from Britain with parliamentary government itself. Generally, ministers remember that they are not the people's masters but the Queen's servants, answerable to the Queen's faithful Commons, bound to let Parliament meet, bound to let it vote, bound to abide by its verdict unless there are substantial reasons of public policy for appealing to the electorate. But if a Prime Minister tries to turn parliamentary responsible government into unparliamentary irresponsible government, then only the Crown can stop him; only the Crown can keep Government responsible to Parliament and Parliament to the people; only the Crown can prevent Parliament from degenerating into a rubber stamp for the Prime Minister, elections into mere plebiscites – plebiscites whose verdict the Prime Minister accepts only if it suits him – only the Crown can prevent the Prime Minister, prime servant, from degenerating into a prime despot, the whole process into an elaborate farce, swindling the public at the public expense, with the public helpless to protect itself.

The Crown is the embodiment of the interests of the whole people, the indispensable centre of the whole parliamentary democratic order, the guardian of the Constitution, ultimately the sole protection of the people if M.P.s or M.L.A.s or ministers forget their duty and try to become masters, not servants. The Crown's reserve power to refuse the advice of ministers when that advice imperils the Constitution still remains, as Lord Attlee reminded us in 1952 and 1959; and if parliamentary government is to survive, it must remain. Parliament is the very Ark of the Covenant of the Canadian tradition. But a system in which Parliament exists, debates, votes, only at the pleasure of a jack-in-office, is a snare and a delusion. In Pym's words, "Parliaments without parliamentary liberty are but a fair and plausible way into bondage. Freedom of debate being once foreclosed, the essence of the liberty of Parliament is withal dissolved."

Responsible government means not only responsibility to Parliament, or to the electorate, but also responsibility for the interests of the nation as a whole. It has been maintained, by a distinguished Canadian professor, that a Prime Minister's supreme duty is to keep his party united and in office. That was not the doctrine which led Peel to carry the repeal of the Corn Laws, at the price of destroying his party. It was not the doctrine which led Wellington to support him. The true doctrine is that "The Queen's Government must be carried on", that "there are times", as

Meighen said, "when no Prime Minister can be true to his trust to the nation he has sworn to serve, save at the temporary sacrifice of the party he is appointed to lead." That is something Prime Ministers are a good deal more likely to remember if they think of themselves first and foremost as the Queen's servants, not just party leaders with "an ambition to be re-elected".

The Crown stands also for something else which is essential in the Canadian tradition: for a Canadianism which, while utterly loyal to Canada, looks beyond Canada. It reminds us that *nationalism* is not enough. Another distinguished Canadian professor, some dozen years ago, extolled the "pure" Canadian, "who knows only Canada", "for whom the Old World has virtually ceased to exist". It apparently did not occur to him to ask what use this monstrosity would be in NATO or the U.N.; if he had had any conception of loyalty to a Queen of a world-wide Commonwealth, such pernicious nonsense would never even have entered his head.

The Crown is in truth "the imperial fountain of our freedom". If we abolished it, and substituted a national President and ten little presidents for the provinces, then of two things one: either we should have to change our whole system of government and replace it by an American or Gaullist or Soviet or other totally alien system; or we should have to give the presidents substantially the same powers as the Queen, the Governor-General and the Lieutenant-Governors now have. If we go for Gaullism, or plump for "popular democracy", or even the American congressional variety, we shall be entering on an enterprise which will be a violent break with our whole history, our whole constitution, all our political ideas, habits and practices; an exercise in political and constitutional bedlam, the issue of which no man can even dimly foresee. If we embark on the more modest attempt simply to replace the Crown by presidents, in the innocent hope that we can leave the structure of parliamentary responsible government otherwise intact, we shall still face formidable problems. Unless we give the presidents the reserve powers, we shall run the risk of Prime Ministerial dictatorship. But the reserve powers are not easy to define in precise terms, and the constitutional draftsman might end up by giving the head of state, and his provincial counterparts, either too much power or too little.[4] Even if he were successful, his troubles (and ours) would not be over; for he would have to devise a method of election which would provide some hope that the presidents would be reasonably impartial politically; no small task.

And all this effort, all this ingenuity, all this tearing up of our roots, all the time, all the strife the process would involve: for what? What would it all accomplish? What good would it do? Who would be the better for it? Heaven knows, we have problems enough, constitutional and otherwise, to occupy us, problems national and international, constitutional, political, social, economic; urgent, practical problems to which

4. See, for example, the attempt in Marcel Faribault and Robert M. Fowler, *Ten to One: The Confederation Wager*, Toronto and Montreal: McClelland and Stewart 1965, in Articles 32 and 33 of their proposed new constitution, at pp. 128-9.

we must find some tolerable solutions if Canada is to preserve any life at all, let alone a good life. Surely they are enough to tax all the intellectual, spiritual, moral resources as we have, without gratuitously adding anything extra that can be avoided?

Unless the proponents of a Canadian republic can produce massive evidence that the change is a matter of urgent public importance, the whole notion must be summed up in the verdict of Sir Robert Borden on a very different subject: "One of the most absurd suggestions ever to come to my attention".

12

*The Canadian Parliament and Cabinet in the Face of Modern Demands**

R. G. ROBERTSON

Some of the more facile purveyors of the conventional wisdom would have it that the great difference between ministers and civil servants – apart from the rather insecure tenure of the former – is that ministers make policy, while civil servants carry it out. I doubt if I need spend much time in saying what nonsense this distinction is. Any civil servant above clerical or stenographic grades who has spent any substantial time in a job without contributing to some degree to the policy he administers should be fired – whatever the security of his employment is supposed to be. In government, whether federal or provincial, the distinction is not between those who contribute to the "making" of policy and those who do not – but between those who finally decide and those who try to carry out the decided policy, whether it is the policy they contributed to making, a caricature of it, or the very opposite. Since we, as administrators, must execute the policies ultimately decided upon by our political masters, we have an enormous interest in the quality of those policies – and in the efficiency of the decision-making process through which they are arrived at.

Obviously our interest is not solely that of administrators. Every citizen should have the most profound concern for the policy determination that is going to decide the course and direction our country takes. Comments day by day in the press make it apparent that such concern does exist, and that many people are disturbed at deficiencies they see or sense or suspect in the way public policy is decided upon, whether at the Parliamentary and legislative level, or at those of governments and cabinets. I think there is valid ground for the worries people have, but I doubt if they are right in thinking, as some so often seem to, that the defect is in the quality of our political leadership or in the character of the politicians who decide our public issues. The truth, I think, is that Canadians are, on the whole, extremely fortunate in the quality of people who are prepared to face the hazards and uncertainties of politics. . . .

*Reprinted, with permission, from *Canadian Public Administration*, Vol. XI, No. 3, Fall, 1968.

If we have problems in the conduct of our government at the political level, and if they are not basically because of the quality of our politicians, what then are they? More important, perhaps, are they ephemeral or with us to stay – and can we do anything about them?

Without pretending to have more access to wisdom or truth than comes from a "worm's eye view" of the governmental process by a civil servant, I think our problems are not ephemeral and that they are likely to grow worse rather than better – but that there are a few things we may be able to do to palliate them.

In contemplating the situation at the national level it seems to me that of our most difficult problems, only one is of long standing; the rest are new – and all are with us to stay.

The "old" problem is, of course, the phenomenally difficult nature of Canada as a country to govern. Sir John A. Macdonald remarked on it and every Prime Minister since has become acutely aware of it if he did not start with the knowledge. Other countries may have to wrestle with plural cultures and languages, regional rivalries, the centrifugal forces of geographical vastness, fractious lords of powerful provinces, the shadow of an overwhelming neighbour, the endless demands of an electorate that wants everything that affluent neighbour has without producing as much to provide it, and other problems we do not know – but few if any have quite such a wealth of complications as we have. These problems may change in emphasis or form or priority, but they are part of our heritage. Constitutional adjustment may help in some respects, but I think we would be wildly unrealistic to think it will affect the underlying reality of our national complexity, from which so much of the difficulty of our public administration arises.

The other, newer problems are all, I think, the inevitable products of our modern industrialized society, the welfare state, and the high level of expectations that Canadians have developed. Translated into the difficulties with which Parliament and government must cope these become problems of magnitude, detail, technical and scientific complexity, and of infinitely intricate selection and priority. If freedom requires that politicians decide on our public measures and determine governmental policies, it means that they must, in some fashion, cope with the enormous difficulty of these new conditions.

I think the public generally and perhaps we ourselves fail to realize fully the extent to which the nature, scope and complications of government have changed in the last few years. In his excellent paper on administration for a bicultural society,[1] Mr. Cloutier referred to government moving in the last thirty or forty years "from a passive, regulatory role to a positive, action-oriented one". So far as we in Canada are concerned that change had not proceeded far before the Second World War. Indeed I think it is only in the last ten years that the cumulative effects of the change in the nature of government have been fully felt.

Because government must now deal with so many aspects of life, the sheer mass of Legislation for Parliament to deal with, and the mass of material on which the Federal Cabinet must decide, are enormously greater than ever before in our history. It is hard to produce any meaningful index of the increase, although everyone close to things would agree on the fact. In trying to gain some rough idea of comparisons I have looked at the ten years from 1957-1967, comparing the operations of Parliament and the Cabinet in the last five years with the same operations in the first five years of that decade. I found that, in the five year period from 1957-1962, the greatest number of days per Parliamentary session was 174; in the five years between 1962 and 1967 we had sessions of 248 and 250 days. Between 1957 and 1962 the largest number of bills passed in any session was 64; at the last session of 1967 the number was 97. Our largest printed volume of statutes in the first five year period had 583 pages of legal text; in 1964-65, Parliament passed 751 pages of statutes, and in 1966-67, 1273 pages. By every one of these indexes we have an increase from one five year period to the next of something between 40 and 100%.

For Cabinet business useful indexes are almost impossible to find. The only crude one that has seemed to have no relation to sheer discursiveness by ministers is the number of documents requiring Cabinet consideration. In the years 1957 – 1959 they averaged 382 per year; from 1964 – 1966 the average was 656 – an increase of 70%. By August 23 of 1967, the Cabinet had had 532 documents before it.

The increased mass of business is not the whole story. It is also far more complex than it used to be.

Beyond this mass of scale and detail, we come to a further problem: the difficulty of coping, in our industrial society with that "dark side of the moon" – the problems and needs of science and technology on which our growth and productivity depend. If we have "two solitudes" in Canada, it takes different forms – and one form is the solitude between political and scientific man. We are not likely to have many highly qualified scientists running for political office, so somehow those who do run, and who achieve office, have to cope with the policy problems of a whole new world for which they were never trained or equipped. Science is increasingly important in public policy, but how do we fit it into a system of lay control and decision?

And, finally, we have all those things competing for the tax dollar. We may once have been a frugal people in Canada but that was long ago. Now we want everything – and we want it now, at no increase in the tax rate. There are a thousand demands, all of them laudable, of which only some hundreds can be satisfied – but which hundreds? Is HARP more needed than more school rooms for Eskimos? Is it more important to provide the financing for another 20,000 houses than to reduce the strain on the borrowing capacity of the federal government? Should we invest millions in an Intense Neutron Generator in the hope – with no guarantees – that it will lead to great new developments, or should we invest the same millions in the alleviation of poverty in New Brunswick? These are problems that have

1. Sylvan Cloutier, "Senior Public Service Officials in a Bicultural Society," a paper at the Annual Conference of the Institute of Public Administration of Canada, September, 1967.

to be understood, evaluated, compared and decided by people with no special qualifications except that they ran for public office and got elected.

We have inherited in Canada one of the most successful systems yet devised for the conduct of government in a free society. The Parliamentary system provides a balance between sensitivity and responsiveness to the public will on the one hand and the need for certainty and responsibility on the other, that can be rivaled by few if any other systems. However, the unitary, homogeneous, aristocratic environment of eighteenth and nineteenth century England in which it was developed was about as different from the circumstances of Canada today as anything could be. The problem we must face is how to adapt that system to cope with a different place and time. We must not fear to shape the Parliamentary system to meet Canada's twentieth century federal needs. The main problem is to reconcile the mass, complexity, and technical sophistication of the decisions required for government today with the continued handling of those decisions by the representatives of the people under a Parliamentary system.

I think there is no question but that we have a real problem, and it is the reflection of this problem that we see in complaints about the waste of time by Parliament, the length of Parliamentary sessions, confusion in government and lack of leadership. The immediate task is not to grope about for a different system, but to see if we can make ours work better.

It seems to me that the main adjustment must begin in Parliament, and must accept that it is no solution to make Parliament a full time occupation. If the vital political basis of our democracy is to remain intact, the representatives of the people must have time to be in touch with their constituents. Democracy will not work well, and it will probably not last if Members of Parliament and Ministers have as little immediate contact with the people as recent pressures of work have imposed. The work of Parliament must somehow be done in seven or eight months rather than in the nine or ten it has been taking. Nor is there any point in thinking we can "catch up" in some session, after which things will again be "normal". The blunt fact is that "normal" is the sort of mountainous program Parliament has had to face in the last few years.

One device that has been adopted is an increasing use of Parliamentary committees. This has helped and can help more. Yet there are dangers. A central feature of our system is the responsibility of the Cabinet, with its collective neck on the block, for the entire program of public policy and public legislation at the federal level. Committees tend to take on a life of their own, and it is not always easy to reconcile their increased use with Cabinet control. Parliamentary Committees cannot have the free-wheeling autonomy of Congressional Committees in the United States without affecting the central doctrine of Cabinet responsibility.

This we have always regarded as one of the best features of our system, for it provides a coherence and consistency in action that adds to the effectiveness of government, but one must recognize that there are disadvantages which may become steadily more important. The American system may be better suited in some respects to these times than the British. It may be that we will have to accept compromises to make the principle of Ministerial responsibility flexible enough to work today. Perhaps one of these is the development of a doctrine by which changes in legislation in committee can be regarded not as matters of confidence unless the government so decides.

In the face of the mass of work Ministers must do – and it is almost beyond human capacity – a real problem arises in the way in which the day-to-day responsibility to Parliament is to be made real and effective. It seems to me that there must be changes from present methods or else we run the risk of a steady reduction in the efficiency of government in coping with growing needs, together with a shift of effective decision-making from the Ministers, where it ought to be, into the hands of civil servants. Somehow we must lessen the relentless daily servitude our Ministers now face when Parliament is in session. The scale of the task of governing is simply incompatible with it. The Congressional system does not face this problem at all: Ministers do not sit in Congress; they do not appear each day to answer the questions of its members, and the life of the government is not constantly at hazard before it. The saving in time and energy, and the added capacity to devote to the needs and decisions of running a government must be enormous. I suspect that several undramatic things would help make our system work better. Limitation of each Minister's responsibility to answer questions in Parliament to two days a week instead of five would provide about six hours of extra time per Minister per week, without in any way reducing the legitimate pleasure of the Opposition in harpooning the Minister on the two days when he is present. Requirement of notice for all questions would eliminate a lot of time now spent in "boning up" on questions that are never asked – and eliminate some of the public damage that now results from wrong or confusing replies by unprepared Ministers.[2]

The greatest single gain, however, for every aspect of our governing process would come from shorter sessions of Parliament. These would not only enable the Members to better discharge their role of keeping contact with the people, but they would add dramatically to the time that Ministers could spend on *their* main role – that of governing. Today our federal Ministers have perhaps two months in the year – at most three – when they can concentrate on governing rather than on legislating and debating. A reduction of two months in the length of sessions would add almost 100% to the time they could put without distraction on the decisions of administration and policy that only they can take.

I am convinced that shorter sessions are possible with no loss of either the realities of Parliamentary control of the government or of the effectiveness of Parliamentary review of legislation. The British deal in their Parliament with the legislative needs we handle at two levels of government, the federal and the provincial. They cope with a larger budget and with many things that are covered here even at the municipal level. I found on comparing performances in 1956-1967, that, in nine full sessions they averaged 1329 pages of legislation in 151 days of session – about 9 pages per sitting

2. The number of days per week which Ministers are in the House for Question Period was reduced by the Trudeau Government in October, 1968. See *House of Commons Debates*, Vol. 113, No. 17.

day. In the same years our Parliament averaged 532 pages of legislation in 158 sitting days – about 3.3 pages per sitting day. It is certainly not an adequate or perfect test of performance or even comparison, but on the basis of it the British Parliament looks about three times as efficient as ours.

Whatever the defects of this particular standard, I think few observers would question that the Parliament at Westminster handles its program with more order and efficiency than ours does. They do it by planning the allocation of time, by selecting the items that deserve the attention of Parliament as a whole, by having shorter speeches, and by dealing with their estimates and supply mostly in committee and with only selective debate in Parliament. None of these things can be regarded as inconsistent with democracy in general, or freedom of speech in particular.

So far we have failed in Canada to assess realistically the functions Parliament must discharge and to allocate its time among them with some sensible priority. If we want our system to be able to meet the needs of today and tomorrow, Parliament must give a higher priority than it has so far to selection of business, planning of time, and curtailment of debate, leaving enough opportunity to the Ministry to discharge its task of governing.

The other place we have to strive for improvement is in the structure and operation of our Cabinet. No problem has received more thought in recent years. A good deal has been done through greater use of Cabinet Committees where a limited group of Ministers can have an initial discussion of questions with the officials most knowledgeable about them. Beyond this, the device that has been most often suggested is the one the British have adopted of a distinction between the "Cabinet" and the "Ministry". There is no question but that the Cabinet is too big for effective discussion. There is equally no question but that many departments are too big for control by a single Minister. The solution of more Ministers with fewer in the Cabinet seems obvious. The main problem is the geographical, economic, cultural and social diversity of Canada that finds its reflection in our federal structure.

The Cabinet is the locus of representation of the elements of our diversity in the policy-making process of the nation. Which Province or which region is to be unrepresented in that process? Even if one or another part of our totality would agree to omission from the Cabinet, would we buy "efficiency" at too high a price in a country like Canada? Our Cabinet is not simply the place where policy is made and questions are decided. It is the place, above all others, where a reconciliation is reached among the attitudes and interests of the diversities to which I have referred. Ministers bring into the Cabinet Chamber a knowledge of those interests and attitudes; they understand the provinces or regions from which they come; they provide some reflection and give their colleagues an understanding of the principles and prejudices, worries and wishes, of cultural, linguistic, economic, religious, and other groups in our total mosaic. It is behind the closed doors of the Cabinet, and in the frankness of its confidence, that we achieve much of the vital process of accommodation and compromise that is essential to making this country work. We must consider carefully any time-saving devices that might sacrifice this most important means of cementing the cracks and rifts of our national structure.

As to the scientific and technological complications of policy to which I have referred, I doubt if the best means of coping with them at the political level has yet been worked out. The establishment of the Science Council and the Science Secretariat in the last few years is a major improvement. There is now what there was not previously – an agency – indeed two agencies in association – to which the Cabinet can turn for advice on scientific matters, agencies which are not themselves "interested parties" through having an area of scientific administration of their own. But Ministers are still left with the infinitely difficult problem of deciding the balance of priority and the claims on the Treasury as between scientific research and other needs of government and between competing scientific projects. I see no new machinery that can release Ministers from this difficult and confusing responsibility. We may simply have to improve as much as we can the provision of disinterested scientific advice, the discussion among politicians, scientists and administrators that can produce at least a minimum of comprehension, and then accept the imperfections of human devices.

I am conscious that I have dealt with only a small part of the total problem presented by the demands of the present on our system of government in Canada. I have said nothing about the administrative aspect, nor have I dealt with our federal-provincial complications. Their importance is reflected in the dramatic increase in the number of federal-provincial meetings each year – and in various proposals to give them more formal status and definition as institutional portions of the government of Canada. I suspect that clarity and definition would be bought at far too high a price in the flexibility that is now possible. It is at times argued that the need for so many meetings is because of deficiencies in Sections 91 and 92 of the British North America Act. I doubt if that is so. The steady growth in the need for federal-provincial contacts is not so much because of a lack of precision in our distribution of powers as it is but another reflection of the growing complexity of government in coping with the intricacies of human relationships today. No definition of powers will ever produce lines so clear and neat that steadily more intimate cooperation will not be necessary.

Finally, I have said nothing of some of our major policy and constitutional problems in Canada. All of these are areas where we clearly face difficulties in making our government work. I have chosen, rather, to concentrate on two points – Parliament and Cabinet – because these seem to me to be the two places where our core of democratic control is under the most relentless pressure from our changing needs.

We have seen democracy fail with disconcerting speed in many new countries where free government had been established with glowing hopes. It is not going to fail in any such way in Canada. However, it is continuing to succeed, and to operate effectively in only a handful of countries, and I think the problems are mounting in almost all. It would be inspiring – and it would make tomorrow's headlines – to be able to announce a shining new formula that would ensure the continued success of our free system under its growing pressures. Unfortunately, I have no such recipe. What is wanted is not revolution; nor, I think, is it a drastic re-casting of our governmental process. What is required is the application of a number of work-a-day improvements to a political system that remains as good a means as has yet been found of providing government on a basis of free choice and free decision. . . .

13

The Influence of the
Cabinet Minister*

SENATOR MAURICE LAMONTAGNE

A paper given at the Annual Conference of the Institute of Public Administration, at McMaster University, Hamilton.

First, let us see how the rise and fall of Ministers came about. To describe this most interesting evolution, I wish to rely on an article published by the *Economist* in 1947 and entitled "The Twilight of Ministers". Those of you who have already read that article will undoubtedly remember its opening paragraph:

"The principle of complete royal subjection to ministerial control was firmly embedded in the British Constitution in the course of the nineteenth century. Though theoretically all powerful the Monarch had, by the end of Queen Victoria's reign, completely accepted the position that he could do nothing without ministerial advice and, indeed, that he could not refuse to do anything that his Ministers advised him to do."

In Canada, a similar evolution took place at about the same time. It started in 1791 and reached a very important moment in 1848 when the principle of responsible government was recognized. The Byng incident in 1926 merely served to formalize what was already implicit. But this rise of Ministers to a position of great influence was not to last very long.

The correspondent of the *Economist* goes on to say:

"But there is no such thing as finality in human development. The cabinet had no sooner removed the last formal checks on its power than it, too, began to be something of an outward show and the reality of power began to move elsewhere. Ministers, in the middle of the twentieth century, were subject to three pressures which together made it impossible for them to fulfil the role that the Constitution, as then understood, assigned to them. In the first place, with the advent of socialism, the subject-matter of state action was enormously extended. Secondly, the subject-matter of public

---

*Originally entitled, "The Influence of the Politician", Reprinted, with permission, from *Canadian Public Administration*, Vol. XI, No. 3, Fall, 1968.

*affairs became much more technical and difficult and this, coinciding with
the growth of the belief that it was a positive advantage for a politician to
have spent his formative years in the mine or at the bench, made it a rarity
for a Minister to be able to understand the papers that were put before
him, even if he had time to read them. Thirdly, the number of personal
appearances required of a Minister – in Parliament, at conferences, and at
luncheons, dinners and meetings of all kinds – increased so greatly that
even these activities, hitherto pre-eminently those of the Minister himself,
came to be beyond the powers of a single man, except with the assistance of
a Public Relations officer. Under these pressures, the Minister, gradually
became a figure-head ... only those Ministers who combined the most force-
ful personalities with a willingness to work cruelly long hours could really
be said to be responsible for their own words and actions, let alone those of
the Department they nominally controlled.*

*But this gradual change was not apparent for many years. The perma-
nent civil servants, while engrossing more and more of the reality of power,
studiously preserved the outward forms of Ministerial supremacy – as,
indeed, Ministers in their turn did the King. Just as laws were still enacted
"by the King's Most Excellent Majesty", and Ministers spoke of their "loyal
duty" to the Crown, so also the most eminent and powerful civil servant
would still refer to his Minister as "my master", and would begin his
letters, "I am directed by the Secretary of State ..."*

This long quotation sums up very well also what happened in Canada.
... The civil service began to emerge as a new force with the recognition
of the merit system and the creation of the Civil Service Commission in
1917. Fifty years later, the peak of its rise was reached when ... full bargaining rights were granted by Parliament to the staff associations. Some objections were raised before the adoption of this important piece of legislation.
Her Majesty the Queen could not bargain with her subjects. The supremacy of Parliament could not be encroached upon by collective agreements.
The fact that these arguments were not even considered seriously shows
how removed our political symbolism has become from the new reality.

Meanwhile, especially after 1935, the Establishment emerged and gradually became the centre of power within the federal administration. ...
Generally speaking, at least until recently, when the Establishment was
united behind or against a certain policy, its advice was accepted by the
Cabinet; when there was a division of opinion between the officials of a
particular department and those of the Department of Finance, including
the Treasury Board, then the views of the latter would prevail at the
Cabinet table. I have seen situations when two important groups of the
Establishment had not been able to reconcile their views on vital policy
issues. In those circumstances, the Cabinet failed to act.

The supremacy of the Establishment may have reached its peak recently
when, as a result of the implementation of the Glassco report, deputy-
ministers were given important managerial responsibilities which had been
viewed before as being too sensitive to be exercised by Ministers and had
been transferred to the Civil Service Commission. The special position of
influence of the Establishment was underlined again not long ago when

a Minister was asked to resign by the Opposition for having consulted outside experts and when another Minister had to resign for having reached a decision without proper consultation with his civil servants. . . .

However, we mustn't conclude that the civil servants' power has always manifested itself in this same manner or that it knows no bounds. In my opinion, the peak of their positive influence coincided with the last days of the St. Laurent administration. During the Diefenbaker administration, their role was particularly negative, as was often confirmed by the Honourable Alvin Hamilton. According to his belief, all of the Conservative Government's projects were systematically blocked by the civil servants. This admission would do much to explain the Ministers' helplessness during this period. On the other hand, during the famed first 60 days of the Pearson administration, the civil servants' influence amounted almost to nil. This newly found independence led to errors which will not soon be forgotten and the traditional imbalance of opposing forces was rapidly restored.

I am convinced, however, that we have already reached the first stages of a new period. The Liberal Party, in opposition, and with the aid of advisors who were, of course, not involved in public functions, had prepared a precise and detailed program. The mistake made, when coming to power, of putting it in effect, secretly and too rapidly, will have no long term consequence, except for the method used for the formulation of their program which, in fact, was inspired by that of the Jean Lesage team before 1960. I feel that the experience gained by the Liberal Party, while in opposition, will be repeated in future by every principal political party, even by those who have come to power. This is one of the factors which leads me to believe that a new era, in regards to the sources of political influence, has begun in Canada.

Thus, a new period is emerging in our country. I would describe it as "the twilight of civil servants". I do not mean by this that the fall of the civil servant will be as dramatic as that of the politician many years ago or that it will correspond to the rise of Ministers to a new position of influence. I mean, however, that the Establishment will play a more limited role than in the past 25 years and that it will have to share its privileged position near Ministers with new sources of political influence.

In the first place, I believe that civil servants will have less and less to do with the development of new policies. Conversely, the intellectual community outside the Civil Service will play an increasing role in the determination of new policy objectives and proposals. The rising number of Royal Commissions, task forces, advisory boards and councils is an obvious sign of the shift which is taking place. But it is only part of the new story. Let me explain more fully what I mean.

In the past, political parties could win elections by making vague promises, by relying on their record or merely by attacking their opponents. When they assumed office, they were not committed to an overall political program and they were free to accept the advice of civil servants even in connection with the formulation of policy. This situation is changing rapidly. The public and the press now expect political parties to be identified with a concrete, detailed and co-ordinated set of policy proposals especially during electoral campaigns. Moreover, this identification has become almost inevitable since political parties have decided to hold national conventions every two years. Their public image would greatly suffer if such meetings were not devoted to serious thinking and discussion. But such an identification means that when a given party is newly elected or even is returned to office, it will be committed to a detailed set of policies which will have been developed with little, if any, consultation with civil servants.

The politician . . . will not be more responsible for the formulation of policy than he was before, but he will have new masters. The new pattern for the preparation of political platforms is already set. It involves the consultation of the public by taking polls and conducting motivation surveys in order to know the priorities of its needs and pre-occupations and also, more and more frequently, the calling of a Thinkers' conference to determine how those priorities can best be met. Resolutions based on this preliminary work will then be adopted in a more or less modified form by national conventions and become the official platform of our political parties. Thus, the public, without really knowing it, and the intellectual community will become new sources of political influence and will play an increasing role in the selection and the formulation of policies.

There is another new pattern which is emerging and which will tend also to reduce the influence of civil servants while not contributing to increase the importance of Ministers. It has to do with the working of Parliament. In the immediate past, Parliament had really very little to do with legislation. The legislative program originated mainly from the Establishment which also prepared the ministerial speeches required for its presentation to the House of Commons. It was expected that once a bill had been accepted by Cabinet on the advice of the Establishment it would also be approved without modification by Parliament. In the House of Commons, the opposition could speak as long as it wished, but it would have been a great sign of weakness on the part of a Minister to accept any of its suggestions. As to the government backbenchers, they were expected to be seen when votes were called but not to be heard.

That situation is changing rapidly. We can even speak of a quiet revolution in Parliament. The private member, after having lost his administrative influence, which is a disguised definition of patronage, is now acquiring a legislative role which he should have had all along.

Several factors account for this change: the improvement in the quality of members; the succession of minority governments; and the length of sessions. It is fair to say that the evolution really originated from the government side. Competent backbenchers became tired of having to sit in the House with very little to do. They began to present their grievances at party caucuses and to press for more and better organized parliamentary committees. Ministers were not in a very good position to resist these pressures. It is indeed interesting to note that, with the minority situation and the length of sessions, Ministers have never been more exposed to the influence of their own backbenchers. This is even more so when they have long-term political ambitions. In certain cases, it is not exaggerated to say that they meet private members more often than their own officials. As a result, parliamentary committees have never been more influential. . . . They have proposed new legislation which the government will have to bring forward, and they have substantially modified several important bills. Such an intrusion of Parliament in the legislative process would not have been tolerated just a few years ago.

Parliamentary reform has been long overdue. It has now become inevitable. When it comes, you will see that a lot of frivolities which the House of Commons is now engaged in will be removed, that Parliament will be more interested in the substance and less in the detail of legislative proposals and that greater emphasis will be placed on parliamentary committees.

We are moving towards a compromise between British and American political institutions. As we reach it, the influence of civil servants in the legislative process will be less important. At least one type of politician will become more influential since the legislative role of the private member will be expanding.

Finally, I would like to mention a third and undoubtedly the most important new force which is competing with civil servants to influence Ministers. I mean the press, broadly speaking, or the so-called mass media. If the correspondent of the *Economist* quoted at the beginning of my remarks is right when he says that the Cabinet has become "something of an outward show", then the main objective of a Minister who wants to be successful and remain in the show ought to be to develop and maintain a good public image. Save the surface and you save all. Hence, the growing importance for a Minister to be friendly with reporters and to have an efficient executive assistant or public relations officer.

Here again, substantial changes have taken place. In the past, the relationship between Ministers and the means of communication was quite different. Television and even radio did not establish themselves as influential image-makers before the mid 50's. The press had a partisan approach to politics. Its owners, generally speaking, were closely identified with a political party and they made sure that their newspapers and their reporters faithfully reflected their political views. In that context, the public image of the politician was largely determined by the good or bad relationship which existed between himself or, more precisely, his political party, and individual publishers. Once that relationship had been defined, Ministers could do very little about their image, especially on a day-to-day basis. It was not, therefore, one of their main daily preoccupations.

The philisophy of the mass media has changed drastically in the last decade. They have become businesses, and competition among them is acute. Party affiliation has disappeared or barely survives in the editorial page. The number of readers, or audience rating, has become the golden rule. In addition, there is the cynical assumption that the public has a strong preference for sensation.

This approach leads to a new code of ethics for reporters. From now on, they do not have to reflect the political views of their employers; thus, they can transmit their own in their articles. The thing they cannot afford is to be dull. But straight and objective information is not supposed to be interesting. So, the reporter who wants to be successful looks for rumours, scoops and leaks. He writes today on the news of tomorrow. He puts the emphasis on personalities rather than on events. He appraises rather than informs. He is interested in the surface rather than in performance. He has few real friends but he is grateful to those who enable him to produce his daily article or his news broadcast "every hour on the hour." In previous days, he used to work hard to find an official source for his information; nowadays it is easier for him to rely on Cabinet leaks originating from Ministers' offices.

I do not feel that I have exaggerated reality to a great extent. I have seen Ministers who have been put on a pedestal by reporters, later be demolished by those same reporters, when they had shown that they were merely human. I have known of Ministers who went on receiving a "good press" although they had accomplished nothing of substantial value. Finally, I have heard some reporters say that they had left journalism because, during the time of the so-called scandals, they would come home at night, feeling that they had bloodied their hands to the elbows.

This general situation was always tempered by noble exceptions and has improved recently. It remains, however, that the Minister who is pre-occupied by his public image, as projected by the mass media, faces a difficult challenge. But, if he is not worried by it, he cannot continue for long to be a successful politician. There is, here, a paradoxical situation which I would like to explore more fully.

My contention is . . . that the mass media do not have a decisive impact on public opinion, at least in so far as politics is concerned. . . . Most politicians share my view and recognize, in theory, that the mass media do not effectively guide or faithfully reflect public opinion. Ministers could, therefore, afford to ignore them, at least up to a point. Some successful politicians have done just that.

In fact, however, most politicians are "newsworms". They are as fond of rumours, scoops and personal stories as most reporters. Both groups live in the same isolated world, although they usually despise each other. This cohabitation produces strange results. In most cases, the politician is almost unconsciously mystified by the reporter. Thus, while the mass media have little impact on the public, they have a great deal of influence on the politician. There lies the secret of the rising power of the press.

It is in this restricted context that a Minister cannot ignore the mass media with impunity. If he enjoys a good press, he will be envied and respected or feared by his colleagues. If he has no press, he has no future. And, if he has a bad press, he is in serious trouble, because he will be viewed even by his own associates as a political liability, in spite of the qualities he may have.

That is why it has become almost essential for a successful Minister to have a dual personality, to smile even if he does not feel like it, to talk when he should remain silent, to say the "right" thing in spite of his own convictions. That is also why Ministers have two ears: one for the press and one for their policy advisers. What they hear from both ears may often be incompatible. The danger is that the desire to preserve the public image may prevail over the requirements of the public interest. In any case, it should be obvious by now that civil servants must be prepared to share with the press the monopolistic influence they used to have on Ministers. From now on, Ministers have to live in the limelight. This new position also contributes to the twilight of civil servants.

My general thesis can be summed up very briefly. To begin with, I make the distinction between the symbol of power and the reality of power or the real source of political influence. Then I contend that we have gone through different phases of a long evolution. It started with absolute monarchy which coincided, broadly speaking, with the colonial period. Then, with the development of our democratic institutions and the granting of responsible government, the Cabinet was recognized as the supreme political authority. Since World War II, gradually and for a variety of reasons, the Civil Service Establishment became identified with the reality of power. Although Ministers could still do wrong and continued to be held responsible for their Departments, they merely represented, in most cases, the authentic symbol of power. As the Monarch, he could do no wrong and therefore could do nothing. He had become a very remote and almost undefinable political entity.

A new phase of this long evolution is now emerging. I have described it as the twilight of civil servants. I do not mean by this expression that the Establishment is following the same pattern as the Cabinet and is tending to become another symbol of power. What I do mean is that it will have to share the monopolistic influence it had on Ministers in the past with others, namely the public, the intellectual community, the private member of Parliament and the press. In other words, the reality of power will be less concentrated on one group; it will be more diffuse.

What will happen to Ministers in this complex new world? Generally speaking, a dependent becomes more independent when he has several masters instead of one. But I am inclined to think that this will not be true in this case. Ministers will have to devote a growing portion of their time to their symbolic role. They will find it harder to reconcile their different loyalties. In the process of reaching a compromise which will make their masters at least equally dissatisfied, their true personality will be weakened and their convictions will become blurred. Their devilish activities will affect their health and their private lives. In the outward show which will be theirs as symbols of power, they will try to wear a mask to hide their tiredness and their boredom.

One might ask who will want to become a Minister under such dismal conditions. My answer would be that we do not need to worry: to many people and to a great number of politicians, the symbols of power are more attractive than the reality of power.

14
A Century of Constituencies*

NORMAN WARD

The drawing of constituency boundaries for the representation of a people in a House of Commons may strike one as an elementary though fundamental exercise. Canadian experience offers conclusive proof that an apparently simple task can become almost hopelessly complex, involving bitter partisan quarrels, tortuous rules for dividing the available seats among the Provinces, mutually exclusive rules within any one Province for the recognition of such varied phenomena as the sanctity of municipal boundaries and the rapid growth of suburbia, and all but endless arguments about the kind of body best suited for drawing constituencies at all. The burden of the Canadian record, indeed, is that there is no single permanent solution to any of these problems, except in the sense that a continuing series of *ad hoc* compromises can be considered permanent.

On the whole the division of seats among the Provinces has occasioned less partisan controversy than any other major aspect of redistribution. Quebec had sixty-five seats in the legislature of the Province of Canada, and the least upsetting way of starting the new House of Commons in 1867 was to give Quebec the same sixty-five seats, and permit the other Provinces representation in proportion; this produced constituencies whose populations averaged less than 20,000.

To protect any Province from a sudden diminution in the number of seats allotted to it after any one census, it was provided that a Province could not lose any seats unless its population, considered as a fraction of the Dominion total, declined by one-twentieth between censuses. Except for the addition of a constitutional amendment in 1915 which guaranteed that no Province could have fewer Members of Parliament than it had senators, these relatively simple rules remained in force unchanged until 1946....

An amendment to the British North America Act in 1946 created new rules for dividing seats among the Provinces, which were amended in detail but not in principle in 1952. The rules currently in force, unlike their predecessors, fix a ceiling of 263 on the membership of the Commons. Two of these seats are reserved for Yukon and Mackenzie River, and each Province's share of the rest is initially calculated on a strict "rep-by-pop" basis. However, the senatorial floor under each Province's representation

*Reprinted, with permission, from *Canadian Public Administration*, Vol. X, No. 1, March, 1967.

still applies, and if the foregoing calculation gives any Province fewer M.P.'s than senators, it is given the requisite number of additional members and the mathematical calculation is done over, omitting any Province or Provinces affected by the senatorial rule. In addition, since 1952 no Province in a redistribution can be deprived of more than 15 per cent of the representation to which it was entitled at the last redistribution, nor can a Province lose seats if that loss would give it fewer M.P.'s than a Province with a smaller population. . . .

The division of seats among the Provinces . . . bears no necessary relationship to the division of any one Province into constituencies and, as suggested earlier, the manner in which this is done can be productive of profound differences of opinion. There are two fundamental questions: the rules, if any, to be followed in drawing boundaries; and the agency which does the actual drawing. The first of these questions in Canada always received a simple answer: until 1964 the House of Commons applied no rules whatever to the drawing of boundaries. Occasional attempts to adopt rules . . . were made, but in the event each redistribution down to the latest was carried out as a free-lance operation in which any rational boundary drawing was likely to be the result of coincidence or accident. Depending on the convenience of the influential, local or municipal lines were sometimes followed, sometimes not; new representation was sometimes given to those parts of a Province which had grown most rapidly, sometimes not; seats were sometimes made as compact as possible, sometimes not; blocks of constituencies were sometimes given fairly equal populations, sometimes not. The one practice that was followed with reasonable consistency was that urban divisions were generally made more populous than rural, but even here urban divisions themselves varied enormously in size, and some rural divisions were larger than the smaller urban seats.

The results of all this can be shown by a few examples. The redistribution law currently in force was passed by a Parliament whose M.P.'s were elected in 1963. The Chief Electoral Officer's report on the election of that year included, among other anomalies, the following statistics on constituencies. The smallest constituency in the country was Iles-de-la-Madeleine, Quebec, with a population in 1961 of 12,479, and the largest was the suburban Toronto seat of York Scarborough, at 267,252. The urban seats of Montreal ranged from 34,020 to 233,964, and those of Toronto (exclusive of the Yorks) from 53,155 to 88,988; the Yorks, surrounding Toronto, ranged from 89,709 to 267,252. The Winnipeg seats contained 42.7 per cent of Manitoba's total population of 921,686, but comprised only four of the Province's allotment of thirteen constituencies. In Prince Edward Island, Kings had a population of 17,893, and Prince 40,894. New Brunswick's seats ranged from 23,285 to 101,736, and Nova Scotia's (exclusive of the two-member riding of Halifax, at 225,723) from 27,634 to 85,001. Saskatchewan, with no metropolitan areas, nonetheless had ridings whose populations varied from 37,937 to 95,575. Every Province, in short, showed remarkable variations in the populations of its constituencies, and almost all the discrepancies had grown worse by the election of 1965, held on the same boundaries.

It would be easy to blame all this on the agencies that severally drew the constituencies' boundaries, but the agencies themselves were only partly to blame. The failure of the House of Commons to establish any rules to govern the drawing of boundaries was one factor. Time and social changes provided another, for the constituencies established in 1952 . . . while they varied markedly in population when created, had become far more varied by the elections of the early 1960's, after more than a decade of brisk urbanization around Canada's major cities, with parallel declines in population in some rural areas.

The agencies, nonetheless, were far from blameless, not only because they were too often dominated by partisan motives, but also because they permitted themselves to be forced to work hastily, and with inadequate information at their disposal. This was particularly true of the redistributions of 1872, 1882, and 1892, which were carried out through a government bill; in each case the government introduced a proposal which included a definition of the proposed ridings, based on the assumptions that the voting habits of electors were constant, and that Liberals and Conservatives reached voting age and died off, and moved in and out of constituencies, in fixed ratios. The first three redistributions were plainly intended to benefit the party in power, the second two particularly so; none of the three was spectacularly successful in attaining its obvious purpose, and that of 1892, after which the governing party was all but annihilated in the areas it had most carefully gerrymandered, was a dismal failure.

The next six redistributions (1903, 1914, 1924, 1933, 1947, and 1952) were effected by committees of the House of Commons; the standard procedure in each instance was for the government to introduce a general bill ordering a redistribution as provided for by the British North America Act and the latest census, but including no details on individual ridings. The bill was then (commonly after second reading) referred to a committee of the House, on which the governing party's majority was frequently conspicuous. . . .

The redistribution that followed the census of 1961 revealed two marked departures from previous practice: the use of committees of M.P.'s was abandoned outright in favour of redistribution by non-parliamentary commissions; and the commissions were given statutory guidelines to follow in the drawing of boundaries. The second of these proposals, as noted above, had been made as early as 1903, when the Leader of the Opposition sought to provide rules for the first redistribution committee. The proposal to have boundaries drawn by a non-partisan body has a history going back before Confederation.

The first draft of the British North America Act noted of constituencies: "The readjustment to be made by an independent authority, as some of the Judges, to be specified in the Imperial Act."[1] The final draft of the Act evaded the issue by providing in section 51 for redistribution "by such authority, in such manner, and from such time, as the Parliament of Canada from time to time provides"; subsequent cabinets, as we have seen, interpreted this to suit themselves. Since 1867 proposals for a non-parliamentary commission have been made sporadically, not just during redistributions and not just by suffering Opposition M.P.'s. In 1899 and 1900 the Liberal government proposed a board of high court judges to make what were considered corrections in the federal ridings in Ontario, and was thwarted each time by the Senate. In this century support for outside commissions has been variously expressed, and with increasing frequency, by spokesmen for the Co-operative Commonwealth Federation (later the New Democratic Party), the Liberal, and the Progressive Conservative parties, with leading members from each showing a particular interest in the topic. The interest culminated in a resolution offered to the House of Commons in 1962 by the Prime Minister, Mr. Diefenbaker. . . .

Mr. Diefenbaker's proposal . . . provided for "an electoral boundaries commission" which could employ "such technical advisers and other staff . . . as it deems necessary."[2] "Parliamentary approval would be required" before the commission's electoral districts became effective.[3] The commission was "to recommend such change in the total membership of the house that would make a just and equitable re-allocation of seats without serious dislocation or hardship arising from its recommendations on the number of seats in any one Province."[4] The names of the commissioners were to be placed before the House, "and our present purpose is to see to it that four of them will be superior court judges and one the electoral commissioner. We hope that one of the judges will be a judge of the Supreme Court of Canada. Another will be a chief justice of a province, a man who in years past participated in public affairs . . . and two others will be chief justices who have not participated in either parliament or legislature."[5] Mr. Diefenbaker's resolution passed, and the relevant bill was given first reading; the dissolution of 1962 prevented further progress in that Parliament, and no bill was introduced in the short Parliament of 1962-63.

The next major steps concerning redistribution fell to the Liberal government which took office in April of 1963. Like Mr. Diefenbaker's earlier resolution, the Liberals' plans included no changes in the rules for dividing constituencies among the provinces, so that no hope was held out that Saskatchewan would not suffer a major loss of representation. In other ways, the Liberal proposals departed markedly from Mr. Diefenbaker's. On November 26, 1963, Mr. Pickersgill, then Secretary of State, introduced a long resolution which prepared the way for two bills, one to establish the office of Representation Commissioner, the other to provide for the establishment of electoral boundaries commissions. . . . Mr. Pickersgill made it clear, and later repeated several times, that both bills were

1. Joseph Pope, *Confederation Documents*, Toronto, 1895, First Draft of British North America Bill, s. 25.
2. *Ibid.*, 1962, p. 2645.
3. *Ibid.*, p. 2646.
4. *Ibid.*, p. 2649.
5. *Ibid.*, 1962, p. 3044. The commission here described by Mr. Diefenbaker refers in the original text to a commission of six members, not five, apparently in error.

only technically government bills, and that in fact the government was ready to accept improvements suggested by any M.P. Already, in anticipation of the measures, the Chief Electoral Officer had visited other countries to study redistributions there, and informal all-party conferences to facilitate agreement had been held in Canada.

Despite all this preparation, the second of Mr. Pickersgill's bills had a protracted and occasionally stormy passage through the House; the first, providing for a Representation Commissioner, passed readily, and members of the House expressed satisfaction with the appointment in the bill of the Chief Electoral Officer, Nelson Castonguay, as Commissioner. The bill providing for the boundaries commissions took a full year to get through Parliament, with prolonged delays because of disagreements over its major clauses.

In essence, the bill to provide for boundaries commissions was based on five propositions which . . . were as follows:[6]

1. Ten commissions, one for each Province, were to be established. Mr. Pickersgill's argument for ten commissions was based primarily on the time which redistribution was expected to take, although mention was also made of the desirability of having local commissions familiar with local conditions. . . . Since the Conservatives had committed themselves to a single commission in 1962, they were sharply critical of the Liberal scheme but offered no amendment to it; a motion for four regional commissions was rejected by the House on April 16, 1964, and Mr. Pickrsgill's proposal for ten was approved the same day.

2. Each commission, in the original bill, was to consist of the Representation Commissioner, a chairman appointed by the chief justice of the Province from among the members of his court, one member appointed by the Prime Minister, and one by the Leader of the Opposition. . . .

The proposed personnel of the commissions was so productive of controversy that the parties reached an impasse, and debate on the bill was suspended for weeks at a time. Concern over personnel took several forms. Despite the high regard in which the Chief Electoral Officer was held, for example, it was nonetheless feared that in his capacity as Representation Commissioner he might exercise a centralized control over all the maps, with the ten commissions acting merely as rubber stamps. Suspicion was also expressed over the preliminary exercises being drawn in his office before the commissions were even established (a duty imposed on him by the statute creating his office) particularly when the government refused to accept responsibility for making them public; the suspicion was partially but not entirely allayed when a delegation from each party was invited to view the exercises in the Commissioner's office. A Conservative motion to require production of the exercises was defeated 101-60 on May 14, 1964, in a division which belied the claim that the debate was entirely non-partisan.

More serious difficulty arose over the other members of each of the ten commissions. No objection was made to the use of judges as chairmen; but the New Democratic Party took the lead in pointing to the potential dangers, in a supposedly non-partisan set of commissions, of having half the members in each instance appointed by the Prime Minister and the Leader of the Opposition, and on April 16, 1964, Stanley Knowles moved to have the chief justice of each Province appoint the two additional members from among a stated list of qualified persons, including provincial public servants, university presidents, etc. Mr. Knowles was strongly influenced by the provincial redistribution commission in Manitoba, as was Mr. Pickersgill himself; but since the Conservatives had already accepted in preliminary discussions the proposal to have appointments made by the two major party leaders, they were chagrined and annoyed to find Mr. Pickersgill taking the Knowles amendment seriously. Debate on the relevant clauses was suspended from April to November, 1964, while a compromise solution was sought, and on November 10 the minister indicated that he now felt that the necessary appointments could be made by the Speaker. The Conservatives still favoured the original bill, and Mr. Knowles still favoured limiting the Speaker to appointments from specified classes of people; Mr. Pickersgill's motion for appointments by the Speaker, "from among such persons resident in that Province as he deems suitable" passed on November 12.

3. The bill declared that constituencies were to "correspond as nearly as may be to the electoral quota for the province"; i.e. the province's population divided by its number of seats. A commission could "depart from the strict application" of this rule to take into account special geographic considerations, such as sparsity or density of population, accessibility, size or shape; and to allow for community or diversity of interests. But in no case could a constituency's population vary more than 20 per cent above or below the electoral quota.

The proposal to have constituencies conform as nearby as possible to the provincial electoral quota did not of itself produce much discussion; what did arouse the members' interest was the series of conditions considered significant enough to justify deviations from the quota, and particularly the statistical tolerance to be allowed above and below it. Mr. J. J. Greene, a Liberal member, pointed out on March 12, 1964, that the commissions were not empowered to take "historical connotations" into account in departing from strict "rep by pop," but made no motion to require it. Another Liberal, Mr. M. J. Moreau, supported by spokesmen for all parties, late in the debate moved an amendment to permit commissions to consider not only the sparsity or density of population, but also the "relative rate of growth," and it passed on November 13.

Differences of opinion over the 20 per cent tolerance to be allowed around the electoral quota not unnaturally divided the parties with strong rural support from those with strong urban bases, and the differences were marked. . . . In general, the Conservatives, Social Crediters, and members of the Ralliement des Créditistes, wanted the quota to be as large as possible, the bidding on their side ranging from $33\frac{1}{3}$ per cent to

6. The proposals are in Bill C-131, House of Commons, First Session, Twenty-sixth Parliament.

40 per cent; the Liberal and New Democratic spokesmen favoured a low quota, the smallest figure mentioned on their side being 10 per cent. Disagreement over the tolerance necessitated further delays in the bill's progress, and again it was not until November of 1964, after informal consultations, that the relevant clause was passed. An Alberta Conservative, Mr. Eldon Woolliams, moved on November 12 for a tolerance of 25 per cent above and below the electoral quota, and his amendment passed the following day.

4. Commissions were permitted but not obliged by the original bill to hold hearings of representations by interested persons before making a report. Any such hearings were to be preceded by a least fifteen days' notice in the *Canada Gazette*, accompanied by a map showing the proposed boundaries. Any person intending to present a brief had to give the commission ten days' notice in writing.

No one objected in principle to having the commissions hold sittings to permit the general public to make representations about the proposed maps, and debate on the topic turned largely on the M.P.'s' desires to make the public hearings as effective as possible. The clause finally agreed on without serious division obliged each commision to hold at least one public sitting on its map, the sitting to be announced not only in the *Canada Gazette* but also in "at least one newspaper of general circulation in the Province", the advertisement to include a copy of the map and a description of each constituency. Interested parties were given twenty-three days from the appearance of the advertisement to notify the commission of their intention to present a brief, and the commissions were expressly forbidden to hear representations which did not comply with this proviso. Representations received by the commissions could be disposed of as the commissions saw fit.

5. The bill gave each commission one year in which to prepare its map, which was to be transmitted through the Representation Commissioner to the Speaker and thence to the House of Commons. Within thirty days (later amended to forty-five sitting days) of its presentation to the House of Commons, one-third of the M.P.'s from any province could object in writing to their province's map, and the House by resolution could refer a map back to a commission for reconsideration. The commission then had thirty days to dispose of the objection as it saw fit, and report back through the Representation Commissioner to the Speaker. After that, the House could take no further action under the proposed legislation. . . .

Opposition members from the beginning objected that any significant group of members, not a majority of those present, should be sufficient to require the reconsideration of a map. They also argued that one-third of the members from a Province was too high a proportion for the consideration by the House of any provincial map; such a proportion, they pointed out, would make it impossible for the Conservatives from Ontario to protest any Ontario map on their own, since they could not muster enough members, while it left the Liberal majority from Ontario free either to accept or protest the map as they saw fit. The same problem in reverse applied to provinces where the Liberals held fewer than one-third of the seats, and to the smaller parties everywhere. The final clause, again after extensive discussion, provided that any ten members could object to any map and precipitate a debate in the House, after which the objection and a transcript of the relevant Hansard would be sent to the Commission involved without a resolution of the House. . . .

The five major points outlined above do not exhaust the list of criticisms and amendments made to the bill (it was amended, for example, to permit the continuation of the two-member seats of Queens and Halifax if desired), but they cover the commissions constitutions. In sum, Parliament created ten independent commissions, on each of which the Representation Commissioner was a full member (a fact which, coincidentally, neatly ensured that each commission initially had on it at least one French-speaking Catholic); the Chief Justice of each Province appointed the chairman; and the Speaker appointed the two other commisioners from within each province. The commissions had one year in which to draw maps based on instructions which specified that they were for each constituency to adhere to the electoral quota, from which they could depart up to a maximum of 25 per cent in either direction for reasons spelled out in the statute. Provision was made for public hearings on the maps, and parliamentary review, but in both cases the commissions' decisions were final. Any changes made in the boundaries after the one parliamentary debate on each were thus subject to no further public scrutiny, either in commission sittings or in Parliament.

The policy followed by the Speaker in making his appointments was not, as some M.P.'s seemed to expect, to consult the party leaders in the Commons. Instead he consulted the Chief Justice in each Province and, if he had been already selected, the chairman of each commission. In general, the Speaker attempted to find in each Province a team consisting of a university head or professor, and a provincial civil servant whose position was likely to be some indication of his impartiality, such as the clerk of the assembly, or the chief electoral officer; where this failed, the Speaker sought other citizens of integrity. In some areas the Speaker paid particular attention to the religious and ethnic backgrounds of possible appointees. As a matter of courtesy, the Speaker sent each party leader in the House a list of his appointments.

The commissions began work early in 1965, and for several months thereafter little was heard from any of them. By late spring and early summer all the commissions had prepared their preliminary maps for publication in the *Canada Gazette* and "at least one newspaper of general circulation," and the requisite public hearings were held from early June through to October. None of the commissions limited itself to the single sitting required by law; each scheduled several hearings in various parts of each province.

The nature and scope of the hearings, and the presentations made at them, varied widely from Province to Province. The Quebec commission heard 152 representations at eight centres, Ontario 75 at seven centres, British Columbia 44 at eight; on the other hand, the Nova Scotia commission heard only 11 briefs in five centres and the New Brunswick 3, though it had scheduled five sittings. The briefs ranged from requests to change a name to comprehensive attempts to redraft the commission's map. Since the law required the scheduling of hearings before it was known what representations, if any, were to be made at each, some commissions found themselves in the awkward position of having to travel considerable distances to open a sitting at which nobody was expected to appear, but without statutory power to cancel the advertised meeting. A few citizens, having failed to meet the deadline in giving notice of their intention to appear, found themselves willing and able to express opinion on a map, except that they could not legally be heard. Most briefs that were presented not unnaturally concentrated on one or a few constituencies within each province, and thus did not take into account each commission's responsibility to draw a whole map, not just a partial one aimed exclusively at satisfying only local interests. Few of the public hearings thus swayed the relevant commission to any great extent, and while a few changes of widely varying significance were made in a majority of the maps, most parts of most maps survived the sittings unscathed. The Ontario map sustained the greatest alteration as the result of public hearings.

When in due course maps reached the House of Commons they survived, in the main, again, although amendments were made to four. Since the Conservative whip, Mr. Eric Winkler, let it be known early that his party intended to challenge as many maps as possible as a matter of principle (and the New Brunswick commission invited challenge by producing majority and minority reports), it was inevitable that many objections would be registered, and that Conservative members would play a leading role in speaking to them; nonetheless, it would be inaccurate to conclude that Conservatives alone protested the maps, for spokesmen for all parties had points to make, and it was indeed a Liberal who said: "In my humble opinion no elected body of men sitting in this house or anywhere else could possibly have made a redistribution on this basis or could possibly have made a worse redistribution than has been done in this case."[7]

One hundred and fifty-eight M.P.'s signed thirty-five objections involving all the Provinces except Newfoundland. . . . allowed in section 13(c). Member after member complained of the commissions' slavish addiction to numbers, and spoke well of "relative rate of growth," "accessibility," and "community of interests." "Apparently," the main Quebec objection read, "the commission was much more concerned with numerical balance than with demographic, geographic and historical facts." To this general observation, echoed by many M.P.'s, the maps' critics added a second objection: the commissioners had confined themselves strictly to the census of 1961, instead of using annual estimates of population changes published thereafter by the Dominion Bureau of Statistics. (A reading of the act suggests that the law gave the commissions no alternative but to adhere to the census of 1961, on which the division of seats among the provinces was based.) A motion of Mr. Ian Watson's on May 4, 1966, to direct the commissions to "further consider all objections legally made to the respective commissions in the light of section 13(c)(i) and (ii)" failed because he was unable to obtain the unanimous consent he needed for procedural reasons.

A few members, it should be added, took advantage of the objections to the maps to say that they were completely satisfied with the new redistribution. . . .

In the event, only the maps of British Columbia, Ontario, Quebec and Manitoba were ultimately returned to the House with substantive amendments. The alterations again varied from changes of name to changes of boundaries, and the Ontario commission, in quanitative terms at least, was most responsive to parliamentary criticism, effecting twenty-four amendments; the Quebec commission changed three names and four boundaries involving eight seats; the Manitoba commission one name and one boundary involving two seats; the British Columbia commission altered six seats. Most of the commissions' original boundaries thus stood throughout the public sittings and the formal objections in the House of Commons. . . .

The maps the commissions drew are not susceptible of ready generalization, but a few significant points may be made. The tolerance established by Parliament meant the end of the enormous disparities in constituency populations hitherto so common. At that, a total tolerance of 50 per cent around a norm still permits substantial variation: the map for British Columbia, to take a random example, includes ridings whose populations on the 1961 census run from barely 55,000 to over 78,000. The tolerance has also reduced the massive rural-urban differentiation that was formerly considered acceptable: the riding named York-Scarborough has been reduced from 267,252 to 80,715, and Mercier from 233,964 to 74,204. It is still true that urban seats are larger than rural, a fact clearly acceptable to Parliament.

At the same time, the redistribution of the 1960's did not eliminate the anomalies that arise from guaranteeing each Province at least as many M.P.'s as it has senators: the largest of Prince Edward Island's four seats is barely 30,000 and the electoral quota for New Brunswick was 59,794, as compared with 67,001 for Nova Scotia, which has just one constituency more. Other results included the elimination of the two surviving two-member seats of Halifax and Queens, and a substantial increase in the number of seats allotted to the major metropolitan areas. The metropolitan area of Toronto . . . now includes at least twenty seats as compared with the eighteen it previously held, and Montreal twenty-five as against twenty-one.

The nature and extent of the shifts in constituencies occasioned by the redistribution of the 1960's has inevitably stimulated speculation about the effects on the fortunes of political parties, a consideration which was of course not within the purview of any of the commissions as they drew their boundaries. The most striking single aspect of the latest redistribution, indeed, was its impartiality, a characteristic which revealed itself in two unprecedented ways. The debates on the maps in the House of Commons, since they concentrated on objections, gave few opportunities to members who wished to speak in favour of the new system; even so, the

7. *Debates*, April 29, 1968 (daily ed.), p. 4552.

debates were far less disputatious than those which had accompanied any previous redistribution. The official Opposition took the lead in criticizing the maps, but nonetheless a leading Conservative, Hon. Walter Dinsdale, said of the Manitoba map, "Under the circumstances I feel that the commission did the best job possible.[8] Furthermore no critic of the maps, whatever views he held of the ignorance, arrogance, or incompetence of the commission in his Province, even raised the charge of partisanship. In the light of the debates which led up to the *Electoral Boundaries Readjustment Act* of 1964, the redistribution which followed must be regarded as a considerable success: Parliament succeeded in eliminating the vast disparities in constituency populations, and succeeded in taking the readjustment of boundaries out of partisan hands. Anyone who thinks these are not remarkable parliamentary achievements should examine closely some of the previous redistributions. It is perhaps fortunate that not all political problems in Canada take ninety-nine years to find a working solution; even so, the objections registered in the House of Commons to the results of the Act of 1964 suggest that the new system too may not be permanent.

8. *Debates*, May 4, 1966 (daily ed.), p. 4703.

15

The Speakership of the Canadian House of Commons: Some Proposals*

DENIS SMITH

The status and responsibilities of the Speaker of the Canadian House of Commons are governed by the BNA Act, the Senate and House of Commons Act, the House of Commons Act, the Standing Orders of the House of Commons, and the conventions of the constitution relating to the practices of the House of Commons. The significance of the office derives above all from its representative character: the Speaker is the "first commoner," the spokesman and representative of the House of Commons in its relations with other institutions, and the chief servant of the House of Commons in the conduct of its own affairs. The central importance of the office thus rests upon the importance of the House of Commons. Because the House of Commons is the "superior power" in the constitution of the United Kingdom, the Canadian House of Commons is, similarly, the superior power in the Canadian constitution, since the preamble to the BNA Act establishes the convention that Canada shall have a constitution "similar in principle to that of the United Kingdom". The first member of the House of Commons, its presiding officer and representative, should occupy a position of dignity and eminence in keeping with the preeminence of the institution itself.[1] Canadian parliamentary experience, extending from before the Confederation of the Provinces, has demonstrated the advantages of a free House of Commons in Canada, and the importance to that free House of Commons of a Speaker who commands universal respect and honour.

---

*A paper prepared for the House of Commons Special Committee on Procedure and Organization, April, 1965.

1. "Excepting only the Sovereign herself, no personage throughout the structure of British parliamentary government occupies a higher pinnacle of prestige than the Speaker of the House of Commons. He embodies in his own person the dignity of the nation's representative assembly. The honour which is accorded his office is such as to sustain the authority of any incumbent. weak and strong alike . . . whoever assumes the Speaker's historic mantle inherits the dignity that goes with it, a dignity that is unfailingly maintained and enhanced at every opportunity." (Philip Laundy, *The Office of Speaker*, p. 7.)

In its conduct and supervision of the nation's affairs, the House of Commons is guided by certain long-recognized principles. Among these are the responsibilities

> . . . to protect a minority and restrain the improvidence or tyranny of a majority; to secure the transaction of public business in an orderly manner; to enable every member to express his opinion within limits necessary to preserve decorum and prevent an unnecessary waste of time; to give abundant opportunity for the consideration of every measure, and to prevent any legislative action being taken upon sudden impulse.[2]

These constitutional duties of the House of Commons are distinctly different from the duties of the Cabinet, and even from those of the majority party in the House of Commons; they require a balancing of the rights and interests of majority and minority in order both that the public business may be efficiently transacted, and that the interests of every section of the public may be advocated and protected against the use of arbitrary authority. The rules of procedure established in the Standing Orders reflect the dual responsibility of the House, and the Speaker of the House of Commons, as the House's chief servant, is given the responsibility of applying the rules in this spirit. The Speaker is the servant, not of any part of the House, nor of any temporary majority in the House, but of the best interest of the House as this interest has been distilled in the practices of the House over many generations.

Members of the Canadian House of Commons have always recognized that the successful exercise of his duty requiries above all that the Speaker shall be impartial and shall be seen to be impartial. "Confidence in the impartiality of the Speaker is an indispensable condition of the working of procedure, and many conventions exist which have as their object not only to ensure the impartiality of the Speaker but also to ensure that his impartiality is generally recognized."[3] From the time of the first election to the Chair of the House in 1867, members of all parties have echoed their belief in the absolute need for an impartial Speaker, and on more than one occasion have reflected wistfully that the conventions and rules governing the Canadian Speakership make achievement of the ideal difficult. Canadian observers of the Speakership have almost always been kind in their judgments of those who have occupied the Chair, but have been disappointed by the weakness or absence of practical buttresses which will support and guarantee the good intentions of the incumbents. This paper will examine what institutional weaknesses may make it difficult for Speakers in the Canadian House of Commons to assure their own independence and the appearance of independence; and it will consider whether the Speakership, as presently provided for, possesses the prestige and distinction that the office should reasonably have as the symbol of the House of Commons' authority.

THE ELECTION OF THE SPEAKER

Section 44 of the BNA Act provides that "the House of Commons on its first assembling after a general election shall proceed with all practicable speed to elect one of its members to be speaker." Section 45 of the Act provides for the election in the same manner of a Speaker during the life of a Parliament in the event of a vacancy occurring in the Chair through resignation, dismissal, or death. The ritual of election, the Speaker's claim to the Governor-General for the rights and privileges of the Commons, the Governor-General's grant to the House of its ancient rights and privileges, are familiar and need no special comment.

One aspect of the Speaker's election, however, deserves reconsideration: this is the custom that the nomination to the Chair is proposed by the Prime Minister and seconded by a Minister.[4]

It is natural that the Prime Minister, as the leader of the House of Commons, should take the initiative in seeking a candidate for the office of Speaker. But it is less fitting that he should actually propose the nomination to the Chair. This practice is likely to create the impression among members of the House of Commons and the public that the choice of a Speaker is the prerogative of the Prime Minister; and this is especially likely if a change of government has occurred. The selection of a candidate for Speaker by the Prime Minister in this circumstance easily becomes confused with the process of selecting a cabinet. The Prime Minister may be encouraged to think of the Speakership as just one of the offices within his patronage, for distribution among his colleagues according to the same political calculations that apply to the nomination of Ministers; and if the Prime Minister has a higher concept of his duty, the public at least may be confused.

Members of the House of Commons acknowledged long ago that to emphasize the independence of the Chair, it would be desirable to begin by treating the nomination in a conspicuously non-partisan way. The form of nomination should demonstrate, as other conventions do, that "the House chooses and elects its Speaker; he is in no sense the choice of the Government – in no sense the choice of the Prime Minister."[5] The Speaker's position as the independent servant of the entire House could be symbolized by arranging for his formal nomination to be made by two private members, one from the government side and one from the opposition side, after consultation and agreement among all parties on a suitable candidate. While possessing the confidence of the majority party, he would not be its official candidate for this office. The means of nomination would discourage the suspicion that the Speakership is given as a reward for party services.

2. Sir J. G. Bourinot, quoted in Beauchesne, Arthur, *Rules and Forms of the House of Commons of Canada*, 4th edition, Toronto: Carswell 1958, citation 4, p. 8.

3. *Ibid.*, citation 68 (1), pp. 56-57.

4. On three occasions, in 1953, 1957, and 1958, the nomination has been seconded by the leader of the Opposition as a mark of the official Opposition's confidence in the candidate. While this practice improves upon the usual one by requiring consultation and by taking part of the responsibility for the nomination out of the hands of the Government, it is still not ideal. The nomination remains, in appearance, that of the leaders of the House, rather than of the whole House.

5. Rt. Hon. Arthur Meighen, *Canada, House of Commons Debates*, March 8, 1922, quoted in Beauchesne, *op. cit.*, citation 28(1), p. 22.

The adoption of this reform would require only a change in practice on the part of the Prime Minister. He would have to ensure consultation among the parties on the nominee, through the usual channels, and arrange for the candidate's nomination by backbenchers on both sides of the House.

Although five Canadian Speakers have been re-elected to the Chair for a second term,[6] and one of these for a third term, the normal Canadian practice has been to elect a new Speaker at the opening of each new Parliament. Occupation of the Chair has never effectively been regarded as a career by members of the House of Commons, but rather as a three, four or five year interlude in a political career. The nomination to the Speakership has been regarded as one of the gifts in the hands of the leader of the majority party, and never has the nomination gone to a member of any other but the party forming the Government. In the four cases in which the incumbents were re-elected to the Chair, no change of government had occurred; the former party affiliation of the Speaker thus remained with the government party. . . .

What is the case for continuity in the Chair? It has been made repeatedly in this country and in the United Kingdom, and it is straightforward. Sir Robert Peel expressed it succintly in proposing the re-election of the Speaker at Westminister in 1841:

First, I do not think it for the public advantage that the election for the Chair should necessarily be made the object of a party.

Secondly, I do not think it would be just towards a Speaker who has shown himself well qualified for his office, and has in my opinion acted fairly and impartially, to reject him.

Thirdly, I think that the late Speaker, if he be re-elected with the general goodwill of the House, will have greater authority and power to preserve order than a Speaker elected after a party contest.[7]

In spite of the virtually unanimous professions of confidence in the particular occupants of the Chair in Canada made by parliamentarians since 1867, there has lingered in Ottawa a feeling that the Speaker's impartiality cannot always be taken for granted. This feeling has been most evident among members of the opposition parties. While no decisive evidence of collusion between the Government and the Chair has ever been presented in the House, and while the record of Canadian Speakers as independent men seems, in retrospect, remarkably good, at various times members of the opposition have suspected bias against them in the rulings of the Speaker. The suspicion has been given support by the conventions governing the Speaker's election, and especially the convention that the Speakership changes hands at the beginning of each Parliament. The nomination, as has been mentioned, frequently becomes confused with the choice of a cabinet. The successful nominee, knowing that he can expect only a short term in the Chair, is discouraged from regarding the election as the beginning of a non-partisan career as Speaker; and members of the Opposition are forever wary that he will make his rulings in the knowledge that his future career depends on the favour of the majority party. There is always likely to be a doubt among the Opposition that the Speaker, what ever his claim to independence, regards his years in the Chair as simply an interruption in a party career: a period of suspended loyalty, but one nevertheless in which party loyalty remains present at some level of his consciousness. The office does not quite inspire the judicial trust that it should, because members know that the Speaker may shortly become a partisan again. It is the uncertain expectation that above all destroys absolute trust. And yet the authority of the Speaker in guiding the House depends essenially upon the absence of suspicion, on "perfect confidence . . . on the part of all the members of the House of Commons."[8]

To have perfect confidence, the House must know that the Speaker "has nothing to lose by doing right and nothing to gain by doing wrong."[9] The most certain guarantee of this is to give the Speaker secure tenure in the Chair, and to remove his future entirely from the patronage of any one party in the House. If the Speaker is to possess the confidence that members of the judiciary are normally accorded, he must hold office on judicial terms; he should not have to plan for another career, most possibly political, after a short term in the Chair. He should be encouraged by a guarantee of secure tenure to regard the Speakership as a career which needs to be undertaken for its own sake alone. He should be able to expect ten, fifteen, or twenty years in the office, rather than four or five.[10]

The argument for competence in the Chair reinforces the case for continuity. A Speaker with long experience is not only likely to be above suspicion of partisanship, but also to be a more capable Speaker than a temporary one. Mastery in the Chair is not something that can be acquired without practice. At the least, the present custom involves frequent periods of breaking-in to the Chair during which the Speakers' knowledge of their task and their authority may be shaky.[11]

6. Cockburn, Rhodes, Lemieúx, Michener, and Lamoureux.

7. Quoted in W. I. Jennings, *Parliament*, Cambridge: The University Press, 1961, p. 66.

8. J. H. Aitchison, *The Speakership in 1962*, a talk on the CBC National Network, July 19, 1962.

9. J. H. Aitchison, "The Speakership of the Canadian House of Commons," in R. M. Clark (ed.), *Canadian Issues*, Toronto: University of Toronto Press, 1961.

10. The longest tenures of the Speakership at Westminster have been those of Onslow (1728-1761), Abbott (1802-1817), Manners-Sutton (1817-1835), Shaw-Lefevre (1839-1857), Denison (1857-1872), and Lowther (1905-1921). The average tenure of the five twentieth century Speakers preceding the present one has been eleven years. The former incumbent, Sir Harry Hylton-Foster, was first elected to the Chair in 1959, and was sustained in office after the change of government in October, 1964.

11. "After a Canadian Speaker has spent his first few years in this precarious position he finds that a new election has been held and that he is quietly dropped, just as he is reaching maturity in office." W. F. Dawson, *Procedure in the Canadian House of Commons*, Toronto: University of Toronto Press, 1962, pp. 80-81.

Continuity in the office is desirable; but, it needs to be more carefully defined. Proposals for an extended term do not call for literal permanence in the Chair. The House must remain the master of its own affairs, and the Speaker must remain the servant of the House in the application of the rules adopted by the House. If, in spite of the best will of the House, a Speaker is seriously incompetent, or biased, the House must possess the means of showing its dissatisfaction and replacing him. "Permanency" in the Chair should mean only that the Speaker will be re-elected without opposition by the House at the opening of each new Parliament for as long as he is able and willing to serve and continues to possess the confidence of the House. The elected term would still be for a single Parliament, and an unsatisfactory Speaker could be replaced in the next Parliament. The same convention of confidence in the Speaker would apply as at present: the possibility of a substantive motion of censure would remain, and the support of such a motion by a substantial minority would be a sign that the Speaker's position had become untenable.

This reform can be achieved without any change in the Standing Orders. It requires only the agreement of the parties in the House, a public commitment by the party leaders in each Parliament, before dissolution, to support the incumbent Speaker for re-election in the new House *whatever party wins the intervening election,* an electoral agreement in the Speaker's constituency, and the good faith of the parties in carrying out the commitment in the new Parliament. In 1958 and 1962, appeals were made to the party leaders to commit themselves to support the re-election of Mr. Speaker Michener to the Chair in advance of, and whatever the outcome of, the general elections. But the party leaders failed to act. Some firm public commitment seems necessary if the existing practice is to be altered: the mere expression of general interest in reform, without commitment to it, has proven futile. The long-term maintenance of the convention would depend upon the will of the House to do so in subsequent Parliaments; but if one Speaker survived a change of government the custom would have passed its most severe test.

The establishment of continuity in the Chair should make no difference to the practice of alternating between English-speaking and French-speaking incumbents. The existing custom would be maintained as a matter of course; and it should be taken for granted that every Speaker will be fluent in both the languages of Parliament.

THE SPEAKER AT GENERAL ELECTIONS

If the Speaker is to be re-elected to the Chair for more than a single term, the Speaker's role in general elections is inevitably complicated. The chief purposes of continuity are to encourage the fact and the appearance of impartiality, and to ensure competence in the Chair. But in the present situation, however impartial and aloof from party activity the Speaker may be during the life of a Parliament, if he wishes to run for Parliament again, he is forced to fall back into the partisan struggle at each general election, and to risk defeat. He is opposed by partisan candidates, and is faced with an awkward dilemma: he must either discourage his constituency organization from conducting a partisan campaign (in which case he places himself at a disadvantage in comparison with opponents who lack similar restraint), or he must throw himself and his organization fully into the battle at the expense of his reputation for non-partisanship. The immediacy of this dilemma was painfully revealed in the 1962 general election, when Mr. Speaker Michener, whose conduct of the Speakership was universally admired, and who might well have been re-elected to the Chair in the 25th Parliament, was defeated in his constituency. . . .

The reluctance of the parties to protect the Speaker from partisan conflict in his constituency has, understandably, prompted advocates of a continuing Speakership to accuse the parties of hypocrisy. Professor Aitchison remarked in 1962 that "I am angry . . . because those with power to act, though they profess to be committed to the principle of a permanent Speakership, refused to do what was easy and simple to put the principle into effect."[12] Perhaps the lesson of 1958, 1962 and 1963 is less simple. It seems evident that no electoral arrangement between the parties in the Speaker's constituency can be made quickly, after a parliamentary dissolution, since by this time the momentum of party conflict in the constituency, the commitment of volunteers and the organizaion of the compaign, is too far advanced to be halted. No party is willing to consider such an act of restraint unless it is sure the others will do the same; but the parties have neither the time, nor are they in the mood at this stage, to consider such an agreement. The decentralized nature of party organization in Canada, too, makes it necessary to gain agreement both at the national and the constituency levels; and the diffusion of responsibility relieves any one level of blame for the failure of an all-party arrangement.

In addition, as previously noted, there has never been any formal guarantee that the incumbent Speaker would in fact be renominated to the Chair even if he were acclaimed in in his constituency. No Prime Minister has ever publicly committed himself in advance to the re-election of the incumbent to the Speakership in the next House. . . . The public understanding of the Speaker's special position of independence is probably not as general as it is in the United Kingdom, and a party contest in his constituency is taken for granted as the usual practice rather than the exception in Canada. An uncontested election would require explanation and justification, even among those active in party work and presumably relatively familiar with the nature of parliamentary government, and such justification, to be sufficiently convincing, would require time. It would also require authority behind it: the authority of a few concerned citizens has been shown to be insufficient.

The familiar criticisms of uncontested elections in the Speaker's constituency are that they result in the atrophy of party organizations in the constituency, and that they deprive the electors in the constituency of the opportunity to exercise their fundamental right to choose among party

12. Aitchison, *The Speakership In 1962.*

candidates at general elections. The further argument is frequently made that after his election to the Chair, the Speaker's constituents are virtually deprived of normal representation in Parliament.

The first complaint is, within limits, justified. The acceptance of the principle of acclamation for the Speaker in his constituency would mean the intentional weakening of party associations in the constituency for the period that that member holds the Chair. To be acceptable, such an act of self-denial would have to be undertaken equally by all parties. One of Mr. Coldwell's complaints in 1958 was that as long as the Speaker himself was proposed by a party association as a party candidate, the opposition parties could hardly be expected to treat him as an independent. The Speaker's party organization would be free to exercise its muscles in the campaign, but the opposition organizations would be expected not to do so. When the Speaker finally retired and normal party competition returned to the constituency, the opposition organizations might well be moribund. The fair solution would seem to be for each party association to nominate the Speaker as a non-partisan candidate, and for each association to participate in the campaign for his re-election. While political activity in the constituency would be low, this would at least stimulate some continuity in the associations during the Speaker's term of office; and the party from which the Speaker was originally chosen would not gain any special advantage as 'the Speaker's party.'

The second criticism, that all electors should have the right to choose among party candidates, can only be met with the argument that, while this is a fundamental right in a free parliamentary system, the successful operation of that very system requires that one constituency should temporarily give up this right in order to support an independent Speaker of the House, the protector of the rights of all parties in the House. Two conflicting principles, both of them basic ones in a parliamentary system, must be reconciled, and the parties must weigh the importance of the Speaker's position against the right of voters in his constituency to express partisan choices. It can be argued in support of all-party co-operation in the Speaker's constituency that two-party or all-party co-operation has frequently occurred for other reasons in various constituencies, formally or informally, without any serious objection on principle that the electors are being deprived of a free choice. What is proposed is not, in any case, that all possibility of an alternative choice should be eliminated in the constituency: only that there should be no *official* party opponents. If an independent candidate wished to contest the Speaker's seat, there would of course be no means of preventing his candidacy.

The third complaint about the Speaker's constituency is that, while he is in the Chair, the Speaker ceases to be an effective representative of his constituents' interests. This claim is not justified by experience. The Speaker does give up his public advocacy of these interests from the floor of the House; but he continues to perform many private tasks for his constituents, as any private member does; and he continues to speak informally for his constituents to the various ministries. His position of eminence in the House is probably advantageous for his constituents,

. . . because none of us is under any illusion at all that a request to a minister from yourself, Mr. Speaker, would probably produce much faster results than would be achieved by one of the political proletariat here.[13]

The Hon. Marcel Lambert has suggested that this judgment is applicable also to the Speaker of the Canadian House of Commons.[14]

There seems to be no unanswerable objection to the acclamation of the Speaker in his constituency; and it is evident that no determined effort has yet been made by the parties to arrange for his acclamation in any general election in Canada. It would be appropriate, as the most simple step toward the re-election of the Speaker without a party contest, for the parties in the House now to make a real and coordinated effort to arrange for his acclamation at the next general election. A public show of common purpose by all parties in the House, and support for it in the Speaker's constituency by the local party associations, are essential if the precedent is to be established. A commitment to acclaim the Speaker should be declared long enough in advance of the general election to illustrate its sincerity and to permit time for the principle to be publicly defended. And it would have to be accompanied by the commitment recommended earlier, to support the renomination of the same person to the Chair in the next House.

AN ALTERNATIVE PROPOSAL FOR THE SPEAKER'S CONSTITUENCY

Acclamation of the Speaker in his constituency would require political agreement. If the parties believe in the importance of an impartial and continuing Speaker, this agreement should be possible to obtain through patient discussion and negotiation officially supported by the party caucuses and organizations. But, as the British experience has shown, such gentlemen's agreements are by their nature temporary and insecure, and must frequently be defended and renewed. . . . The relative autonomy of Canadian constituency associations from their parent bodies would probably make agreements to acclaim the Speaker even more precarious in Canada than in the United Kingdom. If agreement were seriously attempted in Canada and failed, the Speaker would again face political opposition and the possibility of defeat in his constituency; Mr. Speaker Michener's defeat while in the Chair showed that this unfortunate possibility is real.

The expected difficulty of acclaiming the Speaker, along with the 1962 example, has prompted some supporters of a continuing Speakership in Canada to propose another arrangement for the Speaker's seat. This involves the creation of a special constituency of Parliament Hill, whose electors would be the members of the House of Commons, and whose member would be the Speaker of the House of Commons. Upon election to the

13. Richard Marsh, M.P., speaking in the United Kingdom House of Commons in 1963, *U.K. Parliamentary Debates (Hansard)*, Session 1962-63, Vol. 676, Column 230.

14. Conversation with Mr. Lambert, February 19, 1965.

Chair, the Speaker would cease to sit for an ordinary constituency; his former constituency would be opened to a by-election, and the Speaker would no longer face the danger of partisan opposition on the hustings. Aside from the special nature of his constituency, the Speaker's election to the Chair would be governed by the existing practices. An election to the Chair would occur on the first day of meeting of a new Parliament, or immediately upon the resignation or death of an incumbent Speaker. The existing rule governing a substantive motion of censure of the Speaker would stand. But, since the purpose of the proposal is to encourage continuity in the Chair, it would be assumed that the Speaker, once elected as the member for Parliament Hill, would be re-elected without opposition by the House as long as he was a satisfactory Speaker and wished to serve.

The conception of a special constituency for the Speaker of the House of Commons is not new. In 1939, a *Select Committee on Parliamentary Elections (Mr. Speaker's Seat)* considered and reported upon such a proposal for the Speaker's seat at Westminster. It had been asked to examine

What steps, if any, should be taken to ensure that, having due regard to the constitutional rights of the electors, the Speaker, during his continuance in office, shall not be required to take part in a contested parliamentary election.[15]

But the Committee recommended no change in the existing arrangements for the Speaker's seat. After considering the suggestion for a special Speaker's constituency, the Committee concluded that

To alter the status of the Speaker so that he ceased to be returned to the House of Commons by the same electoral methods as other members or as a representative of a Parliamentary constituency would be ... repugnant to the custom and tradition of the House ... The proper aloofness of the Speaker from the political actions of members would in time deteriorate into the detachment of the official.[16]

A further overriding consideration influencing the Committee was that, since the Speakership at Westminster was already successfully non-partisan and continuing, it would be unwise to recommend any departure from tradition which might itself make the Speakership an object of political controversy during discussion of the recommendation. It is impossible to tell from the document which objection to change weighed most heavily with the Committee: the desire to avoid controversy, the generalized complaint that a special seat would be "repugnant to the custom and tradition of the House," or the fear that a specially elected Speaker might grow aloof from the other members of the House. Given the already generally satisfactory conventions surrounding the British Speakership, the Committee's conclusion seems readily justifiable. But it is also apparent that the Committee's conclusion does not necessarily apply to the different circumstances of Canada.

The argument for avoiding controversy, for one thing, carries little weight here. The Canadian Speakership has unfortunately been a recent object of controversy, is not yet satisfactorily protected from political pressures, and needs public defence. There would be little sense in claiming in Canada that certain reforms should not be considered because they might involve the Chair in political controversy: they *need* to be considered precisely to remove the Chair from political controversy. The Canadian Speakership has suffered from recurrent suspicions of bias, from a severe motion of censure, and from the electoral defeat of an incumbent Speaker. These are all complaints peculiar to the Canadian situation, and demand the application of special remedies. A special constituency for the Speaker seems at least worth considerate study.

The argument from tradition has strength: it suggests caution in the application of parliamentary reform, to ensure that valuable features of the parliamentary system will not be lost unwittingly in the pursuit of change. But Parliament is not an institution based upon an unchangeable or logical pattern. It is full of incongruities that exist because they work. The test for parliamentary devices should be whether they actually achieve what they are meant to achieve; if they do not, then other devices may legitimately be adopted. It is not "repugnant to the custom and tradition of the House" to have an independent Speaker: members since 1867 have held this to be desirable. If the creation of a special constituency will make this possible, without creating any very obvious difficulties, it should be worth the trial.

The suggestion that a Speaker elected from a special constituency of Parliament Hill would cease to look upon himself as one Commoner among others, and would grow superior, aloof, and bureaucratic in his approach to the Speakership, is difficult to assess because it rests upon conjecture. But it is open to some doubt. For one thing, it is inaccurate to say that the Canadian Speaker in his present situation is a member of the House like any other. He is already an extraordinary M.P., not an ordinary one. He has great powers in the conduct of debate not possessed by other members; he is non-partisan; he has a special position in the order of precedence; he has the authority of a long tradition to sustain him; he alone among the members of the House continues to exercise his authority as an officer of the House after a parliamentary dissolution. To create a special constituency for the Speaker would not suddenly and unalterably set him apart from his fellows in the House: it would merely confirm in one more way that he is, and must be, a member apart. The constituency of Parliament Hill would be a "constitutional fiction", but there are already many commonly accepted and convenient constitutional fictions in the Canadian parliamentary system. In many senses, the Speaker already acts, in effect, as "the member for Parliament Hill", since the statutes require him to do so.

On the other hand, a Speaker elected from a special constituency would be influenced in many ways to remain the servant of the House, and sympathetic to it. Above all, his function would be what it is today, and he would carry it out within the House, not apart from it. He would have to be re-elected at the commencement of each Parliament. If he failed to act

15. Quoted in *The Times*, April 14, 1939.
16. *Ibid.*

fairly or competently during the life of a Parliament, he would still be subject to a motion of censure; which it would be in his interest to avoid by acting in the best traditions of the Chair. He would invariably be a person with some previous experience in the House, and familiar with it. If it is now possible for a member who is elected Speaker to throw off his former political commitments by an act of will and imagination, it should equally be possible for a Speaker elected from a special Speaker's constituency to continue to regard himself essentially as a member of the House of Commons.

The creation of a constituency of Parliament Hill would permanently solve the problem of partisan competition in the Speaker's constituency. It might be easier to achieve than acclamation for the Speaker in a normal constituency, since it would involve the decision only of members of Parliament; the interests of local party associations and prospective candidates would not be influencing factors. Once established, there would be no need for the renewal of any all-party agreements except the agreement on the initial choice of a candidate by the whole House.

Because the special constituency is an unusual departure from existing practice, it might be held in reserve by the House as a reform to be adopted *if* the parties fail at the next election to make any progress toward acclamation of the Speaker in his constituency. There might possibly be a commitment by the House, and by the parties in their platforms, to support a Bill to create a special constituency at the beginning of the next Parliament if acclamation fails.

THE SPEAKER'S AUTHORITY

However competent he may be, the Canadian Speaker suffers from one fatal disadvantage. He is simply unable to establish his authority in the House because the Standing Orders provide for appeals against his rulings.[17] The appeals rule is unfortunate from every point of view. The confidence of a Speaker who attempts to apply the rules judiciously and fairly can constantly be undermined by members of the House who are not always careful students of the rules, but who may challenge his rulings on irrelevant grounds. Appeals can be used by members of the opposition as weapons of delay and harassment against the government; in this case, the government majority normally comes to the support of the Speaker and creates the unfortunate impression that the Speaker is an agent of the government in the application of the rules. If, on the other hand, the majority is unhappy enough with a ruling to challenge it, the ruling can be overridden on appeal, whatever its merits, merely on the grounds that it does not serve the interests of the majority. A majority which resorts frequently to such a practice will entirely destroy the authority of the Speaker and the consistency with which the rules are applied. Such a possibility denies the very purpose of the Standing Orders. In both cases, the interpretation of the rules is taken out of the hands of the Speaker, whose object is to be impartial, and thrown into the political battle between parties. . . . There is no justification for the retention of the appeals rule.

Two simple reforms are possible. (Both are suggested by Professor Dawson in his *Procedure In the Canadian House of Commons*.[18]) Standing Order 12(1) could be amended to remove the opportunity for appeal. If this change in the rules were accompanied by the institution of continuity in the Chair, it would further strengthen the authority of the Speaker and remove one more suggestion of his dependence upon the Government. Given a Speaker whose future career is no longer at the mercy of the Government, the Opposition should be prepared to signify its full confidence in his independence by giving up its present right to challenge his rulings.

The Speaker, however, may sometimes make mistakes in applying the rules, and occasionally invites appeals on this ground. . . . The simple abolition of appeals would provide no recourse for the House against patently mistaken rulings, except the extreme recourse of a substantive motion of censure. An intermediate measure of reform might provide that an appeal could only be made by substantive motion accompanied by the citation of authorities and precedents in writing, and that such an appeal would be referred automatically by the House either to the Committee on Privileges and Elections or to the Committee on Procedure (if it were to become a Standing Committee). The appropriate Committee would examine the merits of the appeal, and report to the House, which would act upon the recommendation of the Committee to sustain the ruling or allow the appeal. This deliberate and formal procedure would eliminate most nuisance appeals, but would permit legitimate appeals based upon careful study of the rules.

THE DIGNITY OF THE SPEAKER

Two points are involved, one practical and one symbolic. The Speaker must be rewarded sufficiently to balance the tension, the sacrifice of a party career, and the abandonment of a private occupation, that commitment to the Chair involves. The rewards of the office must be enough consistently to attract men of talent; and they must be enough to free the Speaker from any financial dependence which might compromise his position as the servant of the whole House. The Speaker's perquisites should, further, illustrate and reinforce his prestige as the leading member of the House of Commons: they must be the sufficient outward and visible signs of his pre-eminence.

The demands upon the Speaker's time and energies are extraordinary. He is tied to Parliament Hill during a session even more securely than is a Minister of the Crown; he is responsible for a great volume of official entertainment; his alertness is constantly required while he is actually in

17. *Standing Order 12(1)*: "Mr. Speaker shall preserve order and decorum, and shall decide questions of order, subject to an appeal to the House without debate. In explaining a point of order or practice, he shall state the standing order or authority applicable to the case."

18. W. F. Dawson, *Procedure in the Canadian House of Commons*, Toronto, 1962, p. 84.

the Chair; he has the responsibility for managing frequent delicate negotiations among the parties; and he is the head of a large administrative department. Merely to relieve the Speaker from any unnecessary distractions and to encourage the full concentration of his energies upon his duties requires substantial material rewards.

It would be appropriate, in the light of both of his onerous duties and his symbolic position as representative of the House of Commons, to make the salary of the Speaker at least equivalent to that of a Minister. At present, the Speaker's income, including allowances, falls $6,500 short of this.[19] The Speakership should be recognized in the estimates as the equivalent of a Cabinet office.

In addition, the Speaker should be provided at the commencement of his term with a moving allowance which would permit him to bring his family and possessions to Ottawa at parliamentary expense. This allowance should probably be in the range of $1,000 to $1,500. His residential allowance should be somewhat increased – perhaps to $5,000 – or renewed provision should be made for a Speaker's residence in the Parliament Buildings. An entertainment allowance should be provided as a specific item in the Speaker's estimates. The Speaker should be assured the permanent use of the country residence at Kingsmere.

Certain other reforms are desirable to enhance the dignity of the office of Speaker. The Canadian Speaker now ranks tenth in the order of precedence, below ambassadors and high commissions, Cabinet Ministers, Lieutenant-Governors, members of the Privy Council, and the Speaker of the Senate. He is given a relatively inconspicuous place in official ceremonies. The elevation of the Speaker to third place in the order of precedence, following the Governor-General and the Prime Minister, would emphasize the significance both of the Speakership and of the House it represents. The Speaker's official wardrobe might contain, besides the black gown and the tricorn hat, a more colorful ceremonial robe for use in formal processions and ceremonies outside the House.

The Speaker's integrity as the spokesman for Parliament must be more scrupulously recognized by the ministry and the civil service than has been customary in Canada. The Speaker's jurisdiction over Parliament Hill as a representative of the House should be clearly established. Ceremonies and conferences on the Hill should be the Speaker's responsibility, rather than the responsibility of the ministry, and the Cabinet should not take for granted that whatever arrangements it wishes to make will be satisfactory to the Speaker. The Speaker should have a certain clearly established power to requisition the use of facilities by the House of Commons for its purposes, without having to appeal as a supplicant to the ministry.

The Speaker's ambiguous relationship to the Commissioners of Internal Economy, and through them to the Treasury Board and the Cabinet, should be clarified. Since the Commissioners are given responsibility for the preparation and support of the estimates of the House of Commons, and the House and Speaker are, in theory, independent of the government, the Commissioners too should have a formal independence of the government. At present, the four Commissioners of Internal Economy provided for by the House of Commons Act in addition to the Speaker are all members of the Cabinet. While it is obviously necessary for the Cabinet to be represented on a Commission which prepares estimates for the approval of the Treasury Board, it is not necessary that they should dominate it. In view of the Speaker's essential independence, it is transparently undersirable that they should do so. An amendment to the House of Commons Act should provide that two of the Commissioners of Internal Economy shall be appointed from the Opposition benches upon the advice of the Opposition parties. A portion of the Speaker's revenues, too, including the salary and allowances of the Speaker and Deputy Speaker, might be made a statutory charge upon the Consolidated Revenue Fund and therefore not subject to annual review by the Commissioners, the Treasury Board, the Cabinet, and Parliament.

THE SPEAKER IN RETIREMENT

If the Speakership is to gain the reputation for absolute aloofness from politics that the office requires, the nature of the Speaker's retirement is also a matter of concern. An ex-Speaker must be as neutral in politics as he was during his tenure of office if he is to avoid casting doubt retrospectively upon his impartiality, or upon the impartiality of his successors. The convention must be established that a retiring Speaker departs altogether from the partisan political scene. This convention, like others involved in the creation of a continuing Speakership, demands a substantial sacrifice from Speakers, and must be offset by compensating privileges, if it is to be acceptable.

The ex-Speaker must be assured of financial security, so that he will not be forced for economic reasons to turn again to a political career. A special pension in addition to his normal parliamentary pension is desirable: perhaps in the range of $10,000 per year; and this pension should be made a statutory charge upon the Consolidated Fund.

Careful consideration must be given to whether a Speaker should be free to accept any kind of public office upon retirement. If such an appointment is made at the discretion of the ministry, the Speaker's future remains subject to partisan considerations. . . .

Public appointments of ex-Speakers must certainly be governed by scrupulous conditions. They must either be automatic, involving no individual discretion by the Prime Minister, or they must be made only after consultation and agreement with the leaders of the opposition parties. The offices themselves must be above political reproach, like the Speakership. An automatic appointment to the Senate is a possibility, providing the ex-Speaker recognizes that his role as a Senator cannot be that of an ordinary

---

19. The Speaker receives $18,000 as an M.P. ($6,000 tax-free), $9,000 as Speaker, a $3,000 allowance in lieu of residence, and a $1,000 motor car allowance. A Minister receives $18,000 as an M.P. ($6,000 tax-free), $15,000 as a Minister, a $2,000 motor car allowance, and a $1,500 allowance in lieu of residence. *(Estimates for the Fiscal Year 1964-1965,)*

partisan. Appointments to major Royal Commissions of investigation are a possibility. Appointments to senior diplomatic positions may similarly be appropriate. The possibility of elevation to the Governor-Generalship is perhaps the most attractive one, since the two positions are alike in their essential natures. It would be wise in Canada to cultivate the special talents needed for such non-political offices of state, and to encourage those citizens of appropriate skills and ambitions to prepare themselves for this kind of service. The changes in the practices surrounding the Speakership recommended in this paper may thus be seen within the larger perspective of the national interest: the cultivation of a habit of service to the nation which transcends the ordinary interests of party. For the political parties themselves to promote the strengthening of such a habit would surely do credit to their own national spirit and generosity.

16
*The Role of the Senate**

THE GOVERNMENT OF THE PROVINCE OF ONTARIO

The Senate was originally envisaged as fulfilling two main functions: to take a second look at legislation; and to represent and protect provincial and regional interests.

The Senate has been useful in fulfilling the first function. Senators have often made valuable suggestions for improving legislation, and have participated in a variety of worthwhile committees of enquiry and research.

However, the Senate has been much less successful in fulfilling its second function. Provincial and regional representation has instead devolved on the Federal cabinet and on the provincial governments.

There are three areas to consider if the Senate is to be reformed to represent these interests more effectively:
i) the pattern of representation in the Senate;
ii) provincial participation in the process by which senators are chosen; and
iii) the powers and responsibilities assigned to the Senate.

Representation Pattern

Representation in second chambers is not ordinarily on the basis of population. In federations, such representation is usually based on the federated units having equal or weighted representation. The latter method is the one now used in Canada, though in reviewing the Senate serious examination should be made of the former method, particularly if representation by population is to be applied more rigorously in the Lower House.

The Selection Process

At present, senators are appointed by the federal government. If the Senate is to represent more effectively the interests of Provinces or groups of Provinces, and if the federal character of Canada is to be preserved, provision must be made for provincial participation in the process by which senators are chosen.

---

*Included in the *Propositions of the Government of Ontario,* submitted to the Continuing Committee of Officials on the Constitution, December, 1968.

Powers and Responsibilities of the Senate

While there are many considerations under this topic, one deserves special mention at this time. The increasing importance of federal-provincial relationships within the Canadian federation warrants a forum for these matters to be discussed publicly, most suitably in a prominent, national institution. The federal Cabinet is unable to Provide such a public forum. Consideration should, therefore, be given to assigning the Upper House a specific and major role in the discussion of federal-provincial affairs.

17

*The Upper House**

THE GOVERNMENT OF THE PROVINCE OF QUEBEC

If the Parliamentary system is maintained, it would be preferable to have the members of the Upper House act as spokesmen for the state governments. To this end, they should be appointed by the states for a limited period. The Upper House might have power merely to delay passage of legislation, similar to that exercised by the British House of Lords. The number of members for each state could equal the number of Senators each Province has now, although state populations might profitably be taken into closer account.

The measures taken to ensure state participation in the Central legislature's work vary greatly from one federation to another. In most cases, however, such participation is an essential element of the federal system.

The Senate, which was to perform this function in Canada, has failed completely, mainly because senators are appointed by the central government and remain in office until age seventy-five.

If the Upper House is truly to represent the states, its members must be appointed by the state governments and for a limited period of time.

To prevent some or all states from paralyzing the central legislature, the Upper House should not be allowed to stop legislation but merely to delay it.

In the long run, effective state participation in its work does not weaken the central legislature but rather confers on it prestige and authority that it can hardly obtain otherwise. As well, it is an important guarantee of harmonious relations between the central and state governments.

---

*Included in the *Working Documents* submitted by the Province of Quebec to the Continuing Committee of Officials on the Constitution, July, 1968.

18

*The Future of the Senate**

THE GOVERNMENT OF CANADA

In *Federalism for the Future*[1] the Government of Canada suggested that the role and the powers of the Senate should be reviewed. We felt that it could be reconstituted to enable it to play a more vital role in reflecting the federal character of our country. We also felt that if the role and the powers of the Senate were to be changed, we should consider changes in the method of appointment to that body.

An important feature of federal systems is the provision for an Upper House in which the constituent states or Provinces are represented, either on the basis of equality or in a manner which takes into account some principle of equitable balance among the regions. In other major federal systems such as the United States, Australia, Federal Republic of Germany, Switzerland and India, representation is based directly on the constituent unit – that is, the state, canton, or province. In Canada the system is unique, with four divisions of the country – the Maritimes, Quebec, Ontario, and the West – equally represented. Only in the cases of Ontario and Quebec – and now Newfoundland – do the divisions coincide with provincial boundaries.

Various reasons have been put forward to explain why the Canadian Senate has not functioned more effectively as an institution of federalism in which regional interests are more positively and clearly voiced. It is often said that the regions have other and more effective means of protection and expression open to them – the power and influence of their own provincial governments, the courts if the legal rights of the provincial legislatures are infringed, the ballot box if the interests of the people of the provinces or region are imperilled or neglected by federal policy, and the practice of giving representation to each province in the Cabinet where possible.

In other federal systems previously mentioned, the political divisions or regions participate in an organ of the central government. The members of these upper chambers are selected by direct appointment by the political subdivisions, or by direct or indirect election. Terms of office are generally for six years or at the discretion of the state or provincial government. The Canadian system, on the other hand, is doubly unique in providing only

*Included in *The Constitution and the People of Canada*, published by the Government of Canada on the occasion of the Second Meeting of the Constitutional Conference, February, 1969.

for federal appointment and for life-tenure (or now, tenure until age seventy-five).

The Government of Canada feels that the Senate should be reorganized to provide for the expression in it, in a more direct and formal manner than at present, of the interests of the provinces. At the same time, the interests of the country as a whole should continue to find expression in the Senate to maintain there an influence for the unity of Canada.

The Government of Canada would therefore propose a new approach to the organization of the Senate to achieve this end. The Senate could be partly selected by the federal government and partly selected by provincial governments. The method of selection of Senators by the Provinces could be by nomination of the provincial governments, acting with or without the approval of their legislatures, depending on the provisions of each provincial constitution. The term of office for Senators could be limited to a specific number of years – perhaps six.

Equitable transitional arrangements would of course be required in respect of those holding Senate appointments at the time these changes come into effect. These arrangements would have to be considered with care, ensuring that no injustice is done while at the same time permitting those changes required in the interests of the Canada of the future.

It may be asked why the Government does not propose an elected Senate. The reason is threefold. One factor is the importance of giving to the provincial governments themselves a means of naming people who could give direct and clear expression to the views and interests of the provinces, with such appointments being for a limited term to ensure that their holders are responsive to major changes in provincial attitudes. A second factor relates to our parliamentary system. In the present Canadian Constitution, as in those of other federal states, a veto in the Upper House is not regarded as a non-confidence vote. The Government is therefore not defeated if its measures are rejected in the Upper House. In Canada the federal Cabinet should continue to be responsible only to the House of Commons – the body elected directly by the people on a basis of representation by population. If both Houses were elected, it would be difficult to maintain this distinction in authority. Each would claim to represent directly the views of the people in different ways, and new uncertainties could creep into our system with consequent harm to the effectiveness of government. The third factor relates to the desirability of being able to name particular types of people to the Senate to help it meet special powers and responsibilities we propose for it.

A revised Senate should be able to deal with the same range of matters as it now does, but provision would have to be made that in the general legislative process the Senate's rejection of a bill will be overcome by futher action of the House of Commons acting in accordance with specific procedures to be set out in the Constitution.

We feel, however, that a reconstituted Senate should have certain special

1. The Government of Canada, *Federalism for the Future*, A statement of policy prepaired for the Constitutional Conference, February, 1968.

powers flowing from its role as an important institution of federalism. It should have a new jurisdiction to approve nominations by the federal government of judges of the Supreme Court of Canada, ambassadors and heads of cultural agencies. For the same reason it should be considered to have a special responsibility in dealing with legislative measures concerning official languages and human rights. In these matters of special concern to the Senate, its powers should not be subject to procedures which would allow the House of Commons to override its decisions.

In our view such a system would provide the best balance between the principles of responsible and representative government and the need in a federal state for the adequate protection of regional and cultural interests.

There has been no review since Confederation of the basis of distribution of membership in the Senate as among the various regions and provinces of Canada. Yet the original concept was altered to some extent at the time Newfoundland joined Canada. The Government of Canada would therefore also suggest a review of the distribution of Senate membership.

For a revised Senate, we would hope and expect that the Government of Canada and the governments of the provinces would engage in healthy competition to ensure that the best men available are appointed to represent their points of view and to discharge the special responsibilities the Senate would have. In this way it may be possible to develop in the Senate a strong instrument of federalism, in which there will be effective expression of the interests of all citizens – both their interests as Canadians and their interests as residents of particular regions.

SECTION FOUR

PUBLIC SERVICE

This section begins with an article by J. E. Hodgetts on the changing nature of the federal public service. The author provides a character sketch of the public service and discusses certain issues influencing its growth.

In Canada, as elsewhere, public service employment has been mushrooming since the Second World War. An article by J. E. Hodgetts and O. P. Dwivedi examines the factors which have influenced the vast expansion of government employment at all three levels of government in Canada. It also presents a projection of such employment until 1981 and analyzes the implications of this projected growth for the future. The third article in this section, by J. J. Carson, examines those issues which will influence the scope of public administration in Canada, and the final article, by two of the editors, identifies and discusses an important issue facing public servants today: whether or not the necessity of a politically neutral public service requires the continuation of restrictions on the right to political activity by all public servants.

19
The Changing Nature
*of the Public Service**

J. E. HODGETTS

The study of nation-building and political development in the remoter quarters of the globe is now so much in fashion that one might think the winds of change sweep only through the so-called developing nations. In truth, they blow with monsoon force in our own backyards and it behooves us to cast an occasional glance at the institutional adjustments required to hold our domestic ships of state on a steady course. The changing nature of the Canadian public service alone is a subject worthy of a book for which in this short paper I can provide little more than some speculative foot-notes.

We may take it as given that a public service has certain features that can be delineated and that, by the same token, one can identify significant alterations in its lineaments. It is not necessary to embrace a mystical, organic theory of the state to argue that a human institution, rather like a living organism, may change its contour and nature by reason of adaptation to an external field of forces in which it operates or by virtue of its own internal response to physiological laws of growth and decay.

One cannot, of course, speak of changes in an institution until one has said something about the features that have hitherto characterized the institution. In my view, a character sketch of the Canadian public service would have to draw heavily on an ecological analysis. That is, the major contours of the public service have been largely shaped by outside environmental pressures. Later I shall argue that the most important forces now altering the nature of the public service derive from internal pressures of sheer growth.

EARLY DEVELOPMENT

The nature of the Canadian public service was moulded from the outset by the practical problems of administering a sparsely populated domain

---

* Reprinted with permission of Lloyd D. Musolf, ed., *The Changing Public Service,* California: University of California Press, 1968, pp. 7-18.

stretching across a broad continent, subject to the pervasive and pursuasive cultural shock of a larger southern neighbour and, as a former colony, the heir to a persistent British political tradition.

Physical Dispersion

The organizational response to geography has been a wide-spread physical dispersion of the public service, a feature that has persisted to the present day with a constant seventy-five per cent of the work force operating outside headquarters. At the same time, the adoption of ministerial departments and collegial cabinet responsibility – the British heritage – has acted as a steady counter-pull against the physical forces of dispersion, for ministerial responsibility is best preserved by keeping policy decisions under tight rein in Ottawa. As a result, physical dispersion has not been accompanied by genuine devolutions: "ministers," as Sir George Murray succinctly concluded in 1912, "both have too much to do and try to do too much."

The physical setting not only molded the organizational contours of the public service, it dictated in large measure the major programs: opening up the land, encouraging settlement, developing transportation and exploiting the potential wealth in Canada's staple products of fur, wheat, fish, timber and minerals – these constituted the major activities of the public service and are still significant. There was never at any time in Canada's history a period of genuine laissez-faire; the self-reliant pioneer was a romantic fiction and the state, from the earliest days, was a leading entrepreneur in an economy that has always been mixed.

Administrative Proliferation

The active and early involvement of the state in the economic life of the nation has significantly affected the structure of the public service. Beginning its life with far too many departments for the limited functions expected of it, Canada was able for some time to absorb the mounting buden of programs. But, unwilling to adopt either the American pattern of huge holding company departments or the British pattern of numerous small departments, Canada soon faced a "spill-over" problem that could only be met by resorting to an increasing number of extra-departmental administrative entities. Boards, commissions, corporations and crown companies have proliferated in perplexing confusion, distorting the conventional lines of responsibility and, in effect, creating a second public service approximating in size and importance the regular civil service embraced within the old departmental rubric. In essence the mixed economy has given rise to an organizational "mix" in the public service that is a feature now shared by both provincial and federal governments.

Response to Federalism

The federal constitutional structure has left as enduring marks on the Canadian public service as has the physical environment. The allocation of functions and responsibilities initially was precise enough to permit provincial and federal public services to operate with little reference to one another. It is interesting to observe, however, that the provinces looked upon the new central authority as a surrogate version of the former Imperial powers located in Whitehall and the central government, itself, confirmed this suspicion by creating a short-lived Secretary of State for the Provinces. The view taken of the central government as an alien force in the life of Provinces was reinforced by the federal appointment of Lieutenant Governors who, in the early days of poor communication, were expected by the central government to act as regional administrative overlords for all federal activities in the Provinces. (The renowned Joseph Trutch in command of British Columbia was an outstanding example.)

Improved communications and the consequent evolution of a highly interdependent economy have not obliterated this early antagonism between the regions and the central authority. On the other hand, as the areas assigned respectively by the British North American Act to the Provinces and the federal government were occupied by both sets of authorities, public services tended to overlap. Overlapping and the possibilities of friction and conflict were enhanced by the twentieth century expansion of welfare functions. While the increasing concern of all levels of government for conserving and developing physical resources brought provincial and federal public servants into direct confrontation, the expanding need to conserve and develop human resources carried the confrontation right down to the doorstep of the individual citizen.

In accommodating to the legal rigidities of the federal allocation of duties, the public service has assumed another set of characteristic features. First, much ingenuity has been displayed in devising administrative expedients for transforming potential conflict situations into opportunities for collaboration. Most of these are *ad hoc* and piecemeal approaches, characterized by extensive use of representative advisory committees, annual official conferences and sporadic Dominion-Provincial diplomatic meetings; there has also been some joint use of one set of officials, typified by the provincial contracts for the services of the Royal Canadian Mounted Police.

On the program side, as distinct from organization, the Canadian public service's response to federalism has evolved in stages. Centralized collection of statistics, culminating in the Dominion Bureau of Statistics, was followed by the assumption of responsibility for research in such fields as geology, agriculture, mining, fisheries, forests and more recently in health, welfare and the applied and pure sciences – especially those relating to atomic energy. The other significant response has been the creation of machinery to handle the enormous transfer programs associated with federal grants to provincially-administered health and welfare programs.

One peculiar legacy of the federal structure that warrants special consideration is the special status conferred on the French language. The current impassioned attention being devoted to the place of French Canada in the partnership with the English-speaking provinces suggests that the public service failed to respond to this unique feature of its cultural and constitutional environment. It is important to remind ourselves that, during the pre-Confederation period of legislative union between what are now the Provinces of Quebec and Ontario, the political and administrative concessions made to the concept of equal partnership of the two groups went well beyond anything provided, for example, by the United States to keep South and North in a more perfect union. Here was a system topped by a hyphenated premiership, often organized in double-barrelled ministries, staffed in dual divisions and, to cap it all, a system of rotating capitals. All this came to an abrupt end in 1867 and Quebec, like the American South, found itself outvoted politically and forced to accept as a nucleus for the new central civil service, a staff drawn largely from the Province of Ontario, housed in a new, permanent capital in an alien backwoods Ontario town of Ottawa and rapidly conditioned to conducting all official business in English. The wonder is that it has taken the better part of a century for the aggravations implicit in this uneven partnership to erupt into the agonized and understandably extremist complaints that are now a matter of profound scrutiny by the Royal Commission on Bilingualism and Biculturalism. In my view, what is really at stake is the broad issue of how to create a genuinely representative national public service; unfortunately, the issue is likely to be too narrowly construed as a problem of how to placate French Canada alone.

Political and Legal Setting

In highlighting what seem to be the essential features of the Canadian public service let us consider finally the impact of the political and legal setting. Politically, the task confronting Canadian parties has been comparable to that facing their American counterparts – namely, the mobilization of majorities on a regional basis across a continental domain. In practice, the response was the same in both countries: each was sufficiently wealthy to be able to afford a prolonged abuse of public employment as a means of cementing loyal party support in substitution for the discipline of ideological identification. The evils of patronage could be eliminated only by a formal act of self-denial, confirmed by a civil service act and administered by a politically-neutralized civil service commission. In all the discussions leading up to this decision it is curious to note that Canadian reformers thought they were emulating British precedents when, in fact, there never was (and still is not) a comparable civil service act in Britain. The fact was that Canadians were unwittingly following American practices, with long-term consequences that were the same in both countries. Personnel administration in both Canada and the United States was plagued by the negative philosophy engendered by the desire to fumigate patronage from the public service. Civil service commissions were to be the conscience of the elected representatives and were to stand on guard at the portals of the public service denying entrance to the blatantly unqualified patronage-seekers. But, in addition to being confirmed as guardians of the "merit system", civil service commissions in both countries (and unlike their British namesakes) were vested with extensive authority over most aspects of personnel management. Unfortunately, the negative policing function dominated the positive management function until well on into the 1930's.

Two important characteristics of the Canadian public service became deeply entrenched as a result of these arrangements. First, personnel management was over-centralized and oriented toward control rather than service. The inept were excluded but the very best recruits would not have been found through this system; they appeared not by virtue of positive recruitment but largely because the depression fortuitously drove them from the private to the public market place.

The second and largely overlooked consequence of introducing civil service commissions into the Canadian system has been the creation of what might be called a legal ambivalence. The statutes clearly state that the ministerial head shall have the care and management of his department; yet, with its other hand, Parliament has conferred substantial managerial powers on the Civil Service Commission. The confusion is further compounded by the long-standing existence of the committee of Cabinet, the Treasury Board, which has also acquired by statute and squatter's privileges an important share of the management function. The ambivalence is further confused by the uncertain legal status of the Civil Service Commission which for its negative policing function may be regarded as Parliament's agent, but for its positive management tasks may be regarded as an extension of the Executive.

Canadian observers are wont to smile in a somewhat superior fashion when they compare the virtues of their system of unified powers with the American model of separated powers and checks and balances. The fact is that in elaborating its central management and control agencies Canada has created within the public service its own version of checks and balances which is all the more difficult to operate because it is grafted on to a constitutional system that ostensibly unites the Executive and Legislative branches. If the ambivalence of the system has hitherto attracted little notice, the current consideration of collective bargaining and compulsory arbitration will undoubtedly stumble over the ambiguities that give rise to such awkward questions as: who is to represent management and who is the real employer of the public servant?

THE IMPACT OF GROWTH: CHANGE FROM WITHIN

The foregoing conspectus of some of the major characteristics of the Canadian public service provides a basis for speculating on the impact of recent developments on the service. The single, most significant change since the second world war is the tremendous transformation in the scale of operations. In 1939 the total number of public servants was not much larger than the present staff of the Department of National Defense. The significance of growth in size does not reside in the increase in the target area provided for the critical darts of the popular press inveighing against the evils of a swollen bureaucracy. The true impact of growth is to be found in the attention that must now be directed to what in the vernacular is referred to as the care and feeding of the organization. One cannot expect this problem to rest heavily on the minds of any but those who have to work within the public service. Consequently, most of the efforts currently directed at the re-shaping and improvement of the public service – however much the general public or its legislators may benefit from these improvements – are not mounted from the outside but stimulated from within. After all who is likely to care more for a well-run ship than the sailors who have to live and work aboard her! It is true that the initial motive for reforms may be the outsider's simple-minded belief that gigantic savings can be effected. But once set an investigation afoot and the economy motive gets quickly overlaid with the more subtle and difficult problems of improved service and efficiency. This was certainly the experience with the late Royal (Glassco) Commission on Government Organization[1] and, I believe, has been the experience with its more modest contemporary counterpart in Saskatchewan.

It is unnecessary to develop here the familiar reasons for the expansion of state activities which, in turn, give rise to the significant alteration in the scale of operations. It is suggested, however, that the nature of the public service is increasingly likely to be influenced by the internal pressures stemming from the necessary adjustments to the change in scale of operations, rather than by the outside environmental factors which have been so influential in the past. The precise nature of these modifications may best be traced by noting the thought and activity currently being devoted to improving the management and auxiliary or house-keeping functions within the civil service.

Personnel Administration

The take-off point may be identified with the publication dates of the Glassco Commission reports, although it is clear that most of the ideas and proposals presented by the Commission merely echoed what many civil servants had been thinking for years. The Commission provided an uncommitted instrument for screening and publicly endorsing the views of the civil service on many management matters.

In the field of personnel administration or what the Commission, reflecting the new orientation, termed "manpower management", the contradictions between the old pattern and the new needs were particularly pronounced. The old pattern, as noted, was a centralized Civil Service Commission with most of the significant personnel functions concentrated in it and also empowered to police the merit system. The new conditions clearly demonstrated that the dimensions of the job had grown beyond the reach of a central body with concentrated powers and that much of the criticism of the Civil Service Commission could be attributed to the procedures it had developed to defend departments against patronage.

1. A three-man commission set up in 1960 to investigate the organization and operations of departments and agencies of the Canadian government, and to recommend changes which would improve efficiency and economy. Its four volume report was published in Ottawa in 1962-1963.

Extensive devolution to the operating departments of the hitherto concentrated personnel management functions was the obvious solution which, even before it was advocated by the Glassco Commission, had been reluctantly embraced by the Civil Service Commission itself. On the other hand, greater devolution presumably placed the protection of the merit system in greater jeopardy and yet, in the view of the management purists, this negative policing function would only foul up the positive management functions. The temptation – particularly for a Commission's staff drawn from private management firms – was to dismiss the possibility of patronage as a paper dragon long since slain. However, there were others who recognized that here was a peculiar difference between public and private administration and that past history could not be dismissed by wishful thinking. In the result, the policing or at least personnel audit function had to be preserved, the Commission had to be retained for this purpose and, in a typical compromise, the deconcentration of personnel responsibilities was to be conducted in stages under the paternal and experienced eye of the Civil Service Commission. Thus, while the outward forms of the old pattern remain unchanged, the inner working arrangements are in process of a very significant alteration that will divest the Commission of its detailed personnel functions and leave it with an auditing, guiding, appellate role and possibly some common recruiting and examining operations for clerical and other grades shared by most departments.

But whatever the internal re-allocation of the various elements of the personnel function, it is clear that the troika of department, Commission and Treasury Board will continue and that there will never be an entirely satisfactory, clear-cut division of personnel management tasks between them. There are already uncertainties about the proper location of such new tasks as developing and maintaining a manpower inventory, lists of eligibles for promotion competitions, the Pay Research Bureau, and most recently, the proper authority to undertake the tremendous job of reviewing the classification system. Moreover, as the old notion of the sovereign state, the unapproachable task master, is softened by demands that it become a model employer and accept collective bargaining and compulsory arbitration the problem of fitting this triumvirate of management agencies into the new machinery is most intractable and complex. Indeed, these issues of collective bargaining and classification are inextricably linked, for in the effort to devise proper bargaining units, the traditional detailed classification plan is found wanting; and, insofar as the organizations of civil service associations have been geared to the traditional classification plan, they too will be drastically affected by changes in the classification plan and proposals for bargaining units.

All these problems affecting personnel management are churning within the civil service and are now a matter for strictly private and internal scrutiny. When these studies and reports are made and action follows, as has occurred gradually with the recommendations from the Glassco Commission, the nature of the public service is bound to be affected. It is perhaps not too fanciful to say that the Canadian public service has become much more introspective; that its future form and character are largely dependent on the thought and attention civil servants themselves are prepared to give to meeting the organizing and managing challenge posed by the vastly enlarged scale of operations. Needless to say, one cannot dismiss the environmental factors that moulded the earlier civil service for they still pose political, physical, financial and even cultural limits to the "do it yourself approach" within the civil service.

Financial Administration

I have concentrated on the changing nature of personnel administration to illustrate what appears to be a rather general change in the public service. If a significant alteration in scale can induce a basic re-thinking and re-allocation of personnel management responsibilities, it is natural that other basic activities such as financial administration and various housekeeping services should respond to the same unsettling force.

Financial administration in the Canadian public service followed much the same pattern as personnel administration, in response to the same negative though legitimate concern to prevent abuses. Central machinery was inserted on top of the departments to control and check at every possible stage between the initial departmental requests for money and the final expenditure of money. The manifold increase in the sums expended, from the start of World War II, stretched the resources of the ever-enlarging central control apparatus, but failed to reduce the amount of niggling detail or the energy used to argue the pros and cons of a tiny expense account. Devolution of financial management was once again the key-note in the recommendations of the Glassco Commission; these were accepted in principle by the government and detailed feasibility studies followed which, in due course, will prepare the entire public service for the transfer of financial management to departments. Devolution, once again, is to be a phased, controlled operation under the surveillance of Treasury Board, aided and abetted by the management consultants who have been retained to do the studies, install the pilot programs and hold the hands of the departments through the teething stages. (It is impossible to resist the parenthetical comment that first reports of the new devolution indicate departments are now complaining bitterly that their own finance officers are more stiff-necked than their ex-masters in Treasury Board!)

Once again, while this remodelling and adjustment goes on within the civil service, Parliament as a potential major beneficiary is apparently scarcely conscious of these changes. It should shortly be receiving estimates couched in the more meaningful form of programs and accompanied by descriptions that should, if Members take their job seriously, vastly improve legislative scrutiny of the public services.

Supply and Housekeeping Services

The intense preoccupation with recasting personnel and financial management procedures and machinery carries over to the provision of various supply and housekeeping services. The importance of such services to an enlarged public organization has necessitated a careful re-examination of the scattered agencies and somewhat haphazard methods employed. In apparent contradiction of the pattern of devolution emerging in the areas of personnel and financial management, supply and housekeeping services have tended to be consolidated and centralized in a few specialized agencies. The benefits of bulk purchasing, common warehousing, consolidated inventories, and so on, provide strong arguments for this particular development. The complaint commonly registered against centralized servicing agencies is that they are slow and generally seek to control their client departments even as they are allegedly servicing them. The solution, as envisaged in the Glassco Commission reports on "supporting services", is to cost these services and then charge the user departments for the services as the most direct way of preventing abuses. In this way, centralized provision of common services is made compatible with the over-riding concern to keep management decisions mainly in the hands of operating departments.

OUTLOOK FOR THE PUBLIC SERVICE

Enough evidence has probably been mustered to support the proposition that the changing nature of the Canadian public service today is in large part due to the important internal adjustments being made by civil servants themselves in response to the organizational and management problems deriving from the tremendous increase in the scale of operations. Lest I leave the impression that I am now disposed to discard the ecological approach with which this paper began, let me conclude by reverting to a significant environmental change that is undoubtedly affecting the nature of the public service.

The environmental factor in question is a compound of federalism and geography that has created what might be called a different "interrelatedness" of things to be administered. The assignment of functions in the British North America Act always provided for a limited area of concurrent jurisdiction which either or both the Provinces and the national government could occupy. Constitutional authorities now anticipate that these areas of concurrency are going to broaden and perhaps become the critical testing ground for judicial determination of the respective rights and authority of provinces and dominion.

Contributing to this tendency to blend and merge (and perhaps even to trade) legal jurisdictional areas, is the contemporary resort to new administrative areas that cut through or consolidate older ones based upon the traditional political boundaries of towns, townships, counties and so forth. This process is going on at the local, provincial and federal levels; it suggests that new functions cannot find a congenial home within the old boundaries and must search for a more viable administrative base. In, short, we appear to be confronting an increasing number of situations where the administrative regions, basically tied to traditional political boundaries, are proving unsatisfactory. In addition, the historic departmental portfolios which group programs largely on a purpose basis prove increasingly inadequate because they simply do not contain the right combination of skills, resources and authority. Consequently, it becomes necessary to extract some of these elements from the traditional packages and recombine them in a different pattern more closely related to the new functions to be performed. Resource administration and conservation typify the areas where this recasting of the organizational framework appears to be most active and necessary. These efforts to substitute new administrative lamps for the old cannot, of course, be permitted to extinguish the flame of the old lamps. Further, the presence of a growing number of new regional entities raises such important problems as how to preserve conventional lines of responsibility, and what is the most appropriate method of financing these new combinations of old functions. . . . It is clear that what I have called the "new interrelatedness of things" is going to be a major pressure in re-shaping the public service structures at all levels in Canada.

It is a common belief that the public service is, of all our institutions, perhaps the least susceptible to forces of change. If this brief character sketch of the Canadian public service is at all accurate, then this commonly-held stereotype requires substantial amendment. While the public service has had to make its peace with such fixed elements of the environment as geography, politics and constitutional structure, it has nevertheless shown much more ingenuity and zeal in adapting itself to the changing demands of the environment than have, for example, our legislatures. . . .

20

The Growth of Government
Employment in Canada*

J. E. HODGETTS and O. P. DWIVEDI

Governments function in an economic, social, and political context by adopting policies which both reflect and shape the societies of which they are a part. So important and far-reaching are these policies that practically every aspect of an individual's life is influenced and in many important ways even controlled by governmental decisions. The processing, implementing, enforcing, and adjudicating of such governmental decisions have aggrandized the power of the executive and expanded government employment. Much attention has been directed to the increasing powers of the bureaucracy but there is surprisingly little accurate information on the much more immediately obvious phenomenon – its sheer numerical growth. This article is a first attempt to come to grips with the elusive data on the growth of government employment at all three levels of government (federal, provincial, and municipal) in Canada. As part of the effort to calculate the dimensions of this growth a tentative projection of growth patterns is also presented and certain lessons for future manpower planning are drawn.

FACTORS INFLUENCING THE GROWTH OF
GOVERNMENTAL FUNCTIONS

Expansion of government employment is, of course, closely related to the growth and change in governmental functions. One of the most obvious determinants is to be found in a nation's vital statistics: even if functions remain unchanged, a growing population necessitates an expansion of the public service. If, at the same time, the demand schedule of growing population inclines upward (as has happened in mass democracies), the pressures build up on the administrative branch for new services and even more personnel.

Since the turn of the century, Canada's population has nearly quadrupled – from 5.37 million in 1901 to 20.01 million in 1966. During this

---

*Reprinted with permission from *Canadian Public Administration*, Volume XI, 1969, pp. 224-238.

same period and at an accelerating pace, Canada has been transformed from a rural, localized society with a solid agricultural base to an urban interdependent community sharing marked signs of rapid industrialization. These changes have been reflected in a dramatic shift in the occupations of Canadians, most notably the "flight from the land" which is described in the *Second Annual Review* of the Economic Council of Canada: "Perhaps the most striking impression of a half-century of population history of Canada is one of volatility and dynamic change. The rate of growth of urban population has been substantially higher than even in the U.S.A. Over the forty-year period from 1921 to 1961 movement out of farm areas was twice as great, and movement into non-farm areas three times as great as total net immigration into Canada. Although every province experienced some population growth, the increase was entirely concentrated in the non-farm population."[1]

In this period, 1921-61, total population more than doubled, from 8.78 million to 18.24 million, with the urban population commanding the lion's share of this increase (8.65 million or 91.6 per cent of the total). This impressive urban and suburban growth created a community that was much more dependent on certain services provided by government than the former rural-agricultural community. Urbanization was causally related to industrialism; and both, taken in conjunction with population growth, placed heavier demands on transportation, communication, financial, utility, and service enterprises. Government became more deeply involved as regulator, planner, stimulator and even entrepreneur in many significant areas. World War II accelerated these developments and governments penetrated more and more sectors of the citizen's life.

Added to this complex interaction – partly cause, partly effect – was the changing attitude of the public towards the role of government, characterized by Corry and Hodgetts as a shift from the negative to the positive state: "The government was to regulate industry so as to ensure operation in the public interest. Secondly, an attempt was made to reduce the glaring inequalities of income and improve the security of the less-fortunate members of society through social services or social security measures such as health insurance, unemployment insurance, and old-age pensions . . . [These] significant breaches made in the principle of laisser-faire, its inhibiting power was greatly diminished and finally it almost disappeared as an influence on public policy. . . . The negative state is now only a memory and we are faced with what is called, by contrast, the positive state."[2]

The ideological change was reinforced by the depression of the '30s, and all three levels of government assumed an unparalleled burden of new welfare responsibilities. Expenditures on relief, work relief, public works, and transportation soared. Later, World War II further increased

1. Economic Council of Canada, *Second Annual Review*, Ottawa, December 1965, p. 109.
2. J. A. Corry and J. E. Hodgetts, *Democratic Government and Politics*, Toronto, University of Toronto Press, 1963, pp. 119-20.

the involvement of government in the social and economic life of the country, thereby vanquishing the remaining ramparts of the negative state.

The consequent increase and change in composition of governmental functions was mirrored in governmental spending patterns. Table I shows the functional breakdown of net general expenditure expressed in terms of percentage, of all levels of government for selected years in the post-World War II period. The most notable features of governmental expenditure patterns revealed in the Table are the marked decline in the portion of the

TABLE I

EXPENDITURES BY MAJOR PURPOSES, EXPRESSED AS A PERCENTAGE
OF TOTAL NET GENERAL EXPENDITURE, ALL LEVELS OF GOVERNMENT
COMBINED, CANADA, SELECTED YEARS, 1946-66

Fiscal year	Defence	Health and social welfare	Education	Transportation and communications	Natural resources	Debt charges	General govt. and misc.
1946	31.8	14.9	6.7	7.6	5.2	15.2	18.6
1951	30.3	17.1	9.3	10.2	3.8	9.8	19.5
1956	26.2	20.0	11.5	12.6	3.6	7.5	18.6
1961	16.9	25.1	14.9	12.1	5.1	7.9	18.0
1966	11.5	21.5	14.1	12.3	5.1	11.8	23.7

SOURCE: Canada, Dominion Bureau of Statistics, *Comparative Statistics of Public Finance*, 1946, 1951, 1952-1962; and *Canadian Statistical Review*, May 1968.

total budget spent on defence (from about 32 per cent to 11.5 per cent) and the rise in expenditures devoted to the three fields of health and social welfare, education, and transportation and communications. Since the Table shows only combined expenditures, it fails to reveal that expanding responsibilities of provinces and local authorities account in large measure for the substantial increases in these three areas. It is also interesting to observe that the traditional or basic government services – grouped in this Table under the heading "General Government" and "Miscellaneous" – constitute a relatively small and static proportion of total budgetary expenditures.

Although government employment does not necessarily vary directly with spending, nevertheless it is fair to assume from this tabulation of changing priorities in government spending that many new programs have been added and that these, along with increasing budgets, necessarily expand the public service payrolls. Moreover, without seeking to invoke a rigid Parkinsonian Law, it is fair to suggest that growth in one sector often generates growth in related sectors – a self-generating aspect of bureaucracy.

This summary sketch of factors contributing to the growth of public service employment (or serving as indices of such growth, in the case of expenditure patterns) is sufficient to establish the obvious point: the change in size and composition of the government's own labour force does not occur in a vacuum. Without labouring this point further, we turn to the difficult task of calculating the dimensions of the growth of public service employment.

THE DIMENSIONS OF GROWTH

Two preliminary comments must be made for purposes of clarification and as a necessary precaution in viewing the figures presented below. First, the term "total government employment" means the sum total of all persons employed by government (at any level) who work in operating departments, departmental corporations and agencies, public enterprises, institutions of education, and workmen's compensation boards. The total also includes other "seasonally employed" persons. This term is much more inclusive than the more familiar term "civil servants" (in some jurisdictions referred to as public servants) who are recruited and appointed by a civil or public service commission and are working in regular operating departments. This more restrictive nomenclature excludes persons working in other governmental agencies, such as the Canadian National Railways, who are not referred to as civil servants because of their varying systems of employment and working conditions.[3]

The second precautionary word concerns the adequacy and reliability of data on government employment at all the three levels of government. To begin with, we lack historical series based on uniform and constant statistical concepts. Accordingly, precise measurements of growth over a long period of time are fraught with peril. Even the Royal Commission on Government Organization (Glassco Commission) encountered many problems in providing historical data for federal civil service employement.[4] Although the Dominion Bureau of Statistics has produced figures for federal government employment going back to 1924, it made no serious attempt to collect provincial government employment data until October 1959. Provincial sources of statistics are equally spotty and historical data on provincial government employment exist only for Saskatchewan, where the Royal Commission on Government Administration managed to collect data on civil service employment back to 1925. Data on

3. For instance, on December 31, 1965, according to the Dominion Bureau of Statistics publications, there were 796,573 listed as the total number of government employees working for the federal, provincial, and municipal governments. Of this number, 140,206 were "civil servants" working for the federal government and 132,853 were working for the provincial governments; there is no such distinction made for municipal employees. Thus, in all, there were 273,059 "civil servants" constituting only 34.3 per cent of the total government employment in Canada.

4. *Royal Commission on Government Organization*, vol. 1, Ottawa, Queen's Printer, 1962, p. 306.

municipal government employment became available only in April 1968 with the publication by the Dominion Bureau of Statistics of *Municipal Government Employment*. This series goes back to 1961. Even this information is incomplete, for it excludes employees working in municipal enterprises, municipally-owned hospitals, school boards, and other joint boards and commissions. One source, which has the merit of having been compiled on a consistent basis and refers to all three levels of government, is *Taxation Statistics*, and annual publication of the Department of National Revenue, which contains data on the number of employees working for federal, provincial, and municipal governments who submitted annual individual income-tax returns. Unfortunately, this publication goes back only to 1946 and does not include those government employees who work for public enterprises and other corporations or employees of educational institutions. In the absence of other historical series and because of the need to establish certain growth trends for our analysis, we have, perforce, relied on this source (as did the Saskatchewan Royal Commission on Government Administration).

With these qualifying remarks, it is in order to consider the general trends in growth of government employment insofar as they can be ascertained from the elusive and somewhat inconsistent data at hand. Over the hundred-year period since the foundation of Canada, the growth of government employment has been truly remarkable. During this period, Canada's labour force has increased about seven and a half times, but the total number of federal government employees alone has increased a hundred fold. In 1867, less than one out of every hundred of the labour force was employed by any level of government. In 1967 more than one in every eight of the labour force was on a government payroll.[5] Considering only the period 1946 to 1966, the total number of government employees in Canada, excluding persons in the armed forces, grew from 223,458 or 46 employees per thousand of the labour force to 710,155 or slightly more than 95 employees per thousand of the working population. Expressed in terms of growth in population and labour force, we find that in the same period population grew from 12,292,000 to 20,015,000 or approximately 63 per cent and the labour force increased from 4,829,000 to 7,420,000 or about 54 per cent. During the same period, government employment witnessed a remarkable increase of no less than 218 per cent. Table II illustrates the growth and distribution of employees at all the three levels of government.

Surprising though it may appear, the increase in the gross number of government employees in Canada has occurred mainly at the provincial and municipal levels. For example, whereas, between 1946 and 1966, total government employment increased by 218 per cent, the combined provincial and municipal government employment grew by a spectacular 351 per cent. . . .

In 1946, provincial and municipal government employees together constituted less than half of the total employment; however, by 1966, provincial and municipal employment accounted for two-thirds of all government employment in Canada. In absolute terms, between 1946 and

TABLE II

GROWTH OF GOVERNMENT EMPLOYEES IN CANADA,
(ALL LEVELS OF GOVERNMENT) 1946-66

| Year | Employees | | | Total |
	Federal	Provincial	Municipal	
1946	116,657	50,041	56,760	223,458
1947	93,686	46,401	52,040	192,127
1948	107,730	63,250	62,920	233,900
1949	98,310	58,620	49,970	206,900
1950	95,120	63,630	53,640	212,390
1951	106,040	70,100	65,540	241,680
1952	122,380	84,420	77,030	283,830
1953	135,140	92,910	86,100	314,150
1954	145,000	99,000	93,820	337,820
1955	149,360	103,700	99,850	352,929
1956	155,892	108,775	101,942	366,609
1957	168,981	125,321	110,956	405,258
1958	173,510	134,881	118,986	427,377
1959	177,431	148,328	126,680	452,439
1960	186,800	154,943	142,780	484,523
1961	196,563	162,442	153,771	512,776
1962	193,117	178,016	163,606	534,739
1963	198,225	191,938	179,760	569,923
1964	206,873	217,499	190,688	615,060
1965	214,859	237,574	196,860	649,293
1966	228,325	257,115	224,715	710,155

SOURCE: Canada, Department of National Revenue, *Taxation Statistics*, 1946.–66 (fiscal years).

1966, total government employment has experienced more than a three-fold increase. This expansion, to be kept in perspective, should be viewed in relation to the increase in the population as a whole and the growing labour force of the nation. From Table III, we see that in 1946 for every 1,000 citizens there were 18 government employees; twenty years later the figure had just about doubled to 35 per thousand. So, in relative terms, the growth of government employment at all levels of government has doubled rather than tripled. Similarly, while there were 46 government employees for every 1,000 members of the labour force in 1946, by 1966 the number had slightly more than doubled to 96 per thousand.

From Tables II and III, . . . one can readily underline the most significant features of the last two decades: combined provincial and municipal government employment has been increasing at a much more rapid rate

5. J. J. Deutsch, "The Public Service in a Changing Society", *Canadian Public Administration*, vol. IX, Spring 1968, p. 1.

TABLE III

NUMBER OF GOVERNMENT EMPLOYEES PER THOUSAND OF CANADIAN POPULATION AND
LABOUR FORCE, 1946-66 (ALL LEVELS OF GOVERNMENT)

| | | | | No. of employees per thousand of: | | | |
| | | | | Population | | Labour force | |
Year	Employees	Population (000)	Labour force (000)	A*	B	A*	B
1946	223,458	12,292	4,862	18.17	9.49	45.96	23.99
1947	192,127	12,551	4,954	15.31	7.46	38.78	18.91
1948	233,900	12,823	5,032	18.24	8.40	46.45	21.39
1949	206,900	13,447	5,092	15.39	7.31	40.63	19.31
1950	212,390	13,712	5,198	15.49	6.94	40.86	18.29
1951	241,680	14,009	5,236	17.25	7.57	46.16	20.25
1952	283,830	14,459	5,344	19.63	8.46	53.11	22.90
1953	314,150	14,845	5,386	21.16	9.10	58.32	25.09
1954	337,820	15,287	5,476	22.09	9.48	61.69	26.48
1955	352,929	15,698	5,585	22.48	9.51	63.19	26.74
1956	366,609	16,081	5,738	22.79	9.69	63.89	27.17
1957	405,258	16,610	5,970	24.39	10.17	67.88	28.31
1958	427,377	17,080	6,120	25.02	10.16	69.83	28.35
1959	452,439	17,483	6,186	25.88	10.15	73.14	28.68
1960	484,523	17,870	6,391	27.11	10.45	75.81	29.23
1961	512,776	18,238	6,521	28.11	10.77	78.63	30.14
1962	534,739	18,570	6,615	28.79	10.40	80.84	29.19
1963	569,923	18,896	6,748	30.16	10.49	84.46	29.38
1964	615,060	19,235	6,933	31.98	10.76	88.71	29.84
1965	649,293	19,571	7,141	33.18	10.99	90.92	30.09
1966	710,155	20,015	7,420	35.48	11.41	95.71	30.77

*A represents proportion of total government employees whereas B relates to federal government employees only.

SOURCE: For government employment, see Table II.

Population and the labour force data are from *Canada Year Book, 1946–67.*

than federal government employment. Between 1946 and 1966, federal employment has grown only from 0.9 to 1.14 per cent of the population and from 2.4 to 3.0 per cent of the labour force. On the other hand, combined employment by the other two levels has increased, over the same period, from 0.8 to 4.0 per cent of population and from 2.17 to 10.0 per cent of the labour force. A detailed analysis of the reasons for this change is beyond the limits of this article, but, broadly speaking, provincial and municipal governments have been the main recipients of additional operating programs mounted over the last fifteen years. The factors discussed briefly at the outset have contributed to changing priorities and shifts in workload to provincial and local authorities. Since these are likely to persist, there is reason to predict that combined provincial and municipal employment will continue to rise at a more rapid pace than federal government employment.

Though information on qualitative changes in the government work force is extremely limited and incomplete, there is enough evidence, confirmed by world-wide trends, to justify a brief addendum to the statistics of absolute and relative growth of government employment. Table IV assembles a scattered sampling of figures drawn from federal and several

TABLE IV

OCCUPATIONAL DISTRIBUTION OF GOVERNMENT EMPLOYEES AT FEDERAL AND
SOME PROVINCIAL JURISDICTIONS, PERCENTAGE DISTRIBUTION

Occupational groups	Federal 1966	Ontario 1966	B.C. 1966	N.B. 1965	Quebec 1964	Sask. 1964
Administrative	8.6	6.3	1.8	5.8	17.3	14.0
Professional & scientific	6.7	} 28.4	18.6	18.8	14.0	20.0
Technical	11.0		36.2	22.4	8.8	19.0
SUB-TOTAL	26.3	34.7	56.6	47.0	30.1	53.0
Clerical	26.8	21.5	29.5	32.4	39.9	27.0
Operational & maintenance	46.9	43.8	13.9	20.6	20.0	20.0
TOTAL	100.0	100.0	100.0	100.0	100.0	100.0

SOURCES: For Government of Canada see *the Special Joint Committee of the Senate and of the House of Commons on the Public Service of Canada*, (Minutes of Proceedings and Evidence), November 1, 1966, Ottawa: Queen's Printer, 1966, p. 726; Ontario: information received from the Department of Civil Service, Toronto, October, 1966; British Columbia: information received from the Civil Service Commission, Victoria, August 1966; New Brunswick: H. G. Thorburn, *Ethnic Participation and Language use in the Public Service of New Brunswick*, a study prepared for the Royal Commission on Bilingualism and Biculturalism, February 1966, p. 35; Quebec: Commission du Service Civil, *La Composition du Service Civil*, Quebec, août 1964; and Saskatchewan: *Royal Commission on Government Administration*, Regina, 1965, pp. 454–5.

provincial sources which suggest that the more highly-trained, highly-educated personnel in the administrative, professional, and technical groupings of the public service are now numerically strong contenders for first place in an occupation traditionally viewed as the great repository of clerical and operational personnel. Indeed, the figures for the provinces indicate that from one-third to one-half of their employees now fall in this superior category of "high-level manpower".

If these sketchy figures do, in fact, indicate a qualitative change in public service employment then, taken in conjunction with the awesome quantitative demands on Canada's manpower reserves which we now tentatively project, those responsible for staffing the public service of tomorrow face an up-hill battle.

PROJECTION OF GOVERNMENT EMPLOYMENT

Projections are only as reliable as the data which are used for establishing past trends or used as predictive indicators of what will happen in the future. We have already expressed our reservations about the state of available historical statistics of public service employment. The one series used in developing our tables is less than complete, but has been assembled on a comparable basis since the end of World War II. Thus, it is fair to use these figures to establish past trends on a significant twenty-year period.

However, it is obvious that these figures, excluding as they do important segments of the public service, give a very conservative picture of the growth of total governmental employment. In moving beyond the present, we experimented with several indicators, including projections of population growth and estimates of the rate of growth of Gross National Product. Even assuming a reasonably close relationship between growth of governmental employment and growth of the population, a projection of the former would be only as good as the projections we had for population growth. The same is true of the use of GNP growth rate – an indicator used in an Australian study.[6] In the end, we relied on a purely mathematical formula for plotting the curve of past employment trends and projecting the path of that curve to the not-too-distant future of 1981. This procedure seemed to impose no greater restraints than other projection techniques – all of which must assume no significant economic, social, and political disruption that would distort the bases used for projection (e.g., economic growth indices, employment-unemployment ratios, population increase, etc.).

Using the "least squares" method, three non-linear trend lines were plotted for each governmental employer and Table V summarizes the final results of the complex computations. It is apparent that in the fifteen years, 1966-1981, total government employment will have more than doubled. From 35 government employees per 1,000 of population, there will be an increase to a projected 52 employees per 1,000 of estimated population in 1981.[7] What is of striking significance is that, during the next fifteen years, of the projected additional three-quarters of a million em-

TABLE V

PROJECTION OF GOVERNMENT EMPLOYEES 1966–81

Levels of Government	1966 (Actual)	Number of Employees Estimated		
		1971	1976	1981
Federal	228,325	270,049	315,912	365,227
Provincial	257,115	346,616	462,704	597,770
Municipal	224,715	301,708	400,493	515,516
TOTAL	710,155	918,373	1,179,109	1,478,513

ployees, over 631,000 will have to be found by provincial and municipal government.

IMPLICATIONS FOR THE FUTURE

The implications of the preceding figures of absolute, relative, and projected growth should be clear to those who must face them. First, provincial and especially municipal governments begin to appear as major competitors with the federal government and private industry for scarce manpower resources. The federal government took every advantage of a glutted labour market in depression years and built on its early success during wartime. Provincial and municipal authorities have faced the need for positive recruiting programs only in more recent years and obviously still have much to do if they are indeed to capture their rapidly enlarging share of the labour market.

In the effort to mount more positive recruiting programs, governments face a public relations job to improve their "image" as employers. Scattered surveys of public attitudes towards government as employer[8] indicate that all three levels, but particularly provincial and municipal, have a large and prejudiced public to educate if its better-trained members are to look with any marked degree of favour on careers in government service.

If the scattered evidence now available attests not only to an increasing governmental pressure on the labour market as a whole but a growing demand in particular for those with managerial, professional, and technical skills, governments as employers are going to have to devote more attention to forecasting their manpower requirements and planning their staffing or training programs. The starting point for such a program is an inventory of government employees for all three jurisdictions – a recommendation to the federal government that emerged spontaneously from the task force on manpower management of the Glassco Commission as a result of its difficulty in securing reliable data. Such an inventory would have to be maintained on a continuing basis if it is to provide the foundation for the kind of intensive manpower planning that our projection of staffing requirements obviously entails.[9] Conceivably, a central bureau should be established to compile and maintain the inventory and to act as a clearing

6. See Australia, *Report of the Committee of Inquiry into Public Service Recruitment*, Canberra, 1959.

7. According to T. M. Brown, *Canadian Economic Growth*, Ottawa, Queen's Printer, 1964, the estimated population of Canada will be 28,247,000 in 1981.

8. See, for example, J. Fred Dawe, "The Image of the Public Service: Survey of Student Opinion," Civil Service Commission, Ottawa, published in *Public Personnel Review*, vol. 25, October 1964, pp. 233–6; and *High School Attitude Survey* (unpublished), conducted by the Ontario Civil Service Commission in February 1964.

9. The U.S. Civil Service Commission has already shown the way by initiating its annual publication *Federal Workforce Outlook* in which short-range projections are published and revised each year.

house for all government employers and would-be candidates for employment. There is need here for intergovernmental collaboration rather than competition for the large number of highly-trained personnel each level will require. The time may fast be approaching when employees in this scarce pool of manpower will have to be shared and interchanged among the various levels of government. Further, because universities and technical institutions must be looked to for producing the kinds of skills and knowledge in increasing demand by governments, the central bureau would provide an admirable liaison between government employers and educational sources of supply.

The foregoing proposals for immediate initiation of inventories of current government manpower and some kind of control body to compile and update on a continuing basis have been made in the light of our projections of staffing requirements for all three levels of government over the next fifteen years. The requirements in terms of numbers alone are formidable and even so, as we have suggested, are definitely on the low side. When

TABLE VI

COMPUTATION OF TREND — LEAST SQUARES METHOD — SECOND DEGREE PARABOLA: GROWTH OF FEDERAL GOVERNMENT EMPLOYMENT IN CANADA, 1946–66

Year	X	$Y*$ Number of employees	XY	X^2	X^2Y	X^3	X^4
1946	0	116657	0	0	0	0	0
1947	1	93686	93686	1	93686	1	1
1948	2	107730	215460	4	430920	8	16
1949	3	98310	294930	9	884790	27	81
1950	4	95120	380480	16	1521920	64	256
1951	5	106040	530200	25	2651000	125	625
1952	6	122380	734280	36	4405680	216	1296
1953	7	135140	945980	49	6621860	343	2401
1954	8	145000	1160000	64	9280000	512	4096
1955	9	149360	1344240	81	12098160	729	6561
1956	10	155892	1558920	100	15589200	1000	10000
1957	11	168981	1858791	121	20446701	1331	14641
1958	12	173510	2082120	144	24985440	1728	20736
1959	13	177431	2306603	169	29985839	2197	28561
1960	14	186800	2615200	196	36612800	2744	38416
1961	15	196563	2948445	225	44226675	3375	50625
1962	16	193117	3089872	256	49437952	4096	65536
1963	17	198225	3369825	289	57287025	4913	83521
1964	18	206873	3723714	324	67026852	5832	104976
1965	19	214859	4082321	361	77564099	6859	130321
1966	20	228325	4566500	400	91330000	8000	160000
Σ	210	3269999	37901567	2870	552480599	44100	722666

*For the value of Y see Table II in the text.

we note also that the more highly trained and educated will constitute a growing proportion of this large net addition, the need for forward planning cannot be evaded. The effort required to assemble the global totals presented in this study indicates that much laborious detailed work will have to be undertaken at once if we are to have even a minimum amount of reliable statistical data on current governmental employment. Only after this material has been assembled, on the basis of agreed definitions of such terms as civil service, public service, or total government employment, can the more sophisticated qualitative inventories be undertaken. And, only after this task has been completed can we initiate a genuine manpower planning program, preferably mounted on an intergovernmental basis.

APPENDIX

For projecting government employment, we have used the "least squares method". It is a complicated mathematical calculation. The following is an example of the application of this method on Federal Government Employment. The same method has been used for projecting provincial and municipal government employment.

The application of the least squares method for the determination of the trend for the growth of federal government employment in Canada is shown in Table VI. As the parabola is the simplest type of curve used to describe the trend of data, the equation for a curve of the simplest parabolic type is: $Y = a + bX + cX^2$ from which the three "normal" equations are obtained:

$$\Sigma(Y) = Na + b\Sigma(X) + c\Sigma(X^2) \qquad 1$$
$$\Sigma(XY) = a\Sigma(X) + b\Sigma(X^2) + c\Sigma(X^3) \qquad 2$$
$$\Sigma(X^2Y) = a\Sigma(X^2) + b\Sigma(X^3) + c\Sigma(X^4) \qquad 3$$

The value of a, b, and c are given by

$$a = \begin{vmatrix} \Sigma Y & \Sigma X & \Sigma X^2 \\ \Sigma XY & \Sigma X^2 & \Sigma X^3 \\ \Sigma X^2Y & \Sigma X^3 & \Sigma X^4 \end{vmatrix} \div D$$

$$b = \begin{vmatrix} N & \Sigma Y & \Sigma X^2 \\ \Sigma X & \Sigma XY & \Sigma X^3 \\ \Sigma X^2 & \Sigma X^2Y & \Sigma X^4 \end{vmatrix} \div D$$

and

$$c = \begin{vmatrix} \Sigma N & \Sigma X & \Sigma Y \\ \Sigma X & \Sigma X^2 & \Sigma XY \\ \Sigma X^2 & \Sigma X^3 & \Sigma X^2Y \end{vmatrix} \div D$$

where

$$D = \begin{vmatrix} N^1 & \Sigma X & \Sigma X^2 \\ \Sigma X & \Sigma X^2 & \Sigma X^3 \\ \Sigma X^2 & \Sigma X^3 & \Sigma X^4 \end{vmatrix}$$

and $N = 21$, i.e., the number of years.

Now, from Table VI,

ΣX = the sum of the X-values = 210
ΣY = the sum of the Y-values = 3269999
ΣXY = the sum of the product of X and Y-values = 37901567
$\Sigma X^2 Y$ = the sum of the product of the squares of X and Y-values =
$$552480599$$

ΣX^2 = the sum of the squares of X-values = 2870
ΣX^3 = the sum of the cubes of X-values = 44100
ΣX^4 = the sum of the fourth powers of X-values = 722666.

Substituting these values in the above determinants we obtain the following values:

$a = 92535.15$
$b = 5374.09$
$c = 69.06$

The final trend equation then reads: *Trend of Federal Government Employment in Canada, 1946-1966,* $Y = 92535 \cdot 15 + 5374 \cdot 09X + 69 \cdot 06X^2$. The trend values for the various years may now be obtained by substituting the appropriate values of X as indicated in Table VI. Thus, for the year 1956, substituting 10 for X we get the following figure:

$Y = 92535 \cdot 15 + 5374 \cdot 09(10) + 69 \cdot 09(100)$
$Y = 153,182 \cdot 05$.

The process is repeated until the trend value for several years is calculated. These calculated values are then plotted on the graph in order that a trend line may be drawn. For purposes of comparison, the actual growth pattern is plotted on the graph.

Projection of Employment: The above trend equation can also be used to project the growth of employment at a given year. Thus for the year 1971, substituting 25 for X, we get the following:

$Y = 92535 \cdot 15 + 5374 \cdot 09(25) + 69 \cdot 09(625)$
$Y = 270,049 \cdot 90$.

Similarly, the projected employment figures for the years 1976 and 1981 may be obtained:

$1976 = 315,911 \cdot 85$
$1981 = 365,226 \cdot 80$.

21

The Changing Scope of the Public Servant*

J. J. CARSON

The rapid social, economic and technical changes in our society have touched all of us, from the "hippie" who opts out, to the manager who wonders if he will become obsolete in the advancing age of automation. There is little doubt that our society is changing at a pace never before witnessed: concepts, techniques, and environments – all are changing. We are likely to have a greater number and a greater variety of problems in the next ten years than we have had in the last hundred. As public administrators we must be able to respond to these changes, and that response will not always be easy.

I believe there are at least six major changes that will directly alter the scope of public administration in Canada; automation, biculturalism, the growth of the welfare state, international service, collective bargaining, and the managerial philosophy of J. Grant Glassco.

I have not listed these in an order of importance because they will vary in importance for each individual public servant. But sooner or later they will affect nearly all of us whether we are employed at the federal, the provincial or the municipal level. If there is a member here from the City of Victoria, listening in disbelief, let me challenge you to hear me out. The image of the whole public service depends on the resiliency and the imagination of all of its members. Our capacity to respond to change at all levels may well help to determine the future of this country.

AUTOMATION

The first change force that I have listed is automation, or more properly cybernation – the science of communication and control. This particular change alone will give us the ability to organize technical and social processes rationally on a scale never before possible.

In the years since the industrial revolution, knowledge of the techniques of production has led to widespread industrialization. This has been

*Reprinted with permission from *Canadian Public Administration*, Vol. XI, No. 4, Winter 1968, pp. 407-413.

an extremely rapid development if one considers how long man lived in the agricultural age. But for all its rapidity, this will be seen as a relatively slow process in comparison with the changes taking place today.

All of us are dimly aware of the potential uses of the computer in public administration and much experimental activity is under way. However, public services generally are still lagging behind their industrial counterparts in embracing the full potential and implications of the cybernetic age.

Computers are not just capable of giving us better mechanization in our present organizations. They give us the potential for something entirely different. Computers can enable us to analyze the whole of our operations in a detail and scope never before possible. In fact, computers are misused if they are merely a means of speeding up present calculating processes. They should be used for insight, not reckoning. This will call for an ability and perceptiveness that many a maintenance-oriented manager lacks. Information provided by automation will be a key resource, and in the future, governments are likely to have a near monopoly of it. For this reason it is essential that the public administrator of tomorrow have understanding and conviction about the potentialities of these new tools – and that he embrace them with confidence.

Automation can drastically change the scope of the public servant – but only if he is prepared for change.

BICULTURALISM

This represents a change and challenge of a different order. At the federal level we are deeply committed to building a bilingual and bicultural public service. Only in this way can we ensure that public policy and its administration will adequately reflect the values and sentiments of the two founding races. This is no easy task and for middle-aged public servants like myself it is a slow and painful process. Fortunately for our young university graduates it is proving to be much easier.

Regardless of the difficulty, we are determined to have a bilingual and hopefully bicultural administration within ten years. This will indeed change the scope of the federal public servant. For those who work with the provinces and the municipalities there is an important challenge in this development that I hope will not be ignored nor brushed aside. Expo demonstrated to the world that we purport to be a bicultural nation. Whether this turns out to be just a massive piece of window-dressing depends on what happens in the hearts and minds of provincial and municipal administrators as much as it does on what we accomplish at the federal level.

For example, most schools in Canada that teach French to English-speaking Canadians do not produce bilingual students. Why not? Because French is taught as a dead language. The same applies, to a lesser degree, in the teaching of English to French-speaking Canadians. In our secondary schools emphasis is on reading comprehension, so grammar translation methods are used. Little is done to understand or to speak the language. Fortunately, in Ontario at least, elementary school children are now being taught to understand and to speak French. But unfortunately what is taught will be lost altogether if the secondary schools continue to use the grammar translation method.

I understand quite well why secondary schools continue this method. They are preparing students for university, and at most universities a language is only studied as literature. But pedagogically it seems unsound to teach a young child to speak and to understand a language and then proceed to ignore his training for the rest of his school days.

Considering the nature of our country, we should be aiming a lot higher. Why continue to prepare a minority of students to study literature when we can easily prepare the majority of students to learn a living language?

We have found in our federal language schools that after 1,200 hours of instruction, starting from total ignorance, a person can speak a second language quite fluently. On the basis of 200 teaching days a year and one hour a day a student could become bilingual in six years. Surely this is an attainable objective in the Canadian public school systems.

As long as Canadians can barely read their second official language, let alone speak it, there can be little real communication among us, and our present difficulties will not be resolved. When English- and French-speaking Canadians can talk to one another in their mother tongues and at last understand one another, we will have taken an enormous step forward in preserving this bicultural country of ours. The responsibility for this advance rests with the provinces and the municipalities.

For those of us in the federal public service there is the new and very real challenge of working in a truly bicultural milieu. For those who are willing to accept this challenge there will be a broader scope than most of us have known before.

THE GROWTH OF THE WELFARE STATE

This rather hackneyed phrase is used to describe the continual growth and proliferation of government activity in all facets of our society. The demands for increased services from all levels of government seems relentless and insatiable.

The plaintive cries of a Barry Goldwater seem to be about as effective as those of King Canute. We must accept that, regardless of a government's political persuasion, it will inevitably find itself providing more and hopefully better services to its citizens than did its predecessors – short, of course, of a national emergency.

This will mean a continually expanding public service with more and more interesting and potentially rewarding jobs to be performed. I say "potentially rewarding" because so much depends on our being able to organize these tasks in a way that makes them meaningful and challenging to the public servant. If we merely expand our bureaucratic army of clerical workers whenever a new program is launched, we will have done little to satisfy the demands of the citizenry and even less to make the public service a vital and demanding career.

Too often we embark on socially useful programs with inadequately trained staff. The result is a paper-pushing, highly regulated exercise that often seems devoid of human understanding or imagination. Because we are sometimes forced to entrust the administration of funds to individuals lacking professional qualifications, we find it necessary to hedge them in with controls and rule books. Nothing is more deadening or emasculating to a dedicated public servant than to discover that in certain circumstances "the law is an ass" but that he must defend it.

Hopefully we are breaking out of these traditional patterns. Risk-taking is more and more recognized as the only valid approach to some of today's complicated social problems, particularly in the field of corrections and some of our related community disorders. I was alternately dismayed and then reluctantly proud of the Executive Director of the Company of Young Canadians in his defence of one of his staff members who had been incarcerated in Toronto's Don Jail for involvement with the hippies of Yorkville. Like Voltaire, I found myself thinking, "I disapprove of what you say, but I will defend to the death your right to say it." The point is that the growth of the welfare state is going to bring new and grave challenges to the public servant. If we are to deal with these problems effectively we must assume new attitudes and new approaches to public administration. We must become more courageous, more imaginative and more virile.

One has only to look sadly across our Southern border to see evidence of magnificently conceived programs going up in the smoke and gunfire that seem to have resulted from the frustration of disillusioned recipients of badly administered welfare activity.

As professional public administrators, let us resolve to grasp the challenges of the welfare state and its demands with new vigour – bureaucratic methods will not be good enough.

INTERNATIONAL SERVICE

The increasing opportunities for Canadian citizens to work abroad represent another aspect of our changing scope. For years Canada has had a distinguished but relatively small foreign service. It has been composed of a rather élite group of public servants who have brought great distinction to the nation and upon themselves.

A foreign service officer appointment still ranks as a prized goal amongst the ablest young people in the country, as evidenced by the number and quality of university graduates who enter our annual foreign service competitions.

However, the diplomatic monopoly on international service is becoming a thing of the past. This year there are thousands of young and not so young Canadians serving abroad with External Aid, Canadian University Students Overseas, the Ford Foundation, our own Immigration Branch and the various agencies of the United Nations family. They are sharing the skills and experiences of Canada with the developing nations of Asia and Africa, particularly in the field of public administration. By and large their performance has been impressive and their cumulative contribution significant. These efforts are not the kind that win individual Nobel Prizes but they are building a solid reputation for the competency, the integrity and the goodwill of Canadians. And, perhaps most important of all, they are broadening the horizons of those involved. My own work with the International Civil Service Advisory Board over the past two years has given me a new and wholesome respect for my fellow Canadians who are serving abroad in what, for want of a better name, I shall call "The International Public Service". They are sought after, listened to and warmly regarded – what greater tribute can be paid to a public servant!

As Canada expands its aid programs and its support of international agencies, there will be increasing opportunities for public administrators from all levels of government to volunteer their skills and know-how in the field of international service. I am hoping that a prerequisite of entry into our new federal service Executive Category will be a two-year rotational stint outside of our own jurisdiction.

International service can and will change the scope of the public servant who is courageous enough to take it on.

COLLECTIVE BARGAINING

Some months ago the federal Parliament enacted legislation that formally introduced collective bargaining as a legal method for regulating relationships between the State as employer and public servants as employees.

There is no need to dwell on the details of this legislation because they are probably well known to those who are interested in such things. In some respects the federal government was merely following the municipalities and certain provinces in taking this step. In other respects it was pioneering. I am thinking particularly of the decision to design a special piece of legislation tailored to the special needs of the public service and, it is hoped, one that sets the stage for a more mature and civilized relationship than generally exists across the country. Whether all of these high hopes will be realized only time can tell.

However, there is already abundant evidence within the federal service that the new collective bargaining regime is paving the way for a more wholesome approach to the whole business of staff relations. The old rather sentimental, sometimes sloppy, sometimes indifferent, *noblesse oblige* approach is quickly going out the window. Public administrators are waking up to the fact that they have a responsibility for staff relations and that their administration must be fair, sensible and consistent. No longer can the individual supervisor shift blame to some mysterious "they" – presumably the old Civil Service Commission or the Treasury Board. Now he must stand on his own feet, assume responsibility for his own actions or decisions and then be prepared to have them challenged through the grievance procedure all the way up to independent and binding adjudication. This can be a very cathartic experience. Inevitably there will be some growing pains during the first few years. Old-time administrators will resent and misinterpret their nakedness. Some over-zealous staff association officials will attempt to take advantage of management's suddenly revealed nakedness for short-term advantage. Given time, these trial-and-error struggles will settle down into a healthy, mutually self-respecting relationship between the public administrator and organized labour.

This development will bring a very real change in the scope of the public administrator. Some may well feel that this is a change "that they need as much as a hole in the head" – but change it is! It is an irreversible change in the federal service and I should think an inevitable one in the provincial services. Let me challenge you to embrace this change in the role of the administrator. Prepare for it and harness it to the objective of better public administration throughout Canada. (I believe it was Confucius who offered some immortal advice for people who find themselves in such circumstances.)

THE GHOST OF GLASSCO

Finally I come to the potential for change resulting from the managerial philosophy set forth by J. Grant Glassco in the Report of the Royal Commission on Government Organization.

In effect, Glassco said, "Let the managers manage." Indeed he said more than that. He said, "Not only *let* them manage – require them to manage!"

Regardless of how much one may quarrel with Glassco on detail (and it may surprise some to know that I am one who does), I think there is no question that his philosophy of management responsibility is going to have an enduring effect on the future of public administration in Canada. It took almost two decades for the Brownlow report to influence public administration in the United States but eventually the political science students who read Brownlow in their college days became the senior administrators of government. And change came about!

In Canada, change is occurring more rapidly. Admittedly we were many years riper and, paradoxically, the introduction of collective bargaining for employees is making a redefinition of management responsibility an absolute essential.

But no matter how one tries to explain or rationalize our present situation, the facts of life are that Glassco is here to stay. His ghost will not be exorcised by the Cassandra-like mutterings of political science professors nor will his spirit be contained by the misgivings of politicians. A new generation of public administrators has read Glassco and by and large they like what they have read.

This quiet revolution within the ranks of public administrators does not trouble me because I happen to believe rather passionately in Glassco's philosophy. (If I had not, I could not have stood by, aiding and abetting the dismembering of those historic prerogatives of the old Civil Service Commission which intruded on managerial responsibility.)

However, I feel it my responsibility to warn those who think of Glassco as a disquieting voice that ultimately will prove to be as much a will-o'-the-wisp as Sigmund Freud and those who want to dismiss him as an unfortunate aberration of the "Diefenbaker Years" that Glassco's philosophy does not belong to one man, one royal commission or one party. It is a philosophy that is well supported by all theorists and practitioners who have seriously studied the problems of administration in large-scale, dispersed organizations.

So let us embrace this philosophy of management responsibility in the public service. Let us genuinely show that we are capable of acting responsibly, that we are willing to be held accountable, that we do care about the taxpayers' dollars – in a word, that we can manage. Too long the public administrator has been caricatured as an empire-building bureaucrat who if given half a chance will fulfil all of Professor Parkinson's worst fears, and the fact that none of us has spoken up to give the lie to that mischievous cynic has given tacit credibility to his charges. It is time we set about to correct that caricature.

We are doing everything we can to eradicate this image at the federal level. I like to think we are having some success as evidenced by this year's recruiting efforts at the universities across the country (a 100 per cent improvement over previous years in quantity – and early indications are that quality has not suffered). But recruiting figures and external image-building are not a complete answer. We must set about to create a really lively, invigorating atmosphere within the public service and at all levels.

I am just as concerned with creating a climate that will encourage stenographers to tell their bosses that stenography is an inefficient and obsolete art as I am with encouraging managers to face up to the fact that automation may relieve them of half their staff but enable them to be twice as effective. This is the kind of environment that the public service must generate.

I am confident that we are heading in this direction. How fast we go depends on the initiative, the vigour and the courage of individual public administrators at all levels of government. The ghost of Glassco will not disappear from the ramparts. It will always be there – challenging the public servant and offering the key that will enable him to enlarge his scope – *if* he is prepared to assume the risks of managerial responsibility.

22

Political Rights of Canada's Public Servants

O. P. DWIVEDI and J. P. KYBA

One of the major assumptions on which western liberal democracies have been founded is the belief that, with rare exception, all adult citizens should have the right to participate fully in the political affairs of their nation. All such countries have attempted to put this theory into practice, but, in each of them, one substantial group has been denied this right to a greater or lesser degree: their public servants. There is conflict between the principle that all citizens should possess an unrestricted right to political activity and the belief that a politically inactive and neutral public service is necessary for the proper functioning of government. The purpose of this article is to analyse this conflict in the context of the federal public service of Canada, and to attempt its resolution through suggestions for the improvement of the existing situation.

Canadian public servants[1] were not always denied unrestricted political activity. Although the Act of Parliament which established the federal public service in 1868 included a provision to create a Board of Examiners to consider and appoint the nominees of Ministers (in effect an attempt to institute a politically neutral public service), this regulation was ignored by successive governments whenever opportunities arose for them to improve their parties' fortunes. The patronage system spread rapidly throughout the public service, and, for fifty years large numbers of public servants worked actively for their political bosses in order to secure promotions or other favours.[2] This system, although entrenched for half a century, could not survive the First World War. The exigencies of the war years demanded an able and efficient public service, and the outburst of patriotic fervour which accompanied the onset of the war insisted upon a politically neutral one. In the words of one Member of Parliament: "Patronage in this country is one of the worst things that exist today in the civil government. It is one of the most corrupt methods of canvassing for votes."[3]

In 1918, the Borden Government, urged on by public, press, and Parliament, gave way to the pressures for a patronage-free public service. The Civil Service Act of that year increased the jurisdiction of the Civil Service Commission (established in 1908 with responsibility limited to public servants residing in Ottawa), and set out as its main objective the eradication of appointment and preferment on the basis of political patronage. This provision was undeniably necessary, and it served its purpose – today the merit system is an integral part of the Canadian public service. However, the same Act restricted all public servants in the exercise of all their political rights except the right to vote. These restrictions did not alter greatly in the next forty-five years. Although an Order-in-Council passed in 1960 allowed public servants to participate in and be elected at municipal elections, the revised Civil Service Act of 1961 still forbade public servants to:

a. *engage in partisan work in connection with any election of a member of the House of Commons, a member of the legislature of a province . . .*
b. *contribute, receive, or in any way deal with any money for the funds of any political party.*[4]

The punishment for those found guilty of violating the above restrictions was dismissal. This Act was the last victory for those who insisted on a politically neutral public service, for within six years the emphasis on politically neutral public service was relaxed. In 1967, on the basis of the recommendations of a Joint Committee of the Senate and of the House of Commons on employer-employee relations in the public service of Canada,[5] the Pearson Government agreed to loosen some of the restrictions on the political activities of public servants contained in the 1961 Act. The 1967 Public Service Employment Act marked the first step away from the belief that a politically neutral public service requires the denial of most political rights to all public servants and towards the understanding that political inactivity by all public servants is not necessarily prerequisite to their efficiency and loyalty.

The political rights of Canadian public servants, as they exist today, fall into five categories: those rights not mentioned in the Public Service Employment Act of 1967 but understood to be possessed by all public servants; those rights mentioned in the Act and granted explicitly to public

1. We have used the term "public service" or "public servants" constantly in this article. However, until early 1967, federal government employees were divided into three distinct groups: "civil servants" included employees working in the executive departments only; "Public servants" were employees working in departmental and some other public corporations and "civil servants"; and "other government employees" were those not included in the above two groups. In historical perspective, the term "public servants" would actually mean "civil servants".

2. Nevertheless, it would be erroneous to leave the impression that Canada had a "spoils system" in the Jacksonian sense of the word in its public service. See Canada, *Report of the Civil Service Commission*, "Personnel Administration in the Public Service," Ottawa, Queen's Printer, 1959, p. 4.

3. Quoted in R. M. Dawson, *The Civil Service of Canada*, London, 1929, p. 93.

4. Canada, *The Civil Service Act, 1961*, Section 61, sub section (1).

5. Canada, The Special Joint Committee of the Senate and of the House of Commons on employer-employee relations in the Public Service of Canada, *Minutes of Proceedings and Evidence*, Ottawa, Queen's Printer, 1966-67, pp. 1297-1339.

servants; those rights mentioned in and restricted by the Act; those rights not mentioned in the Act but restricted in law elsewhere; and those rights not mentioned in the Act but understood to be restricted.

The only political right which falls into the first category is the right to vote. Although there is no provision in the Act, it is understood that no public servant is prohibited from voting in any election. It was due to the absence of such statutory provision that the Heeney Report recommended that no public servant "shall be debarred from voting in any election if, under the laws governing said election, he has the right to vote".[6] It is surprising that the above recommendation was not incorporated into the new Public Service Employment Act, 1967, but the present practice is not to interfere with this fundamental political right.

There are two types of political activity specifically guaranteed to public servants by the 1967 Act. In the words of the Act, a public servant does not commit an offence "by reason only of his attending a political meeting or contributing money for the funds of a candidate for election".[7] The Government, in 1967, appears to have made a distinction between public and private acts of political partisanship. Public servants were granted the right to attend political meetings and to contribute to the campaign coffers of candidates apparently because such acts are usually carried out without publicity and will not affect the reputation of the Public Service for political neutrality. It is not clear, however, what a public servant's position will be if he is not circumspect in his support for a political party, either at a political gathering or in his method of donation. According to the Act, nothing should happen to him, but, in practice, he might be disciplined. This clause in the Act does not contain sufficient detail for absolute clarity, but at least it recognizes the fact that public servants do have the same political beliefs and prejudices as ordinary citizens, and in granting public servants the right of political attendance and donation, the Government departed from a pattern which had been constant for nearly fifty years.

The Act of 1967 by no means restored the right of full political partici-pation to Canadian public servants, however, for according to its pro-visions any public acts of political partisanship are still prohibited. In the words of the Act itself:

No deputy head and . . . no employee shall
a. engage in work for, on behalf of or against a candidate for election as a member of the House of Commons, a member of the legislature of a province or a member of the Council of the Yukon Territory or the North West Territories, or engage in work for, on behalf of or against a political party; or,
b. be a candidate for election as a member described in paragraph (a)[8]

The wording of sub-section (a) effectively prevents any public servant from performing àny political service for any candidate or political party. Can-vassing during a campaign is regarded as direct participation in the election and, hence, is strictly forbidden. Even the display of any political symbol on his person, vehicle, or residence by a public servant is considered as "engaging in work for . . ." and thus is subject to disciplinary action. There are no qualifications whatsoever to this clause, and in localities where public servants constitute a substantial section of the voting population, candidates often have a difficult time finding sufficient workers to wage an effective campaign. It is, in fact, easier for a public servant to become a candidate than to work for one according to the provisions of the Public Service Employment Act. It is not clear why the Government made a distinction between these two types of political activity; but the Act, while denying without qualification the right of public servants to work for candidates during an election campaign, does qualify its previous denial of the right of public servants to stand for election. According to the Act:

upon application made to the Commission by an employee the Commission may . . . grant to the employee leave of absence without pay to seek nomination as a candidate and to be a candidate for election . . .[9]

This is an improvement on the 1961 Act, which absolutely forbade public servants to be candidates for federal or provincial election; but the right of public servants to be candidates is by no means guaranteed. A public servant may be a candidate, but only if the Public Service Commission, in the words of the Act, "is of the opinion that the usefulness to the Public Service of the employee in the position he then occupies would not be impaired by reason of his having been a candidate for election . . ."[10] Thus, although the Act appears to admit the right of every citizen to stand for election to Parliament and Provincial Legislature, it gives the Public Service Commission the power to grant or deny this right to individual public servants as it sees fit.

The loosened restrictions on the rights of public servants to political activity in the 1961 and 1967 Acts emphasized the need of some procedure for hearing charges brought against public servants under the new regulations. Under the 1918 Act, public servants had no right to fair hearing or appeal in the event of their dismissal. Until 1922, in fact, a public servant could be dismissed without inquiry of any kind simply if a Member of Parliament directed an oral complaint against him. This abuse was rectified somewhat in 1922 when an Order-in-Council made it necessary for a Member to level his charge in writing and for an investigation of the charge to be conducted prior to the order of dismissal.[11] This procedure was not satisfactory, however, for it was neither permissive nor mandatory. The Heeney Report in 1959 proposed, therefore, that:

a. Charges shall be laid in writing, addressed to a Minister of the Crown, and supported by an affidavit;

6. "Personnel Administration in the Public Service", *op. cit.*, p. 93.
7. Canada, *The Public Service Employment Act, 1967*, Section 32.
8. *Ibid.*, sub section (1).
9. *Ibid.*, sub section (3).
10. *Ibid.*
11. Canada, *Order-in Council*, P. C. 1467, July 22, 1922.

b. When the charges have been laid . . . the Deputy Head shall suspend the employee who was so charged and the Minister shall request the Minister of Justice to initiate an enquiry;

c. The Minister of Justice . . . shall set us a Commission of Enquiry, under the provisions of the Enquiries Act, to investigate and report upon the charges;

d. The report of the Commission of Enquiry shall state the Commission's opinion as to whether there has or has not been a violation, and the report shall be tabled in Parliament;

e. If the Commission of Enquiry is of the opinion that there has been no violation the employee shall be reinstated without loss of pay;

f. If the Commission of Enquiry is of the opinion that the employee is guilty of the violation, the employee shall be dismissed by the Governor-in-Council.[12]

The more important of these recommendations were incorporated in Section 32 of the existing Public Service Employment Act, which provides that:

Where any allegation is made to the Commission by a person who is or has been a candidate for election . . . that a deputy head or employee has contravened subsection (1), the allegation shall be referred to a board established by the Commission to conduct an inquiry at which the person making the allegation and the deputy head or employee concerned, or their representatives, are given an opportunity of being heard, and upon being notified of the board's decision on the inquiry the Commission,

a. in the case of a deputy head, shall report the decision to the Governor in Council who may, if the board has decided that the deputy head has contravened subsection (1), dismiss him; and

b. in the case of an employee, may, if the board has decided that the employee has contravened subsection (1), dismiss the employee.[13]

The new Act thus makes it clear that a public servant, when charged with political partisanship, is entitled to a hearing before he can be dismissed, and that he can be represented at the hearing by legal counsel.

Freedom of speech is intimately conjoined with the right to political activity, and the exercise of this freedom by Canadian public servants is undeniably restricted. These restrictions are not found in the Public Service Employment Act, but rather, in the Official Secrets Act and in the Oath of Secrecy which a public servant swears when he enters the employment of the Government of Canada. Canadian public servants, by the terms of the Official Secrets Act, are forbidden to divulge any official secret or to pass any official information to any person with whom they are not authorized to communicate.[14] They are further restricted by their Oath of Secrecy, which binds them not to disclose or make known any matter that comes to their attention by reason of their employment.[15] The maximum punishment for a felony committed in violation of either Act or Oath is fourteen years of penal servitude. The maximum punishment for a misdemeanour is imprisonment for twelve months, or a fine of five hundred dollars, or both.[16]

Other restrictions of the right of Canadian public servants to exercise their freedom of speech on political matters are not found in any Act of the Canadian Parliament, but rather in the traditions of the Service itself. These restrictions stem from the tradition that public servants should remain neutral on all political issues, and, since 1918, the Canadian Public Service has put into practice the belief expressed by the Masterman Committee that:

the efficient and smooth working of democratic government depends very largely upon maintaining that confidence and on people believing that . . . the civil service will give completely loyal service to the Government of the day.[17]

Canadian public servants, therefore, have restricted themselves in any expression of their views on any political controversy. They indicate publicly neither their approval or disapproval of government policy nor express themselves on matters of party politics. There are no statutory restrictions whatsoever preventing Canadian public servants from criticising governments. They do not criticise simply because they adhere to the traditions of "civil service neutrality" and "ministerial responsibility". In their desire to serve all political parties when in power with equal devotion and detached impartiality they have effectively deprived themselves of their right to discuss matters of public concern, whether political or non-political in nature.

The above discussion demonstrates the conflict between the belief in the necessity of a politically neutral public service and the belief that all citizens should have the right to participate fully in the political affairs of their nation. In the context of the Canadian public service this conflict appears as a problem of reconciling a determination to preserve the integrity and efficiency of the public service with a desire to permit public servants to exercise the same civil liberties as their fellow citizens. There is no doubt that the creation and maintenance of public confidence in the neutrality of the public service is very important to the proper functioning of any democratic institution. It has been recognized for some time in Canada that the merit system fosters this confidence, and that this system can best be maintained if public servants are politically neutral and able to render impartial service to whichever political party is in power. It is also admitted that the abolition of political neutrality throughout the public service would have severe repercussions on the doctrine of ministerial responsibility, and that both unified direction of policy and parliamentary control of the executive would suffer if the Government's chief

12. "Personnel Administration in the Public Service," *op. cit.*, p. 94.

13. *Public Service Employment Act*, section 32, sub section (6).

14. Canada, *Official Secrets Act*, R. S. C. 1952, Chapter 198, Section 4.

15. "*Public Service Employment Act*," Schedule C.

16. *Official Secrets Act*, Section 15.

17. U. K., *Report of the Committee on Political Activities of the Civil Servants*, Cmnd. 7718, London, 1949, p. 14.

advisers were politically partisan. Further, the doctrine of political neutrality protects the public servant. He does not have to defend his actions publicly, and:

His anonymity preserves the constitutional fiction of his political non-commitment and thus ensures his permanency in office whenever there is a change in the governing political party.[18]

Few would deny the need to maintain the integrity of public servants, but the issue here is whether this must be done by politically emasculating the public service. There is another objective which is at least equally important: the exercise of the right of full political participation by as many citizens as is compatible with the effective functioning of government; and if this right is denied to any group, it must be only for the most compelling of reasons. If the denial or restriction of this right is based on a doubt that public servants can be trusted not to create an embarrassing situation for a government if they are restored to full freedom of political action, then there is an urgent need to re-examine the existing restrictions. If it can be demonstrated that public servants, given the fundamental right of political participation, can maintain their efficiency and integrity then there is no logical reason to deny them this right.

The Civil (now Public) Service Commission itself suggests that an efficient and loyal public service can be reconciled with political participation by public servants. In its brief to the Joint Committee of the Senate and of the House of Commons on employer-employee relations in the public service of Canada, the Commission furnished ample evidence to prove that in countries such as Great Britain, which adhere to the doctrine of ministerial responsibility, public servants have been granted the right to political participation without adverse effects on the functioning of government.[19] The practice in these countries points to a solution of the problem confronting the Canadian Public Service today. None of these countries pursues the extremes of complete denial or complete conferal of the right to political activity. Rather, each has granted or restricted this right as best suits its own particular situation. We in Canada would be well advised to follow a like procedure. In Canada, a fair and proper solution of the conflict between the twin objectives of political participation and political neutrality might be achieved if those public servants who, because of their status in the public service, have no influence whatsoever in the process of policy formation were given the freedom to participate fully in all forms of political activity. The implementation of this suggestion would necessitate the division of the Public Service into two groups: those possessing a restricted, and those possessing an unrestricted, right of political participation; but the problem of distinguishing between the two should create no difficulty. Under the terms of the Public Service Staff Relations Act of 1967, public servants are already divided into two broad categories: those who perform managerial functions in a confidential capacity and those who do not.[20] Those public servants who are employed in a managerial or confidential capacity are excluded from the exercise of trade union rights, particularly those of striking and of collective bargaining, and thus the Act provides a convenient distinction within the Public Service which could be used if the Government saw fit to alter the existing Public Service Employment Act. Those public servants in the higher echelons of the Public Service would be denied the right to full participation in the political affairs of the nation, but, because they are the officials who plan and develop government programs, there seems to be no other way to reconcile the necessity of a politically nonpartisan public service with the desirability of political activity by public servants in their capacity as citizens. They might be permitted to stand for election to Parliament or to a provincial legislature, as they are permitted to do under the existing Public Service Employment Act, but only if the Public Service Commission were "of the opinion that the usefulness to the Public Service of the employee in the position he then occupies would not be impaired by reason of his having been a candidate. . . ."[21] The division of public servants into two groups, and the conferal or denial of the right to full political activity on the basis of the functions they perform, not only reconciles the dual objectives of a politically neutral public service and political participation by public servants, but it also maintains the doctrine of ministerial responsibility. Ministers, individually and collectively, would continue to be held accountable for the actions of their employees while these employees were performing their duties as public servants, but not while they were exercising their political rights as responsible citizens. On these grounds, therefore, we propose that all public servants, except those excluded from the collective bargaining process, be permitted to exercise those political rights guaranteed to all citizens by the common law and the federal Bill of Rights.[22] All public servants would, of course, continue to be bound by the Official Secrets Act and the Oath of Secrecy, and no public servant would be permitted to engage in political activity during normal working hours.

Whether this proposal to restore the right of full political participation to most public servants is accepted or not, there are several minor modifications to the existing Public Service Employment Act which should be

18. J. E. Hodgetts, "Challenge and Response: A Restrospective View of the Public Service of Canada", *Canadian Public Administration*, vol. 7, no. 4, December 1964, p. 414.
19. Joint Committee of the Senate and of the House of Commons, *op. cit.*, pp. 327-329.
20. Canada, *The Public Service Staff Relations Act, 1967*, Section 2, sub section (U). According to this Section, in part, a public servant who performs managerial functions or is employed in a confidential capacity is that person:
   (a) who has executive duties and responsibilities in relation to the development and administration of government programs;
   (b) whose duties include those of a personnel adminstrator or who is directly involved in the process of collective bargaining on behalf of the employer-Government of Canada, and
   (c) who is employed as the deputy head of a department or the chief executive officer in the public service.
21. Canada, *The Public Service Employment Act, 1967*, Section 32, sub section (3).
22. Canada, *Bill of Rights, 1960*, Section 1, sub section (d).

made. The act, in its present form, does not give guidance on all matters of political concern to public servants, nor are its clauses completely clear. One matter not mentioned in the Act concerns the right of public servants to participate in municipal elections. It appears that they are permitted to do so under the terms of the 1960 Order-in-Council,[23] but the conferral of this right should be clearly specified in the Act, especially since it appears likely that candidates at future municipal elections will be campaigning under the labels of federal and provincial political parties. Section 32, sub-section 3, of the existing Act, which gives the Public Service Commission the power to permit or forbid all public servants to stand for election, should be altered to give all public servants not in a managerial or confidential capacity leave of absence to run if they are nominated. This leave of absence should be automatically granted without exception by Department Heads, and the Public Service Commission should be duly informed of such action. The effective functioning of government does not require such control over public servants who have no influence on the formation of public policy. Section 32, sub-section (5) of the Act stipulates that once a public servant is elected to the Federal House or to a provincial legislature he ceases to be an employee of the Crown. This means that, once elected, a person loses his right of tenure in the Public Service. It seems unjust that a public servant who exercises his right to stand for election is penalized if he is elected. Public servants who are elected to public office should have the option to rejoin the Public Service after their terms of office are completed, and if they decide to return their re-entry at their former level should be automatic.

A final matter for consideration concerns the allegations of and penalties for political partisanship which can be made against public servants. Sub-section (6) of the Act restricts the types of individuals who can bring charges of political partisanship against a public servant, but appears not to restrict the time at which they can make them.[24] The Act permits only those who are or were candidates for election to the federal, provincial, or territorial Houses to bring charges against a public servant, but the use of the phrase "a person *who is or has been* a candidate for election" opens the possibility that a candidate at a previous election could bring a charge of political partisanship against a public servant for an act alleged to have occurred during a present campaign, or vice-versa. It may be, perhaps, that the drafters of the Act assumed that such charges would concern only those acts alleged to have been committed during the most recent election campaign, but the addition to the Act of a simple statement to this effect would preclude any misunderstanding. Further, it is not clear whether a charge of political partisanship can be brought against a public servant who entered or re-entered the Public Service after having been defeated at the polls. This situation could very easily arise, and a suitable amendment to the Act would be one that effectively prevented the laying of charges against public servants who failed in their attempt to serve their country in another capacity.

In conclusion, the authors of this article believe the Section on political partisanship in the existing Public Service Employment Act to be imperfect in two ways: in the deficiency and ambiguity of its sub-sections; and in the assumption on which the Section on political activity itself is based. New sub-sections should be added to the Section, and several existing sub-sections need clarification; suggestions have been made above for the achievement of these ends. More important, however, is the fact that the basic assumption on which this Section is founded needs to be re-examined. The Section, although a first step away from the tradition of a half-century, is still a product of the belief that a politically non-partisan public service is essential at all costs. Consequently, the Section denies all public servants many of the fundamental political rights enjoyed by all other Canadian citizens. The authors reject the validity of this belief, and suggest that the benefits of a politically neutral public service can be attained without a prohibition on the political activity of all public servants. We agree that the effective functioning of government demands political impartiality on the part of those public servants involved in the formation of public policy. However, we submit that the remainder of public servants could be given the right of complete political participation, and we believe that such a reform is possible without endangering the governmental process in Canada or compromising the integrity of the Public Service. The experience of other countries has demonstrated that the assumption on which the existing Section on political partisanship is based is no longer valid, and that, in fact, the twin objectives of political neutrality on the part of the Public Service and political activity on the part of all but a few public servants can be reconciled. It is our contention, therefore, that this country would gain much more than it would lose by a restoration of the right of political participation to all but a few of its public servants, and further that it would be more in accordance with the principles of our liberal democracy to do so.

23. Canada, *Memorandum: Public Office- Municipal or Civic*, P. C. 1960-1121, August 12, 1960.
24. Canada, *The Public Service Employment Act, 1967*, Section 32, sub section (6).

SECTION FIVE

JUDICIARY

The importance of the judiciary in Canada has been underestimated all too frequently. In recent years, however, it has come to be recognized as a strong force in the Canadian political process, as Edward McWhinney demonstrates in his article on constitutional review.

Jacques-Yvan Morin's thought-provoking article on constitutional adjudication does more than raise doubts about the wisdom of the present judicial system in Canada; it also presents a clear case for a new constitutional court, one which would ensure the preservation of the "two Canadian nations", and correct the "imbalance" brought about by the Supreme Court of Canada since 1949.

S. R. Peck brings the section to a close with a scalogram analysis of the Supreme Court of Canada, demonstrating how the methodology of behavioural science can assist us to understand the forces and influences which affect judicial decision-making at the highest level of the Canadian judiciary.

23

The Canadian Supreme Court and Constitutional Reviews*

EDWARD McWHINNEY

THE INHERENTLY POLITICAL CHARACTER OF CONSTITUTIONAL REVIEW

Shortly after the appearance of the first edition of my book, *Judicial Review in the English-Speaking World*, a little over a decade ago, one of the older-generation English law professors charged me, in effect, with introducing "left-of-centre" political attitudes into the task of judicial criticism. It had been one of my theses that the historical record of judicial interpretation of social and economic legislation, in the United Kingdom itself and also in the Colonial Empire and the Commonwealth, – not less than in the United States in the so-called "Gilded Era" (liberty-of-contract-in-the-abstract period) of American capitalism which lasted, roughly, from the end of the Civil War until the Roosevelt "New Deal" era – revealed a more or less conscious judicial preoccupation with questions of social and economic basic values. I had further suggested that this judicial preoccupation had been all too frequently manifested in a direct injection of judicial value preferences into the cases that the judges were deciding. In this same context, another English professor of the same era charged me with being "unfair" to the Privy Council – the highest appellate tribunal of the old British Colonial Empire and of the Commonwealth – and in particular "unfair" to two of the most dominant judicial personalities in its modern history, Lord Watson and Lord Haldane, in my analysis and appraisal of the detailed record of the Privy Council's interpretation of the Canadian Constitution.

Looking back, – and though it is now only a decade ago – these particular English criticisms seem curiously jejune and out-dated, so much have the Legal Realist teachings of the law-making, law-creating role of the final appellate judge become received opinion, since that time, in Commonwealth, and not less perhaps by now, in English law schools. On any empirically-based study, it hardly seems possible to deny that the particular decisions referred to, given by the English and Commonwealth judges in

---

*Reprinted, with permission, from the *Canadian Bar Review*, vol. XLV, 1967.

regard to social and economic legislation, were neither necessary nor inevitable in terms of the positive law as written; and that the judicial interventionism, at the value level, involved the judicial projection, in positive law form, of the values of an earlier, usually more laissez-faire-attuned, era of society in place of the rather more contemporary legislative majorities.

As to the Privy Council and its record of interpretation of the Canadian Constitution,[1] my criticism had been directed specifically to the failure of the Privy Council frankly to acknowledge and admit, in its formal opinions accompanying its decisions, that it was engaging in constitutional elaborations that were neither expressly warranted by the text of the constitution, nor supported by the original historical intentions of the Founding Fathers of the constitution, in reaching the results that the Privy Council did, in the period from 1896 onwards, in relation to social and economic planning legislation and Dominion-provincial relations generally. The judicial policy-maker surely has certain obligations of public candour, in order to expose the judicial policy choices to the democratic corrective of public discussion and criticism. The failure of the Privy Council, in relation to the Canadian Constitution, to be frank and explicit as to the policy bases of its opinions, meant that the reasons for the actual policy choices too often remained obscured and concealed, with the policy considerations necessarily operating then as "inarticulate major premises" to the final decision.[2] And the failure to articulate these same policy bases meant, in turn, that the judges were not directly assisted by counsel, through the *Brandeis Brief* technique of bringing social and economic facts before the court, or otherwise, in the building of an appropriate factual record that might inform and assist a judicial conclusion on complex social and economic issues. If we had judicial policy-making on the part of the Privy Council in relation to the Canadian Constitution, in the period from 1896 onwards, it was, necessarily, because of these very omissions, a species of policy-making in the dark, – at best, loosely impressionistic and in the end rather hit-and-miss.

It is possible in this regard to argue that a good number of the past decisions of the Privy Council, – viewed, now, in policy terms, – whatever their relationships to particular social and economic predilections on the part of the individual members of the judiciary taking part in them, happen to make sense also – that is to say, can be justified pragmatically – in terms of the development of a community consensus in the individual countries for whom the Privy Council was deciding. In this regard, while it may be difficult to think of a more aridly conceptual decision, viewed now in strict positive law terms, than the Privy Council's Labour Conventions decision of 1937,[3] it is a fact that the policy consequences of the decision are at the

1. Judicial Review in the English-Speaking World, Toronto: University of Toronto Press 1956, footnote 1. ch. 4.

2. See per Holmes J., dissenting, in *Lochner* v. *New York* (1905), 98 U.S. 45, at p. 74.

3. *Attorney-General for Canada* v. *Attorney-General for Ontario*, [1937] A.C. 326 (P.C.).

core of the present great constitutional debate in Canada. Nevertheless, Lord Wright, one of the main judicial authors of the Labour Conventions decision, in his informed second thoughts about the decision, had such grave reservations as to its rationality, from the viewpoint of the "black-letter law" and the traditional rules of construction, that, many years after the decision, he took the unusual step, for a judge, of uttering his own public *mea culpa* – in effect, a retrospective dissent.[4] The Privy Council's official opinion, in the Labour Conventions case, is pitched in "black-letter law" terms alone, and singularly barren of the policy-type arguments which might serve to redeem or justify it today as a conscious value-choice among competing key concepts as to federalism and the desirable location and distribution of community decision-making power in a plural-cultural society.

THE DILEMMAS OF JUDICIAL POLICY-MAKING IN CANADA

Important changes of judicial personnel, in recent years, on several of the final appellate tribunals of the English-speaking countries, go to the core of the intellectual conflict between the proponents of judicial activism and the proponents of judicial self-restraint. The political changes foreshadowed in the case of the Supreme Court of Canada, in the late 1950's by the departure of Mr. Justice Rand on his reaching the compulsory retirement age of seventy-five in 1959, and by the voluntary retirement, a little earlier, of Mr. Justice Kellock, his closest intellectual associate on the court, seem to have been realised. In retrospect, the period of liberal activism on the Canadian Supreme Court – lasting about a decade – can be seen substantially as having come to an end with the Roncarelli case decision in 1959, the last great decision in which Mr. Justice Rand participated.[5] The explanation for this lies only partly, however, in changes in judicial personnel on the court and the fact that the successors to Justices Rand and Kellock seem to be much more in the tradition of judicial self-abnegation than to be adherents to the liberal activist credo. Part of the explanation undoubtedly lies in the practical disappearance, or at least muting, of the sort of great political *causes célèbres* that are especially ripe for sweeping policy pronouncements. With the death of their political arch-enemy, Premier Duplessis of Quebec, in 1959, the Jehovah's Witnesses have apparently been directing the main thrust of their aggressive religious proselytising activities elsewhere than in the predominantly French-speaking and Roman Catholic Province of Quebec. In any case, no major direct confrontations between the Jehovah's Witnesses on the one hand and the Quebec provincial governmental authorities or the Quebec police have in fact taken place since that time. This all recalls, of course, Jeremy Bentham's maxim that the law is not made by judge alone, but by "judge and company" – which specifically includes counsel who are prepared and competent to take cases right through to the final appellate level. Virtually all of the great Canadian civil liberties cases of the decade up to 1959 arose, originally, from cases involving individual Jehovah's Witnesses; for these cases provided, in effect, the vehicles for judicial legislation in an area not heretofore specifically covered in any constitutional bill of rights or other fundamental law charter. It is important to recognize how much, practically, the state of Canadian constitutional law-in-action today is the product of the energies of a litigation-minded, and politically unpopular, minority pressure group like the Jehovah's Witnesses.

The seeds of the judicial conflict originally planted in these Jehovah's Witnesses-derived cases remain, however. In the first place, the Canadian Supreme Court split unmistakably, in these cases, along general ethnic-cultural lines, with an Anglo-Saxon, essentially (though not exclusively) Protestant, common law majority deciding the cases, over the strong dissent of the two French-speaking. Roman Catholic, civil law[6] judges. In cases whose fact-complexes fairly uniformly had their origins in the public assault made by the Jehovah's Witnesses in the Province of Quebec upon the Roman Catholic Church – the religion of the majority of the inhabitants of the Province of Quebec – and in correlative attempts by the Quebec provincial governmental authorities to control or to suppress this activity, the Canadian Supreme Court majority imposed, in effect, what it undoubtedly conceived of as the more comprehensive or general, *national* values upon the more specialised, provincial or *local* values. It seems quite clear, in any case, that in situations involving competitions or conflicts between the interests in speech and communication on the one hand and interests in public order, the Anglo-Saxon, common law judges on the Canadian Supreme court tended, in the decade of the 1950's ending in 1959, to strike the balance of the competing interests in a quite different way to their French-speaking, civil law colleagues. More than that, it seems clear, from the judicial dispositions of the Jehovah's Witnesses cases arising from Quebec, that particular fact-complexes that the Anglo-Saxon judges on the Canadian Supreme Court characterised fairly uniformly as civil liberties situations, were characterised quite otherwise by the minority, French-speaking judges – presumably as simple situations involving the community protection of public safety or public morals.

4. See Lord Wright's comments on the Labour Conventions decision, in the course of his tribute to Chief Justice Sir Lyman Duff of the Canadian Supreme Court, in (1955), 33 *Can. Bar Rev.* 1123.

5. *Roncarelli* v. *Duplessis* (1959), 16 D.L.R. (2d) 689, [1959] S.C.R. 122: analysed in detail in (1959). 37 *Can. Bar Rev.* 503.

6. The third civil law member of the court, — required in terms of the express stipulation in the Supreme Court Act (Canada) 1949, R.S.C., 1952, c. 259, as am., that three of the nine members of the court should come from the Province of Quebec — Mr. Justice Abbott, is of course, in terms of language classification, English-speaking. As a matter of record, Mr. Justice Abbott, in those of the Jehovah's Witnesses-derived *causes célèbres* of the 1950's in which he himself participated, parted company with his French-speaking civil law colleagues and joined with the English-speaking common law majority.

THE RELATION OF CONSTITUTIONAL REVIEW TO NATIONAL CONSTITUTIONAL CONSENSUS

The role of a Supreme Court functioning as a federal institution becomes especially difficult under circumstances when there are, in effect, two or more radically different *Weltanschauungen* within the one country. If the conflict between particularistic, regionally-based, ethnic-cultural attitudes and values on the one hand, and over-all or majority *national* attitudes and values on the other, be not too extreme, a mutually satisfying accommodation may no doubt be reached on a federalistic principle (along lines generally favoured by the late Mr. Justice Felix Frankfurter of the United States Supreme Court), of deference to the regional authority, and in particular of deference to the decisions and determinations of the regional authority's supreme court or other tribunals. Unarticulated philosophic considerations of this nature certainly seem to base, in part at least, various political proposals being advanced in Canada at the present time that the highest tribunal of the Province of Quebec, the Quebec Court of Appeal, be made the final appellate tribunal for cases arising under the Quebec Civil Code (without appeal therefrom to the Canadian Supreme Court); or that the Canadian Supreme Court should be divided into bancs or chambers specialised by subject matter, with a civil law banc, composed of judges trained in the civil law, having sole competence over the Quebec Civil Code.

Where the issues involved are of the nature, for example, of parental custody of minor children and whether the mother or the father should have primacy as to this[7] – something on which the Quebec civil law, and the common law as practised in the English-speaking provinces, might seem to reach different results, the price of such accommodation, and of any consequent national deference to provincial values, may not be felt to be oppressive.[8]

Where, however, as in the case of the issue in the United States, of racial segregation in education, the social consensus eventually emerges, nationally, that tolerance to regionally-based diversity in basic values on this particular issue is no longer compatible with democratic constitutionalism, then compromise may cease to be possible any longer. One may be left, in this situation, with the ultimate choice either of imposition of national values by national instrumentalities (of which, of course, a federal Supreme Court is necessarily one), or else perhaps of outright political separatism.

A federal Supreme Court, with its undoubted national prestige and authority, can certainly assist, by the course of its decisions, in promoting, in time, a genuine national consensus that will increasingly reconcile the particularist regional values with over-all national values. Yet this public educational function of a Supreme Court is undoubtedly a difficult one to execute, and it will normally require making an ally of time and proceeding slowly. The ultimate result in the United States, in 1954, in *Brown* v. *Board of Education*,[9] was undoubtedly predictable, after the series of rather modest, essentially fact-oriented decisions, usually under the rubric of the "separate but equal" formula, that the United States Supreme Court had begun to give in State education cases from the late 1930's onwards. But it did take a rather long time to reach the ultimate Supreme Court decision outlawing segregation in education, as such. And the practical effectuation of the 1954 decision was hardly assisted by the substantial inaction in race relations matters, during most of the 1950's, of the Presidency and of Congress – the two organs, after all, charged under the constitution with prime responsibility for governmental activism in the major areas of community social policy. In this light, it hardly seems fair to criticise the United States Supreme Court too much for the frequent deference to considerations of judicial self-restraint which refined or moderated its judicial policy-making during that same time period.

LIMITS OF RELEVANCE, AND UNIVERSALITY, TO AMERICAN-STYLE CONSTITUTIONAL REVIEW. SPECIAL "AMERICAN" FACTORS IN THE POLITICAL SUCCESS OF THE UNITED STATES SUPREME COURT

A Supreme Court is not the only possible, nor even necessarily at all times the most useful or most desirable, instrument of constitutional review. Recognition of the undoubted political success and also the fairly wide-spread public acceptance of judicially-based constitutional review in the United States should not blind us to the special facts that have contributed so largely to the viability of judicial review as a prime instrument of democratic constitutionalism in the United States, in comparison to other methods and forms of constitutional review and constitutional checks and balances that might have been tried there and that have certainly been historically tested in other legal systems.

First, the essential constitutional law character of the jurisdiction of the United States Supreme Court has emancipated its members from the irksome necessity of too much technical training and experience prior to appointment to the court, or of too much specialist expertise in too many different and largely unrelated fields of law – the latter, in any case, a largely unattainable ideal – and so facilitated the growth of a free-wheeling, philosophically unencumbered and, in end result, largely pragmatic approach to constitutional adjudication, that emphasises what is politically sensible and socially useful – in effect, what will work, today – as distinct from what may have been constitutionally pre-ordained in some bygone age.

Second, the largely "men-of-affairs" background of appointees to the

7. *Donaldson* v. *Taillon*, [1953] 2 S.C.R. 257. And see Lalande. Puissance paternelle – déchéance – droit civil et jurisprudence de Québec – composition de la Cour suprême du Canada (1953), 33 *Can. Bar. Rev.* 950.

8. Lalande, *ibid*. Also Lalande. "Audition des appels de Québec à la Cour suprême" (1955). 33 *Can. Bar Rev.* 1104. And see generally Legal Theory and Philosophy of Law in Canada, in *Canadian Jurisprudence. The Civil Law and Common Law in Canada* (1958), p. 1, especially at p. 9; Baudouin. *Methode d'interprétation judiciaire du Code civil du Québec* (1950), 10 R. du B. 397.

9. (1954), 347 U.S. 483; and see generally. "An End to Racial Discrimination in the United States? The school-Segregation Decisions (1954)", 32 *Can. Bar Rev.* 545.

United States Supreme Court – with direct political experience in public life (as Attorney-General or Solicitor-General or as a senator) looming largely as a qualification for Presidential nomination to the court and Senate confirmation of the actual presidential choices – has encouraged a broad, legislative approach to constitutional adjudication in which policy is generally emphasised and preferred to a narrowly technical, essentially abstract, "legalistic" approach.

Third, the discretionary control that the United States Supreme Court is able to exercise over the nature and timing of the cases coming before it, allied to the very large number of cases among which, in effect, it may pick and choose the very limited number that it will finally elect to hear and decide on the merits, facilitates a continuing, staged or planned, gradualist, step-by-step, approach to judicial legislation, in all the major areas of community policy-making.

Fourth, in spite of the apparent surface vehemence of many contemporary American political *causes célèbres*, the United States has in fact achieved a substantial degree of national consensus as to the "American way of life" and the key concepts or basic values of American society, which the Supreme Court, for its part, has usually been fairly easily able to apprehend and to concretise in constitutional law decisions. While, for example, the school-segregation disputes in the late 1940's and early 1950's might have seemed, in the early stages at least, to mirror what Roscoe Pound, following Kohler, used to identify as differing or opposing "civilisation-areas", in this case national and local (State), each with their own distinct and separate value system, any absolutist conceptions of a politically un-bridgeable gap between national and local societal attitudes as to racial segregation in education were demonstrated to be greatly exaggerated, and in the final analysis untrue, as the aftermath of the United States Supreme Court's decision in *Brown* v. *Board of Education* in 1954 has demonstrated. These earlier, historically fatalist and pessimistic attitudes simply failed to appreciate the extent to which original white supremacist positions of the erstwhile political *élite* in the Southern States had been eroded, or at least mitigated in their impact upon underlying societal attitudes in the Southern States, by the passage of national political events in the years since the post-Civil War "Reconstruction" period and its immediate aftermath.

Fifth, the very fact of exercising judicial review, for a period of a century and a half and more, has given the United States Supreme Court a certain political confidence and political *savoir-faire*, and more important perhaps, a certain continuing oral tradition of specialist judicial experience in the constitutional handling and legal moderation of great political *causes célèbres*, particularly when these political *causes célèbres* threaten to involve the judiciary in adverse relationships or power struggles with countervailing executive or legislative authority. This immense back-log of past experience in handling great political issues is especially helpful in deciding when the Supreme Court should choose to follow the path of political prudence either by immunising itself procedurally from the necessity of passing upon a particular political issue or else by exercising self-restraint and caution in its actual pronouncement on that issue; and in deciding when, by contrast, the Supreme Court should try to strike out boldly and seek to elaborate or apply a new community norm for the future. . . .

A SPECIALIST, FEDERAL CONSTITUTIONAL COURT FOR A BICULTURAL CANADA?

The constitutional lawyer of today, of course, is likely to be far more modest than were his predecessors in that era of rationalised constitutionalism between the two World Wars. For he will normally be much more aware of the extent to which constitutional forms and institutions follow on, and do not precede, fundamental societal consensus. On this approach, the wise constitutional lawyer today is apt to argue that the business of constitutional novation or constitutional drafting generally should wait upon solution of other, more pressing community problems, usually of social and economic, and non-constitutional, character.

If, however, the stage should be reached, in the present Canadian constitutional "great debate", of consideration of over-all constitutional change or re-casting, involving the function and role of the Canadian Supreme Court, it is difficult to avoid the conclusion that the case for the principle of judicial specialisation, in some form or other more clamant than the court's present loose, all-ranging, "general" competence and jurisdiction, can hardly be denied. The apparent absence of any backward glances, with which the court ventured upon accepting jurisidiction in the Offshore Oil Reference from the Dominion government is not merely a commentary upon the inherent limitations of the court's advisory opinion jurisdiction, un-fact-oriented and abstract as such constitutional references invariably must be. It is also a commentary upon the perils that attend a non-specialist tribunal venturing into a difficult and complex area of positive law where black-letter law precedents from one's own law tend to be lacking; and where also American precedents, with their own special, internal policy elements, seem much less relevant than usual to a wise policy decision in a specifically contemporary, "bicultural", Canadian context. A politically more tried and tested, specialist constitutional tribunal in another country, facing a policy choice of similar dimensions without compelling pre-existing positive law criteria to help it in its task, would by now, I think, have recognised the high political character of the choice that it was being called upon to make – going beyond the ordinary political elements necessarily inherent in any constitutional decision-making – and it would by now, I think, have returned the Offshore Oil Reference to the executive-legislative authority whence it originally stemmed, as being a non-justiciable "political question".[10] The content and scope of what is non-justiciable as being a "political question" will, as with any other legal category that

10. For criticism of the advisory opinion jurisdiction of the Canadian Supreme Court, and the actual practice under it, as conducing to an extreme abstractness in the court's constitutional opinions, see Freund, *A Supreme Court in a Federation: Some Lessons from Legal History* (1953), 53 Col. L. Rev. 597, at pp. 617-618.

requires judicial evaluation on the particular facts, necessarily vary according to time and place; yet the doctrine of *non liquet* must surely have a place in the political armoury of any specialist appellate tribunal called upon to exercise the high policy-making function inherent in public law adjudication.

If judicial specialisation is to be achieved, as an objective in Supreme Court jurisdictional reorganisation consequent upon any fundamental constitutional rewriting, it might take several forms. The simplest mode, meeting some well-documented, but so far hardly very persuasive, complaints about the Supreme Court's actual record of review of civil law cases arising under the Quebec Civil Code,[11] might be to establish a specialist civil law banc within the court to hear civil law cases, composed entirely of civil law judges. By the same logic, of course, we could hardly, then, avoid having a specialist common law banc, and another specialist banc to hear criminal law appeals, – something that would probably, by itself, necessitate a considerable increase in the court's present membership of nine judges if a constitutional law banc were to be retained and anything like minimum specialist legal expertise assured on each of these specialist bancs so created, which would presumably have to have a minimum of at least five judges apiece.

It is for reasons of what they consider to be an extreme cumbersomeness in any multi-banc system in a final appellate tribunal (though such a system, as we all know, works fairly simply and easily with the French *Cour de Cassation*), as well as for reasons of the obvious intellectual attractiveness and the general political effectiveness of specialist Continental legal tribunals like the French *Conseil d'Etat* and the West German *Bundesverfassungsgericht*, that a number of Canadian jurists have been favouring having specialist, autonomous, and separate tribunals at the final appellate level in Canada, meaning here essentially a Supreme Court of Appeals for civil law matters; a Supreme Court of Appeals for common law matters; and finally a federal Constitutional Court having a jurisdiction that would also include criminal law and civil liberties.[12]

An alternative suggestion, that recognises as amply as the others the advantages of judicial specialisation, would involve building up the authority and status of the provincial supreme courts on lines analogous to those of the state supreme courts in the United States. This would mean, in effect, confining common law and civil law matters, criminal law appeals, provincial constitutional questions and the like, to the provincial court systems and hierarchies, with the highest provincial courts' decisions being final except in so far as federal constitutional (including civil liberties) issues might be involved. In these latter situations the cases might go up to the Canadian Supreme Court, either directly, or else on appeal after all provincial remedies and appeals had been exhausted. But in general, this particular suggestion of favouring the provincial supreme courts would seem to involve, as a correlative, transferring the power of nomination and appointment of provincial supreme court judges and of the provincial judiciary generally to the provincial governments, – something, indeed, that is the constitutional rule and practice in virtually every other federal system than Canada's.

The point is, of course, that once the principle of judicial specialisation has been accepted, the question of how best to effect it is not lacking in comparative law precedents that should be readily capable of adaptation to Canada's special needs today; and the problem of choice between these different modes does not seem an especially difficult one.

CANONS OF SELF-RESTRAINT FOR THE CANADIAN SUPREME COURT, (AS PRESENTLY CONSTITUTED), IN AN ERA OF MARKED POLITICAL ("BICULTURAL") CONFLICT

Constitutional problems tend, as we have suggested earlier, to be subordinate to other, non-constitutional problems. If it should be concluded, therefore, at the political level, that the issue of reform of the structure and jurisdiction of the Supreme Court of Canada should wait upon solution of other, non-constitutional (presumably social and economic), problems of a pressing character; or if it should be concluded, even, that at the level of constitutional law change itself, reform of the court is to be given less priority than many other measures, (for example, redistribution and re-allocation of taxation and fiscal powers as between the federal authority and the provinces), ways certainly remain open for the court, within its presently existing jurisdictional limits and its presently settled practice, to respond flexibly and prudently to the political facts-of-life of Canadian federalism of today, with the new emphasis on ethnic-cultural diversity and political pluralism. Among these judicial "rules of reason" we might advance the following list.

First, and quite obviously, in cases originating under the Quebec Civil Code and raising what might be called "pure" civil law questions unaffected by civil liberties or general constitutional law issues, the common law majority on the court should sensibly exercise judicial self-restraint and in general defer to the views of their civil law brethren on the court. Beyond this, the facilities available within the Supreme Court's present rules for ensuring that, of any panel of judges hearing a civil law case, a majority of the judges will always be drawn from the civil law (if need be by summoning *ad hoc* judges to sit on the court specially for that case), should be exercised to the full.[13]

Second, on matters affecting the provincial constitutions or indeed, involving provincial public law exercises in general, the Supreme Court

11. In a study first made in 1958, I advanced the hypothesis that cases like *Donaldson* v. *Taillon, supra*, footnote 7, were the rare exception rather than the rule, and that in general there was no significant difference between the record of the civil law judges and the common law judges on the Supreme Court of Canada in regard to cases arising under the Quebec Civil Code. "Legal Theory and Philosophy of Law in Canada," in *Canadian Jurisprudence*. The Civil Law and Common Law in Canada (1958), p. 6 *et seq.*

12. See, for example, Morin. "A Constitutional Court for Canada" (1956), 43 *Can. Bar Rev.* 545.

13. See, in this regard, the concrete suggestions advanced by Lalande, *loc. cit.*, footnote 8.

should be loath to strike down provincial legislation or provincial administrative action – at least in the absence of a positive conflict with federal constitutional law concretely evidenced by an active, adversary, federal governmental intervention against the provincial legislation or provincial action in the case actually before the court. The court should particularly avoid enunciating federal-provincial constitutional conflicts in the abstract; and in the absence of positive federal governmental intervention, the court should apply the ordinary rule of judicial self-restraint and uphold the challenged provincial legislation or provincial administrative action accordingly, in effect conceding a presumption of constitutionality to the provincial measure.[14]

Third, where there is positive conflict between a provincial law or provincial governmental action and the federal governmental authorities, as concretely evidenced by an active or adversary, federal governmental intervention in the instant case, the Supreme Court's role necessarily becomes politically far more complicated. It is difficult to avoid the conclusion that, in such cases, the integrity of the judicial process demands, in the present era of cultural conflicts and differences where no new, clear over-all national constitutional consensus seems as yet to have emerged, an even greater exercise than usual of the principles of judicial auto-limitation. The court, in this sense, should try to immunise itself from the exigent here-and-now of partisan politics as far as possible by insisting on observance of a strict jurisdictional base before it rules upon any issue, and by insisting upon a proper factual record so as to avoid constitutional rulings that are, in effect, abstract general philosophical pronouncements. In particular, the court would seem to be wise to make an ally of time in great political *causes célèbres* arising from the current bicultural debate, and to avoid rushing to judgment as far as possible. By way of some comparison, the West German Federal Constitutional Court had the issue of the banning of the West German Communist Party before it for five years before it at last rendered a decision in 1956, and even then it only gave its decision because it was assumed (quite wrongly, I believe) that the court's rules required it then.[15] Looking back, it can be assumed that it might have done no harm for the West German court to have held the *Communist Party* case for another ten years, by which time the case might have been already resolved by political, and not judicial, means, and so have become legally otiose, or moot, as actually happened to the West German court, for example, in the complex affair, in the middle 1950's, of the various processes coming before it concerning constitutionality of the European Defence Community projects.[16]

The point is, of course, that there are periods in the life of any policy-making constitutional court that are ripe for judicial innovation and ultimately for judicial legislation, and other periods that are not. In these latter cases, the courts sensibly should recognise and accept the practical limits on judicial policy-making and, as an exercise in wise judicial statesmanship, leave the social problem-solving for other, cognate arenas of government. In the present circumstances of the Canadian constitutional debate, the federal government could help by trying not to pass on its own political "hot potatoes" over to court. The federal government, in this regard, has hardly done the court a service by giving it a *cause célèbre* of such high partisan and sectional political intensity, and such low technical legal authority, as the offshore oil issue. The court might, perhaps, properly return the compliment by recognising that this latter is a "political question", better resolved by the ordinary political processes of give-and-take and compromise in the specialised arena of the Dominion-provincial conferences. The Dominion-provincial conferences now seem to be the main *locus* for community problem-solving in Canada, in the absence of an over-all national constitutional consensus which purely federal agencies, like the Supreme Court, can expect to discern and apply with any real prospect of general community acceptance and support, nation-wide.[17]

As a fourth point, where cases arise involving fundamental civil liberties allegedly infringed by provincial legislation or provincial governmental action, the Supreme Court may be faced with its cruellest political dilemma. It would be a distortion of the court's past jurisprudence not to recognise that this particular type of case provided the great political *causes célèbres* coming before the court in the decade beginning with the close of the 1940's and ending, with the close of the 1950's, with the handing down of the decision in the Roncarelli case[18] and, almost contemporaneously, the retirement of Mr. Justice Ivan C. Rand from the court. It would also be doing less than a service to the truth in recounting Canadian constitutional history not to recognise frankly that, in these cases, the Supreme Court's judges in general split along essentially ethnic-cultural lines, with the Anglophonic judges on the court making up the majority and the Francophonic judges composing the minority. I wrote on another occasion,[19] of these cases, that they revealed two radically different, if not indeed sometimes directly opposing, judicial *Weltanschauungen* or value systems, going to the basic values of a constitutional society. For in situations involving conflicts between the interests in speech and communication on the one hand and the interests in public order on the other, it became apparent, in these cases, that the English-speaking common law judges and the French-speaking civil law judges would strike the balance of the competing interests in different ways: or, putting it in other and simpler terms, what

14. This particular point is developed more fully in the author's recent article: "The New, Pluralistic Federalism in Canada" (1967), 2 *Thémis* 139, at pp. 142-143.

15. Edward McWhinney *Constitutionalism in Germany and the Federal Constitutional Court* (1962), p. 32 *et seq.* Leyden: A. W. Sythoff Ltd., 1962.

16. *Ibid.*, p. 40.

17. Compare Pigeon, "The Meaning of Provincial Autonomy" (1951), 29 *Can. Bar Rev.* 1126, at p. 1134; "Report of the Royal Commission of Inquiry on Constitutional Problems." Province of Quebec (1956), vol. 2, pp. 35-37 [*The Tremblay Report*].

18. *Roncarelli* v. *Duplessis, supra*, footnote 5.

19. A Supreme Court in a Bicultural Society: The Future Role of the Canadian Supreme Court," in Ontario Advisory Committee on Confederation. *Background Papers and Reports* (1967), vol. 1: and see more generally *Judicial Review in the English-Speaking World* (3rd ed., 1965). p. 200 *et seq.*

the common law judges characterised as a civil liberties issue the civil law judges would either characterise as not involving civil liberties at all or else involving a civil liberty of Quebec citizens not to be subjected to aggressive or insulting religious proselytising activities.

I do not pretend to have found the wise solution, as yet, to this particular dilemma of judicial policy-making, and I certainly recognize its magnitude; for it goes to the core of a constitutional debate that, in Canada today, involves plural, and sometimes competing, constitutional philosophies. *Le Devoir* of Montreal, in a thoughtful and well-reasoned editorial[20] responding to some of my own comments on this point in a special report to Premier Robarts of Ontario's Advisory Committee on Confederation,[21] suggested that the existence of a double system of constitutional values and consequently also of constitutional characterisations rooted in the philosophic key concepts of the two main ethnic-cultural systems making up Canada today, pointed up the need for reflecting these special societal facts in constitutional reorganisation involving the Canadian Supreme Court, – presumably by way of establishment of a federal constitutional court composed equally of judges from English-speaking and French-speaking Canada and with equal voting rights as between the two groups of judges. For my own part, I have the impression that these value differences, at least where they affect claimed interests of the citizen and the social group in the speech and communication area, may be more relevant and meaningful in the case of older legal generations and hence also, by definition, the judicial members of the present Canadian legal establishment. For the young civil lawyers who are currently spearheading the "Quiet Revolution" in Quebec seem in many respects far more activist in the support of speech and communication interests and civil liberties generally than their English-speaking, common law contemporaries, and so any philosophic differences between the two main components of the Canadian community, in this area at least, can be expected to diminish markedly with time, and not to be perpetuated.

Perhaps the answer, in political-institutional terms at least, may lie in uniform provincial and federal Bills of Rights, adopted by all of the provinces (both French-speaking and English-speaking) and the Dominion. This particular proposal was first noted by Premier John Robarts of Ontario and his constitutional advisers,[22] at the time that an entrenched constitutional Bill of Rights, within the provincial constitution of the Province of Quebec, was being advocated by Premier Daniel Johnson and Opposition Leader Jean Lesage of Quebec,[23] and the idea was later taken up by Prime Minister Lester Pearson.[24] It would be a gain, of course, if the nature and the extent of the dilemma could be more generally realised, – by the judiciary of course (both common law and civil law), and by the general public. Judicial activism, even granted a fairly general or over-all national consensus and popular support as in the case of the United States, can only do so much to atone for the sins of omission of executive and legislative authority, and for their frequent inefficiency and inaction, and occasional simple political cowardice. In the end, the preservation of national minimum standards of constitutional liberties and the Rule of

Law generally must rest on public opinion and on political action expressed through the ordinary political processes; and no amount of judicial liberalism can be expected to fill the gap in constitutional law created by a combination of weak or timorous executive-legislative authority and an apathetic and indifferent, or downright intolerant, general public.

20. Editorial by Paul Sauriol, *Le Devoir*, Montreal, May 13th, 1967.

21. *Supra*, footnote 18.

22. See, for example, the report, "The Provinces and the Protection of Civil Liberties in Canada," in Ontario Advisory Committee on Confederation. *Background papers and Reports.* (1967), vol. 2.

23. See, for example, speech of the Hon. Daniel Johnson reported in *La Tribune de Sherbrooke, The Montreal Gazette,* and the *Montreal Star,* March 21st, 1966. And see also speech by Hon. Jean Lesage, reported in *Le Devoir,* Montreal, May 18th, 1966.

24. See Prime Minister Pearson's proposal to the provincial Premiers for a meeting in Ottawa on July 5th, 1967, to arrive at an accord in principle on a declaration of the rights and liberties of citizens. See the Editorial by Vincent Prince. "Le droit des citoyens et ceux des minorités," *Le Devoir,* Montreal, May 15th, 1967.

24

Quebec and Constitutional Arbitration: Between Scylla and Charybdis*

JACQUES-YVAN MORIN

The intervention of an independent and impartial third party in the disputes that oppose individuals is essential, in internal law, for the existence of effective legislation. The same is true in the case of the differences and conflicts that arise between States or nations. To be sure, the intervention of the judge or international arbitrator is surrounded by many obstacles and restrictions, because of the considerable interests that are at stake, but the States are admitting more and more the necessity of submitting their disputes to international bodies.

Nor could there be any political or even economic union without the existence of courts capable of reconciling the interests of the member-States and of interpreting their agreements. It is in this way that the courts of the economic community and the European Court of Human Rights were formed in Europe about twenty years ago.

Similarly, few federations or confederations are formed that do not include a court empowered by the constitution to end disputes between the member-States and the central power over the interpretation of the fundamental law and the validity of their respective laws. In fact, no stable politicial structure could exist without the presence of the judicial power; the more uniform the structure is on the ethnic level and unified on the socio-economic level, the easier is the task of the judges.

Even today, however, some instances still exist in which the minority ethnic groups, in order to settle their differences with the majority, must rely on courts organized and selected by this majority. All the relationships of political dependence and particularly the colonial structures have engendered situations of this kind; many examples could be given in which the conquered people, even more numerous than the population of the mother country, nevertheless saw their rights and institutions subjected to foreign courts and their methods of interpretation.

Canada has been subjected to this system since 1949, and Quebec is still

---

*Reprinted with permission from *The Canadian Bar Review* XLV, No. 3, September 1967. Originally published under the the title "Le Québec Et L'arbitrage Constitutionnel: De Charybde En Scylla." Translation provided by the publisher.

undergoing it, with the sole difference that the Quebec judges belong to the Supreme Court of Canada, although in it they still constitute a minority group, while the Judicial Committee of the Privy Council was composed only of Britishers. In other respects, the Judicial Committee belonged to the government of London, and the members were not chosen by Ottawa, whereas all judges of the Supreme Court, which in 1949 became the final court of appeal for Canadian affairs, are appointed by the federal government.

Moreover, the Judicial Committee had acquired, as arbitrator of a vast empire, a certain tradition of impartiality and detachment in the face of the problems raised by the co-existence of a great number of peoples; of all the metropolitan courts created by the European States in the last century, this was certainly not the most oppressive, and it has even been attributed, with reason, a certain liberalism.

Nor should it be astonishing to see Quebec, which has escaped from imperial institutions only to fall into a new peril, regretting the arbitration of the former court, in spite of all the disadvantages that it implied for French Canada, and insistently claiming the establishment of a constitutional forum that would not leave it at the mercy of the federal power. While accepting the retention of a certain number of political ties with English-speaking Canada and the principle of constitutional arbitration, Quebec is seeking a judicial system that would correspond to the more complete autonomy to which it aspires as "national seat" and "fundamental political 'milieu' " of French Canada; it demands the creation of a constitutional court that would be consistent with the existence of the two Canadian nations.

Is it possible to conceive and realize such an institution? After having studied the nature and the structure of the existing constitutional forum as well as the attitude of Quebec since the Supreme Court replaced the Judicial Committee, we will try to define what might be the jurisdiction, the status, and the composition of a constitutional forum appropriate to Canadian realities.

I. THE TWO NATIONS BEFORE THE SUPREME COURT

The general evolution of the judgements of the Judicial Committee of the Privy Council resulted in modifying the grand plan of certain "Fathers of Confederation", in putting an end to the subordination of the Canadian Provinces with regard to the federal power. Although the decentralizing tendency of the Judicial Committee has experienced some fluctuations and regressions, the *Hodge vs. the Queen* case (1883), followed by the *Maritime Bank* case (1892), set the tone for this jurisprudence. Thus, within the limits of their powers, the provincial legislatures were forced to recognize a "sovereign power".

Such an interpretation of the British North America Act could only arouse the opposition, indeed the annoyance, of the partisans of a strong central power, especially at the time of the economic crisis when attitudes favourable to the intervention of the State in the socio-economic areas began to spread to Canada. When the Judicial Committee made its famous decisions of the year 1937, especially in the matter of the international labour unions and in the dispute concerning the law on work and social insurance, the Anglo-Canadian jurists raised a real outcry. Dean V. C. Macdonald became the spokesman of a great number of his colleagues when he declared that the cases revealed "the necessity of seriously considering the opportunity of ending appeals in constitutional matters."[1]

In a report submitted to the Senate in 1939, the judicial counsellor of that chamber maintained that the court had departed from the wording of the constitution in the gravest and most unremitting fashion.[2] Dean W. P. M. Kennedy, for his part, concluded from this that the abolition of recourse to the Judicial Committee was the only way "to get rid of all its past decisions."[3] Ten years later, a simple federal law definitively removed appeals to the Privy Council, and the Supreme Court of Canada became the court of final appeal in constitutional matters.

The Supreme Court was created in 1875 by the Canadian Parliament, under the terms of Article 101 of the British North America Act which authorized it to constitute a general court of appeal for Canada. The federal government at that time would have liked to have made it a real constitutional court, capable of settling the disputes between the two levels of government and among the Provinces, as well as all questions relative to the validity of the federal and provincial laws, but, as the Minister of Justice regretfully acknowledged, the Constitution did not authorize Parliament to create such a court. However, the government had envisioned "an expedient according to which, with the consent of the provincial governments involved, the decisions passed by the Supreme Court would be given full effect."[4] Moreover, the court would be forced to acknowledge a "special jurisdiction" under the terms of which the Governor-General-in-Council could submit to it directly questions relative to the interpretation of the British North America Act or the constitutionality of federal or provincial laws, but without the opinion expressed by the Court being considered as a peremptory judgment.

The present government would also have liked to have abolished appeals to the Privy Council, but hesitated to carry through this measure, which might perhaps have troubled the Quebec outlook, which was very sensitive about the matter of civil rights; a resolution of Deputy Minister Irving, aiming at putting an end to appeals was accordingly excluded from the motion. For that reason, the Law regarding the Supreme Court, as adopted in 1875, did not create a constitutional court except to the extent that the provincial governments would consent to it; at that time they had not acceded to the request of the central power, and the provisions relative to the constitutional jurisdiction of the Court had to be abandoned. However, the federal high court acquired, over the years, an actual power in constitutional matters. As a court of appeal, in fact, it was called upon to make decisions more than 180 times on the validity of federal or provincial laws; moreover, its "special" jurisdiction permitted it to give counsel many times (on about 70 occasions).

With the definite abolition of appeals in 1949, the Supreme Court became in actual fact the court of final appeal in constitutional matters, without having acquired the status of a constitutional court, however. In that way, this Court, which is constantly called upon to express its opinion on the validity of the federal and provincial laws, depends solely on the federal government, which appoints all of its members. This outcome is reminiscent of the situation that prevails in the United States, in which the federal Supreme Court, in the *Marbury vs. Madison* case (1803), claimed the power to judge the validity of the laws, even though the American constitution does not expressly confer the power of judicial review on any court. This Supreme Court, appointed entirely by the Executive of the federal government, has played an important part, particularly since the New Deal era.

The Quebec government was not long in reacting against this new politico-judicial situation, established unilaterally by the Parliament at Ottawa. At the federal-provincial Conference in September 1950, the memorandum submitted by the Quebec delegation stated the question in the following terms:

"We consider that the Supreme Court of Canada, in constitutional matters and in Canadian intergovernmental relations must fulfil all the requirements of an arbitrator."[5]

Quebec realized, perhaps a little late, the dangers presented by a court appointed exclusively by the central power. Moreover, several cases had confirmed these fears at a very early date. In the Johanneson case, tried in 1952,[6] the theory of "national dimensions" which had been deferred by the Judicial Committee in 1937, was re-established, and in 1956, in the *Francis vs. The Queen* case, the Chief Justice implied that it might perhaps be necessary to review the Privy Council's decision relating to the incompetence of Federal Parliament with regard to the carrying out of treaties that involved the provinces. The Quebec Justices could also read in scholarly journals articles that left them wondering.

The research of the Tremblay Commission presented the opportunity to study the question in detail. In fact, numerous associations and institutions came before the commissioners to express their doubts about the Supreme Court. The Commission summarized the criticisms in two points. First of all, the Court "is the creation of the central government", and no provision of the constitution foresaw the existence of a constitutional

1. "The Canadian Constitution Seventy Years After" (1937), 15 Canadian Bar Review, 401, p. 427.

2. The O'Connor Report, annex I, p. 11 (Ottawa: 1939).

3. "The British North America Act: Past and Future" (1937) 15 Canadian Bar Review, p. 393.

4. Debates of the House of Commons, 1875, p. 354.

5. Compte-Rendu des Délibérations de la Conférence Fédérale-Provinciale (1950), p. 101.

6. *Johanneson* v. *Municipality of West St. Paul*, (1952) 1 R.C.S. 303.

court. In the second place, Parliament never ceased extending the jurisdiction of the Court from year to year, and all the judges are appointed by the Ottawa government, so that the court resembles the Senate, in that sense.

"It would be sufficient, for example, to establish the custom of appointing to it former deputies or federal ministers. It would have been satisfactory if it had only been a matter of judging ordinary civil and criminal cases, but in constitutional conflicts it is neither normal nor satisfactory that a single party choose, appoint, and pay all the arbitrators."[7]

The reforms suggested by the Commission tend to give the Supreme Court the character of "an impartial and independent arbitrator". This high court should be given a real constitutional status, "as in the other federative constitutions",[8] and this status could not be modified unilaterally either by the Parliament or by the Legislatures. Furthermore, the commissioners thought it would be fitting to restrict the jurisdiction of the Court. They wrote, in fact:

"The province of Quebec, which possesses its own civil code, would be quite justified in demanding and being granted that cases of a civil nature in the province be tried without appeal by a Quebec supreme court. This would be just and reasonable, as well as a guarantee that this court would pronounce judgment according to the letter and the spirit of our civil code, and not according to the British common law."[9]

The Commission recommends that Quebec, lacking the power to reserve cases relating to civil law from the federal Court, should require that such cases be tried by a court composed of five Supreme Court judges including those three judges with Quebec legal experience, the last three having to give a unanimous decision each time it were a matter of reviewing a decision of the highest Quebec court.

Finally, on the example of some foreign constitutions, the commissioners recommended that the method of appointing the judges be specified in the Constitution. It would even be fitting to establish a special constitutional court and to involve the provinces in appointing the members of this high court. This participation could be assured in various ways, either that the constitutional court be made up of the nine Supreme Court judges and of the chief justices of the ten provinces, or that it include five Supreme Court judges and four others chosen by the four large regions of which the country is composed, or even that the Constitution follow the pattern of the different international courts on that point.

At the 1960 federal-provincial Conference, M. Jean Lesage took up briefly the argument of the Tremblay Commission, which was also that of the former government. In speaking of the "repatriation" of the Constitution before the premiers gathered at Ottawa, he declared:

"We must not forget to make provisions at the same time for a constitutional court in keeping with the basic principles of a federal system. In fact, the fundamental principle of a federal system requires that neither

one nor the other of the two levels of government may affect the division of power established by the constitution. It follows that the arbitrator of the conflicts cannot depend exclusively on one of them."[10]

If English-speaking Canada can congratulate itself on having abolished appeals to the Judicial Committee and on having granted itself a truly "national" constitutional court, such is not the case for Quebec. For the English-Canadian majority, the Supreme Court, as it stands, is worthy of the utmost confidence and favourably replaces a British court guilty of having given the British North America Act terms that were too favourable to the provinces. For French Quebec, on the other hand, the Court represents the ever-present dangers of centralization and imperialism. Since 1960, the Quebeckers have had the opportunity to study their entire political and constitutional position, and their desire for change is no longer in doubt. What would be the role and the form of a constitutional court that could fit into the dualistic context of binational Canada?

II. STATUS AND JURISDICTION OF THE CONSTITUTIONAL COURT

The first reform that should be brought to the Canadian constitutional forum consists of determining precisely the jurisdiction of the court of final appeal and of incorporating it in the Constitution. The court should have *an original and exclusive* jurisdiction over all the disputes that arise between the federal government and Quebec, or any other Province, or between one Province and another. It should, moreover, be invested with the power of interpreting the federal Constitution and of verifying the validity of all the laws of Canada, Quebec, and the English-speaking provinces.

Should these duties be entrusted to the present Supreme Court? In the majority of the federal States, including the United States, Australia, India and the Latin-American federations, it is, in fact, the federal Supreme Court that plays the part of constitutional arbitrator, but besides the control that the central power can therefore exert over the action of the court through the power of appointment, one may wonder whether constitutional questions should be treated in the same way as difficulties relating to the interpretation or the application of ordinary laws. That is one of the reasons for which the three European federations and Italy, a unitary State that has several autonomous regions, opted for a specialized constitutional court. In the author's opinion, Canada would have every advantage in taking its inspiration from this formula, which is more in keeping with the spirit of federalism and the circumstances that prevail here.

7. Tremblay Commission *Report*, vol. III, p. 297.

8. *Ibid.*, p. 298.

9. *Ibid.*, p. 300.

10. Compte-Rendu de la Conférence fédérale-provinciale (1960), p. 33.

The Austrian Constitution of 1919 established the equality of the *Bund* and *Länder* in the constitution. It also established a "constitutional Court" separate from the federal courts.[11] Similarly, the Fundamental Law of the German Federal Republic (1949) created two separate courts: the Supreme Court, which hears appeals in civil and penal matters, and the Constitutional Court (*Bundesverfassungsgericht*), in which are vested the interpretation of the Fundamental Law, questions relating to the compatibility of federal and local laws with constitutional norms, or the carrying out of federal laws by the *Länder*, as well as the disputes of a public nature between the Federation and its members.

Finally, the Yugoslavian Constitution also established a Supreme Court and a constitutional Court, which verifies the validity of the laws and judges disputes between the federal Republic and the federated Republics or among the latter.[12]

Such a solution is, without a doubt, not in keeping with the tradition that prevails in the Anglo-American world, according to which the courts of final appeal must be courts of appeal of general jurisdiction. The spirit and techniques of "common law" are better adapted, in fact, to a system that does not establish too close distinctions among constitutional law, private law, and statutory law; the whole British tradition, with the preponderant part it accords to the judge, and the emphasis it places on customary law, runs contrary to specialization of the courts. Dean Le Dain even wrote recently that a court that does not have jurisdiction of general appeal is not in a position to knowingly express its opinion on constitutional questions; according to him, specialization tends to favour abstract opinions in which questions of principle take precedence over concrete problems.

If we agree to place ourselves in an Anglo-American perspective, we cannot deny the force of these arguments, but, beside the fact that they do not take into account the European tradition, they have been forcing French Canadians for two centuries to let themselves be invaded by a system which is, to a great extent, alien to the spirit of their judicial institutions. Moreover, as Professor E. McWhinney points out, the tradition of general courts of appeal is somewhat fetishistic in many countries today, and even for those who have undergone British influence, the tendency is toward specialization in the principal domains of the law, particularly in administrative matters. And if one could validate these arguments in favour of such specialization in these different domains, are they not even more convincing when it is a question of the constitutional right of a binational country? It would be advantageous in Canada's particular circumstances to take its inspiration on this matter from the tradition of the European continent.

The Canadian constitutional court should be endowed by the constitution with an independent status relative to the Supreme Court, or it could also constitute a separate chamber in this Court. The first solution is preferable, however, since it would permit placing the Constitutional Court beyond the Supreme Court and the governments involved.

In Germany, any federal or provincial court that considers a legislative provision unconstitutional must postpone ruling and appeal to the Court in order to obtain a hearing on that matter; otherwise, if the lower court considers the law to be valid, it does not have to have recourse to the Court, but the party that invokes the invalidity may submit the matter to the Court, after exhausting the ordinary recourses. One could also follow the pattern of the Nigerian system, according to which the lower regional court must, upon request of one of the parties, refer any question involving the validity of the laws or the interpretation of the Constitution to the regional High Court, which must resolve the point under dispute, unless it is forced, in turn, to refer the point of law to the federal Supreme Court, if the interested party so demands; the courts may also bring about the postponement *propio motu*.[13] The two systems, German and Nigerian, are founded on the same principle, but the first seems to us more expeditious and less susceptible to abuse by the parties to a conflict. Finally, in both cases, the higher court judging the point contested must resolve it and return the dossier to the original court, which pronounces judgment in light of the reply received. Let us note that the Law concerning the Supreme Court of Canada already contains provisions authorizing the courts to defer any constitutional matter that arises in a civil affair to the Supreme Court, on condition that the provincial legislature pass a law authorizing the judges to use this procedure. One could also observe that a striking similarity exists between the postponement by the minor courts and the procedure of consultative advice, which is none other than a postponement to the Supreme Court by the federal Executive. It should be foreseen that the Canadian constitution Court would not be at all competent to pronounce on questions relating to the compatibility of Quebec laws with the Quebec constitution; these questions should be resolved by the highest Quebec court. Such is the rule applicable in the German federation, and it conforms to the principle of the autonomy of the member-States. In a general manner, it would be fitting to distinguish better the two judicial orders by granting to the provincial courts (those of Quebec, at least) exclusive jurisdiction over those matters which concern the application and interpretation of provincial laws except the questions that deal with constitutionality; there should be no appeal to the Supreme Court (distinct from the Constitutional Court) except with regard to the federal laws.

All these propositions give rise to some difficulties, it is true, as to the "qualification" of disputes, since the same matter may include different aspects which depend either on the civil code, or on federal laws, or on constitutional law. However, once the idea of specialization and of a greater jurisdictional autonomy for Quebec have been accepted, there are different techniques, namely the creation of a Court of Conflicts, by which these problems can be resolved. For those who might see in it insurmountable difficulties, one must keep in mind that the Canadian political reality is also very complex, and that the common law system does not necessarily contain possible and reasonable solutions.

11. The Constitution of the Republic of Austria, arts. 137 and 138.

12. The Constitution of Yugoslavia, arts. 132, 145 to 151, 160, 241, 244 to 246, 249.

13. The Constitution of Nigeria, arts. 107 to 114.

III. COMPOSITION OF THE CONSTITUTIONAL COURT

In several federal States, we have observed that the role of constitutional arbitrator is granted by the Constitution to the federal Supreme Court. This system invariably entails the nomination of constitutional judges by the federal bodies. In this way, in Canada, the members of the Supreme Court are all appointed by the federal Executive. A single provision, added in the course of the 1875 debate on the Supreme Court bill, somewhat restricts the freedom of choice of the government: at least three out of nine judges who make up the Court must be chosen from among the judges of the Court of Appeal or the High Court, or from among the lawyers of Quebec.

One cannot help wondering whether the arbitration of federal-provincial disputes and the control of jurisdiction can be exercised in an impartial way in a federal system which adopts such a means of nomination. Several authors view this procedure as an exercise of the sovereignty of the central power. Jurisdiction in the federal States, wrote the late Professor M. Mouskhély, shows that the federal judicial body "is trying to reinforce the central power and to increase its authority."[14] It would, of course, be a mistake to believe that the constitutional courts alone are responsible for the centralizing tendencies that are found in most federations; one must also take into account the action of the social and economic factors, as well as the popular will, which, in States that are homogeneous on the ethnic level, constitutes a powerful element of uniformity and integration. Moreover, one could also cite more than one case in which the supreme court of certain federations has favoured the member-States.

Nevertheless, it remains true that, in a general way, the constitutional courts appointed by the central governments have contributed to the centralization. And when they refused to do it, particularly in critical periods, the other federal bodies were tempted to intervene in order to break down their resistance. In this way, in 1870, the American Congress increased the number of judges in such a way as to transform rapidly the composition and orientation of the Court's jurisdiction. Moreover, the President sometimes appointed to this high court partisans of his policies or persons from federal political milieus, in the hope of modifying the orientation of the Court. Roosevelt himself did not hesitate to use this means between 1937 and 1941, when he was trying to promote his "New Deal".

In Canada, the attitude of the Privy Council provoked the well-known reaction, which eventually brought about the abolition of appeals to the Judicial Committee by a unilateral act of Parliament. Such methods are perhaps justifiable, on the political level, when they are supported by the majority of citizens of a culturally homogeneous federation; but in a bi-national or pluralistic State, it could only be effected by risking the loss of confidence of an important part of the population.

Since the abolition of appeals, the percentage of cases favourable to the federal power in constitutional matters increased from 51.3 percent to 56.9 percent, out of a total of 51 decisions made between 1949 and 1965. Certainly, it is difficult to give an account in quantitative terms of such a qualitative phenomenon as that. But these percentages nevertheless reveal a tendency which, moreover, confirms the reading of several capital cases such as The Validity and Applicability of the Industrial Relations Disputes Investigation Act, in which it was decided that federal legislation on labour disputes applied to the dockers of Toronto harbour because of the authority of the central Parliament in navigation matters. A more recent example is the case of the *Minimum Wage Commission versus The Bell Telephone Co. of Canada*, because of which the employees of this company are not covered by the Quebec minimum wage law because the enterprise was classified by the central Parliament among those that "benefit the whole of Canada in general." Thus, by a subtle and gradual increase of federal powers, an increasing part of the legislative power of the Provinces, and even of their territory, has come under the thumb of the central Parliament. One needs only to read the Winner and Munro cases besides the cases already mentioned, to be convinced of this.

It is interesting to note also that the percentage of opinions favourable to the central power is rising to nearly 60 percent among the judges who were formerly ministers or federal under-secretaries (nine since the establishment of the Court). As A. V. Dicey observed, with traditional British realism, if the court of final appeal depends on the federal bodies, there will always be a danger that it will twist the meaning of the constitution in favour of the central power, just as a court created by a province would be tempted to distort it in favour of autonomy.

What would be the composition of a constitutional court that would escape these dangers, and how would its members be appointed? In the first place, the court would constitute one of the chambers of a renewed supreme Court, or would form, as Dean P. Azard suggested, the entire assembly of a Court composed of a Civil Chamber and a Chamber of common law. If this solution were adopted, it would be appropriate to increase the number of the judges of the Civil Law Chamber to five, in order for it to be sufficiently numerous, and that of the judges of the Common law Chamber in a similar proportion such as ten. When a dispute between the federal government and a Province other than Quebec, or when a question of constitutional law concerning one of the Provinces, was brought before the Court, the entire assembly of fifteen judges (or a bench of nine judges including three common law judges) would put the question to the majority. However, the composition of the court or of the bench would have to be different in disputes between the federal power and Quebec or when the question of law submitted to the Court involved the particular jurisdiction of the Quebec parliament or the application of federal legislation to Quebec. In such a case it is especially necessary to avoid placing the fate of the French-Canadian nation in the hands of an English-Canadian majority. The constitutional Chamber could therefore be composed of ten judges taken equally from the other two Chambers, and the decisions of the majority would rule, on condition that this majority include three judges of the civil law Chamber. This system would not be without disadvantages,

14. Théorie juridique de l'Etat féderal (1931), p. 137.

since it might be possible that no majority could be attained in one direction or the other with regard to an appropriate interpretation of the Consitution. It would be equally possible for two different systems of jurisprudence or of interpretation to develop, one of which would apply to the English-speaking provinces and the other exclusively to Quebec. Nevertheless, when one considers, on the one hand, the necessity of maintaining a common constitutional forum, and on the other hand, the obstacle that a court composed of a majority of English-Canadian judges presents for Quebec, one must admit that a solution of this kind is reasonable. As for matters for which the required majority cannot be attained, it is no doubt a matter of questions affecting very important interests, that the constitution should from then on accede to direct negotiation between the Ottawa and Quebec governments. Although such questions would doubtless seldom arise, their existence cannot be denied, as proved by Quebec's refusal to accept the arbitration of the Supreme Court in the dispute relating to the mineral deposits on the continental shelf.

In the second place, the constitutional court could be separate from the Supreme Court. In Austria, where this situation prevails, the High Court is composed of a president, a vice-president, twelve other members, and six substitute members. The Court has no permanent sitting, but is called together when it is required. In the German Federal Republic, the framers oscillated between the union of the constitutional court with the Supreme Court, and the establishment of an independent court. The report of the Herrenchiemsee Commission (1948), entrusted with planning the Fundamental Law project, nevertheless insisted on the necessity of independent constitutional jurisdiction with regard to political power, so that it could effectively protect the rights of the *Länder*. Parliament was supposed to have resolved these questions at the time of the adoption of the federal law that determined the composition of the court. They opted for a court independent of the common law courts and composed of sixteen members divided into two colleges or senates which would share constitutional jurisdiction, but must meet together when there was a difference of opinion between the two colleges about a decree made by one of them, or when the occasion arose to decide between their respective jurisdictions. Although the court has hardly lacked work since its establishment, it has no permanent sitting; several of its members are public law specialists and teach in German universities.

Canada should take its inspiration from these models, to a certain extent. The experiment of the special High Court created in 1946 to arbitrate constitutional disputes between the Italian central power and the region of Sicily, whose members are appointed in equal proportion by the Assemblies of the State and the Region, could also serve as an example. Its function was satisfactory until Rome undertook a centralizing policy and tried to strongly restrict the autonomy of the Italian Regions. As far as Quebec is concerned, a special jurisdiction, independent of the common law courts, seems necessary from now on; the political incidences of constitutional cases, particularly important in a binational country, require a solution of this kind. The court could be composed of fifteen members, five of whom would be common law judges, and would function according to the system described above. The Supreme Court could, for its part, become the object of a separate reform; or it could remain as it is, if the Quebec Court of Appeal were designated as the court of last resort in civil law cases.

It remains to discuss the means of appointing the members of the constitutional court. In Austria, the members of the High Court are appointed by the president of the Federation; the president, the vice-president, the six members and three substitutes are appointed by recommendation of the federal government; and the others,, by recommendation of the federal chambers. The High Chamber (*Bundesrat*), composed of representatives elected by the local legislatures, elects three members and a substitute. The federal bodies, therefore, always elect the judges, but an attempt has been made to diversify the electoral body and to assure a certain participation of the *Länder*. The means of nomination adopted in Germany accords a more considerable role to the member-States. The members of the constitutional Court are elected to it in equal number by the federal Diet (or Lower Chamber) and by the federal Council, which is composed of delegates of the *Länder*.[15] The candidates cannot belong either to the federal legislative and executive bodies, or to those of a Land; they cannot exercise any other function except that of professor of law. Six must be chosen from among the judges of the federal high courts and are appointed for life; the others are elected for eight years and may be re-elected. As might be observed, there is no lack of solutions; each federation invented its own on the basis of its needs and the equilibrium that prevails between centralization factors and the decentralizing forces.

Which means of nomination would be most appropriate to the Canadian circumstances? For the reasons we have given, it seems essential to assure the participation of Quebec and of the Provinces in this critical stage of the establishment of the constitutional Court, for it will not be sufficient to create Chambers of civil law and common law to restore the necessary confidence between the central power and the member-States, if all the judges continue to be appointed by the Governor-General-in-Council. It is not certain, for example, that the French-Canadian judges appointed by Ottawa after 1875 were very far removed from the tendencies of their English-speaking colleagues. Certainly, it is not a matter of questioning the intellectual qualities of the ten French-Canadian jurists who have sat on the Supreme Court all this time, and who have been, for the most part, excellent officers of the law; but it must be noted that they were prisoners of the system. Their situation can be better understood once one is aware that the French-speaking judges deliver their opinions in English, in the majority of cases relating to constitutional questions. Judge H.-E. Taschereau, although he was a ferocious adversary of Confederation in the course of the 1865 debates, delivered 33 out of 35 of his opinions in English; Judge P.-B. Mignault delivered 17 out of 19; Judge S. Girouard, all his opinions; Judge I. Brodeau, 17 out of 20; and Judge T. Rinfret, 28 out of 35.

15. The Fundamental law of the Federal German Republic, art. 94.

Many formulas exist that would ensure the participation of Quebec and the provinces in the appointing of constitutional judges. We should adopt only the means that seem the most appropriate to the kind of court proposed above. If the constitutional court were composed of fifteen members, in fact, the federal power and the English-speaking Provinces could share the nominations of the ten *common law* members, either equally, or by granting the majority of the nominations to one or the other levels of government, the provinces being grouped by regions for this purpose. Quebec, for its part, would name three members of the common law group, and the nomination of the two others would return to the central Power. In this way, all the interests involved would be represented.

To ensure the greatest possible objectivity in the choice of members of the constitutional court, it would be appropriate for nominations to be submitted to the vote of the federal Parliament in the case of the judges chosen by the central Executive, and to the approval of the legislatures in the case of the members appointed by the provinces or regions. The two-thirds majority should be required for these ratifications.

Having gone from Charybdis to Scylla with the abolition of appeals to the Judicial Committee of the Privy Council, and the accession of the Supreme Court of Canada as a constitutional court of final appeal, Quebec demands the creation of a constitutional forum that takes into account the place it must occupy in the Federation as the fundamental political milieu of French Canada. After having expressed very early her fear of seeing the Supreme Court alter the constitutional equilibrium established by the Judicial Committee to the federal government's advantage, Quebec is able to claim that her premonitions were well founded; the Supreme Court soon let it be known, in fact, that it would be appropriate to revise several fundamental decrees of the Judicial Committee and it inclined, in fact, toward positions more favourable to the central power.

As long as Quebec chooses to belong to the Canadian union, whatever constitutional or conventional formula is adopted, the need must be recognized for a forum where the majority of the questions of interpretation of the fundamental law and the disputes that arise between member-States or between the latter and the central Power can be resolved. Most of the questions involving the interpretation or the validity of the laws arise in the disputes between individuals, and it is important in the normal course of events to be in a position to arrange them quickly.

However, any system of constitutional arbitration that would result in systematically submitting Quebec to the decisions of a court whose members would be mainly English-Canadian or mainly appointed by the central government, would not rally the confidence and the support of the Quebeckers. One could not raise an objection to all the States', even the sovereign ones, agreeing from now on to submit their disputes to the courts, for, in this case, almost all the judges or arbitrators belong to third States, while in the present Canadian system, the central power is both judge and litigant at the same time. Neither could one maintain that this question is of little importance, as the partisans of the status quo sometimes assert; in fact, it suffices to imagine the attitude in federal circles if the provinces named all the Supreme Court judges. . . .

Canadian constitutional arbitration, such as it is now, is accompanied by all sorts of vestiges of the Victorian Age and of British colonialism: it places Quebec in the dependence of the central power, which gradually replaced imperial power. Any judicial system that tried to perpetuate such a state of affairs would present a constant source of tension, indeed of contention, between Quebec and the Canadian Federation.

25
Scalogram Analysis of the
Supreme Court of Canada*

S. R. PECK

I wish to present and discuss scalograms of recent taxation and of criminal law decisions of the Supreme Court of Canada. Each scalogram contains relevant appeals heard by the court after January 15, 1958 and reported in the 1958 to 1966 volumes of the *Supreme Court Reports*. A period starting on January 15, 1958, was selected as only three justices (Kerwin C. J., and Rand and Locke JJ.) on the court on that date left the court up to the time of writing.[1] The period chosen is long enough to contain a moderately large number of appeals of each type, and short enough to limit the number of judges represented on the scales to twelve. A scale covering a longer period will contain decisions of a larger number of justices and, therefore, a larger number of non-participations. The scalograms produced below cover the entire terms of office of Martland, Judson, Ritchie, Hall and Spence JJ., two-thirds of Mr. Justice Abbott's term of office, one-half of Mr. Justice Cartwright's and Mr. Justice Fauteux's terms of office and not quite one-third of Chief Justice Taschereau's term of office.[2] Accordingly, conclusions drawn about the voting behaviour of Taschereau C. J. and Cartwright, Fauteux and Abbott JJ. must remain tentative until all relevant decisions of these justices during their entire terms of office have been studied.

On the scalograms, each justice is designated by the first letter of his surname, with the exception of Rand J., for whom the letters Ra are used, to avoid confusion with Ritchie J. Each case is designated by the year and page number of its location in the *Supreme Court Reports*. Thus, the designation 58-441 indicates the appeal reported in [1958] S.C.R. 441.

THE TAXATION SCALE

The Taxation Scale (T) contains twenty-eight divided decisions in taxation appeals heard by the Supreme Court of Canada after January 15, 1958, and reported in the 1958 to 1966 volumes of the *Supreme Court Reports*. The T scale includes fourteen cases arising under the federal Income Tax Act, six

---

*Reprinted, with permission, from *The Canadian Bar Review*, vol. XLV, 1967.

cases arising under the federal Excise Tax Act, three cases concerning federal death duties, one case arising under the federal Customs Act, one case arising under the British Columbia Social Services Tax Act, and three cases arising under municipal taxing by-laws.

The T scale is constructed to make possible an examination of the effect of the justices' votes on demands made by government for the payment of taxes, and on attempts by taxpayers to resist such demands. A vote favouring the taxpayer's attempt to resist payment or reducing the amount payable is classified as affirmative, and a vote favouring the government's claim is classified as negative. Accordingly, an affirmative vote upholds the interest of the taxpayer, whether an individual, or a business organization, against the claims of government, and, speaking generally, favours individual and corporate enterprise and the retention of wealth by those who have acquired it through industry, investment, or good fortune. A negative vote, upholding a claim for taxes, is one which supports the revenue demands of government and thereby makes possible the fulfilment of government commitments and the expansion of government functions, including the expansion of social services. At least where the tax imposed is "progressive", a negative vote tends to redistribute wealth from those who have more to those who have less.

The R and S coefficients[3] are 9.3 and .77 respectively. As the difference between the observed consistency and the least possible consistency (computed for cases)[4] given the structure of the scale is .20, the increase in consistency is considerable. Therefore, if the scale is taken to be a cumulative scale and if scalability at the conventional levels is accepted as establishing unidimensionality, one would conclude that the scale indicates that the justices reach their decisions on the basis of their attitudes to taxation. As I indicated above, I am not prepared to draw such a conclusion from scales of decisions of the Supreme Court of Canada.

In spite of the incidence of non-participation[5] resulting from the court's practice of sitting in panels, the T scale identifies with relative clarity four types of voting behaviour.

1 Kerwin C. J. died on February 2nd, 1963. Rand J. retired on April 27th, 1959, and Locke J. on September 18th, 1962.

2. The justices on the court on July 1st, 1967 and their dates of appointment are as follows: Taschereau C. J. (February 9th, 1940); Cartwright and Fauteux J. J. (December 22nd, 1949); Abbott J. (July 1st, 1954); Martland J. (January 15th, 1958); Judson J. (February 5th, 1958); Ritchie J. (May 5th, 1959); Hall J. (November 23rd, 1962), and Spence J. (June 11th, 1963).

3. I have included in the computation of R, decisions in which the court divided 4-1 and 1-4.

4. MMR for justices is .68; MMR for cases is .73.

5. The scale contains 146 votes. If nine justices participated in each of the twenty-eight cases, the scale would contain 252 votes. Accordingly, 106 non-participations result from the court's practice of sitting in panels. An additional eighty-four non-responses result from the inclusion on the scale of a column for each of the twelve justices who were on the court at any time during the eight years investigated.

TAXATION SCALE (T)

Voting Division	Scale score	.78 .89 C	.58 .54 T	.50 .39 R	.56 .14 S	.53 .071 M	.40 .036 H	.60 −.036 L	.22 −.43 A	.30 −.57 K	.25 −.75 F	.14 −.75 J	Ra	
Toronto Gen. Trusts	58–499	+	+			(−)		+		+		+		4–1
Dom. Eng. Works	58–652	(−)	+			+				+	+	+	—	4–1
Alaska Pine	60–686	+ +		+		+ +				+		+		4–1
Can. Gen. Elec.	62–3	+	+			+	+		+(−)+ +					4–1
Seneca & Cayuga	64–569	+ +	+	+	+	+ +		+						4–1
Smith	60–477	+ + + + (−) +	+ + +	+ (−) +	+	+ + + +								3–2
North Bay Mica	58–597					+								3–2
Worldwide Evang.	60–49													3–2
Evans	60–391							+						3–2
Premier Mouton	61–361	+	(−)	+ (−) +	+	+ + + +	+	+ + +			(+)			3–2
Irrigation Ind.	62–346													3–2
Falconer	62–664	(−)	(−)	+ + +		+		−		−				3–2
Montreal Trust	62–570	+				+ +		− −	−					3–2
Premium Iron Ores	66–685					+ +	+		−					3–2
Imperial Oil	60–735	(−)	(−)		+	+ + + + +	− −		−					3–2
Sedgwick	64–177		+ +	+ +		−		−	− −					3–4
Highway Sawmills	66–384	+ + + + +	+ −	− − −	− −	− − − −		− −	−	−	− −	−		1–4
Pfizer Corpn.	66–449	+ + +	− −	− − −	−	−			− −	− −				1–4
Mead Johnson	66–457	+ +				−			−	−				1–4
Curran	59–850	+												1–4
Beaver Lamb	60–505								−					1–4
Regal Heights	60–902								−	−				1–4
Orlando	62–261								−	−				1–4
Denison Mines	66–8				−				−					1–4
Rexair of Canada	58–577								−		−			1–4
Oxford Motors	59–548								−					1–4
Bickle	66–479	−		−	(+) (+)	−		−	−	−	−			1–4
Royal Trust Co.	64–526	−		−	−		− −	−	−	−	−	−		1–8

28 appeals

	C	T	R	S	M	H	L	A	K	F	J	Ra
+	14	7	7	5	10	2	6	4	3	2	3	0
−	4	5	7	4	9	3	4	14	7	6	19	1
	18	12	14	9	19	5	10	18	10	8	22	1

146 participations

+ = pro-taxpayer
− = pro-government
( ) inconsistent votes are shown in brackets

R = .93
S = .77
R−MMR (computed for cases) = 20

INCOME TAX SUBSCALE (I)

Voting division		C	T	R	S	M	H	L	A	F	K	J	Ra
Voting division		.80	.50	.63	.67	.64	.50	.57	.13	.00	.00	.00	—
Scale score		1.00	.64	.50	.29	.14	.071	-.071	-.57	-.86	-.93	-.93	—
Can. Gen. Elec.	62–3	+		+		+		+	(—)				4–1
North Bay Mica	58–597	+				+			+		—		3–2
Evans	60–391	(—)	+	+				+				—	3–2
Irrigation Ind.	62–346	+				+		+	—	—			3–2
Falconer	62–664	+		+		+			—		—		3–2
Montreal Trust	62–570			+	+	+			—			—	3–2
Premium Iron Ore	66–685		—		+	+	+					—	3–2
Imperial Oil	60–735	+	—			+		+	—		—	—	3–4
Sedgwick	64–177	(—)	+						—	—		—	1–4
Highway Sawmls.	66–384			+		—		—	—			—	1–4
Curran	59–850		+			—		—		—		—	1–4
Regal Heights	60–902	+		—		—		—				—	1–4
Orlando	62–261	+	—	—		—						—	1–4
Oxford Motors	59–548	+		—	—	—	—					—	1–4
14 appeals +		8	3	5	2	7	1	4	1	0	0	0	
—		2	3	3	1	4	1	3	7	3	3	11	
		10	6	8	3	11	2	7	8	3	3	11	

+ = pro-taxpayer
— = pro-government
( ) inconsistent votes are shown in brackets

72 participations

R = .92
S = .67
R−MMR (computed for justices) = .17

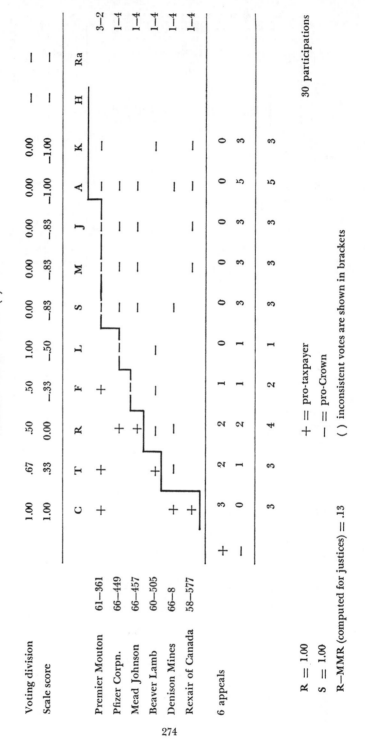

Voting division / Scale score		C	T	R	F	L	S	M	J	A	K	H	Ra
Voting division		1.00	.67	.50	.50	1.00	0.00	0.00	0.00	0.00	0.00	—	—
Scale score		1.00	.33	0.00	−.33	−.50	−.83	−.83	−.83	−1.00	−1.00	—	—
Premier Mouton	61–361	+	+		+				−	−		—	3–2
Pfizer Corpn.	66–449			+			−	−		−	−	—	1–4
Mead Johnson	66–457			+				−	−	−	−	—	1–4
Beaver Lamb	60–505		+	−	−	−	−			−		—	1–4
Denison Mines	66–8	+	−	−			−			−		—	1–4
Rexair of Canada	58–577	+						−	−	−	−	—	1–4
6 appeals +		3	2	2	1	0	0	0	0	0	0		
6 appeals −		0	1	2	1	1	3	3	3	5	3		
		3	3	4	2	1	3	3	3	5	3		

R = 1.00

S = 1.00

R−MMR (computed for justices) = .13

+ = pro-taxpayer

− = pro-Crown

( ) inconsistent votes are shown in brackets

30 participations

1. The voting pattern described for Mr. Justice Cartwright is identified as pro-taxpayer on the basis of his voting division of fourteen affirmative and four negative votes (.78 affirmative). There appears to be no reason to adopt the more extreme classification, highly pro-taxpayer, which is suggested by his scale score of .89, which reflects his break-point located close to the bottom of the scale.

2. The voting patterns described for Taschereau C. J. and for Ritchie, Spence, Martland and Hall JJ. may be classified as neutral as between taxpayer and government.

(a) The voting patterns of Taschereau C. J. and Ritchie J. are identified as pro-taxpayer on the basis of their scale scores of .54 and .39 respectively. However, we adopt the more moderate classification of neutral, indicated by the voting divisions of seven affirmative and five negative votes (.58 affirmative) for the Chief Justice, and seven affirmative and seven negative votes (.50 affirmative) for Ritchie J.[6] (Chief Justice Taschereau's voting division measure is just below the minimum of .60 which we define as pro-taxpayer).

(b) Mr. Justice Spence, Martland and Hall exhibit voting patterns which are neutral as between taxpayer and government both on the basis of their scale scores and their voting divisions. Mr. Justice Spence has a scale score of .14 and a voting division of five affirmative as against four negative votes (.56 affirmative). Mr. Justice Martland has a scale score of .071, and a voting division of ten affirmative and nine negative votes (.53 affirmative). Although Mr. Justice Hall is located within the neutral group, it is suggested that, as he participated in only five cases, any conclusions drawn about his voting pattern are highly tentative and must await confirmation as further data appears.

3. The voting patterns of Abbott and Fauteux JJ. may be characterized as pro-government in taxation appeals.

(a) This classification is given for Abbott J. both by his scale score of −.43 and by his voting division of four votes in favour of taxpayers and fourteen votes in favour of government (.22 affirmative).

(b) Mr. Justice Fauteux's voting pattern is classified as pro-government on the basis of his voting division of two affirmative and six negative votes (.25 affirmative), although his scale score of −.75 suggests classification as highly pro-government.

Note that the voting division of Mr. Justice Abbott is as pro-government (.22 affirmative) as that of Mr. Justice Cartwright is pro-taxpayer (.78 affirmative).

4. Finally, the T scale indicates that Mr. Justice Judson's voting pattern is highly pro-government, on the basis both of his scale score of −.75 and his voting division of nineteen negative votes in twenty-two participations (.14 affirmative). Mr. Justice Judson's voting pattern is especially noteworthy, as he participated in more cases on the T scale than any other

---

6. Mr. Justice Ritchie's break-point would have been lower and his scale score higher if the normal rule requiring cases within the same voting division group to be ordered according to date were followed.

justice (twenty-two out of twenty-eight) and has the most extreme voting pattern.

The T scale describes Chief Justice Kerwin's voting pattern as pro-government on the basis of both his voting division (.30 affirmative) and scale score (−.57), and Mr. Justice Locke's as pro-taxpayer on the basis of his voting division (.60 affirmative) and neutral on the basis of his scale score (−.036). However, no conclusions should be drawn about these justices until scales containing all divided taxation appeals in which they participated during their full terms on the court have been prepared and analysed.

The T scale, of course, gives no information about Mr. Justice Rand's voting pattern in taxation appeals.

Two subscales of the T scale have been prepared to facilitate the description of the justices' voting patterns – the Income Tax subscale (I), and the Excise Tax subscale (E), containing respectively the fourteen income tax appeals and the six excise tax appeals appearing on the T scale.[7] The ranking of the justices on the I subscale is identical with that on the T scale, with the exception of Fauteux J. who precedes Kerwin C. J. on the subscale solely because he did not participate in case number 58-597. The six negative votes which appear inconsistent on the T scale remain inconsistent on the I subscale.

On the E subscale, Fauteux J. ranks fourth by reason of his affirmative vote in 61-361 which appears as an inconsistency on the T scale. The justices in the fifth to tenth positions on the E subscale cast no affirmative votes, and their ranking is based on their non-participations which determine the positions of their break-points. Rand and Hall JJ. cast no votes in appeals appearing on the E subscale.

Mr. Justice Cartwright, who appears at the extreme left side of the T scale, and exhibits the only voting pattern identified as pro-taxpayer, cast affirmative votes in eight of the ten income tax appeals in which he participated, and in the three excise tax appeals, one death duty appeal and two of the three appeals arising under municipal taxing by-laws in which he participated. He cast six affirmative votes in cases appearing on the lower half of the T scale, in which he was in dissent, and in five of those cases he dissented alone. His voting pattern suggests the hypothesis that he may be inclined as a matter of policy to favour the taxpayer in taxation appeals, at least where it is open upon the law for him to do so. I propose to attempt to determine whether the three inconsistent negative votes which he cast in cases on the T scale may be explained consistently with that hypothesis.

In *The Queen* v. *Alaska Pine & Cellulose Ltd.* (60-686), Cartwright J., dissenting in part and voting negatively and inconsistently, held that section 5 of the British Columbia Social Services Tax Act which exempts from sales tax material used as a "direct agent for the . . . manufacture of a product by contact" exempts material which comes in contact with the final product of the manufacturing process, but not material which comes in contact only with waste products. He suggested that if the legislature had intended to exempt the latter material "some such word as 'substance' would have been more appropriate than the word 'product' ". Kerwin C. J., rejecting so narrow an interpretation of the word "product", held the exemption to be applicable.

Mr. Justice Cartwright's second inconsistent negative vote was cast in *Irrigation Industries Ltd.* v. *M.N.R.* (62-346), in which he was joined by Judson J. in dissent. The appellant company purchased certain speculative shares which the directors intended to sell at a profit as quickly as possible, and which the company did, in fact, sell at a profit within a few weeks. Cartwright J., noting that he was not bound by authority to hold such a profit taxable in the hands of a party not engaged in the business of trading in securities, held, however, that the transaction was an adventure in the nature of trade and that the profit was subject to income tax. The effect of his conclusion is to make the determination whether such a profit is income or capital, depend on the taxpayer's intention at the time the purchase is made. That some other justices believed that it was not necessary as a matter of law to adopt this test, is indicated by Mr. Justice Martland's adoption of a broader test on the basis of which he held that the profit was a capital gain and not taxable.

Mr. Justice Cartwright cast his third inconsistent negative vote in *Highway Sawmills Ltd.* v. *M.N.R.* (66-384).[8] Speaking for the majority, he held that to compute the capital cost allowance to which a logging company is entitled, it is necessary to deduct from the cost of the lumber cut, the amount of the proceeds received from the sale of stripped land, despite the fact that, when the company acquired the land and standing timber, the price was attributable wholly to the timber and not to the land, and that the company did not expect to sell the stripped land at a profit. On the question of statutory construction, Cartwright J. held that as the meaning of the words of the statute and regulations was difficult to ascertain, the

7. The I subscale has an R of .92 and an S of .67. The difference between the observed consistency and the least possible consistency, computed for justices) given the structure of the subscale is .17. (MMR for justices is .75; MMR for cases is .70.)

   The E subscale (composed of only six cases) has no inconsistent votes. Accordingly, R and S are each 1.00. MMR for justices is .87; MMR for cases is .77.

8. *Highway Sawmills Ltd.* vs. *M. N. R.* (1966) S.C.R. 384. In placing this appeal (66-384) on the scale, it was necessary to choose whether to assign an inconsistent affirmative vote to Ritchie J., or an inconsistent negative vote to Cartwright J. The inconsistent vote was assigned to Cartwright J., partly because his voting pattern suggests that his negative votes are inconsistencies, and partly because Mr. Justice Ritchie's affirmative vote in *Highway Sawmills* seems to be consistent with his affirmative votes in *Montreal Trust* v. *M.N.R.* (62-570) and *M.N.R.* v. *Imperial Oil* (60-735), all being income tax appeals in which the taxpayers engaged in the extractive industries.

   In placing *M.N.R.* v. *Bickle* (66-479) on the scale, it was necessary to choose whether to assign an inconsistent affirmative vote to Spence J. or an inconsistent negative vote to Ritchie J. In the absence of strong evidence to suggest to whom the inconsistency should be assigned, the normal rule of chronological order was followed, and the inconsistency was assigned to Spence J. This had the added advantage of producing higher break-points for Ritchie and Spence JJ., a result which seems to be consistent with their voting divisions.

court should adopt the construction which conforms to the apparent scheme of the legislation. Accordingly, it appears that Mr. Justice Cartwright's decision against the taxpayer resulted from the application of a broad purposive rule of construction to an ambiguous taxing statute. A decision in favour of the taxpayer might have been reached by adopting a narrow rule of construction. That, in effect, was the course adopted by Ritchie J., who, dissenting, stated that the company's profit was a windfall which "fall[s] clear of . . . the 'rather intricate statutory skein'" of the relevant provisions of the Income Tax Act.

Thus, Mr. Justice Cartwright's three inconsistent votes occur in two cases (*Alaska Pine*, 60-686 and *Highway Sawmills*, 66-384) in which he chose a construction of an ambiguous statute more favourable to the government than to the taxpayer, and in a third case (*Irrigation Industries*, 62-346) in which, to distinguish income from capital receipts, he applied a test favourable to the government. In the *Alaska Pine* case and the *Irrigation Industries* case, the majority of judges chose the construction or rule favourable to the taxpayer, although they appear to Mr. Justice Cartwright's right on the scale and hence generally are less likely to favour taxpayers' claims. In *Highway Sawmills*, Ritchie J. chose the construction favourable to the taxpayer.

Is it possible to reconcile Mr. Justice Cartwright's inconsistent negative votes with the hypothesis suggested by his voting pattern, that as a matter of policy he votes in favour of taxpayers, where it is open for him to do so under the applicable statutory and case law? The inconsistent votes clearly did not promote that policy. On the other hand, it is difficult to say that they were determined by the requirements of the applicable law, in an objective sense, as other justices voted affirmatively.

The explanation may be simply that a justice's view of what the law permits is a highly individual, even personal matter; so that a justice whose decisions generally are based on a certain policy may, in an individual case, believe that the applicable law prevents him from giving effect to that policy, even although other judges, not generally motivated by the policy, believe that the state of the law does not prevent a decision carrying out that policy. Mr. Justic Cartwright's negative inconsistent votes are some evidence that judicial decision-making is determined not only by law and policy, but by the ways in which individual judges in individual cases perceive law and policy.

Chief Justice Taschereau, as may be seen from the I and E subscales, voted affirmatively in three of the six income tax appeals and two of the three excise tax appeals which he heard. Three of his negative votes in income and excise tax appeals occur in appeals in which the taxpayers were engaged in an extractive industry. In *Montreal Trust Co.* v. *M.N.R.* (62-570), he joined Judson J., in dissent, to hold that a well-drilling company which sold part of a mining lease obtained by it in consideration for its promise to drill an oil well, received the proceeds from the sale as income not capital. In *M.N.R.* v. *Imperial Oil Ltd.* (60-735) he concurred with the majority judgment given by Judson J., construing against the interests of the taxpayer a regulation governing the method of calculating the depletion allowance on oil wells.[9] In *Deputy M.N.R.* v. *Consolidated Denison Mines* (66-8), an excise tax appeal, he concurred with Spence J. that certain "rock bolts" used in the construction of mine shafts were structural devices, not safety devices, and accordingly were not exempt from sales tax.

Mr. Justice Martland's voting behaviour in appeals involving the liability of taxpayers engaged in the extractive industries contrasts with that of Taschereau C. J. Martland J. voted in favour of taxpayers engaged in the extractive industries in three income tax appeals and in the provincial sales tax appeal in which such taxpayers were parties. Thus, he voted affirmatively with the majority in the *Montreal Trust Co.* case (62-570) in which Taschereau J., as he then was, voted negatively in dissent; and he voted affirmatively in dissent in the *Imperial Oil* case (60-735), in which Taschereau J., as he then was, voted negatively with the majority. Again, he voted affirmatively in *North Bay Mica Co.* v. *M.N.R.* (58-597), holding that a mica mine abandoned in 1947 and reactivated by new owners in 1950 "came into production" on the latter date, and so qualified for an exemption; and in *The Queen* v. *Alaska Pine and Cellulose Ltd.* (60-686).

Mr. Justice Martland voted negatively in the three excise tax cases in which he participated, holding that the dietary aids "Metrecal" (66-457) and "Limmits" (66-459) are pharmaceutical, rather than foodstuff, and hence subject to sales tax. In *Rexair of Canada* v. *The Queen* (58-577), he agreed with the majority that where articles of trade were manufactured by one company for another to which they were sold, the second company reselling to its distributors, the sales tax was payable on the higher price which obtained in the second sale.

Mr. Justice Abbott, whose voting pattern in taxation cases has been classified as pro-government, voted negatively in the five excise tax appeals and in seven of the eight income tax appeals in which he participated. His four affirmative votes occur in the only appeal on the T scale arising under a provincial taxing statute (60-686), in one of the two appeals in which he was called upon to consider municipal taxing by-laws (64-569), in one of the two death duty appeals which he heard (60-477), and in one income tax appeal (58-597). Prior to his appointment to the court in 1954, Mr. Justice Abbott served as Minister of Finance in the federal government for seven years.

Mr. Justice Fauteux, immediately to the right of Abbott J. on the T scale and with a pro-government voting pattern, voted negatively in six of his eight participations. His inconsistent affirmative vote on the T scale (which appears as a consistent vote on the E subscale) occurred in *The Queen* v. *Premier Mouton Products Inc.* (61-361). In that case, the taxpayer brought a petition of right to recover excise tax paid by it several

---

9. Regulation 1201 passed under the Income Tax Act. The majority held that to compute the profits to establish the base on which the depletion allowance is calculated, it is necessary to deduct from the profits attributable to profitable wells, all losses and costs which the company deducts in determining its taxable income. The minority held that it is necessary to deduct only the expenses related to profitable wells.

CRIMINAL SCALE

Voting division		1.00	.82	.80	.67	.55	.35	.18	.40	.15	.19	0.00	
Scale score		1.00	.55	.38	.38	−.17	−.21	−.48	−.59	−.72	−.90	−1.00	
		C	H	S	K	R	M	A	L	J	T	F	Ra
Batary	65–465	+	+	+		+	+	+		+	+	−	6–1
Rustad	65–555	+	+	+		+					+	−	4–1
More	63–522	+	+	+	(−)	+	+				+	−	5–2
MacDonald	65–831	+		+		+	+		+	+	(+)	−	5–2
Topechka	60–898	+		+	(+)	+	+	(−)			(+)	−	3–2
Brown	62–371	+		+		+	+					−	3–2
Warner	61–144	+	+	+	(−)	+	(−)	+	+		(+)	−	5–4
Kerim	63–124	+		+		+	(−)					−	3–2
Colpitts	65–739	+		+		+	+	−		−		−	4–3
Paul	60–452	+		+		+			−		−	−	3–4
Dennis	58–473	+	+			+				−	−	−	2–3
Cowan	62–476	+				+				−	−	−	2–3
Lemire	65–174	+	+	+		−				−	−	−	3–4
Cumming	62–507	+	+							−	−	−	2–3
Wright, McDermott	63–539	+								−	−	−	2–3
Kipp	65–57	+								−	−	−	2–3
Silvestro	65–155	+				(+)			−	−	−	−	2–4
Workman & Huculak	63–266	+	+	+		−	−	−		−	−	−	3–6
Coté	64–358	+	+	+		−	−	−		−	−	−	3–6
Laroche	64–667	+	+	+		(+)	−	−		−	−	−	3–6
Koury	64–212	+				(+)				−	−	−	1–4
Goldhar	60–60	+								−	−	−	1–4
George	60–871	+							(+)	−	−	−	1–4
Taylor	63–491	+								−	−	−	1–4
Toupin	65–275	+					−	−		−	−	−	1–6
Gordon	65–312	+					−	−		−	−	−	1–6
Salamon	59–404	+				−	−	−		−	−	−	1–6
McDonald	60–186	+				−	−	−		−	−	−	1–6
George	66–267	+				−	−	−		−	−	−	1–6
29 appeals	+	25	9	8	2	12	6	3	2	3	5	0	
	−	0	2	2	1	10	11	14	3	17	21	24	
		25	11	10	3	22	17	17	5	20	26	24	180 participants

− | +

R = .93
S = .68
R–MMR (computed for justices) = .15

+ = pro-accused
− = pro-Crown
( ) inconsistent votes shown in brackets

280

years earlier under protest, in the face of threats by officers of the Department of National Revenue to have the company's licence cancelled. Mr. Justice Fauteux held that the moneys were paid under duress, and, therefore, that the company's claim was not barred by the limitation period applicable to claims for a refund of moneys paid under mistake of law or fact.

Mr. Justice Fauteux clearly viewed the case as one raising, as a primary issue, the question of the proper limits to be placed on the use of threats by civil servants. His inconsistent affirmative vote may perhaps be explained on that basis. Whether Mr. Justice Fauteux's vote in the appeal is in accord with his voting pattern in other cases raising that issue, is beyond the scope of this article.

Mr. Justice Judson, the only justice with a strongly pro-government voting pattern, voted negatively in nineteen of the twenty-two appeals in which he participated, including eight appeals in the top half of the T scale in which he was in dissent. His only affirmative votes appear in a death duty appeal (58-499), an appeal arising under the federal Customs Act (58-652) and *The Queen* v. *Alaska Pine*, the only appeal on the scale arising under a provincial statute (60-686).

THE CRIMINAL LAW SCALE

The Criminal Law Scale (C)[10] contains twenty-nine divided decisions in appeals arising under the Criminal Code and other legislation creating criminal offences, heard by the Supreme Court of Canada after January 15th, 1958, and reported in the 1958 to 1966 volumes of the *Supreme Court Reports*. The C scale includes: nine appeals arising from charges of homicide; four appeals arising from charges of keeping a common gaming or betting house; three appeals in connection with theft and robbery; three appeals arising from charges of fraud and forgery; two appeals in connection with sentences of preventive detention following a finding of habitual criminality; two appeals in connection with summary conviction offences; one appeal in connection with a charge of interfering with the administration of justice; two appeals arising under the Opium and Narcotic Drug Act; and one appeal arising under each of the Food and Drugs Act, the Saskatchewan Coroner's Act, and the Migratory Birds Convention Act.

The C scale is constructed to make possible an examination of the effect of the justices' votes on prosecutions brought by the Crown under the Criminal Code and other statutes creating criminal offences. A vote favouring the acquittal of an accused, or acquittal on the more serious of two

10. In the construction of the C scale. I treat cases with a voting division of 3-2, 4-3 and 5-4 as members of the same voting division group for the purpose of rearranging cases to reduce to a minimum the number of inconsistent votes. After arranging the cases with those voting divisions for that purpose, I arrange them on the scale in groups according to their actual voting division. I deal with cases having a voting division on 4-5, 3-4 and 2-3 in the same way.

charges, or the granting of a new trial or of leave to appeal when requested by the accused, is classified as affirmative; a vote favouring conviction, or conviction on the more serious of two charges, or the granting of a new trial or of leave to appeal when requested by the Crown, is classified as negative. Thus, an affirmative vote has the effect of shielding an accused from prosecution or assuring him of fairer or at least more favourable treatment in a second trial, or benefiting him in some other way. A negative vote has the effect of promoting the Crown's ability to prosecute and obtain a conviction, and of assuring that the Crown receives fairer or more favourable treatment in the lower courts.

The C scale has an R of .93 and an S of .68. The difference between the observed consistency and the minimum consistency possible (computed for justices), given the structure of the scale, is .15. Accordingly, the scale exhibits the degree of consistency conventionally accepted as establishing the unidimensionality of items on a Guttman cumulative scale.

In spite of the incidence of non-participation[11] resulting from the court's practice of sitting in panels, the C scale indicates five fairly clear and distinct types of voting behaviour.

1. The voting pattern described for Mr. Justice Cartwright may be classified as very pro-accused, on the basis both of the high scale score of 1.00 and of his voting division of twenty-five affirmative votes in twenty-five participations (1.00 affirmative).

2. The voting patterns of Mr. Justice Hall and Mr. Justice Spence are identified as pro-accused by the scale scores of .55 and .38 respectively, and as very pro-accused by the voting division of nine affirmative and two negative votes for Hall J. (.82 affirmative), and eight affirmative and two negative votes for Spence J. (.80 affirmative). Adopting the measure which given the less extreme result, the voting patterns should be classified as pro-accused.

3. Mr. Justice Ritchie's voting pattern may be classified as neutral according to the voting division of twelve affirmative votes as against ten negative votes (.55 affirmative), and his scale score of −.17.

4. Two justices, (Martland and Abbott JJ.) exhibit voting patterns which may be classified as pro-Crown.

(a) Mr. Justice Martland's voting pattern characterized by a scale score of −.21 and a voting division of six affirmative votes out of seventeen participations (.35 affirmative) is identified as pro-Crown on the basis of both measures.

(b) Mr. Justice Abbott's voting pattern is identified as pro-Crown on the basis of his scale score of −.48, and highly pro-Crown on the basis of his voting division of fourteen negative votes in seventeen participations (.18 affirmative).

Although the voting patterns of both of these justices are classified as pro-Crown, Mr. Justice Martland's voting pattern is more moderately so than is that of Mr. Justice Abbott.

5. The scale describes highly pro-Crown voting patterns for three justices – Judson J., Taschereau C. J. and Fauteux J. The classification is suggested both by their high scale score (−.72, −.90 and −1.00) and by their voting divisions. Judson J. cast seventeen pro-Crown votes in twenty

participations (.15 affirmative); Taschereau C. J. cast twenty-one pro-Crown votes in twenty-six participations (.19 affirmative) and Fauteux J. upheld the Crown in the twenty-four appeals in which he participated (.0 affirmative).

Mr. Justice Rand did not participate in any of the appeals which appear on the C scale. Chief Justice Kerwin and Mr. Justice Locke participated in three and five appeals respectively. For the reasons expressed in connection with the T scale and the N scale, we are unable to draw any conclusions about the voting patterns of these justices from the C scale.

In deciding the twenty-nine appeals on the C scale, the justices were called upon to consider five general types of legal problems: the adequacy of the charge of the trial judge; questions of statutory construction; whether the court had jurisdiction to hear the appeal; the special pleas of *res judicata, autrefois acquit* and inconsistent verdict; and defects in the procedure followed by one of the parties. It is beyond the scope of this article to discuss the legal considerations which govern each of these matters. I propose, however, to indicate briefly the diversity of the issues considered by the court in these appeals, and to point out that notwithstanding that diversity, Cartwright, Hall and Spence JJ. voted affirmatively in over eighty per cent of the cases in which they participated, and Taschereau C. J., and Abbott, Judson and Fauteux JJ. voted negatively in over eighty per cent of the cases in which they participated.

In eleven appeals, the court considered the adequacy of the directions given by the trial judge to the jury or to himself as the trier of fact. These appeals included: seven cases of homicide and one each of forgery; keeping a common betting house; theft by conversion; and robbery with violence. Mr. Justice Cartwright, Hall and Spence, the three justices located on the left side of the scale, voted affirmatively in all of these appeals in which they participated (nine, six and five participations respectively). Mr. Justice Ritchie, whose voting pattern was identified on the C scale as neutral, voted affirmatively five times and negatively four times. Martland J., who ranks immediately to the right of Ritchie J. on the C scale, voted negatively in five such appeals located in the bottom half of the C scale and voted affirmatively in one. Mr. Justices Abbott and Judson voted negatively in six of their seven participations. Taschereau C. J. and Fauteux J., located on the right side of the C scale and having highly pro-Crown voting patterns, voted negatively in the nine appeals in which they participated.

In the seven appeals raising a question of statutory interpretation, Cartwright J. voted affirmatively in the five cases in which he participated, and Spence J. in his single participation. Abbott, Judson and Fauteux JJ. voted negatively in all appeals in this category in which they participated (three, four and five appeals, respectively). Hall J. voted negatively in two

11 The scale contains 180 votes. If nine justices participated in each of the twenty-nine cases, it would contain 261 votes. Accordingly, eighty-one non-participations result from the courts practice of sitting in panels. An additional eighty-seven non-responses result from the inclusion on the scale of a column for each of the twelve justices who were on the court at any time during the eight years under review.

of the three such appeals which he heard, casting his only negative votes on the C scale. Ritchie J. voted affirmatively in three participations out of five, and Martland J. in three of four. Taschereau C. J. voted affirmatively in two of the six appeals he heard. The two affirmative votes constitute two of his four inconsistent votes on the scale.

There are eight appeals on the C scale in which the primary question was whether the court had jurisdiction to hear the appeal. In five appeals, the court considered whether an appeal was based on a question of law, so as to be within the jurisdiction conferred by sections 597 and 598 of the Criminal Code; in two appeals, the court considered its jurisdiction to hear an appeal against sentence; in one appeal, the court considered its jurisdiction under section 41 of the Supreme Court Act.

Cartwright J. voted affirmatively in all eight jurisdictional appeals. In the five jurisdictional appeals brought by the Crown, he held that the Supreme Court had no jurisdiction to hear the appeal; and in the three jurisdictional appeals brought by the accused he held that the court had jurisdiction. Mr. Justice Fauteux voted negatively in all appeals involving jurisdiction in which he participated, holding that the court had jurisdiction to hear four appeals brought by the Crown, and no jurisdiction to hear three appeals brought by the accused. Mr. Justice Martland held that the court had jurisdiction to hear the five appeals in this group in which he participated, three being appeals by the Crown, and two, appeals by the accused.

In the three appeals considering the special pleas of *res judicata, autrefois acquit* and inconsistent verdicts, Cartwright and Hall JJ. voted affirmatively in the cases in which they participated. All other justices voted negatively in all cases in which they participated, other than Ritchie J., who voted affirmatively in one of the two appeals which he heard.

In the four appeals considering allegations of procedural defects, Cartwright J. voted affirmatively in the three appeals in which he participated, as did Martland J. in the two appeals in which he participated. Taschereau C. J. and Fauteux and Judson JJ. voted negatively in all the appeals of this sort in which they participated.

Ritchie J., with a voting division of twelve affirmative and ten negative votes, is the only justice whose voting pattern is neutral as between the Crown and the accused. He voted affirmatively in five of the six homicide appeals in which he participated, and negatively in the three appeals in connection with theft and robbery; he voted affirmatively in two of the three betting house appeals and in two of the three fraud and forgery appeals in which he participated. In the jurisdictional appeals in which he participated, he held that the court had jurisdiction to hear one of the two appeals brought by the accused and one of the three appeals brought by the Crown.

CONCLUSION

My purpose in this article is to present a report of an initial effort to apply a behavioural method to the work of the Supreme

Court of Canada. I have used only one such method, scalogram analysis, and I have applied it to a relatively small number of decisions. Bearing in mind these limitations in scope, I shall not attempt to anticipate the broad conclusions about the nature of decision-making by the court, which may be warranted after further work has been done. I wish to conclude this report by drawing together some of the findings that emerge from the separate examinations of taxation and criminal law decisions.

The scalogram of each group of cases indicates that some justices consistently uphold or oppose the claims of the taxpayer in taxation appeals . . . or the accused, in criminal appeals. As the appeals on each scale raise a wide variety of legal issues, it is reasonable to hypothesize that such justices (who appear near the left or right sides of the scales and have voting patterns classified as "highly pro" or "pro") base their decisions, at least in part, on the value or policy issue raised by the appeals on each scale. An examination of the two scalograms, taken together, indicates that some justices tend to have one-sided voting patterns on more than one scale. This suggests the hypothesis that these justices pursue policy goals in more than one area of the law.

The voting patterns described on each scalogram for each justice may be conveniently represented by indicating the position of each justice on a profile line, divided into five segments to represent the five categories of highly pro-affirmative, pro-affirmative, neutral, pro-negative and highly pro-negative. The rankings of the justices on the profile lines differ somewhat from those on the scales, as they are based on scale score alone, but on voting patterns classified to both scale score and voting division.

The two justices who appear most frequently near the extremes of the profile lines are Mr. Justice Cartwright and Mr. Justice Abbott. Mr. Justice Cartwright appears near the left side of each of the two lines. His voting pattern is in favour of the taxpayer in taxation appeals and highly in favour of the accused in criminal appeals. Accordingly, he supports the individual or business organization in disputes with government (criminal law and taxation cases) . . .

Mr. Justice Abbott's positions on the profile lines contrast with those of Mr. Justice Cartwright, as he appears near the right side of the two lines. His voting pattern is in favour of the government in taxation appeals, and of the Crown in criminal law appeals. His voting pattern which is never in the "highly pro" category, does not place him at the extreme right side of the taxation or criminal law profile lines. . . . With respect to his support of government in taxation and criminal law appeals, it should be remembered that he was a member of the federal cabinet for many years.

Mr. Justice Hall and Spence resemble Mr. Justice Cartwright in their support . . . of the accused in criminal cases. However, the voting patterns of both are neutral as between taxpayer and government.

The voting patterns described for Mr. Justice Judson and Fauteux have similar characteristics. Both support the government in taxation and in criminal law appeals, and in these respects their voting patterns resemble that of Mr. Justice Abbott. Mr. Justice Judson, whose voting pattern is highly in favour of the Crown in both taxation and criminal law appeals, is the only justice whose voting pattern is classified as "highly pro" on two scales.

Although Chief Justice Taschereau appears as a neutral in taxation appeals, his voting division shows a tendency to support the taxpayer as against the government. . . . In criminal law appeals he is highly in favour of the Crown.

Mr. Justices Ritchie and Martland are the most neutral justices on the two scales. Mr. Justice Ritchie's voting pattern is neutral in taxation, and criminal law appeals. Mr. Justice Martland's voting pattern is neutral in taxation appeals and pro-Crown in criminal law appeals.